Dog-Friendly
NEW YORK

A Complete Guide to New York City and the Empire State

Trisha Blanchet

The Countryman Press
Woodstock, Vermont

ISBN 0-88150-601-X
Library of Congress Cataloging-in-Publication Data has been applied for

Book design, maps, and composition by Hespenheide Design
Maps © 2004 the Countryman Press
Front cover photo of Toby © David Parket
Interior photographs by the author

Published by The Countryman Press,
P.O. Box 748, Woodstock, VT 05091

Distributed by W.W. Norton & Company, Inc.,
500 Fifth Avenue, New York, NY 10110

Printed in the United States of America

10 9 8 7 6 5 4 3 2 1

**For the search-and-rescue dogs and handlers of
September 11, 2001**

Special thanks to

Scott, the world's best copilot;
Mom, who definitely deserves a raise;
and Samantha, a fearless NYC adventurer

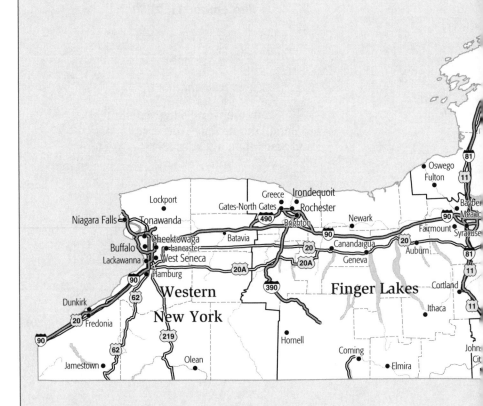

Lockport
Greece · Irondequoit
Gates-North Gates · Rochester
490 · Brighton
Niagara Falls · Tonawanda
Newark
90
Fairmount
Cheektowaga · Batavia
Syracuse
Buffalo · Lancaster
Canandaigua · 20 · Auburn
Lackawanna · West Seneca
20 · Geneva
81
Hamburg · 20A
20A
90 · **Western**
390 · **Finger Lakes** · Cortland
62
Dunkirk
Ithaca
20 · Fredonia · **New York**
90
62 · 219 · Hornell
Corning
Jamestown · Olean
John
Elmira · Cit

Oswego
Fulton
Bay
90 · Mead
81
11

N

0   50
Scale in Miles

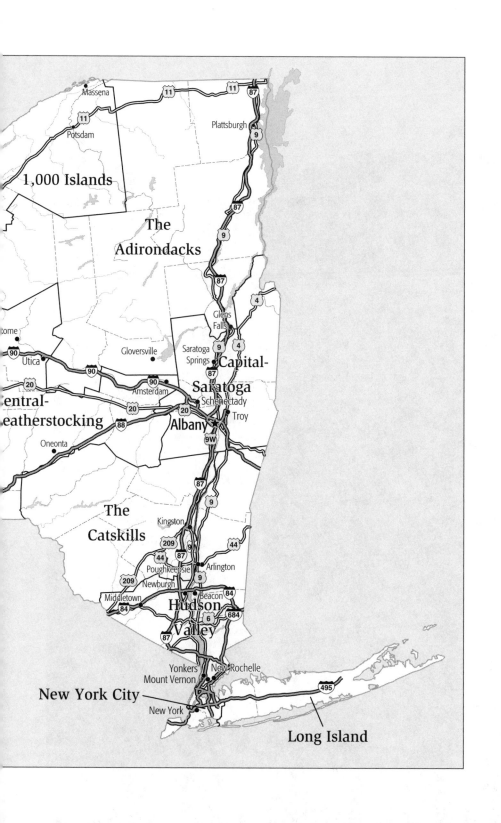

Massena

11

11 87

Potsdam

11

Plattsburgh
9

1,000 Islands

The
Adirondacks

87

9

87

4

Glens
Falls

Rome

90

Utica

20

90

Saratoga
Springs

9

9 4

Capital-

Central-
eatherstocking

Gloversville

90

88

Oneonta

Amsterdam

20

90

20

20

Saratoga

87

Schenectady

Troy

Albany

9W

87

9

The
Catskills

Kingston

209

9

87

44

44

44

Poughkeepsie

Arlington

209

Newburgh

9

Middletown

84

84

Beacon

Hudson

87

6

684

Valley

Yonkers

New Rochelle

Mount Vernon

New York City

495

New York

Long Island

CONTENTS

(LEFT) A RESCUED BORDER COLLIE ENJOYS HIS SURROUNDINGS AT GLEN HIGHLAND FARM IN MORRIS IN THE CENTRAL-LEATHERSTOCKING REGION.

Introduction

There are dog people, and then there are dog people. You know who you are: Milk Bone crumbs in your coat pockets; a pet bed in every room; and the requisite red bandana stashed somewhere in your glove compartment. In a light breeze, clumps of dog hair roll across your kitchen floor like tumbleweed. Your friends, those cat people and people people, might think you're a little weird. After all, who would want the hassle of late-night walks, the mess of muddy paw prints, or the slobber of gooey kisses? You do. And you love every minute of it.

But, as you know, not every person is a dog person. That strange-but-true fact doesn't usually affect your day-to-day life, especially if Rover sticks to chewing up your own shoes and leaves everyone else's alone. Venture out of your home, however, and you're largely at the mercy of a world where dogs are considered, well, animals. And when it comes time to plan a family vacation, you might be surprised to learn that most innkeepers and hotel managers do not consider your pooch to be a family member—even if she *is* wearing a polka-dot hair bow. That seems to leave you with two choices: Leave your best friend alone in a cement-floor kennel for a week, or cancel the vacation plans this year. And next year, and the year after that.

VISITING CANINES DO THE MEET-AND-GREET AT THE THEODORE ROOSEVELT PARK'S DOG RUN IN NEW YORK CITY.

If neither of those options sounds appealing, you're not alone. And you're also in luck, because *Dog-Friendly New York* will help you skip the usual "no pets allowed" chorus and plan a minimum-hassle trip with maximum potential for fun, adventure, relaxation, and escape from the daily grind. Whether you're hoping to tour New York's wine country, swoosh down a mountain, window-shop on Fifth Avenue, cast a line on a fishing charter, hike a trail, or simply stare out at the ocean waves, New York can accommodate every whim. How many states can stake claim to mountain ranges, a 6-million-acre park, famous waterfalls, vineyards, sand dunes, lighthouses, and historic settlements, not to mention the most vibrant city in the world? New York has all these and more to offer visitors, who flock to the Empire State from around the globe—and from around the corner—for a glimpse at the region's attractions.

But a vacation is more than just fun and games; you also have the necessities to consider. *Dog-Friendly New York* will keep your belly full and your pup entertained with listings of pet-supply stores, outdoor cafes, groomers, doggie daycares, take-out food services, and veterinarians in each region. And don't worry about finding a place to hang your hat and leash. We've weeded out the pet-*un*friendly spots to list more than 600 swanky hotels, affordable motels, cozy B&Bs, charming country inns, private homes, and rustic campgrounds where canines are welcomed. As some innkeepers say with a wink: "If your dog can vouch for you, you're welcome, too." From the Adirondack Mountains to Niagara Falls, New York City, the Catskill Mountains, and everywhere in between, the Empire State provides nearly limitless opportunities for day trips, weekend forays, and lengthy vacations—for people *and* for pets. After all, dogs ♥ New York, too.

ACCOMMODATIONS

Some travelers don't spend much time choosing a lodging, not caring where they sleep as long it's cheap and convenient. For other people, accommodations define a vacation and set the tone for the rest of trip. Whether you prefer a plain-and-simple country locale, a luxurious city penthouse, or even a bed under the stars, New York State has a hotel, motel, cottage, cabin, inn, B&B, or campground that's sure to provide just the experience you're looking for.

There's no denying that those traveling with a pooch will have fewer accommodations options than those who take the strictly human route. But that doesn't mean you'll have to compromise. The innkeepers and hotel managers that do allow pets—definitely a small minority in the industry—often do so with open arms, beautiful lodgings, and a friendly attitude that will make your vacation even more memorable. This book divides them into the following categories:

Hotels, Motels, Inns, and Bed & Breakfasts

This group of accommodations offers the most choices, highlighting everything from high-end, high-rise hotels to cozy inns with just a few rooms. Inns and B&Bs are often very similar in style, although inns usually don't include breakfast as part of the overnight package. Rates vary greatly from region to region, but hotels, B&Bs, and inns located near each other tend to have comparable rates. Motels are typically the most economical option, offering fewer amenities in return for more affordable prices. Other variations on the motel theme

TOOTSIE, A SHETLAND SHEEPDOG, VISITS THE WARD POUND RIDGE RESERVATION IN CROSS RIVER IN THE HUDSON VALLEY.

include motor inns, efficiencies (which usually include a kitchen or kitchenette), and "housekeeping cottages," meaning that maid service is not included. If you prefer to keep to yourself and your pup, a hotel or one of the motel varieties would probably be your best bet. But if you enjoy mingling with other guests at the breakfast table and in common rooms, you might be happier at an inn or B&B.

Campgrounds

New York campgrounds are located primarily in the upstate regions, with the most options found in the Adirondack and the Catskill Mountains. Although these two areas are renowned for offering great outdoor experiences, don't limit yourself: Equally wonderful camping areas are scattered throughout western New York, the Finger Lakes and Central-Leatherstocking regions, and even the 1,000 Islands. Many pet owners assume that every campground allows dogs—not true. Nevertheless, camping remains one of the most popular lodging stand-bys for dog lovers. Some of the sites listed here are basic and secluded, offering little more than a place to pitch your tent. Others are jam-packed with amenities such as heated swimming pools, play-grounds, showers, laundry facilities, and lots of scheduled family activities.

Homes, Cottages, and Cabins for Rent

Renting a private vacation home can be a great option for families, couples, or anyone else who wants a little extra elbowroom. The houses, cabins, cottages, estates, condominiums, and apartments listed here are usually rented for one week or longer, although a few do allow night-by-night rentals. Each homeowner has his or her own rules and regulations regarding doggie guests: Some will require the use of pet beds or sleeping crates; others will charge extra fees or an extra security deposit; still others will ask that your pet stays out of certain rooms or areas in the yard; and some will require all these things or nothing at all. If you're interested in learning more about a particular rental, use the contact information to speak to the home-owner directly. Some also offer web sites where you can view pic-tures and learn more details about each property.

A Note about the Dog-Friendly Ratings

Each New York region has been given a dog-friendly rating that ranges from one to five biscuits. A rating on the higher end of the scale indicates that a particular region is one of your best vacation bets, offering a wide variety of dog-welcoming accommodations and activities as well as a general animal-friendly attitude. This is a place where you'll feel at home wandering around with a canine companion. A rating on the lower end does not indicate that a region is necessarily a bad choice; it just means that you might have to work a little bit harder and make compromises to find attractions and lodgings where Fido will be welcome. The criteria for determining a dog-friendly rating are varied. For example, will you have to stay in a motel when you wanted a B&B? Will you encounter lots of other dog lovers there, or just lots of glares? Will you and your dog be able to visit the most popular attractions in the region, or will you be turned away at the gate? Of course, each person's experience and opinions will vary, but the ratings are designed to give you a starting point when planning your trip and deciding on a home base.

Rental Agencies

These real estate specialists can help fulfill your vacation dreams with vast offerings of houses and other rentals in popular tourism areas. The agencies listed here have at least some dog-friendly properties for rent; accommodations options vary wildly from gated mansions to simple fishing cabins in the woods. If you're having trouble finding what you want, give them a call. But be aware that some agencies charge finder's fees, so ask about the relevant charges before you start an agent on the hunt.

IN THE DOGHOUSE

Your dog is cute, cuddly, never barks, and never growls at strangers. You're pretty cute and cuddly, too, and you only growl once in a while. So why do so many innkeepers refuse to let the two of you come through the door? Most naysayers claim the reason is simple:

Too many people have allergies to pet dander, and allowing dogs to stay might affect the health of present and future guests. But when pressed, hotel managers and B&B owners from Niagara Falls to Long Island are also quick to mention a few other annoyances that keep them firmly in the "no dogs allowed" camp. Even those who do allow pet guests cite the same few concerns over and over again when discussing the subject of animals and accommodations. The grievances are many, but here are the top five:

1. **Not cleaning up after your dog.** No, it's not fun. In fact, it's usually disgusting to have to scoop up that pile and carry it around until you find the nearest trash can. But it's even more disgusting to stumble across a pile that someone else's dog has left in your driveway, your front yard, or your favorite park. This is by far the number-one complaint of innkeepers and non-dog owners, and with good reason: There are still too many canine owners who refuse to clean up after their animals, even when scooper bags are provided, signs are posted, and fines are charged. Until that situation changes, we dog lovers are likely to remain pariahs—and the vast majority of lodging owners will maintain their pet-exclusive policies.

A Note about Rates and Dog-Friendly Policies

Rates change almost constantly in the hospitality industry. The rates listed in the "Accommodations" section of each chapter were current at press time, but you may want to ask about possible price increases before making a reservation. Likewise, dog-friendly policies can quickly be altered with each innkeeper or manager's experiences. A formerly dog-friendly accommodation can change to "dog-unfriendly" overnight—or alter its fee structure—after a particularly bad experience with irresponsible pet owners. In some cases, the lodging owners may raise their pet-specific fees; in other cases, they might lower them or do away with them altogether. The same can be said of attractions, restaurants, and other spots where pet-friendly policies were once in place. Before planning your trip around a particular hotel or attraction, it's always a good idea to call and make sure the site is still willing, and able, to accommodate your pooch.

DOGGIE FOOTPRINTS AT FIRE ISLAND ON LONG ISLAND

2. **Leaving your dog alone in the room or at the campsite.** Hotel managers are tired of getting calls from guests who complain that the dog in the room next door has been barking, whimpering, or crying for hours. Even if your pooch never makes a peep at home, he may react differently in a new and strange place. Many accommodations owners are simply unwilling to alienate the majority of customers to please the minority. Some have solved the problem by not allowing guests to leave their pets alone in the rooms. Others, unfortunately, have solved the problem by no longer welcoming doggie guests at all. Even if your B&B, inn, campground, or motel doesn't require it, you can bet they'd appreciate it if you'd take Fido with you whenever you leave the premises.

3. **Letting your animal sleep/sit on the furniture.** Innkeepers who allow pets understand that your fluffy friend will leave some hair behind; it's often unavoidable. But there's a big difference between leaving a few tufts of hair on the floor and leaving an inch of blonde fuzz on the inn's customized upholstery, down comforters, or antique rocking chairs. Many of us allow our dog to curl up in the bed or chair with us at home, and can find it difficult to break the habit when we're on the road. For lodging owners who are trying to control allergy-inflaming pet dander, however, these cozy habits can create costly and annoying problems. Some accommodations forbid animals to venture onto the furniture; others will even ask you to sign an agreement to that effect. Regardless of the rules, however, it's usually just a good

A Note about Dog-Related Fees

Often, lodgings will accept pets only on the condition that the guests pay an extra fee. The charges range from minor ($5–10) to significant ($50–100 and higher). Some of the more hefty fees are refundable at checkout, providing that the dog has not caused any significant damage to the property. Other innkeepers will require a security deposit only if the guest is paying in cash. With the standard fees, lodging managers typically charge in one of two ways: "per night" or "per stay." For example, one hotel will require an extra $25 for each night of your visit, while another will ask for a flat $25 fee, regardless of the length of your stay.

A Note about Breeds

Among many veterinarians, pet professionals, and dog lovers, the common wisdom goes something like this: There are no "bad breeds," only "bad owners." At one time or another, we've all run into sweet-as-pie pit bulls or vicious cocker spaniels that defy stereotypes. Nevertheless, some accommodation owners now include some, but not all, breeds in their dog-friendly policies. The excluded canines are usually pit bulls (Staffordshire bull terriers), rottweilers, German shepherds, Doberman pinschers, and huskies. Sometimes campgrounds and hotels are forced to adopt restrictions by their insurance companies; sometimes not. If you happen to be traveling with one of these breeds, it's usually not a good idea to try and sneak your pooch in by being less than forthcoming with the lodging owners—they can, and will, turn you away at the door if they feel they've been misled. Instead, take a few extra minutes to find that perfect pet-friendly accommodation where your pup will be welcomed with open arms and you'll be able to relax and enjoy your trip.

idea to make sure your pooch keeps all four paws on the floor. Bringing along a padded pet bed or blanket can solve two problems at once by containing hair while also giving your dog a comfortable spot to call her own.

4. **Not adhering to leash requirements.** Even if your friendly mutt is used to roaming free in his own yard, the vast majority of lodging owners would prefer that he stay on a leash during his visit. Some of the reasons for this are purely practical: A leashed dog is less likely to scare, startle, or hurt other guests, thus protecting the innkeeper from liability and ensuring repeat customers. Other reasons are more emotionally based: Some lodgings may be home to other pets or neatly manicured gardens, neither of which may take kindly to visiting animals. Many hotels, motels, inns, and campgrounds have even set aside certain areas for doggie exercise and bathroom breaks.

5. **Leaving the place in a shambles.** So who are those canine-toting travelers who are giving the rest of us a bad name? Most

innkeepers and campground owners have plenty of stories to
share about nightmare guests who leave behind a wake of
property damage and bad karma. Some allow their pup to chew
up the furniture, knock over appliances, and leave "presents"
on the rugs, then check out and bolt without saying a word
about the damage. Some leave their dog locked in a hot car at
the campsite, leading to visits from the local police. Others use
the hotel-room bathtub to wash skunk spray off their pooch's
fur, leaving behind a God-awful stink and a flooded bathroom
floor. This strange breed of dog owner seems to appear everywhere at one time or another, from swanky hotel suites to family resorts. Sometimes, lodging owners chalk it up to the "one
bad apple" syndrome. Others come away from the experience
vowing to never, ever, allow companion animals as guests
again. Of course, these are the innkeepers who have just fin-
ished fumigating one of their rooms when you call to inquire
innocently about an overnight stay for you and Spot. That
would explain the yelling and the sudden dial tone.

Unfortunately, there isn't a whole lot we can do to convince the
majority of hotel managers that dogs make wonderful guests. But we
can, at least, convince the pet-friendly lodgings that they didn't
make a mistake in allowing us to stay. Who knows: Maybe they'll
tell two friends, and they'll tell two friends, and sooner or later the
ranks of dog-friendly accommodations will grow.

OUT AND ABOUT

Finding a great accommodation is only part of the vacation experience. After all, you probably didn't drive for seven hours to stare at
the B&B's pretty wallpaper all day. But how much sightseeing can
you realistically do with a pup by your side?

A lot. True, you won't be able to tour the inside of famous New York
estates and cathedrals, but you can admire the architecture and
grounds from the outside. You can't go to the theater with your dog,
but you can witness dramatic backdrops and stunning scenery that
are far better than any stage set. The "Out and About" listings,
which include pet-friendly parks, boat rides, special events, hiking

trails, lighthouses, historic spots, covered bridges, and even dog camps, are designed to help you make the most out of your trip without ever leaving Fido in the car. The listings are not a complete guide of all the things to see and do in a region—we'd need a lot more than one book to cover all that. But they will help you find the highlights and best-known attractions that can serve as starting points for an unforgettable New York getaway.

QUICK BITES

It might be an understatement to say that mealtime is a problem for traveling pet owners. For most of us, vacationing means eating out. Eating out means restaurants, where pets are prohibited. So what's a hungry dog-lover to do? In most cases, you can't leave your pooch in the car, because severe heat or cold can cause illness or even death. And as any pet-toting traveler will tell you, the fast-food drive-through gets real old, real quick.

The "Quick Bites" section of each chapter will help resolve the quandary with a geographically spaced selection of eateries that offer outdoor seating, takeout, delivery service, or all three. Some regions have much more to offer in this area than others. In New York City, for example, it seems like every other restaurant has sidewalk tables or some kind of delivery service. On the other hand, more rural areas in central and northern New York can prove especially chal-

A GARDENER'S ASSISTANT AT THE BLACK DOG LODGE IN ELLICOTTVILLE IN WESTERN NEW YORK

lenging when it comes to finding cafés and take-out windows. Like "Out and About," these listings are not intended to be complete guides of every culinary choice in a region. But they will help you find a meal in a pinch and hopefully lead you down the road to even more dining options.

One word of caution: Just because a restaurant offers outdoor seating, that doesn't mean they necessarily allow dogs to sit there. Some eatery owners take the letter of the law (in this case, local health codes) seriously, extending the rules that govern the "indoor" boundaries of their restaurant out onto the sidewalk. Others will welcome your pooch but ask that she stay on the other side of a fence or velvet rope. Still others don't mind if Fluffy stays curled up at your feet throughout the meal. And rules change as management changes: Always ask permission before wandering into any patio, garden, or sidewalk-seating areas, even if you've sat there with your pup in the past.

HOT SPOTS FOR SPOT

Your dog is hungry—very hungry. But you've run out of dog food, and now you're driving through a town you've never heard of, searching in vain for a pet shop while your four-legged friend whines in the back seat. Or maybe you've spent the day splashing through the ponds at a state park, and now you'd kill to find a groomer that could wash off that foul, moldy smell from your pooch's fur. Or perhaps you're a marine-biology buff, and you've just learned that a great aquarium is located right down the street from your hotel. You'd love to go, if only you could find someone to keep an eye on your dog for just a few hours.

Whatever your pet-related mission, "Hot Spots for Spot" can help. This section lists pet-supply stores, doggie daycares, groomers, kennels, animal-themed boutiques, and other services to help dog lovers out of nearly any jam. These professionals take pride in providing care and supplies to local and visiting animals of every stripe. Still, leaving your precious family member in someone else's care, even for a short time, is no small matter. A listing in this book is not a recommendation, and pet owners should take the time to research each facility and interview the staffers before signing on to any service. Web site addresses (when available) have been included in each listing; if you're interested in possibly using a kennel or doggie daycare facility for the first time, the web sites often provide pictures and other information that will give you a better idea of what to expect.

IN CASE OF EMERGENCY

Accidents happen, even on vacation. Should an illness, injury, or other misfortune befall your pet, each chapter includes listings of veterinarians that can help. The doctors' locations are scattered geographically throughout each region in the state, so you'll never be too far away to reach at least one of them. Pet lovers should note, however, that these listings are provided strictly for emergencies: Some veterinarians are not accepting new patients for routine care, although they will of course help any animal with an extreme or urgent need. Be sure to carry your pet's up-to-date vet records when you travel, as well, to help the new doctor assess your animal's health history and immediate concerns.

MUST-HAVES

In the hustle-and-bustle of packing and planning your trip, you may easily forget a few things. Use this as a checklist of items that you simply can't leave behind when traveling with a dog:

- **Vaccination certificates and/or vet records:** Keep them in the glove compartment whenever you hit the road. Even if you think no one will ever ask to see the records, you can bet at least one campground owner, park manager, hotel owner, or innkeeper will insist on viewing them (and, in some cases, making a copy for the insurance company). If you're planning on using the services of a doggie daycare center, kennel, or pet sitter, the records become even more vital. In addition, some accommodations require them, but won't necessarily tell you that beforehand. In some cases, your dog's rabies-vaccination collar tag is enough, but not always.

- **Crate/kennel:** I know, I know: Why cart around that big crate when chances are you'll never have to use it? Trust me. Buy a folding model, strap it to the roof of the car, and forget about it. If you never need it, no harm done. But when you stumble across that B&B owner who suddenly insists it's the "crate-way" or the highway, you'll be very glad you brought it along. Some places require your pet to sleep in the crate; others simply ask that you crate your dog when leaving him alone in the room.

- **Towel, towels, towels:** Two are good. Four are better. Pile as many as you can fit into some corner of your car or suitcase. You'll use them when it rains (and it will), if your dog sits on something yucky (and she will), or if your innkeeper won't appreciate muddy paw-prints on the new carpet (which he won't). It never hurts to line your car seats with a few towels, as well, to guard against car sickness and make clean-up a whole lot easier when you return home.

- **Water and water bowls:** Traveling is a thirsty business. All that running, swimming, and hanging his head out the window can make your pup parched. Whether you use plastic bowls and squirt bottles or high-end food-and-water storage systems designed for traveling dogs, always have plenty of water on hand. You and your pup don't need the complications and heartache of dehydration-related health problems.

- **Pooper-scooper bags:** Yucky, but necessary. Most parks and accommodations will require that you clean up any messes; even if you're not required to do so, common courtesy requires us dog lovers to remove the "gifts" our furry friends leave behind. For some, this is as simple as carrying around a few plastic grocery bags. Others prefer to buy specially designed

A Note about Motion Sickness

Unfortunately, car sickness is not just for people. If this is your first road trip with Sparky and you're not sure if he'll become queasy, you don't want to be surprised. Talk to your veterinarian before you hit the highway about possible motion sickness remedies. Also, you might want to prepare for a worst-case scenario by having plenty of paper towels and some kind of fabric cleaner on hand.

scooper bags in the pet store. Whatever your method, make sure to always have a bag or two stashed in your pockets.

- **A spare bag of food:** You just never know. Maybe the local store at your destination won't carry your pup's favorite brand. Maybe all the extra activity will make her eat more than usual. You might end up carrying home an uneaten bag, but chances are it won't go uneaten for long.

- **Treats and chew toys:** No one likes being stuck in a car (or hotel room) for long periods of time, and your dog is no exception. Rawhides, plush squeaky toys, biscuits, and other snacks and goodies will help keep Rover occupied while you navigate the highways or take a break from vacation activities.

You're packed, you're prepared, you're ready to go. Now it's time to leave the gritty details behind and head out for the city streets, rugged wilderness, sandy beaches, river rapids, mountain peaks, or charming byways that make New York such a wonderful state to visit. Few places are more diverse or more enchanting. Whether you want to canoe in a lake, tackle a challenging trail, or just sip coffee in an urban café, rest assured that your pup won't be left out of the fun.

TRAVELER'S TIPS

Empire Passports

Leashed dogs are welcome at most New York state parks, although visitors usually have to pay an entrance fee. If you plan to do a lot of exploring, consider purchasing an Empire Passport, which allows you unlimited access to almost every state park, forest preserve, boat launch, recreational facility, and arboretum. Each pass is valid for one full year, from April 1 to March 31. At press time, the cost was $59 per pass, with discounts given to those who purchase more than one. According to park officials, the pass usually pays for itself after about eight visits. To purchase an Empire Pass or to learn more, call any state park office (the phone numbers are listed throughout this book), write to Empire Passport, New York State Parks, Albany, NY 12238, or visit the New York State Office of Parks,

NEW YORK STATE'S DOG PARKS PROVIDE PLENTY OF OPPORTUNITIES
FOR FROLICKING: THIS ONE IS LOCATED IN LIVERPOOL, NEAR SYRACUSE.

Recreation and Historic Preservation web site at www.nysparks.state.
ny.us.

Recreational Boat Registrations

Boaters planning a short-term vacation need not worry about boat regis-
trations in New York: As long as your boat is legally registered in your
home state, you're covered. But out-of-towners staying longer than 90
days will have to notify the local Department of Motor Vehicles and register the vessel with the state. Within New York, call 1-800-CALL-DMV.
From outside the state, call 518-473-5595.

Camping Reservations

There are several ways to reserve a campsite at one of New York's state
parks: In addition to calling the park directly (see the phone number in
each listing), you can also call the statewide toll-free reservation service
at 1-800-456-CAMP, or reserve on-line using the Reserve America web site
at www.reserveamerica.com. Reservations can be made two days to
eleven months in advance—or you can always try your luck as a walk-in.

Snowmobiles

Any snowmobile used in the state of New York must be registered with
the Department of Motor Vehicles (DMV), even if it is already registered

in another state. (Out-of-staters must provide the ownership documents required in their home state when registering.) To register, call the DMV at 1-800-225-5368. Snowmobilers must also carry proof of insurance while operating the vehicle. New York State has a helmet law and a minimum age requirement of 18 for operators. In addition, snowmobile riders are expected to abide by the state Code of Ethics for the sport, which includes not harassing wildlife, not damaging plants or natural features, and not trespassing on private property. For more information on snowmobile recreational opportunities in the state, contact the New York State Snowmobile Association by writing to P.O. Box 62, Whitesboro, NY 13492, calling 315-736-8187, or visiting www.nyssnowassoc.org.

New York State Traveler's Resources

New York State Department of Economic Development
Division of Tourism
One Commerce Plaza
Albany, NY 12245
(1-800-I-LOVE-NY)

New York State Department of Transportation
Map Information Unit
State Office Building Campus
Building 4, Room 105
Albany, NY 12232
(518-457-3555)

New York City

NO VISITOR TO NYC SHOULD MISS A STROLL THROUGH THE CITY'S URBAN OASIS, CENTRAL PARK.

New York City

DOG-FRIENDLY RATING:

Whether you're visiting for the first time or making one of many return trips, New York City is truly a spectacle. For newcomers, the city's sheer size can be impressive and overwhelming all at once, but don't let that intimidate you. With a good map and some careful preparation, you and your pooch can navigate like natives. And don't believe what you hear: Most New Yorkers are more than willing to provide cheerful directions, advice, and suggestions for making the most of their city.

New York City is made up of five boroughs: Manhattan, the Bronx, Brooklyn, Staten Island, and Queens. Most NYC vacationers head to Manhattan, the home of Broadway, the Empire State Building, Wall Street, Fifth Avenue, the ferry to Ellis Island, Central Park, Little Italy, Soho, and hundreds of other world-famous neighborhoods and landmarks. If you only have a few days or a week, you'll probably opt to

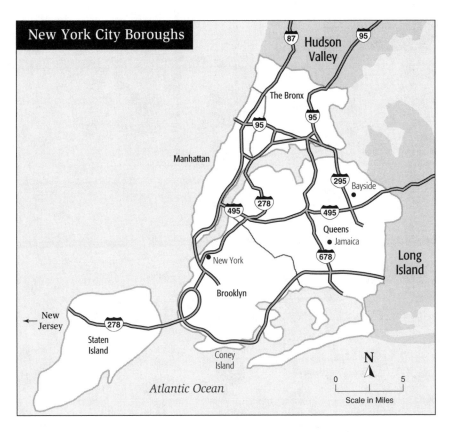

New York City Boroughs

Hudson Valley

The Bronx

Manhattan

Bayside

Queens

Jamaica

New York

Long Island

Brooklyn

New Jersey

Staten Island

Coney Island

Atlantic Ocean

N

0   5

Scale in Miles

start and end your visit here. But if you're blessed with a bit more time, make the effort to wander out into the outer boroughs. These less-visited spots are home to quaint waterfront villages, amusement areas, great restaurants, doggie playgrounds, and the city's largest parks.

Of course, one chapter (or one visit) can hardly do justice to exploring all that a city of this size has to offer. You'll find the don't-miss high-lights listed here, including parks, eateries, doggie daycares, pet bou-tiques, walking trails, and notable sights that are accessible and welcoming to canine-toting travelers. And then there are the accommo-dations: deluxe resorts, historic landmarks, and plain-and-simple hotels, all ready and willing to welcome four-legged guests. (You'll have better luck in Manhattan than in the outer boroughs and airport areas, where hardly any hotels permit pets.) Your concierge can arrange pet-sitting services and suggest dog-friendly activities and restaurants. Or, just ask the manager of the nearby pet shop or a New Yorker holding the end of a leash. This is, after all, a metropolis full of pet lovers. Spend an hour at a dog park, and you'll no doubt make scores of new friends.

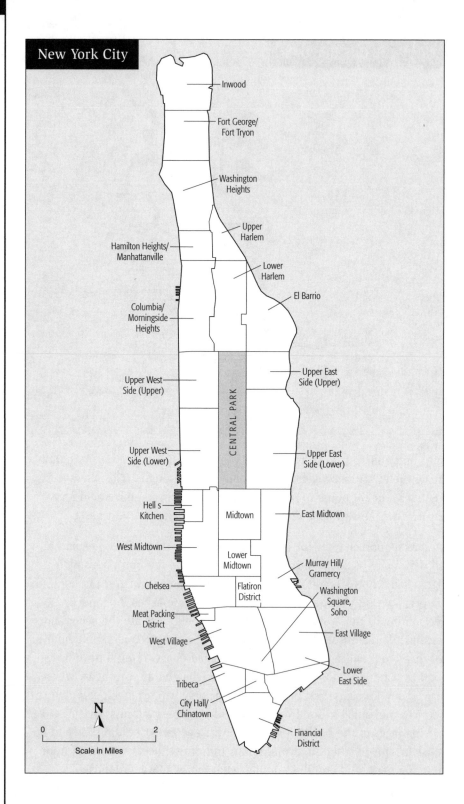

New York City

Inwood

Fort George/
Fort Tryon

Washington
Heights

Upper
Harlem

Hamilton Heights/
Manhattanville

Lower
Harlem

El Barrio

Columbia/
Morningside
Heights

Upper West
Side (Upper)

Upper East
Side (Upper)

CENTRAL PARK

Upper West
Side (Lower)

Upper East
Side (Lower)

Hell s
Kitchen

Midtown

East Midtown

West Midtown

Lower
Midtown

Chelsea

Flatiron
District

Murray Hill/
Gramercy

Meat Packing
District

Washington
Square,
Soho

West Village

East Village

Tribeca

Lower
East Side

City Hall/
Chinatown

Financial
District

N

0   2

Scale in Miles

As wonderful as it is, New York City's pet-friendliness does come with one caveat: Size matters. Shi-tzu people will have a much easier time than golden retriever fans, because many of the city's hotels only welcome pets weighing less than 20–30 pounds or so. Dog owners often find the weight limits baffling. (Is this a boxing match or a vacation?) Logical or not, we're stuck with the rules. If you're traveling with a black lab, a weimaraner, or a similarly hefty pup, be sure to double-check the hotel's size limits when making a reservation. If you're really stuck, ask to speak to the manager; exceptions are sometimes made to allow a slightly larger pooch.

Once you've settled in, lace up a pair of comfortable walking shoes and explore NYC at your own pace. If your dog is already a city dog, he'll feel right at home. If not, he may think he's stumbled into a sniffer's paradise. Dog owners who are used to letting their dog run through open fields at home, however, should know that leash laws and pooper-scooper requirements are deadly serious business to locals. Owners who leave little "presents" on the sidewalk will invite the wrath of passersby—and risk hefty fines. Similarly, newcomers should be aware that many dog parks are paid for and maintained by local residents who often post rules and regulations at the entrance. (For example, if a park entrance is double-gated, be sure to close one of the gates before opening the other.) A little common sense and courtesy will be much appreciated by New Yorkers and help you avoid grief during your visit.

But enough chitchat. The city awaits, and there's a shady spot in Central Park with your name on it.

ACCOMMODATIONS

Hotels, Motels, Inns, and B&Bs

Brooklyn
Bed & Breakfast Marisa, 288 Park Place (718-399-9535; jupti@earthlink.net; www.brooklynbedandbreakfast. net); $85–120 per night. A cozy accommodation in the big city, this brownstone B&B offers two guest rooms—the North and the South—and one large garden apartment. Amenities include hardwood flooring, quilts, built-in bookshelves, refrigerators, dining areas, and a shared bathroom. Discounts are available for stays

of eight nights and longer. Off-street parking is available. Well-behaved dogs are welcome with no additional charges.

Manhattan–East Midtown

Eastgate Tower, 222 E. 39th St. (212-687-8000); $139–369 per night. Pets weighing less than 20 pounds are allowed with an additional $250 security deposit at Eastgate Tower, an all-suite accommodation located in the Murray Hill neighborhood. Guests can enjoy air-conditioning, cable television with premium movie channels, a concierge desk, room service, valet parking, a fitness center, and a grocery-shopping service.

Four Seasons Hotel, 57 E. 57th St. (212-758-5700); $395–1,800 per night. Located between Park and Madison Aves., the famous Four Seasons provides guests with 364 rooms and suites, a restaurant and lounge, valet parking, a spa and fitness center, a business center, 24-hour room service, meeting rooms, and baby-sitting services. The rooms and suites come equipped with terry bathrobes, VCRs, down pillows, CD players, minibars, and hair dryers. Dogs weighing 15 pounds or less are welcome.

The Metropolitan, 569 Lexington Ave. (212-752-7000; 1-800-223-0888); $159–495 per night. Check in to the Metropolitan (formerly known as Loews New York) and take advantage of rooms and deluxe suites—some with whirlpool baths—cable television, a fitness center, in-room movies, and air-conditioning. You can also enjoy dinner in the Lexington Avenue Grill and free continental breakfasts and evening cocktails in the Metropolitan's Club 51 concierge level. Pets are welcome without extra charges, as long as owners don't leave their pup alone in the room. You'll have to sign a pet-policy agreement at check-in.

New York Helmsley Hotel, 212 E. 42nd St. (212-490-8900; www.helmsleyhotels.com); $235–305 per night. Visitors to this hotel will find a concierge desk, a gift and sundry shop, cable television, pay-per-view movies, valet parking, room service, Internet access, a business center, banquet facilities, and meeting rooms. Breakfast, lunch, and dinner are served in the on-site restaurant. Dogs weighing less than 20 pounds are permitted. Pet owners can expect to sign a pet-policy agreement and waiver at check-in.

Plaza Fifty Suites New York, 155 E. 50th St. (212-751-5710); $129–349 per night. This 22-story hotel has 204 guest rooms, studios, and one- and two-bedroom suites. All have air-conditioning, irons and ironing boards, cable television, and access to valet parking, a fitness center, a concierge, room service, and even secretarial and grocery-shopping services. The suites also have full kitchens with microwaves and complimentary coffee. Pets weighing less than 15 pounds are allowed as long as owners sign a pet-policy agreement at check-in.

Swissotel New York–The Drake, 440 Park Ave. (212-421-0900); $225–1,300 per night. Located five blocks from Central Park, The Drake is a landmark hotel with 495 guest rooms and suites, function and banquet rooms, a business center, the Park Avenue Spa & Fitness Center, a restaurant and lounge, 24-hour room service, and valet parking. Each room has high-speed Internet access, voice mail, coffeemakers, and work desks. Pets are welcome for an extra charge of $30–40 per stay; there are no size restrictions for dogs.

W New York, 541 Lexington Ave. (212-319-8344); $239–399 per night. With pillow-top mattresses, an earth-tone décor, CD players, terry bathrobes, snack packs, and 250-thread-count linens, the W New York aims to make your stay as relaxing and enjoyable as possible. Guests can also order up a 24-hour massage service, surf the Internet, meet with clients in the business center, or watch pay-per-view movies. Pets weighing less than 80 pounds are welcome for an extra $25 per night and a one-time $100 cleaning fee.

W New York–The Court, 130 E. 39th St. (212-685-1100); $279–649 per night. Located between Lexington and Park Aves., this W New York hotel location provides a restaurant, a café and bar, a fitness center, meeting and banquet facilities, a concierge desk, valet dry-cleaning services, cell-phone rentals, a 24-hour front desk, luxurious in-room amenities, and special weekend packages. Your pet is welcome for an additional $25 per night and a one-time $100 cleaning fee, as long as she weighs less than 80 pounds.

W New York–Union Square, 201 Park Ave. South (212-253-9119); $319–379 per night. Like the other W New York hotels, the Union Square location welcomes pets weighing less than 80 pounds, although you will pay an extra $25 per night and a one-time $100 cleaning fee. Guests can enjoy rooms and suites with bathrobes, hypoallergenic feather pillows, cable televisions, DVD players, chocolate bars and other snacks, velvet armchairs, and pillow-top mattresses.

Manhattan–Financial District
Holiday Inn Wall Street District, 15 Gold St. (212-232-7700); $230–399 per night. The 138 guest rooms at this Holiday Inn have modern amenities like personal computers, printers, high-speed Internet access, CD players, and video-game consoles. You'll also find a fitness center, a gift shop, meeting rooms, a café, a 24-hour front desk, wake-up calls, a newsstand, room service, a tour desk, a rental-car desk, and on-site parking. Dogs are welcome without extra fees.

The Regent Wall Street, 55 Wall St. (212-845-8600); $350–1,150 per night. Dogs are allowed with no extra fees in designated fifth-floor rooms at the Regent Wall Street, provided owners have proof of vaccinations. The historic 1842 hotel has an impressive lobby, 144 guest rooms and suites, a ballroom with a 70-foot ceiling, meeting and function rooms, a spa, and a fitness center. Guests can also enjoy amenities such as valet parking, 24-hour room service, airport shuttles, CD and DVD players, down pillows, concierge services, and bathrobes and slippers.

The Ritz-Carlton New York Battery Park, 2 West St. (212-344-0800; www.ritzcarlton.com); $299–1,150 per night. This luxury hotel provides guests with 298 rooms and executive suites, featherbeds, marble showers, CD and DVD players, high-speed Internet access, cordless telephones, 24-hour room service, twice-daily maid service, an evening turndown service, and even Ritz-Carlton pajamas in each suite. You'll also find a fitness center, a spa, and fine-art exhibits. Dogs weighing 20 pounds or less are welcome for an additional $30 per night.

Manhattan–Flatiron District/Lower Midtown

Hampton Inn Chelsea, 108 W. 24th St. (212-414-1000); $149–229 per night. Choose from single, double, king/queen, king study, and king deluxe rooms at the Hampton Inn Chelsea, where all rooms have movie channels, coffeemakers, free local calls, irons, and ironing boards. Guests can also take advantage of a 24-hour front desk and freebies like a daily breakfast bar, newspapers, and coffee and tea in the lobby. Dogs weighing 25 pounds or less are welcome for an additional $25 per stay.

Holiday Inn New York City–Martinique, 49 W. 32nd St. (212-736-3800; 1-888-694-6543); $139–369 per night. For an extra

$50 per night, your dog is a welcome guest at this Holiday Inn location. The hotel offers 532 rooms and suites on 18 floors, 2 restaurants, a lounge, on-site parking, a rental-car desk, a fitness center, a 24-hour front desk, a gift shop, dry cleaning and laundry services, wake-up calls, express check-in and checkout services, and a business center.

Hotel Thirty Thirty, 30 E. 30th St. (212-689-1900; info@3030nyc.com; www.3030nyc.com); $125–269 per night. Choose from standard rooms, superior rooms, and deluxe executive rooms at Hotel Thirty Thirty, a convenient and very pet-friendly hotel located just south of Midtown. The rooms vary in size and style, providing marble bathrooms, cozy down comforters, and expansive work spaces for executive travelers. Other services include a concierge, valet dry-cleaning, and Internet access. Pet owners (this hotel permits various pets) pay an extra $10 per night.

The Sherry Netherland, 781 Fifth Ave. (212-355-2800; 1-800-247-4377); $350–795 per night. Built in 1927, the Sherry Netherland was renovated in 2000 and offers features such as a fitness center, air-conditioning, meeting and conference facilities, complimentary continental breakfasts, and free daily newspapers. In the rooms, guests will find bathrobes, hair dryers, radios, and personal grooming extras like lotion, nail files, and shower caps. There are no extra charges and no size restrictions for dogs;

HOTEL THIRTY THIRTY HAS A CONTEMPORARY STYLE AND A DOG-FRIENDLY ATTITUDE.

pet owners are asked to sign a pet-policy agreement at check-in.

Manhattan–Hell's Kitchen

Skyline Hotel, 725 Tenth Ave. (212-586-3400); $119–209 per night. Dogs weighing less than 80 pounds are welcome at the Skyline Hotel, located just west of Midtown within walking distance to Broadway theaters and Times Square. Amenities include a 24-hour front desk, an indoor swimming pool, cable television, Internet access, pay-per-view movies, and 230 rooms on 14 floors. Pet owners leave a credit card imprint as a security deposit against any animal-caused damage.

Manhattan–Midtown

Courtyard by Marriott Times Square South, 114 W. 40th St. (212-391-0088); $159–279 per night. There are no extra charges and no weight limits for companion animals at this Courtyard by Marriott, located near all Times Square attractions and Broadway theaters. Guests will find a restaurant, a coffee shop, a lounge, valet laundry services, a fitness center, high-speed Internet access, work desks, voice mail, and 244 rooms and suites on 32 floors.

Hilton New York, 1335 Avenue of the Americas (212-586-7000); $149–329 per night. Located at Rockefeller Center, this Hilton location provides guests with baby-sitting services, a gift shop, a turndown service, a business center, a tour desk, concierge services, valet dry-cleaning services, and on-call doctors. Room features include cable television with premium movie channels, coffeemakers, alarm clocks, and hair dryers. Dogs weighing 15 pounds or less are permitted with no extra charges.

Hilton Times Square, 234 W. 42nd St. (212-840-8222); $209–429 per night. Walk to theaters, shops and restaurants in this well-located hotel with standard rooms, suites, and executive accommodations on 44 floors.

Guest amenities include a fitness center, a gift shop, a newsstand, meeting rooms, cell-phone rentals, room service, a concierge desk, a tour desk, and laundry services. Dogs are welcome with a $250 security deposit, although some breeds are restricted: Call for details.

Le Parker Meridien, 118 W. 57th St. (212-245-5000; www.parker-meridien.com); $235–700 per night. This hotel boasts an "equal-opportunity pet policy" (no size limits) and very dog-friendly attitude: Pet lovers will even find a room-service menu designed exclusively for cats, dogs, and other types of companion animals. Humans can expect the royal treatment, as well, with ergonomic furniture, valet dry-cleaning service, free high-speed Internet access, voice mail, CD and DVD players, a business center, a 15,000-square-foot fitness center and spa, and two eateries.

Millennium Broadway Hotel, 145 W. 44th St. (212-768-4400); $209–399 per night. Dogs weighing less than 15 pounds are welcome without extra charges at the Millennium Broadway, a hotel with a fitness center, a restaurant, parking facilities, room service, a business center, conference and meeting rooms, and a turndown service. Standard and Premiere rooms have amenities such as bathrobes, air-conditioning, coffeemakers, minibars, cable television, work desks, VCRs, voice mail, irons, and ironing boards.

Muse Hotel, 130 W. 46th St. (212-485-2400; 1-877-NYC-MUSE; www.themusehotel.com); $209–449 per night. The Muse Hotel not only allows companion animals, they welcome them with open arms. Dog lovers can even opt for the extra "Pampered-Pooch Package," which includes a goody basket, food and water bowls in your room, one free room-service meal, and one free dog-walk. Other hotel amenities include a fitness center, cable television with premium movie channels, featherbeds, high-speed Internet access, and valet parking. There are no extra charges for pet guests.

New York Marriott Marquis, 1535 Broadway (212-398-1900); $239–529 per night. With nearly 2,000 guest rooms and suites, the Marquis offers something for everyone, including room service, a coffee shop, a hair salon, valet laundry service, a rental-car desk, baby-sitting services, a gift shop, valet parking, and an activities/tour desk. You can also enjoy dinner at The View, New York's only revolving rooftop restaurant, and then work off the calories in a fitness center overlooking Times Square. There are no extra fees for pets, although the hotel does have some size and breed restrictions; call for details. Dogs must be crated while in the rooms.

Novotel New York, 226 W. 52nd St. (212-315-0100; www.novotel. com); $169–259 per night. One of the more affordable Midtown options, the Novotel offers 480 clean, no-nonsense accommodations with air-conditioning, minibars, pay-per-view movies, radios, voice mail, Internet access, and hair dryers. The hotel also has a restaurant and bar, meeting and conference rooms, a gift shop, parking, a tourist-information desk, and room service. Dog owners must sign a waiver at check-in; there are no extra charges for your pooch.

Peninsula New York, 700 Fifth Ave. (212-956-2888; pny@peninsula.com); $590–12,000 per night. (No, that's not a typo—the rates really do go that high at this ultra-deluxe Midtown hotel.). Rover will appreciate the "canine cuisine" room-service menu, which offers items such as Pekingese Peanut-Butter Cups and Scratch My Belly Bagels. Pet beds, dog-themed movie rentals, and dog-walk services are also available. Two-legged visitors, meanwhile, can enjoy superior and grand-luxe rooms or one-, two-, and three-bedroom suites, along with a spa, a restaurant and three lounges, marble bathrooms, and flat-screen televisions. In general, the hotel accepts dogs weighing less than 25 pounds.

Renaissance New York Hotel Times Square, 2 Times Square, 714 7th Ave. (212-765-7676); $199–650 per night. This Marriott property offers 305 guest rooms and suites on 26 floors in Times Square; features include a restaurant, 24-hour room service, valet parking, turndown services, and express checkout services. In the rooms, guests will find satellite television, voice mail, high-speed Internet access, writing desks,

coffeemakers, hair dryers, irons and ironing boards, and mini-bars. Dogs weighing less than 60 pounds are welcome for an additional $60 per stay.

Royalton Hotel, 44 W. 44th St. (212-869-4400; 1-800-635-9013); $345–650 per night. Locals often stop by the 44 Restaurant and Round Bar at Royalton, a boutique hotel with contemporary styling. Guest room amenities include Internet access, cable television, alarm clocks, minibars, free newspapers, and hair dryers; the hotel also offers a spa, valet laundry services, parking, express checkout services, room service, and a concierge. Dogs weighing less than 10 pounds are allowed; pet owners are asked to sign a pet-policy agreement and waiver at check-in.

W New York–Times Square, 1567 Broadway (212-930-7400); $279–359 per night. Located at the intersection of Broadway and 47th St., this W New York hotel has a dramatic interior waterfall, 509 guest rooms and suites, a promenade, a dance club, a gift shop, 24-hour in-room massage, a restaurant and bar, room service, spa treatments, and in-room Internet access. Sleep soundly on a feather bed or choose a DVD to watch. Your dog is a welcome guest for an additional $25 per night and a one-time $100 cleaning fee, provided he weighs less than 80 pounds.

Manhattan–Murray Hill/Gramercy

Envoy Club New York, 377 E. 33rd St. (212-481-4600); $149–333 per night. Studios and one- and two-bedroom apartments are all available for short- and long-term rental at the Envoy Club. The extended-stay hotel has air-conditioning, cable television, conference rooms, a wake-up service, alarm clocks, bathrobes, fully equipped kitchens, coffee-makers, hair dryers, irons, and ironing boards. Dog owners pay an extra security deposit; there are no weight restrictions for companion animals.

Gramercy Park Hotel,
2 Lexington Ave. (212-475-4320; 1-800-221-4083); $139–400 per night. Overlooking Gramercy Park, this homey accommodation offers single rooms, double rooms, family suites, and deluxe suites—including the two-bedroom Babe Ruth Suite. Guests can also enjoy a lounge, banquet facilities, meeting rooms, complimentary high-speed Internet access, daily breakfasts, and a fitness center. Your well-behaved pet is a welcome guest with no extra charges or weight restrictions.

Manhattan–Upper East Side
The Carlyle, Madison Ave. at 76th St. (212-744-1600; 1-888-767-3966; thecarlyle@rose-woodhotels.com; www.rosewood-hotels.com); $500–3,200 per night. This ultra-deluxe hotel boasts plenty of extras, including 23 suites with grand pianos, Central Park views, original Audubon prints, and the Café Carlyle cabaret. Suites range in size from the 650-square-foot Standard Suites to the 1,800-square-foot Tower Suites, and everything in between. Guests can also choose from standard,

superior, deluxe, and premier rooms. Pets weighing less than 15 pounds are permitted.

Hôtel Plaza Athénée, 37 E. 64th St. (212-606-4635; 1-800-447-8800; www.plaza-athenee.com); $495–3,600 per night. Choose from traditional, superior and grand-deluxe rooms or executive, deluxe and penthouse suites at the Hôtel Plaza Athénée, a European-style accommodation. Guests can also enjoy spa services, child-friendly packages, a restaurant and lounge, concierge services, minibars, Internet access, speakerphones, 24-hour room service, and complimentary shoe-shines. "Small" dogs (call to see if yours qualifies) are welcome.

Melrose Hotel, 140 E. 63rd St. (212-838-5700; 1-800-MELROSE); $169–379 per night. Guests at the Melrose Hotel will find a fitness center and spa, terry bathrobes, cable television, pay-per-view movies, high-speed Internet access, voice mail, a business center, free newspapers, and valet parking. The hotel's twelve Tower Suites provide the ultimate in luxury with terraces and sweeping views. Dogs weighing less than 25 pounds are allowed, although pet owners can expect to pay a nonrefundable cleaning fee of $100 per stay.

The Pierre–Four Seasons, 2 E. 61st St. (212-838-8000; 1-800-332-3442); $380–825 per night. Best known as "The Pierre," this luxury hotel provides guests with 201 individually decorated rooms and suites, elevator operators, valet parking, a fitness center, a business center, a gift shop, and meeting rooms. Central Park is located across the street. Dogs weighing less than 30 pounds are allowed without extra fees, provided they are not left alone in the rooms at any time. The concierge is happy to arrange dog-sitters upon request.

Regency Hotel, 540 Park Ave. (212-759-4100; www.loews-hotels.com); $199–659 per night. "Loews loves pets." So goes the animal-friendly slogan of the company that owns and runs the Regency, an upscale accommodation with rooms and suites, 24-hour room service, bathrobes, complimentary newspapers, mini-bars, voice mail, and even television in some bathrooms. But your dog will have the most pampering here: In addition to dog beds, pet-walking and pet-sitting services, the Regency also provides a room-service menu designed especially for companion animals. And we're not talking about canned Purina here—the chef creates full, deluxe doggie meals ($10–12), including vegetarian options, that you just might want to share.

Manhattan–Upper West Side

Phillips Club, 155 W. 66th St. (212-835-8800; info@phillipsclub-newyork.com; www.phillipsclub.com); $420–525 per night. Designed primarily for long-term stays of 30 days or longer, the Phillips Club offers hotel rooms, suites, and apartments. All guests can take advantage of concierge services, on-site parking, maid services, valet dry-cleaning and

laundry services, refrigerators, stoves, and microwaves. Dogs weighing 40 pounds or less are permitted, as long as they stay on a leash in all public areas.

Mayflower Hotel on the Park, 15 Central Park West (212-265-0060; 1-800-223-4164; resinfo@mayflowerny.com; www.mayflowerhotel.com); $200–1,200 per night. Guests at the Mayflower choose from cozy single rooms, double rooms, suites, and penthouse terrace suites; other features of the hotel include refrigerators, free daily newspapers, valet laundry and dry-cleaning services, Internet access, airport shuttles, and a fitness center. Walk across the street to Central Park. Dogs are welcome with a $300 refundable security deposit.

On the Ave Hotel, Broadway and 77th St. (212-362-1100; 1-800-497-6028; info@ontheave-nyc.com; www.ontheave-nyc.com); $149–359 per night. For an extra $10 per night, your well-behaved dog is always welcome at On the Ave. This newly built Upper West Side hotel offers patios, high-thread-count bedding, Internet access, a contemporary décor, penthouse suites, and "double double" suites. Lincoln Center, the Museum of Natural History, and numerous restaurants are all located within walking distance.

Manhattan–Washington Square/Soho/Tribeca

Off Soho Suites Hotel, 11 Rivington St. (1-800-OFF-SOHO; info@offsoho.com; www.offsoho.com); $66–149 per

THE SOHO GRAND HOTEL PAMPERS BOTH TWO-LEGGED AND FOUR-LEGGED GUESTS.

night. Off Soho Suites bills itself as "the traveler's alternative to New York's overpriced, under-sized hotel rooms." Amenities include two- and four-person suites, an on-site café, and a fitness center. All suites have a full-size kitchen, Internet access, hardwood floors, and satellite television with premium movie channels. Dogs are allowed in deluxe suites only ($99–149 per night) and pet owners must pay with a credit card.

Soho Grand Hotel, 310 West Broadway (1-800-965-3000; www.sohogrand.com); $249–434 per night. "Accommodations" options at the Soho Grand include superior queen rooms, deluxe king rooms, and the 350-square-foot grand corner king rooms. Built in 1996, the hotel also offers 24-hour room service, velour bathrobes, a fitness center, same-day laundry services, valet parking, minibars, express check-in, a salon, and meeting and conference rooms. Pet owners will also be pleased to find lots of goodies for guest animals, including a doggie room-service menu.

Tribeca Grand Hotel, 2 Avenue of the Americas (212-519-6600; www.tribecagrand.com); $189–699 per night. Dogs and cats are always welcome guests at the Tribeca Grand, a relatively new, pet-friendly hotel offering 203 guest rooms and suites, 24-hour room service, a fitness center, a beauty salon, laundry services, cordless telephones, Internet connections, VCRs, and complimentary newspapers. The front desk supplies food bowls, leashes, and doggie toys upon request, and the concierge is happy to arrange dog-sitting and walking services. (If you had to leave your best friend at home, the hotel will even provide an "on-loan" goldfish to keep you company—no joke.) Room service also offers a selection of dog and cat foods on demand.

Queens
Holiday Inn Express Queens–Midtown Tunnel, 38 Hunters Point Ave., Long Island City (718-706-6700); $101–169 per night. A newly built hotel, the Holiday Inn Express of Queens provides visitors with a 24-hour front desk, dry cleaning and laundry services, wake-up calls, a concierge service, free continental breakfasts, fax and photocopying services, interior corridors, and 79 rooms on three floors. The Midtown Tunnel is located a half-mile away. "Small" dogs (call to see if yours qualifies) are welcome for an extra $20 per night.

Radisson Hotel JFK Airport, 135 140th St., Jamaica (718-322-2300); $119–229 per night. Located next to the airport and not too far from Manhattan, this Radisson Hotel has a restaurant and lounge, a gift shop, a fitness center, and a business center that's open 24 hours. The 386 guest rooms come equipped with Internet access, pay-per-view movies, work desks, voice mail, two telephone lines, coffeemakers, free daily newspapers, hair dryers, irons, and ironing boards. Room service is also available. Dogs are allowed with a $50 one-time fee.

Staten Island

Hilton Garden Inn, 1100 South Ave. (718-477-2400); $129–350 per night. Dogs weighing less than 18 pounds are allowed at this Hilton location for an extra $35 per night. The large hotel provides a fitness center, a car-rental desk, baby-sitting services, laundry facilities, meeting rooms, cell-phone rentals, and a gift shop. In the rooms, guests will find double- or king-size beds, work desks, two telephone lines, high-speed Internet access, video-game consoles, coffeemakers, and cable television with premium movie channels.

Staten Island Hotel, 1415 Richmond Ave. (718-698-5000); $116–350 per night. Deluxe rooms at the Staten Island Hotel have cable television, armoires, work desks, coffeemakers, hair dryers, voice mail and either one king, one double, or two double beds. Or, choose a suite, each of which comes equipped with two double beds, separate sleeping and living areas, a kitchenette, a pull-out sofa and the other amenities described above. Dogs are welcome, but can't be left alone in the rooms at any time.

OUT AND ABOUT

The Bronx

Annual Halloween Dinner Dance and Costume Ball, Bobbi & the Strays, P.O. Box 170129, Ozone Park 11417; 718-845-0779; BobbiCares@aol.com. Crazy hats, wild wigs, outrageous outfits: Everything goes at this spooky Halloween celebration thrown every year by Bobbi and the Strays, an award-winning animal protection organization founded by Bobbi Giordano of Ozone Park. The group has been instrumental in rescuing, protecting and finding adoptive homes for thousands of stray cats and dogs throughout Queens County. Partygoers at the Halloween bash can expect to find food, drinks, music, dancing, and of course pets of all stripes (and spots). You can also support Bobbi's

organization at its annual garage sale, adoption events every Saturday at the Howard Beach PETCO (157-20 Cross Bay Blvd.), and appearances at the annual Broadway Barks! galas. (For more information about Broadway Barks!, see the listing below.)

Bronx dog runs, City of New York Parks and Recreation, The Arsenal, Central Park, 830 5th Ave.; www.nycgovparks.org). In addition to the outstanding Van Cortland and Pelham Bay parks (see listings below), the Bronx also offers five other leash-free parks managed by the city's Department of Parks and Recreation: Ewen Park on Riverdale and Johnson Aves.; Frank S. Hackett Park on Riverdale Ave., 245th St., and the Henry Hudson Pkwy.; Seton Park on W. 232nd Street and Independence Ave.; and the Williamsbridge Oval on 3225 Reservoir Oval East. In most cases, canines will have to wear a leash until they reach the designated, fenced-in dog-run area of the park. All dogs visiting the runs must have rabies vaccination tags, flea-and-tick-preventative treatments, and identification tags. Owners are also asked to clean up any messes (trash cans are usually provided) and not leave dogs unattended.

City Island. A visit to this seaside community might leave you feeling like you're closer to Boston than New York City: Dotted with clam shacks, white-picket fences, nautical museums, lighthouses, and piers, the place has a distinctly New England ambiance and makes for a great day trip. Take a lesson at the New York Sailing Center, swing some clubs at the Turtle Cove Golf Complex, pick up some bait at Jack's Bait and Tackle, or enjoy seafood specialties at restaurants like the Lobster House, Sammy's Fish Box, Sea Shore Restaurant and Marina, and Tony's Pier. By car, take I-95 to Exit 8B.

Pelham Bay Park, Pelham Bay Park Exit off of I-95 or Pelham Bridge Rd. off of the Hutchinson Pkwy. (718-430-1890). Feeling penned in by the city? The 2,765-acre Pelham Bay is NYC's largest park—big enough to give you that wonderful "middle-of-nowhere" feeling, but still just a short train ride from Manhattan

and other crowded locales. In addition to the usual park amenities like baseball fields, tennis courts, playgrounds, and a running track, you'll also find a lagoon, marshes, hiking trails, statues, historic sites, the Long Island Sound, a beach, a river, and enough wildlife species to keep you busy with those binoculars. There's also, conveniently enough, a dog run. Canines must be leashed between the hours of 9 AM and 9 PM (everywhere but the dog run).

Van Cortlandt Park, bordered by Gun Hill Rd., Jerome Ave., and Broadway (718-430-1890). New York City's third largest park, Van Cortlandt encompasses 1,146 acres with miles of nature trails, numerous playgrounds, a golf course, meadows, wetlands, sports fields and courts, a lake, a brook, and a variety of wildlife. But dog lovers will especially appreciate the park's Canine Court, a doggie playground and dog-agility course. Half of the 14,000-square-foot fenced-in area is a dog run, and the other half is the dog-agility course. For more park information, contact the Friends of Van Cortlandt Park at 718-601-1460 or visit the group's web site at www.vancortlandt.org.

Brooklyn
BARC Shelter Animal Parade and Show, BARC (Brooklyn Animal Resource Coalition) Shelter, 253 Wythe Ave., Williamsburg (718-486-7489; www.barcshelter.org). Held every fall in McCarren Park, this animal-centered event includes doggie contests, a parade, food

for people and pets, demonstrations, a "Bow Wow Lu'au," and more. The nonprofit organization also hosts an annual art show and auction, regularly scheduled dance parties, and "take your pet's picture with Santa" days in December. Locals and visitors alike are welcome. All money raised benefits the shelter's homeless animals. Call or visit the web site for the updated schedules and dates. The web site also provides news about adopted BARC animals (one of whom went on to become a National Agility Champion!), animals currently available for adoption, and links to animal-rights organizations, other local shelters, trainers, and educational resources. BARC's Picasso Fund, named after a resident pooch, provides grant money to shelters struggling to care for special-needs animals; for more information about the fund, visit www.animalalliancenyc.org/picasso.

Coney Island, Surf Ave. This world-famous landmark is still going strong with amusement park rides (including the historic Cyclone roller-coaster), circus-style sideshows, a beach, an aquarium, wacky museums, batting cages, burlesque, parades, parks, live musical performances, arcades, film festivals, go-cart tracks, and of course lots of food and drink vendors. In the summer, visitors can watch fireworks on the beach every Friday night. Your pup can even get some cool relief by taking a dip at Gravesend Bay Beach, located in Kaiser Park at the end of Bayview Ave.

DiMattina Park, Hicks Coles and Woodhull Sts. This large city park offers two separate dog-run areas and is managed by the city's Department of Parks and Recreation. Owners are required to use a leash in the park until they reach the dog runs, and must clean up after their animals. Dogs must be flea-free and have rabies vaccination tags and identification tags. For more information, write to the City of New York Parks and Recreation, The Arsenal, Central Park, 830 5th Ave., or visit www.nycgovparks. org.

Fort Greene Park, bordered by Myrtle Ave., Washington Park, and Dekalb Ave. Although not the most spectacular park in the city, Fort Greene is popular with dog owners, who appreciate the greenery and camaraderie of other canine lovers they often find here. The 30-acre spot has walking paths, tennis courts, open fields, and a monument to the 11,000 Revolutionary War soldiers who died on board British prison ships docked nearby. Dog lovers will also appreciate the recently installed doggie water spigot. For more information about the park (including directions, pictures, and a complete history), write to the Fort Greene Park Conservancy at P.O. Box 21734, Brooklyn, NY, 11202, call 718-222-1461, or visit the group's web site at www.fortgreene-park.org. For more information about dog-related events and issues in the park, contact Fort Greene PUPS, an advocacy group for canine owners, by writing to

P.O. Box 103, 542 Atlantic Ave., Brooklyn, NY, 11217, or visiting the PUP web site at www.fort-greenepups.org.

Mighty Mutts, P.O. Box 140139, Brooklyn (212-982-6832; 718-946-1074). This all-volunteer group is dedicated to rescuing and finding new homes for the many homeless dogs and cats in New York City. If you happen to be in town on a Saturday, stop by and say hello to some of the volunteers, who can be found at the southwest corner of Union Square, 14th St., and University Place (in Manhattan) between noon and 7 PM; they'll be joined by a group of adorable, four-legged city dwellers in need of new homes.

Prospect Park, Prospect Park W., Flatbush Ave., Park Circle, and Ocean Ave., Brooklyn (info@ prospectpark.org; www.prospect-park.org). One of the hottest spots in New York for canines, the 526-acre Prospect Park offers Dog Beach, the 90-acre Long Meadow, walking trails, a 60-acre lake, wooded areas, a canine memorial area, and special events like "Pup-Nic," "Coffee Bark," pet-themed lectures, and various doggie contests. Pets are not allowed on sports fields, in playground areas, or on equestrian trails. Owners are required to pick up after their animals. Leashes must be used, except during designated off-leash hours: At the time of this writing, the off-leash hours were 9 PM to 9 AM in the Long Meadow and Peninsula areas and 5 PM to 9 AM in the Nethermead area. Parking is available around the perimeter of the park in designated spots. FIDO (Fellowship in the Interest of Dogs and Owners) is an organization that keeps an eye on all happenings at the park, ensures that rules and regs are followed, and lobbies on behalf of dog owners in the area. The group offers a regular newsletter and web site, as well. For more information, call FIDO at 1-888-604-3422, write to fido@fido-brooklyn.com, or visit the organization's web site at www.fido-brooklyn.com.

Manhattan

American Society for the Prevention of Cruelty to Animals (ASPCA), 424 E. 92nd St. (212-876-7700; www.aspca. org). The ASPCA, one of the world's first humane organizations, is headquartered right here in New York City. This nonprofit education and advocacy group provides adoption services, a full-service animal hospital, behavioral therapy and obedience classes, agility programs, a poison-control center, and a Humane Law Enforcement Department, which you may have seen featured on its own show, "Animal Precinct," on the Animal Planet cable network. Call or visit the web site for the latest information about upcoming classes, events and fund-raisers.

Battery Park, Battery Place, Broadway and State St. Pets are not permitted at Liberty Island and Ellis Island, but you can still get a great view of the Statue of Liberty from this famous park located on the southern tip of Manhattan. Walk along the promenade, look out over the water, relax on a bench, throw a Frisbee, or nap under the shade of a tree. Expect crowds on weekends. Dogs are welcome on a leash.

Blessing of the Animals. Each year in early October, the local Catholic and Anglican churches celebrate the Feast Day of St. Francis (the patron Saint of animals) with a Blessing of the Animals religious service. And we're not talking just dogs, here: Churchgoers can expect to see canines, felines, birds, gerbils, fish, goats, and virtually every other type of feathered, furred, and finned friend. The Cathedral of St. John the Divine (1047 Amsterdam Ave.) holds the most popular services, along with vegetarian food, musical performances, and daylong celebratory events. You'll find similar get-togethers at St. George's Episcopal Church (Stuyvesant Square), St. Luke's in the Fields (487 Hudson St.), and Prospect Park in Brooklyn.

Broadway Barks! (212-840-0770; www.officialbroadwaybarks.org). This annual event (2003 marked the fifth) was founded by Mary Tyler Moore and Bernadette Peters and usually includes raffles, auctions, and an ever-changing roster of supportive celebrity hosts from stage and screen. But the main guest stars are the animals from city animal shelters who strut their stuff on the catwalk (or dog-walk?) in the hopes of attracting adoptive families. In addition to bringing together the various shelters and rescue groups in the city, Broadway Barks! also promotes

the issues of responsible pet ownership, pet identification, and spay/neuter education. The yearly event, produced with the support of Broadway Cares/Equity Fights AIDS, usually takes place at the beginning of the summer, although the date may vary from year to year. Corporate sponsors like Animal Planet, Loews Hotels, and Sherpa, along with individual donors, provide financial support to keep the program going from year to year. Call or visit the web site for more information about this year's location and schedule; you'll also find many links to other pet-rescue and adoption organizations in the city and in the immediate region.

Brooklyn Bridge Footbridge, Park Row (across from City Hall Park on the Manhattan side) You and your favorite canine can take a walk through history and get some great views on the Brooklyn Bridge. Cars aren't the only crossers here: The bridge also has a sidewalk/footbridge where you can jog, linger, or just take some pictures. The footbridge entrance is located at the median on the east side of Old City Hall Plaza. For detailed information about the bridge's history, including statistics, pictures, and poetry, visit www.endex.com/gf/buildings/bbridge.

Canine Comedy. This annual event is sponsored by *Animal Fair* magazine to benefit the non-profit local animal welfare group Stray from the Heart. Well-known comedians—many of whom have been on cable-TV's Comedy Central channel, *Saturday Night*

Live, The Late Show with David Letterman, The Tonight Show with Jay Leno, and other shows and venues—gather each year to lend a laugh or two to the cause of animal rescue and humane pet education in the city. For more information about this year's event or to buy tickets, contact Stray from the Heart (P.O. Box 11, New York City; 212-726-DOGS; www.strayfromtheheart.org) or pick up an issue of *Animal Fair* (545 Eighth Ave.; 212-629-0392; www.animalfair.com).

Central Park, bordered by 59th St., Central Park West, 110th St. and Fifth Ave. In 1858, the renowned landscape architects Frederick Law Olmstead and Calvert Vaux drew up a city park sketch they called the "Greensward Plan." Luckily, the name was eventually changed to Central Park, but the designers' vision for a green oasis in the city remained. Today it is one of the best-known parks in the world, providing New York City residents with seemingly endless trails, paved paths, bodies of water, playgrounds, scenic look-outs, sports fields, and quiet corners. It's no surprise that the park is a favorite with dog owners. Indeed, no visit to New York (with or without a dog) would be complete without at least a few jaunts into the park's greenery. Canines are allowed in most areas, but not in others: Luckily, clear signage keeps confusion at bay. So just use a leash, scoop the poop, and enjoy organized walking tours, outdoor music concerts, flower gardens, kids'

programs, catch-and-release fishing, horseback riding, tennis, bird-watching, tai chi classes, cross-country skiing, botany classes, and (best of all) people-watching. For maps, bloom schedules, and information about scheduled events, contact the Central Park Conservancy at 14 E. 60th St., 212-310-6600, or visit the group's web site at www.centralparknyc.org.

Central Park PAWS (webmaster@centralparkpaws. org; www.centralparkpaws.org). This nonprofit committee works tirelessly to improve communications among dog lovers, the Central Park Conservancy, and the Department of Parks and Recreation. It's a noble effort. But as a visitor to NYC, you might especially appreciate the group's exhaustive research and experience that will help you make the most of your trip to this fabled park. The PAWS web site provides all the details you might want to know about rules and regs (leash laws are enforced between 9 AM and 9 PM), advice (look for special dog-drinking fountains), and tips (don't miss the Ramble and the Harlem Meer). The group also helps to organize and publicize events like the My Dog Loves Central Park Country Fair.

Dog-Friendly Walking Tours of New York City, Zuckerman Family Travel (914-633-7397; marscot@worldnet.att.net; www.zuckermanfamilytravel.com /dogwalk). Art and Susan Zuckerman's two golden retrievers can help you and your pooch get acquainted with their city by taking custom-designed tours for two- and four-legged visitors. Depending on your interests, the tour visits popular neighborhoods such as Chinatown, Soho, the East Village, Little Italy, and Midtown, focusing on dog-friendly parks, restaurants, and famous sights. Along the way, you'll learn interesting tidbits and stop by little-known spots, including the "narrowest house in the city," Tammany Hall historic locales, and "the bloody angle." The Zuckermans are lifelong New Yorkers and dog lovers.

DOGNY Sculptures. The DOGNY sculpture show was a temporary exhibit hosted by the American Kennel Club as a tribute to the search-and-rescue dogs of September 11, 2001. Although the display was eventually disassembled, you can still find a few of the dog-themed sculptures in two locations: at Pace Plaza (at Pace University near City Hall); and at Lehman Brothers Park, behind Lehman Brothers's headquarters on 7th Ave. and 49th St. You can also order a fund-raising, 7-inch replica of the original dog sculpture model ($39.95), buy a hardcover book featuring photographs of the exhibit's sculptures ($24.95), or make a donation to the AKC's ongoing relief fund for search-and-rescue programs. For more information, write to the AKC at 260 Madison Ave., 4th Fl., New York, NY, 10016, call 919-816-3560, or visit www.akc.org.

Feast of San Gennaro, Little Italy (www.sangennaro.org). In 2003, this much-loved feast and festival celebrated its 76th anniversary of bringing fun, entertainment, and lots and lots of food to New York City locals and visitors. The weeklong event is typically held in early- to mid-September and includes parades, vendors, live music, cannoli-eating contests, and more diversions sure to please your eyes, ears, and taste buds. For more information, visit the festival's web site or call Little Italy's Most Precious Blood Church at 212-226-6427.

Great American Mutt Event, Mayor's Alliance for NYC's Animals, 244 Fifth Ave., Suite R290, New York (212-252-2350; info@animalalliancenyc.org; www.animalalliancenyc.org). The Mayor's Alliance, a nonprofit animal welfare group, joins forces with the ASPCA each year to host this festival and adoption event that includes demonstrations, "Ask the Vet" and "Ask the Trainer" sessions, food, drink, and even microchip clinics. Fun doggie contests award prizes for "Best Wagger" "Best Kisser," "Best Spots," and other free-wheeling categories. The Alliance also organizes an AdoptaCat Day with Cat Fancier's Association and regular dog and cat adoption days throughout the city; call or visit the web site for upcoming dates, times, and locations. The Alliance was formed as a way for all of the region's various animal welfare organizations to find strength in numbers and work toward making New York City a "no-kill" city.

Harlem Week, Harlem (harlem-chamber@hotmail.com; www.harlemdiscover.com). This annual festival celebrates the cultural history of Harlem with indoor and outdoor events, including jazz breakfasts, Family Unity Day, "Under the Stars" concerts, fashion shows, live performances at Riverbank State Park, sports tournaments, auto shows, children's festivals, art expos, and food vendors. E-mail the Greater Harlem Chamber of Commerce or visit the web site for this year's updated schedules and information.

Have A Heart Gala, Bide-A-Wee, 410 E. 38th St. (212-532-6395; 532-4455; info@bideawee.org; www.bideawee.org). Bide-A-Wee's annual fundraising gala, complete with celebrities, awards ceremonies, and lots of good food and drink, is just one of the group's fun gatherings held throughout the year. The non-profit organization houses and finds new families for homeless pets, offers free spay-and-neuter programs, and plans educational outreach programs in the community. Call or visit the web site for the latest information on upcoming events. The group also has two Long Island shelters: in Wantagh (516-785-4079) and Westhampton (631-325-0200).

Horse & carriage rides. Hansom cabs are a New York tradition that's often used in the movies and on TV. As you ride along with the gentle clip-clop of hooves and take in the sights of the city streets and Central Park, you'll know why the romantic transport persists in these days of yellow cabs and traffic jams. Many of the drivers will also allow you to

bring your pet on board, if you ask nicely enough; you can find the carriages parked and ready for customers at the intersection of 59th St. and Fifth Ave.

Hudson River Park, Hudson River Park Trust (212-791-2530). This waterfront park in lower Manhattan spans 5 miles between Battery Place and 59th St. Dogs are welcome to run free in the two on-site dog parks (one at Leroy St. and the other near 23rd St.), but must be on a leash no longer than 6 feet in the main park area. Popular activities here include boating, biking, dog-walking, gardening in community plots, and fishing. The area is also home to playgrounds, a skate park, volleyball courts, an ecology education center, and even a trapeze school. The park is currently undergoing a $383 million restoration, which will encompass flower gardens, walkways, bikeways, and piers.

Madison Square Park, East 24th St. and Fifth Ave. Set aside as parkland in 1847, this cute open space offers lawns, benches, flower gardens, a 19th-century fountain, a playground, statues, and a reflecting pool. Rover will be happy to know that the park also has a good-sized, leash-free dog run surrounded by distinctive wrought-iron fencing. Clean and well maintained by its regular users, the run is one of the most popular in the city.

Manhattan dog runs, City of New York Parks and Recreation, The Arsenal, Central Park, 830 5th Ave.; www.nycgovparks.org).

In addition to the dog runs and parks listed separately here (including Washington Square Park and Theodore Roosevelt Park), Manhattan also offers numerous other runs for boisterous pups. Try one of these locations: Inwood Hill Park on the corner of Dyckman St. and Payson Ave.; Carl Schurz Park at East End Ave. to the East River and E. 84th to 89th Sts.; Fish Bridge Park on Dover St. between Pearl and Water Streets; DeWitt Clinton Park (two runs) at W. 52nd and W. 54th Sts. between 11th and 12th Aves.; Thomas Smith Park on 11th Ave. between W. 22nd and W. 23rd Sts.; the J. Hood Wright park at Fort Washington and Haven Aves.; Robert Moses Park at E. 42nd St. between First Ave. and FDR Dr.; Fort Tryon Park on Margaret Corbin Ave. in Washington Heights; and the Peter Detmold Park between E. 49th and E. 51st Sts. The dog runs themselves are leash-free, but your pooch will have to remain leashed in other areas of the parks. In addition, pets must display identification tags and rabies-vaccination tags at all times. Trash cans are usually provided to make pooper-scooper duty a little easier to bear. These parks are all managed by the city; you will find other runs in Manhattan, but many are privately run (and paid for) by locals and may not welcome visitors. Be sure to read signs carefully before entering any potentially private property.

Metropolitan Transportation Authority (MTA) Services (www.mta.info). "Small" domestic pets are allowed on MTA buses and trains, as long as they remain crated or leashed at all times. Dogs and cats are not allowed to "take up" a seat; in other words, leave your carrier on the floor or on your lap. These rules apply to MTA buses, the subway, the Long Island Railroad and the Metro-North Railroad. Unofficially, you can often get away with a medium-

CANINES CAN ALWAYS FIND SOME ACTION AT WASHINGTON SQUARE PARK'S DOG RUN.

sized or larger dog, but it's best to try your luck during nonpeak hours. All schedules and rate information can be found on the MTA's web site; or, call 718-330-1234 for New York City Transit, 718-217-LIRR for the Long Island Railroad, or 212-532-4900 for the Metro-North Railroad.

New York City architectural highlights. Although you won't be able to roam inside with Spot at your heels, many of the city's historic structures are equally as impressive when viewed from the outside. During your visit, try to wander by some of these: in Manhattan, the Cathedral Church of St. John the Divine at 1047 Amsterdam Ave.; the Empire State Building (in the Art Deco style) at 350 Fifth Ave., the Morris-Jumel Mansion (Georgian) at 65 Jurnel Terr.; St. Patrick's Cathedral (Gothic Revival) at 14 E. 51st St.; the Eldridge Street Synagogue (currently undergoing renovations) at 12 Eldridge St.; the Merchant's House Museum (Greek Revival) at 29 E. Fourth St.; St. Bartholomew's Church (Byzantine) at 109 E. 50th St.; and in Brooklyn, the Soldiers and Sailors Memorial Arch at Grand Army Plaza.

NYCDOG, P.O. Box 330, Planetarium Station (212-496-1WAG; www.nycdog.org). This coalition of more than 21 dog-owner groups in New York City is an important source of information for local and visiting pet lovers. In addition to providing health and safety information and news about dog happenings, the group also works to improve

and increase off-leash opportunities for city pups and make sure dogowners' voices are heard by politicians. Visit the web site for updated meeting and events information.

Pet Chauffeur (718-752-1767; 1-866-PET-RIDE; info@petride.com; www.petride.com). Taxi drivers aren't always inclined to stop for a passenger with an 80-pound pooch in tow. Luckily, the Pet Chauffeur isn't so finicky. No matter where you're hoping to get to in the city (or elsewhere), this pet-transportation service doesn't mind a little drool and shedding on the journey.

Pet Taxi, 244 Fifth Ave. (212-755-1757; www.pettaxi.com). Pet Taxi drivers can take your mutt to the groomer, to the dog park, to the airport, sightseeing, across town or even across the county. Usually, about one-hour's notice is needed to arrange a ride—a bit more during peak hours and weekends. The business also offers an emergency "ambulance" service to nearby veterinary hospitals.

Riverside Park, Riverside Dr. at W. 87th and W. 105th Sts. A boon for dog lovers, Riverside Park boasts a 4-mile trail that winds beside the Hudson River. The park is also home to three separate dog runs, where visitors will find benches, trees, trash cans, hoses, water bowls, and plenty of friendly faces. Don't be surprised to see a doggie birthday party or two.

Rockefeller Center, 47th to 51st Sts. between Fifth Ave. and

Avenue of the Americas. When most people think of Rockefeller Center, the images of a giant, brightly lit Christmas tree and carefree ice skaters jump to mind. It's no secret that the landmark attracts the most visitors during the winter season. But even if you arrive in spring, summer, or fall, there is plenty to see and do here. You won't be able to tour the NBC studios or Radio City Music Hall with a pup in tow, but you will be able to stroll through the Channel Gardens, peer through the windows at ongoing NBC shows like "The Today Show," grab a coffee or snack at one of the surrounding cafés, or gawk at all the gawking tourists.

Seastreak Ferry Rides, Pier 11 (Wall St.) and E. 34th St. (732-872-2628; www.seastreakusa. com). Well-behaved pets are welcome on the outdoor decks on Seastreak, a ferry service that offers weekday and weekend departures to Atlantic Highlands and South Amboy, cities in northern New Jersey. The company's special-event excursions include fall foliage cruises; fireworks cruises; and holiday cruises with Santa.

Shopping. Notice that doesn't say *window-shopping:* In the city, many of the better known stores, such as Saks Fifth Avenue, Brooks Brothers, Bergdorf Goodman, and The Gap will allow your pet to accompany you while you shop for the necessities of the good life. Coach, which specializes in leather bags and other goods, also sells a variety of high-end leashes, collars,

and dog coats (18 locations in Manhattan). And Burberry's, located at 1350 Avenue of the Americas, also sells a fun line of dog coats, sweaters, and other accessories.

Of course, this doesn't mean the shops will be happy to see you coming with a 120-pound Great Dane in tow. But don't be surprised to see tiny terriers and dainty dachshunds browsing the aisles, their heads poking out of oh-so-fashionable doggie carriers. Some of the smaller boutiques will also allow canine guests, but be sure to ask a staffer before wandering inside with Rover.

South Street Seaport, Financial District. Located on the southern tip of Manhattan, this popular waterfront spot has cobblestone streets, coffee shops, scenic views from every angle, piers, street performers, clothing shops, outdoor concerts, boutiques, and more than 35 restaurants (some with outdoor seating and/or take-out service). It's also a great spot to get a picture of the Statue of Liberty.

Theodore Roosevelt Park, 81st St. and Columbus Ave. Dogs are required to be on a leash on the walking trails and grassy areas, but not in the newly renovated dog run, at this great park. The run is lined with small stones, accessorized with benches and trees, and filled with enthusiastic pooches and people. Stop in and read a book while your pup makes new friends.

Tompkins Square Park, E. 9th St. near Ave. B. This park was home to the very first dog run in New York City—a spot that's still extremely popular today. Local dog owners donate their time and money toward keeping the run in tiptop shape. Amenities include benches, picnic tables, trash cans, and regular events like costume contests and dog-lover gatherings.

Union Square Park, 15th St. and Union Square West. One of the-busiest parks in New York, Union Square also has one of the most crowded dog runs. The area is slated for renovation and expansion; in the meantime, bring a tennis ball and expect to share with the other mutts, mastiffs, and malamutes that come here to spend a little down time. Water, fencing, and benches are all provided.

Washington Square Park and dog run, Fifth Ave. and Washington Square North. (Like Union Square Park, the dog run at Washington Square Park is well known and often bursting at the seams with people and pups.) Even if you don't have a dog, there's always something to see in Washington Square Park; visitors can catch an impromptu musical performance, people-watch, read the paper, or just bask in the sun. Canine owners can rest at the dog run's benches while their pooches play leash-free in the pebble-lined play area.

William Secord Gallery, 52 E. 76th St. (212-249-0075; www. dogpainting.com). Every painting, print, and artifact on display at the William Secord Gallery has

the same subject matter: Dogs. The gallery, which was named after the founding director of The Dog Museum of America, specializes in nineteenth-century works of fine art, with an emphasis on paintings. Canines of all sizes are welcome to join their humans inside.

Queens

Bobbi & the Strays, P. O. Box 170129, Ozone Park 11417; 718-845-0779; BobbiCares@aol.com. This award-winning animal protection organization, founded by Bobbi Giordano of Ozone Park, has been instrumental in rescuing, protecting and finding adoptive homes for thousands of stray cats and dogs throughout Queens County. Every Saturday, you can find Bobbi and her adoptable animals at PETCO at 157-20 Cross Bay Blvd. in Howard Beach. Special events such as garage sales, Broadway Barks! and the Annual Halloween Dance & Costume Ball all help this all-volunteer organization.

Flushing Meadows Corona Park, bordered by the Van Wyck Expressway and Grand Central Pkwy. between 111th and 134th Sts., Flushing (718-760-6565). The former site of the 1939 and 1964 World's Fairs, Flushing Meadows is certainly one of the more distinctive parks in the city's system. The 1,255-acre area is home to many of its borough's best-known attractions, including the Queens Botanical Garden, the World's Fair Theaterama, the Queens Wildlife Center, Shea Stadium, the Queens Museum of

Art, and the Queens Zoo. Of course, you and your pooch will be more interested in the outdoor attractions, including two lakes, hiking and biking trails, and the massive globe "Unisphere" statue that survives from the 1964 fair. Dogs are welcome on a leash.

Forest Park, Woodhaven Blvd. and Forest Park Dr., Kew Gardens (718-235-0815). Sports enthusiasts will love the western end of Forest Park, where you'll find the Victory Field Sports Complex, bocce courts, tennis courts, softball fields, and the like. But you and Spot will probably want to head instead toward the eastern end, where you'll find hiking trails, paved walking paths, bridle paths (you can even "hire out" a horse at one of the stables), oak forests, and pine groves. Leashed dogs are welcome.

Noah's Ark Project, 251-61 Jamaica Ave., Bellerose (718-343-5203; director@arkproject.com; www.arkproject.com). This non-profit animal welfare organization hosts an annual softball game and other events throughout the year; vacationers are always welcome to volunteer or attend. Call, e-mail, or visit the web site to learn more about upcoming outings, happenings, and fund-raisers. The organization aims to spread the word about spaying and neutering, reduce the pet population in New York City, and reach local school-children with a message about kindness to animals.

Queens dog runs, City of New York Parks and Recreation (www.nycgovparks.org). The city operates two leash-free runs for dogs in Queens: The Forest Park Dog Run in Forest Park is located at Park Lane South and 85th St., while the Windmuller Park dog run is located on Woodside Ave. between 54th and 56th Sts. Feel free to unhook the leash once you're inside the fenced-in run, but you'll have to use a leash in other areas of the park. Dog owners are required to clean up any messes, display rabies vaccination tags and identification tags on their pets, and not leave the animals unattended at any time.

Socrates Sculpture Park, 32 Vernon Blvd., Long Island City (718-956-1819; www.socrates sculpturepark.org). Once an abandoned landfill, this unusual spot was transformed by civic- and artistic-minded locals into a huge outdoor exhibition space for local sculptors. Dogs are welcome on a leash, as long as owners clean up after them. The exhibits change regularly, so repeat visits should always provide plenty of eye candy. You'll also find a summer film series, concerts, theatrical performances, and educational programs here throughout the year.

Staten Island

Great Kills Park, Hylan Blvd. 718-351-6970). Despite its somewhat foreboding name, this is a wonderful spot for all types of New York residents and visitors. During your visit, you'll probably see schoolchildren on a field trip, fishermen, birdwatchers, hikers, boaters, Little League players, sunbathers, and every other conceivable variety of park-goer. Your dog is welcome in most beach areas (yes, even in the water!) and she'll also have fun sniffing around on dry land. Part of the Gateway National Recreation Area, the property is managed by the National Park Service.

Staten Island Botanical Garden, 1000 Richmond Terr. (718-273-8200; sibginc@erols.com; www.sibg.org). Get a glimpse of nature's beauty in bloom at the botanical garden, which houses an outdoor collection of widely varied trees, flowers, herbs, and bushes. Visitors will find a butterfly garden, a Chinese garden, a Heritage rose garden, statues, ponds, wetlands, a café, a farm, a visitors center, and a gift shop. Leashed dogs are welcome on the grounds but not in the formal gardens. You won't find a much better spot for the proverbial "walk in the park."

Staten Island Greenbelt, 200 Nevada Ave. A park in its own right, this 2,800-acre space was also designed to connect the borough's most distinctive ecosystems and other designated parks. Get back to nature by exploring the Greenbelt's trails, ponds, wet-

lands, and lakes, or enjoy the sporting life with tennis courts, a golf course, and softball fields. The park is also home to the William T. Davis Wildlife Refuge, the first bird sanctuary in NYC, and the Victory Plant Center. Key areas for exploring are Deer Park, Buck's Hollow, the Egbertville Ravine, and Reed's Basket Willow Swamp. And don't stop there: The Greenbelt is bordered by LaTourette, Willowbrook, and High Rock Parks. Leashed dogs are welcome. For more information, contact the Greenbelt Conservancy, a nonprofit group dedicated to preserving and promoting the park: Call them at 718-667-2165 or visit their web site at www.sigreenbelt.org.

Walkathon, Staten Island Council for Animal Welfare (SICAW), P.O. Box 120125 (718-448-3525). Bring your pup for a fun walk, meet other pet lovers, and raise money for this nonprofit animal welfare organization. SICAW's mission is to rescue homeless pets, shelter them, and work to find each animal a new home. The annual event is typically held in September; call for this year's date, time, and location.

QUICK BITES

The Bronx

Arthur Avenue. This much-loved area is the "Little Italy" of the Bronx; window-shop for a while to gawk at all the cheeses, fresh pastas, breads, and gifts that line the streets' storefronts. Most of the baked goods here are made in vast quantities and shipped to Connecticut, upstate New York, New Jersey, and other areas. But you can still stop into a café or two to taste strong coffees, sweets, sandwiches, and great Italian dinners. Many of the restaurants offer takeout; some have outdoor seating where Fluffy will be welcomed.

Lazy Susan's Mexican Seafood & Grill, 316 City Island Ave. (718-885-3003; www.lazysusans mexicangrill.com). The staff is anything but lazy at this fun restaurant offering outdoor seating, takeout, and delivery. The menu includes dishes like beer-battered fish tacos, veggie burritos, beef enchiladas, fried catfish sandwiches, queso carne, fried shrimp with tartar sauce, and Tex-Mex fusilli.

Liebman's Kosher Deli, 552 W. 235th St. (718-548-4534). One of only a handful of kosher delicatessens left in the Bronx, Liebman's has a dining area and a take-out counter. Choose from deli items such as pastrami sandwiches, matzoh ball soup, sour pickles, stuffed cabbage, noodle pudding, apple pie, knishes, and even salads.

Tito Puente's, 64 City Island Ave. (718-885-3200). This friendly seafood and Latino restaurant offers a few sidewalk tables under a bright green-and-white awning. Dinner entrees include lobster dishes, rice dishes, surf-and-turf, chicken, steaks, and a clam bar; at lunchtime, choose from burgers, fried shrimp, Spanish rice, and the catch of the day. The restaurant is perhaps best known for its live jazz.

Tosca, 4038 E. Tremont Ave. (718-239-3300). Coal-fired-oven pizza, thin and crispy, was made famous in New Haven, Connecticut. Tosca brings that much-raved-about (and hard-to-find) taste to the Bronx, serving up their pizza pies and other meals in a candlelit atmosphere. Outdoor seating area and takeout are both available.

Brooklyn

Brooklyn Ice Cream Factory, Fulton Ferry Landing between Old Fulton and Water Sts. (718-246-3963). Expect great views and crowds at this warm-weather mecca in the so-called DUMBO (Down Under the Manhattan Bridge Overpass) neighborhood. Indulge yourself with a cone, sundae, milkshake, or banana split and enjoy your booty while viewing the Manhattan skyline.

Downtown Atlantic Restaurant and Bakery, 364 Atlantic Ave., (718-852-9945). Takeout and delivery are both available at this unique eatery with a bar, weekend brunch menus, live musical performances, and a host of delicious baked goods, sandwiches, and other treats.

The Garden, 921 Manhattan Ave., Greenpoint (718-389-6448). Here's a good place to pack your picnic basket: This gourmet grocery shop and deli serves plump sandwiches, coffee, and soups, all available to go. You can also pick up some organic fruit and veggies, fresh-baked breads, and more than 80 types of cheese.

Nathan's Famous, Stillwell and Surf Aves., Coney Island (718-946-2202). This is the site of the original stand that started selling Nathan's Famous hot dogs in 1916. Stop by the take-out window and pick up your own bite of history-in-a-bun, smothered with relish and onions, along with some crinkle-cut fries and fresh-squeezed lemonade. The stand still holds its annual hot dog–eating contest every July 4.

Pan Pizza Kitchen, 7401 5th Ave. (718-833-8346; www.panpizza kitchen.com). Delivery is free at this pizza-pie haven, which serves burgers, salads, specialty sandwiches, and pasta in addition to its signature pies. Log on to the web site to view all your choices before calling in an order; pizza toppings include black olive, ricotta cheese, ham, sausage, hot peppers, and garlic.

Manhattan

2nd Avenue Deli, 156 Second Ave. (212-677-0606; www.2ndave deli.com). Take a peek at the menu on-line and order kosher meals and sandwiches from the comfort of your hotel room. Choose from Jewish specialties such as gelfilte fish, matzoh ball soup, knishes, chopped herring salad, and nova lox. Corned beef, pastrami, and brisket sandwiches are also available, as are desserts like rugalach, pareve cheesecake, and halvah.

A & M Roadhouse, 57 Murray St. (212-385-9005). Eat in, take out, or enjoy free delivery from the Roadhouse, a fun barbecue-style eatery. The lunch menu includes soups, salads, sandwiches, and sides like baked beans, "smashed" potatoes, and corn on the cob. At dinnertime, start with chili or nachos and move on to dishes like ribs, beer-battered chicken, lobster, or fried shrimp.

Bagels, bagels, bagels. You can't leave the city without at least one taste of its famous boiled-then-baked round treats. From Zabar's to H&H, Bergen Bagels, and smaller individual shops like Lenny's on Broadway and Tal Bagel on Avenue of the Americas, the plump, crispy-on-the-outside and chewy-on-the-inside breads are great with lox, peanut butter, meats and cheeses, jams, and just about every other topping you can think of. Order a sandwich, a simple toasted bagel, or a baker's dozen, and enjoy them at the park.

Barking Dog Luncheonette, 1678 3rd Ave. (212-831-1800). Dogs, dogs, everywhere: The health code prohibits real pooches from coming inside, but canine lovers will nonetheless get a kick out of the dog-themed décor and merchandise of this Upper East Side spot. Rover can even get some much-needed refreshment at the doggie water bowl near the front door. Outdoor seats, takeout, and delivery are all available.

Big Nick's Burger and Pizza Joint, 2175 Broadway (212-362-9238). Big Nick's calls it "emergency pizza": that pie you just have to have immediately, even if you can't (or won't) leave your hotel room or home. Whether you want a plain-and-simple pepperoni or a more unusual topping, such as chili, hamburger, eggplant, pineapple, and hard-boiled eggs, they aim to please. Delivery is free on the West Side.

Broadway Joe Steakhouse, 315 W. 46th St. (212-246-6513). Broadway Joe's will delight carnivores with its prime rib, sirloin steak, filet mignon, pork chops, and lamb chops. On the lighter side, the restaurant also serves pasta primavera, salads, broiled filet of sole, and grilled salmon. When you call to make reservations, let the staff know you're bringing a pooch and request outdoor seating.

Brother Jimmy's BBQ To Go (212-860-6466; bbqtogo@brother-jimmys.com; www.brotherjim-mys.com). In addition to offering wild-and-crazy restaurants in three locations (1485 Second, 1644 Third, and 428 Amsterdam Aves.), Brother Jimmy's also specializes in "BBQ to Go." The cooks will grill up smoked ribs, pulled pork, barbecue chicken, potato salad, macaroni and

cheese, and other gooey specialties, then wrap your meal in chilled packaging designed to survive your ride to the beach or the park.

Café St. Bart's, 50th St. at Park Ave. (212-888-2664). Located next to the beautiful St. Bartholomew's, this restaurant has a giant outdoor-seating area with great views. Favorites include fish tacos, beer-battered onion rings, fried okra, tortilla soup, chocolate layer cake, and berry-covered waffles. Breakfast and lunch are served year-round; in warmer months, you can also enjoy dinner and Sunday brunch.

Café Sha Sha, 510 Hudson St. (212-242-3021). This cozy coffeehouse provides java lovers with hot, fresh cups of cappuccino, espresso, iced coffee, and the straightforward brews of the day. A vast array of sweet treats and sandwiches ensures that your coffee won't be lonely. You can pick up your drink to go or enjoy it at one of the seasonal outdoor tables.

Cookie Island, 189 Broadway (212-608-5937). You've gotta' love this bakery's slogan: "Every cookie needs a belly!" Your belly is sure to volunteer once you smell the sweet scents wafting out of the door. Coffee, ice cream, and, of course, milk are also available. And if you fall in love with the cookies during your visit, you won't have to do without after you leave—they'll ship to just about anywhere.

Fine & Schapiro, 138 W. 72nd St. (212-877-2721; 212-877-2874; www.fineandschapiro.com). This kosher restaurant and deli has been a Jewish NYC tradition since 1927. Quick delivery service to hotels is always available; you can even view the menu online before you call. Choices range from simple sandwiches and soups to baby potato latkes, egg barley, fried kreplach, stuffed cabbage, and cocktail knishes.

Fred's, 476 Amsterdam Ave. (212-579-3076). This is a must-stop for all dog lovers visiting the city: Not only does Fred's have great food, but it's also filled with canine pictures and memorabilia. Named after a female (yes, female) black lab, the restaurant displays fun pictures of customers' dogs all over the walls—if you frame it, they'll hang it. The menu includes items such as soups, salads, burgers, pasta, chicken, kids' meals, and vegetarian dishes. Customers with dogs can order take-out, delivery, or lounge at a few outdoor tables.

Greenwich Café, 75 Greenwich Ave. (212-366-6004). Located at 7th Ave., this laid-back café provides outdoor tables with umbrellas during the warmer seasons (weather permitting). Whether you're looking to relax with a cup of coffee and pastry or sink your teeth into a hearty meal, you're sure to find something to suit your mood. Choose from appetizers, wines, and entrees like veggie burgers, steak, grilled fish, ravioli, and crab cakes.

Grey Dog's Coffee, 33 Carmine St. (212-462-0041). Sure, Grey Dog's has won a few local "best cup of coffee" contests, but of course we dog lovers really like this cozy café because of its name. Everything is big here, from the large cups of java to the piled-high sandwiches and giant cookies. Place your order to go and sip as you walk.

Hakata Grill, 230 W. 48th St. (212-245-1020). Sushi delivered? You bet. Choose individual pieces, à la carte–style, or combination meals like the sashimi set, the spicy Pacific combination, and the Hawaiian set deluxe. Noodle dishes, Bento boxes, sandwiches, and entrees like shrimp tempura and miso salmon are also available. Nearby delivery is free.

The Harrison, 355 Greenwich St. (212-274-9310). During the warmer months, The Harrison offers an outdoor sidewalk seating area; your dog is welcome to sit beside you, provided she stays on the other side of the stantion barrier. Entrees include items such as black sea bass, roasted crispy chicken, lamb shank, and pork chops. Start your meal with a sunflower salad or potato-wrapped scallops, and end with an almond panna cotta, apple crepe, or chocolate cake.

Hudson Place, 538 3rd Ave. (212-686-6660). Your dog is welcome to join you at Hudson Place's outdoor seating area, as long as he stays on the other side of the small barrier fence. Expect to find dishes such as lamb shank,

THE WALLS AT FRED'S RESTAURANT ARE COVERED WITH FRAMED PHOTOS OF CUSTOMERS' DOGS.

baby-back ribs, seafood risotto, French onion soup, pasta primavera, meatloaf, chicken sandwiches, and fried calamari.

Island Burger and Shakes, 766 9th Ave. (212-307-7934). This Hell's Kitchen "joint" offers an eat-in dining room, take-out service, and delivery. They are probably best known for their hamburgers, including the Bourbon Street (blackened with bacon and Bayou mayo), the Black 'n Bleu (blackened with blue cheese), and the au poivre (sautéed with a black pepper sauce). Of course, you'll need a thick milkshake to wash it all down, and maybe a salad on the side.

Manhattan Chili Company, 1500 Broadway (212-730-8666) and 1697 Broadway (212-246-6555) (www.manhattanchilicony.city-search.com). This funky, colorful restaurant recently started a delivery service: Now you can have jalapeno quesadillas, chorizo nachos, Texas Chain Gang Chili, and spicy BBQ sandwiches dropped off at your hotel room door. You can even view the menu and order on-line. The 1697 Broadway site is located beneath the marquee for Ed Sullivan Theater, where the "Late Show with David Letterman" is filmed.

Mulberry Street. This Little Italy landmark is lined with tempting bakeries and restaurants serving up pasta, pizza, seafood, baked goods, cappuccino, and virtually every other delectable treat you can imagine. If you arrive in warm weather, nearly all of the

eateries have outdoor seating and will welcome your well-behaved pooch at sidewalk tables; in fact, don't be surprised to see staffers calling out menu items and trying to tempt you to choose their restaurant over the neighbor's.

Our Place Shanghai Tea Garden, 141 E. 55th St. (212-753-3900; www.ourplaceteagarden.com). Delivery is free from this upscale East Side Chinese restaurant. Just go on-line to pick out your favorites, then call to order. You'll be able to choose from specialties like sautéed squid, stuffed duck, Szechuan peppery chicken, Mandarin Paradox, General Ching's chicken, tangerine beef, and braised lobster.

Ray Bari Pizza, 201 Amsterdam Ave. (212-595-8400); 930 Third Ave. (212-755-2390); 1330 Third Ave. (212-988-3337); 400 W. 42nd St. (212-695-0300); and 3 Greenwich Ave. (212-620-0200). No matter where you are in Manhattan, chances are that one of the five Ray Bari locations will deliver to your hotel's area. Takeout is also available, as are pasta dishes, salads, cold drinks, and sandwiches.

Serendipity III, 225 E. 60th St. (212-838-3531). Sure, you can get burgers, soups, and even dim sum to go at this café and general store. But Serendipity is really known for its expansive sweet selection, including guilty pleasures such as Cheese Cake Vesuvius, Crème de la Crème, Humble Pie, Celestial Carrot Cake, Lemon Ice Box Pie, and the shop's famous "Frrrozen Hot Chocolate."

SheepMeadow Café, Central Park West (212-396-4100). This convenient snack bar at Central Park has lots of takeout and outdoor seating, wonderful views, and a low-key attitude. In the evening, it switches gears and becomes a sit-down restaurant (still offering outdoor seating) with steaks, fish, salads, and barbecue ribs.

SouthwestNY, 225 Liberty St., 2 World Financial Center (212-945-0528; www.southwestny.com). This southwestern-style restaurant offers outdoor seating, takeout, and delivery in the Financial District: You can check out the menu on-line, then call or e-mail your order. Meal choices include burgers, wraps, salads, tortilla pies, steaks, seafood, and chicken.

Stage Deli, 834 Seventh Ave. (212-245-7850). This delicatessen is famous for its glowing neon sign, but you might best appreciate its "delivery anywhere, anytime" motto. Stop into the eatery and order a meal to go, or have it delivered directly to your hotel room. Stage has a little bit of almost everything, including egg platters, homemade soups, salads, traditional and specialty sandwiches, "triple-deckers" (named after stage and screen celebrities), and burgers.

Theresa's Gourmet Café and Coffee Bar, 215 E. 47th St. (212-355-2833), 51 W. 51st St. (212-265-7988), 220 E. 42nd St. (212-682-4490), and 555 7th Ave. (212-354-9590). When that cold fall and winter wind is blowing, stop into one of Theresa's four Manhattan locations for a café latte, cappuccino, espresso, or coffee of the day. Cold drinks, sandwiches, salads, and soups are also on the take-out menu.

Tossed, 295 Park Ave. South (212-674-6700; www.tossed.com). Billed as "the world's first on-line salad bar," Tossed will deliver its leafy creations in the Park Ave. South delivery area (between Third Ave. and Avenue of the Americas and 14th and 31st Sts.) and the Rockefeller delivery area (between Broadway and Park Ave. and 45th and 55th Sts.). You can call or place your order on-line; selections include "design-your-own" salads, burgers, sandwiches, cold drinks, and desserts.

Queens

Danny Boy's, 64 Dry Harbor Rd., Middle Village (718-894-3488). Oh, Danny Boy... This Ireland-inspired pub and restaurant has a good selection of beers, a kid's menu, and serves breakfast (on weekends), lunch, and dinner. Typical menu items include burgers, chicken, seafood, steak, and sandwiches. In warmer weather, seating is available in an outdoor patio.

El Coyote, 178 Hillside Ave., Jamaica (718-558-6013). Dig into Mexican specialties at El Coyote, a fun-loving restaurant with an outdoor patio seating area and take-out service. Options include chips-and-salsa with guacamole, fajitas, tacos, burritos, enchiladas, seafood, pork, and even Mexican beers.

Lemon Ice King of Corona, 52 108th St. (718-699-5133). Whoever he is, locals really do think he is the king of lemon ice—and strawberry ice, and watermelon ice, and grape ice (you get the idea). On a hot August day, you can't beat an Italian Ice treat, and this is one of the best spots in NYC to get it.

Oneness-Fountain-Heart, 15719 72nd Ave., Flushing (718-591-3663). This strictly vegetarian eatery also serves vegan and macrobiotic meals. Grilled portobella sandwiches, salads, wraps, coffee, and fruit smoothies are some of the menu items offered. You'll find a Japanese garden outside; takeout and delivery are also available.

San Antonio Bakery, 36-20 Astoria Blvd. (718-777-8733). The *Village Voice* chose this spot for its "Tastiest Hot Dog" category a few years back, a testament to the fresh-baked buns and juicy, meaty flavor. All your favorite toppings are here, too, including onions, mustard, relish, and mayo. One for you, one for Fluffy: It's only fair.

Staten Island
Dairy Palace, 2210 Victory Blvd. (718-761-5200). This take-out spot serves a huge variety of foods, including Chinese dishes, sushi, ice cream, kosher options, and lots of vegetarian and vegan meals. This is an ultracasual place with a "move 'em along" mentality, but it can be a convenient eatery for hungry dog-toting travelers.

East Shore Inn, 283 Sand Lane (718-815-1781). East Shore Inn is a casual restaurant with happy hours, a raw bar, early-bird specials, Sunday brunch, daily lunch specials, full dinners, and live music. In the summertime, ask for a sidewalk table next to the barrier; your pup can sit just on the other side. Takeout is also an option.

Goodfellas, 1718 Hyland Blvd. (718-987-2422). A much-loved spot with locals, Goodfellas serves up brick-oven pizza and a host of pasta dishes, salads, desserts, and appetizers. Specialty pie choices include Taco Pizza, Vegetarian Delight, Pizza alla Vodka, and Mushroom Madness. Takeout and delivery are both available.

Neza Mexican Restaurant, 548 Lincoln Ave. (718-351-4929). Staten Island gets spicy at Neza: All of your favorite Mexican specialties are here, including fajitas, tacos, burritos, quesadillas, refried beans, and margaritas. Takeout and delivery are both available.

Ralph's, 501 Port Richmond Ave. (718-448-0853). This is the main site and headquarters for the popular local chain specializing in "famous Italian ices." Wander up to the take-out window and choose from more than 34 flavors, including root beer, Mai Tai, citrus twister, mango, and cherry. You'll also find other Ralph's locations scattered around Long Island, Queens, and New Jersey.

HOT SPOTS FOR SPOT

The Bronx

All Paws Grooming, 3639 Bruckner Blvd. (718-824-3927). Adventuring around the big city can be a messy business: This friendly grooming salon can help Rover look his best once again with washes, cuts, brush-outs, and other pampering services.

Pet Stop, 3605 Riverdale Ave. (718-549-5900). At Pet Stop, you can count on finding all the basic dog supplies you might need, including food, leashes, and flea-and-tick preventative treatments. But you'll also find plenty of products designed purely for pampering, like gourmet biscuits, plush toys, vitamin supplements, grooming brushes, and ergonomically correct dog bowls.

Brooklyn

Brooklyn Dog House, 327 Douglass St., Park Slope (718-222-4900; info@brooklyn-doghouse.com; www.brooklyn-doghouse.com). Daycare and overnight boarding are both available at the Brooklyn Dog House, a facility offering two large pooch playgrounds where dogs spend most of their time playing and socializing. Open 365 days a year, the Dog House also provides baths upon request, drop-off and pickup services, and a staff that keeps an eye on your canine throughout the day. Each pooch has his or her own sleeping area.

Dog Delight, 300 Kings Hwy. (718-339-7800); 756 3rd Ave.

(718-788-7970); and 8510 21st Ave. (718-714-0588). With three locations in Brooklyn, this store stocks brands such as Midwest pet homes, Chewtastics treats, and Marine Dog leashes, as well as a good selection of premium and affordable pet foods.

Monster Mutt, 297 Warren St. (718-858-9028; monstermutt@ monstermutt.com; www.monster-mutt.com). Monster Mutt provides local and visiting pups with doggie daycare services, overnight boarding (otherwise known as "sleepovers"), obedience training, grooming, and even a pet-supply shop called the Bow-Wow Boutique. Canine clients enjoy a cageless experience with plenty of treats, naps, and playtime in the 2,000-square-foot facility. All visiting dogs must have up-to-date vaccinations and flea protection.

Williamsburg Pet Supplies, 253 Wythe Ave. (718-486-7489). All proceeds from this pet-supply store benefit the Brooklyn Animal Resource Coalition (BARC) shelter next door (see Brooklyn in "Out and About"). You'll find every type of necessity and fun extra, including dog and cat foods, chew toys, flea and tick medications, carriers, beds, bowls, leashes, and snacks.

Manhattan

Beasty Feast, 630 Hudson St. (212-620-7099); 237 Bleecker St. (212-243-3261); and 680 Washington St. (212-620-4055).

YOUNG NEW YORKERS GET SOCIALIZATION AND OBEDIENCE TRAINING IN ONE OF BISCUITS AND BATH'S PUPPY CLASSES.

With three locations in Manhattan, this popular pet-supply store provides animal lovers throughout the city with everything from serious supplies—including brand-name foods and vitamins—to silly toys and helpful accessories.

Biscuits & Bath Doggy Gym, 1535 First Ave. (212-794-3600). Like its flagship location on E. 44th St. (see listing below), this Biscuits & Bath facility is an urban oasis for four-legged NYC residents and visitors. Located between 80th and 81st Sts., the gym offers indoor play areas, a gift shop, grooming services, daycare and overnight boarding.

Biscuits & Bath Doggy Village, 227 E. 44th St. (212-692-2323). This extensive 5-floor facility in Midtown is like a doggy heaven for city pooches: Amenities include a canine café, a lap pool, grooming services, indoor "grassy" fields, daycare and overnight boarding, weekly Sunday brunches for people and animals, training and socialization classes, a napping area, a gift and supply shop, dog birthday parties and other special events, and even services for cats. The facility also has an adoption center for homeless dogs and a Doggy Gym at a separate location (see listing above). Most clients have a yearly membership, although short-term visitors can also take advantage of many Biscuits & Bath services.

Blue Sky Dogs, P.O. Box 230532 (212-580-3009; info@bluesky-dogsny.com; www.bluesky-dogsny.com). Dogs and dog lovers have found a soulmate in Blue Sky Dogs, a canine adventure company that caters to four-legged NYC residents and visitors. "We specialize in outdoor adventure trips to wilderness areas and beach areas just outside of the city, and also local travel adventures for busy city dogs and their owners," explains Blue Sky Dogs owner Tammy McCarley. Options include Adventure Days, Weekend Adventure Getaways, Best Friends Weekends, and "slumber parties" (overnight boarding services).

Canine Ranch, 452A Columbus Ave. (212-787-PETS; 1-877-K9-RANCH). Located between 81st and 82nd Sts., only about a block from the dog run in Theodore Roosevelt Park, this packed, friendly store offers grooming services, doggie daycare, a pet "deli," and a wide selection of treats, toys, and accessories for pets—and for the people who love them.

Canine Styles, 830 Lexington Ave. (212-838-2064; info@ caninestyles.com; www.canine-styles.com). Some say New York is the fashion capital of the

world, so why should the humans have all the fun? English-style trench coats, anoraks, fisherman's sweaters, Burberry wool coats, and other fashions for the furry set are all available at Canine Styles. You'll also find dog beds and dog futons, holiday items, plaid leashes and collars and more. Visit the shop or order on-line.

DoggyStyle, NYC, 100 Thompson St. (212-431-9200; www.doggy-stylenyc.com). This cute shop isn't too far from the dog run in Washington Square Park; after a romp with your pooch, you can stop in here for pet-inspired jewelry, treats, leashes, dog beds, and other items.

Dog Wash, 177 MacDougal St. (212-673-3290). As the name implies, this Greenwich Village shop offers full grooming services, including baths, brush-outs, clips, and TLC. But the business also

CANINE RANCH, A POPULAR UPPER WEST SIDE SHOP, OFFERS GROOMING, GOURMET BISCUITS, SUPPLIES, AND OTHER PET PRODUCTS AND SERVICES.

provides doggie daycare, overnight boarding, and even obedience training. Dog guests stay in large, individual dog runs.

Fetch, 43 Greenwich Ave. (212-352-8591; info@fetchpets.com; www.fetchpets.com). Let's face it: Sometimes you just have to have a picture frame shaped like a dog bone. Or a collar charm shaped like a dog bone. Or even a water bowl with cutouts of dog bones. You can fetch all these and more at this pet-centered shop on Greenwich Ave., which also stocks doggie raincoats and sweaters, pet shampoos, travel bags, leashes, dog beds, and even "pet tents."

Inn at Canine Ranch, 72nd and Columbus (212-787-PETS; 1-877-K9-RANCH). At press time, the Inn at Canine Ranch, a "doggie B&B" boarding facility, was getting ready to open in the near future. The inn is owned by the same people who run Canine Ranch up the street (see listing on previous page). Interested customers can call the store for more information and updated schedules.

Katie's Kitty, 170 E. 83rd St. (212-288-5712). Specializing in cat-sitting and dog-walking in the Upper East Side, this service is run by a pet lover and his daughter; the pair provides "sleepovers," pet picnics in the park, kitty-sitting, and pet birthday parties for dogs and cats as well as regular dog-walk outings for pent-up pets. Call ahead for reservations.

New York Dog Spa & Hotel, 145 W. 18th St. and 32 W. 25th St. (212-243-1199; www.dogspa.com). Yes, it's just what it sounds like: Catering exclusively to canines, the New York Dog Spa & Hotel provides overnight stays in private runs, doggie daycare with lots of socialization, obedience classes, veterinary services, baths, and even canine massage. (Don't forget your up-to-date vaccination records.) You can call or visit the web site to make reservations.

NYC Dog Walkers, 27 W. 96th St., #6E (917-912-3968; nyc.dogwalkers@verizon.net; www.nycdogwalkers.com). NYC Dog Walkers staffers will arrive at your home or hotel room to take Fluffy on a solo or group walk. Outings of varying lengths are available, from 30 minutes to 2 hours. The service area includes all Manhattan hotels below 98th St.

Pampered Pets, Inc. (212-772-2181; www.pamperedpetsinc.com). Have tickets to the opera, but your hotel won't allow you to leave Fluffy alone in the room? Just give this pet-care business a call. "We're a full service company," explains Pampered Pets' staffer Jane Stiner. "We come to your home or hotel room with groomers, trainers, and pet-sitters." Customers can also schedule regular or one-time-only dog walks, along with play and socializing sessions for adult dogs and puppies.

PAWS-NYC (212-316-0427; kat@paws-nyc.com). This pet-sitting service provides dog walks, boarding, playtimes, feedings, and transportation to and from the groomer, the veterinarian, and other service providers throughout Manhattan. "Our walkers are available 24 hours a day, seven days a week, including all major holidays," explains PAWS-NYC owner Kathi Vincent. "We're also capable of filling last-minute requests for visitors to New York."

The Pet Bar Pet Supplies, 132 Thompson St. (212-253-9250). Don't be surprised to see a cat napping on one of the dog beds in the window of this cozy store. Filled to the ceiling with supplies, food, and accessories, The Pet Bar can help you stock up on essential items for dogs, cats, and other pets.

Pup Culture, 529 Broome St. (212-925-2090; info@pup-culturenyc.com; www.pup-culturenyc.com). You'll find this doggie daycare and boarding facility on Broome St. between Thompson St. and Avenue of the Americas; the facility also offers grooming services, obedience training, dog-walking services, pickup and delivery services, spa treatments, and other ways to spoil your favorite four-legged friend. Overnight guests and animals in daycare enjoy romping with each other in two play areas with rubber flooring and air-conditioning.

Spoiled Brats Pet Food & Supplies, 340 W. 49th St. (212-459-1615). Maybe you're in the market for a Burt's Bees Furry Friends Deodorizing Candle. Or perhaps Fido is hankering for

some freeze-dried liver treats. Whatever your whim, this shop aims to satisfy. Doggie bow ties, raincoats, sweaters, vitamin supplements, and plush toys are all available in abundance.

Sutton Pets, 311 E. 60th St. (212-355-2850; www.suttonpets. com). Billed as "a country place in the city," Sutton Pets provides air-conditioned overnight boarding with sheepskin rugs, a doggie "playcare" center, daily dog walks for guests, cat "condos," an aviary for bird boarding, grooming services, and even a pet-supply store selling food, toys, vitamins, rawhide bones, collars, leashes, bowls, and numerous other necessities.

Two Dogs & A Goat, 326 E. 34th St. (212-213-6979; char@two-dogsandagoat.com; www.two-dogsandagoat.com). This Manhattan pet-care company provides a special "hotel care" service for visitors to NYC: One of the staffers will visit your pooch in the hotel room for play time and TLC while you're out, or you can elect to have him or her take your dog for a walk around the block or through the park. The company also offers grooming services, obedience training, "sleepover" boarding, and transportation for veterinary visits.

Walkee Doggie (212-925-8100; walkeedoggie@aol.com; www.walkeedoggie.com). The canine clients of this dog-walk company (serving Soho, Tribeca, and the entire East Side) are always walked in groups of three or fewer, allowing for less herding and more genuine exercise. Dogs can expect food and water after each walk; human clients can expect a drop-off and pickup service and progress reports. Some in-house boarding is also available.

Queens

Collars and Scents, serving Queens and Manhattan (718-932-2164; collarsandscents@hotmail.com; www.collarsandscents.com). This pet-care service covers two boroughs with pet sitting, dog walks, "sleepover" overnight boarding, and pet-related errands. "Our dog walks are one-to-one to provide extra attention to each dog," explains Collars and Scents owner Stephen Neagus. "The majority of our clients are cats and dogs, but we also care for a variety of types of pets including rabbits, turtles, fish, and birds."

Janimals, serving Long Island City, Astoria, and Sunnyside (all in Queens) and Manhattan (646-249-9063; janimalsnyc@aol.com; www.janimals.net). Janimals owner Jan Tilley is a lifelong animal lover who turned her passion into a pet-care business serving areas of Queens and Manhattan. You can choose to board your dog or cat in Janimals' "pet hotel" (pickup and drop-off service is available) or have Jan visit your home or hotel room for a dog walk, feeding, or play session.

You Dirty Dog, 60-72 72nd St., Maspeth (718-779-5990). This day spa for pets offers baths, brush-outs, skin and fur conditioning, ear cleanings, nail clippings, and other services for pups in need of a freshening-up. A pickup and delivery service is also available. Call ahead for reservations.

Staten Island
Animal Pantry, 1801 Hylan Blvd. (718-979-1657). This pet-supply store stocks items such as Marine Dog leashes and collars, Noah's Kingdom premium all-natural dog foods, Midwest doghouses, and a good selection of other foods, toys, chewies, and supplies.

Clip & Fluff Boutique, 129 Port Richmond Ave. (718-447-2304). This grooming facility and pet-supply shop can give your pup a wash, a clip, a nail cut, or even just help him stock up on his favorite food and treats.

Country Estate Kennels, Arthur Kill Rd. (718-356-3933). Locals and visitors can opt for overnight boarding or doggie daycare at Country Estate. The kennel facility also hosts regular adoption days for the Staten Island Council for Animal Welfare's homeless pets looking for new families.

Petland Discounts, 2600 Hylan Blvd. (718-351-7811), 1495 Forest Ave. (718-981-0849), 6410 Amboy Rd. (718-227-8077), and 2795 Richmond Ave. (718-983-1158). This discount chain sells a wide variety of dog and cat food, collars and leashes, treats, food and water bowls, grooming supplies, flea-and-tick-control products, pet beds, and animal-related books and magazines. The company also works with local shelters and humane societies to encourage animal adoptions.

IN CASE OF EMERGENCY

The Bronx
Abbey Veterinary Hospital
322 W. 231st St. (718-543-6565)

Animal Hospital of Morris Park
1135 Morris Park Ave. (718-822-3309)

Riverdale Veterinary Group
3607 Riverdale Ave. (718-796-8387)

Throggs Neck Hospital
3800 E. Tremont Ave. (718-430-7000)

Brooklyn
Animal Clinic of Canarsie
9605 Glenwood Rd. (718-257-1010)

Animal Hospital of Brooklyn
2270 Flatbush Ave. (718-258-0500)

Bay Ridge Animal Hospital
6803 5th Ave. (718-748-1047)

Manhattan Beach Animal Clinic
102 West End Ave. (718-616-0964)

Northside Veterinary Clinic
233 Berry St. (718-387-0541)

Yorktown Animal Hospital (holistic/complimentary care)
271 Veterans Road, Yorktown Heights (212-962-3111)

Manhattan
145th Street Animal Clinic (Manhattanville/Hamilton Heights)
454 W. 145th St. (212-234-3489)

Ambuvet (pet ambulance service)
(911@ambuvet.com; 1-800-262-8836)

Animal Emergency Clinic (Upper East Side)
240 E. 80th St. (212-988-1000)

Animal General (Upper West Side)
558 Columbus Ave. (212-501-9600)

Downtown Veterinary House (Tribeca)
295 Greenwich St. (212-619-9119)

East Harlem Veterinary Clinic (El Barrio),
2296 1st Ave. (212-348-8314)

Heart of Chelsea Animal Hospital (traditional and holistic care)
257 West 18th St. (212-924-6116)

House Calls for Your Pet (holistic/complimentary care)
New York City (petvet2k@aol.com; 212-465-1667)

Lexington Veterinary Group (Flatiron District/Lower Midtown)
32 W. 25th St. (212-206-0655)

Rivergate Veterinary Clinic (East Midtown)
227 E. 44th St. (212-213-9885)

Riverside Animal Hospital (holistic/complimentary care),
250 West 100th St., New York City (212-865-2224)

Riverside Veterinary Group (holistic/complimentary care)
219 West 79th St. (212-787-1993)

St. Mark's Veterinary Hospital (Washington Square/Soho)
348 E. 9th St. (212-477-2688)

Urban Vets (East Village)
163 Ave. C (212-674-6200)

Washington Heights Animal Hospital (Washington Heights)
2414 Amsterdam Ave. (212-927-6070)

West Side Animal Hospital (Hell's Kitchen)
733 Ninth Ave. (212-247-8600)

West Village Veterinary Hospital (West Village)
705 Washington St. (212-633-7400)

Queens
Boulevard Animal Clinic
11249 Queens Blvd., Flushing (718-261-1231)

College Point Animal Hospital
1411 College Point Blvd., Flushing (718-321-3202)

North Shore Animal Hospital
21214 Northern Blvd., Flushing (718-423-9600)

Ozone Park Animal Clinic
10730 Rockaway Blvd., Jamaica (718-843-7878)

Veterinary Emergency Group
18711 Hillside Ave., Jamaica (718-454-4141)

Staten Island
Animal Hospital of Staten Island (holistic/complimentary care)
640 Willowbrook Rd. (718-698-1400)

Boulevard Veterinary Group
2300 Hylan Blvd. (718-980-6491)

Emergency Veterinarians Clinic
125 New Dorp Lane (718-370-1102)

Northside Animal Hospital
773 Post Ave. (718-981-4445)

Richmond Valley Animal Hospital
4915 Arthur Kill Rd. (718-948-3331)

Veterinary Emergency Center
1293 Clove Rd. (718-720-4211)

Long Island

THE BLUE DOLPHIN RESORT IN EAST MARION HAS A POOL, A BARBECUE AREA, AND PET-FRIENDLY ROOMS.

Long Island

DOG-FRIENDLY RATING:

While Hamptons celebrities and other bigwigs can probably take their dogs anywhere they darn well please in this sand-and-surf paradise, the rest of us have more limited options when it comes to visiting the island with our pets. For such a large region—and one that is covered from shore to shore with hotels, motels, B&Bs, and inns—this area is home to surprisingly few accommodations that welcome four-legged guests. If you're looking for an especially pet-friendly vacation locale, you can do better than Long Island. (Even the majority of the state parks here are off-limits to animals.) Still, the region does have charms, surprises, and sunsets that can make it worth the extra effort.

Because the western end of the island is largely residential and suburban, most vacationers venture further east to the South Fork, the North Fork, the central-northern shore, or the central-southern shore. The

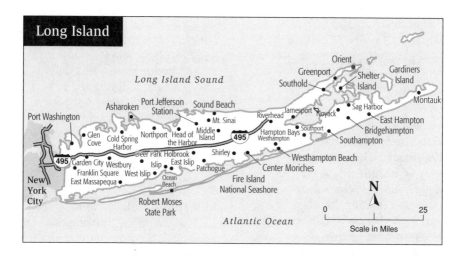

North Fork is well known as "wine country," and you and your pup will be welcomed at the pathways and picnic areas of many of the region's vineyards. The South Fork is home to famous beachfront communities such as Southampton, Hampton Bays, Bridgehampton, East Hampton, and Montauk. On the central-northern shore, you can explore quaint locales like Port Jefferson and Head of the Harbor. And on the central-southern shore, Fire Island beckons with cozy cottages, breathtaking beaches, lighthouses, and fun shops. Although summer is obviously the most popular time of year for Long Island visitation, dog lovers would be better off waiting until spring or fall: In these seasons, the tourist crowds are thinned, the beaches have fewer restrictions for canines, the lodging rates are more affordable, and the weather is still crisp, inviting, and just right for outdoor adventures.

ACCOMMODATIONS

Hotels, Motels, Inns, and Bed & Breakfasts

Cherry Grove (Fire Island)

Dune Point, Lewis Walk (631-597-6261); $125–297 per night or $895–1,295 per week. Dune Point offers a rarity on Fire Island: accommodations that stay open all year long. The upscale spot offers studios and full-size apartments, available for rent by the night, with a two-night minimum, or by the week. (Weekly rentals in the summer are the most popular.) All units have daily housekeeping service, kitchens, stereos, television, and card games. Gay, straight, and four-legged guests are all welcome at this laid-back ocean front resort.

Commack

Howard Johnson Express Inn Commack, 450 Moreland Rd. (631-864-8820); $101–149 per night. The 110 rooms at this HoJo Express Inn have double, queen-, and king-size beds, coffeemakers, irons, ironing boards, alarm clocks, and cable television with premium movie and sports channels. Other hotel features include free newspapers, free daily breakfasts, an outdoor swimming pool, laundry facilities, and safe-deposit boxes. Dogs are welcome for an additional $50 per stay.

Cutchugue

Santorini Hotel and Resort, 3800 Duck Pond Rd. (631-734-6370; www.santorinibeach.com); call for rate information. This motel-style getaway on the North Fork is located on a 500-foot private beach and surrounded by 17 acres of land. Guests can also relax in one of 45 rooms, enjoy breakfast, lunch, or dinner in the recently renovated restaurant, or splash around in the resort's swimming pools—one of which is set aside for children. "Small" dogs (call to see if yours qualifies) are welcome.

East Hampton

Bassett House, 128 Montauk Hwy. (631-324-6127; bassett@ peconic.net; www.peconic.net/ tourism/accommodations/ bassett); $115–275 per night. A full made-to-order breakfast is

included in the rates at Bassett House, a country inn from the 1830s with 12 rooms, some with shared and private baths, lawns and gardens, a dining room, and a sitting room. Two guest rooms have fireplaces and one has a whirlpool bath. East Hampton attractions and restaurants are nearby. Dogs are welcome with prior approval.

Mill House Inn, 31 North Main St. (631-324-9766; innkeeper@ millhouseinn.com; www.millhouseinn.com); $150–550 per night. For an extra $25 per night, well-behaved, friendly doggie-guests are welcome in one guest room and three cottage suites at Mill House Inn. The recently built suites have king-size beds, fireplaces, flat-screen TVs and DVD players, refrigerators, featherbeds, and leather furniture. Visitors can also enjoy freshly baked cookies all day and full breakfasts.

East Marion

Blue Dolphin Resort, 7850 Main Rd. (631-477-0907; info@blue-dolphinresort.com; www.blue-dolphinresort.com); $129–299 per night. Accommodations options at this North Fork motel range from efficiencies and deluxe efficiencies to junior and deluxe suites. Guests can also enjoy an outdoor swimming pool, a barbecue and picnic area, dog runs, a playground, laundry facilities, and a café and lounge. Dogs are welcome in designated rooms.

Garden City

Garden City Hotel, 45 Seventh St. (1-800-547-0400; www.gch. com); $229 per night and higher. Guest pets at this luxury property enjoy "Welcome Pet" gifts and a complimentary dog-walking service; other hotel amenities include a gourmet restaurant, 24-hour room service, free newspapers, turndown services, and personal toiletries in the rooms and suites. Dogs weighing less than 50 pounds are preferred, but larger dogs will not be turned away. Animal owners pay an extra $50 per night and sign a letter agreeing to abide by pet policies.

Great Neck

The Andrew, 75 North Station Plaza (516-482-2900; www. andrewhotel.com); $125–225 per night. The upscale Andrew provides guests with leather-paneled beds, hardwood furniture, bathrobes, Internet access, CD and DVD players, refrigerators, reading chairs, and desks. Other hotel extras include complimentary breakfasts, a concierge, valet parking, valet laundry service, a fitness center, free newspapers, and a lobby lounge area. Your dog is welcome for an extra $50 per night.

Greenport

Greenporter Hotel, 326 Front St. (631-477-0066; info@thegreenporter.com; www.thegreenporter.com); $125–235 per night. Choose from Superior Queen and Deluxe King rooms at the Greenporter, a North Fork resort hotel with spa services, a conference center, and a French bistro and wine bar. "Small" dogs (call to see if yours qualifies) are welcome for an additional $50 per night and a refundable $100 security deposit. Pets cannot be left alone in the rooms at any time.

Hauppauge

Wyndham Wind Watch Long Island, 1717 Vanderbilt Motor Pkwy. (631-232-9800); $169–259 per night. This towering, full-service hotel offers nearly every resort amenity imaginable, including a golf course, a driving range, indoor and outdoor swimming pools, a restaurant, a fitness center, a hot tub and sauna, a concierge, airport shuttles, a grand ballroom, a car-rental desk, tennis courts, and sand volleyball courts. Dogs weighing less than 30 pounds are welcome; pet owners pay a $100 nonrefundable fee for any stay up to 10 days.

Huntington Station

Huntington Country Inn, 270 W. Jericho Turnpike (631-421-3900; 1-800-739-5777; info@ huntingtoncountryinn.com; www.huntingtoncountryinn.com); $159 per night. The recently renovated Huntington Country Inn provides its guests with an outdoor swimming pool, aromatherapy bath products, workout equipment in an updated fitness center, complimentary continental breakfasts, and in-room refrigerators and microwaves. Dogs are welcome guests.

Kings Park

Villa Rosa Bed & Breakfast Inn, 121 Highland Rd., (631-724-4872; villarosainn@aol.com; www. thevillarosainn.com); $130–285 per night. Indoor amenities at Villa Rosa include three guest rooms, one large suite, a fireplace, and a Victorian-era ambiance; outside, the inn offers landscaped gardens, koi ponds, and waterfalls. State parks, beaches, restaurants, and shops are all nearby. Leashed, well-behaved dogs are welcome for an extra $20 per night and can enjoy romping in the fenced-in dog run area.

Montauk
Burcliffe by the Sea, 397 Old Montauk Hwy. (631-668-2800); $85–159 per night. Burcliffe by the Sea offers vacationers four motel-style efficiencies and three cottages with fireplaces. Visitors will also find air-conditioning and cable television, and can request VCRs and Internet access. For an additional $25 per stay, dogs are allowed in the cottages during the off-season.

Plainview
Residence Inn by Marriott Plainview, 9 Gerhard Rd. (516-433-6200; 1-800-331-3131); $160–229 per night. Designed for business travelers and others needing a long-term stay, the Residence Inn is an all-suite facility with separate kitchen, living, and sleeping areas. The Plainview location also offers a

swimming pool, a sauna, air-conditioning, cable television, complimentary continental breakfasts, a game room, a fitness center, and laundry services. Dog owners pay a one-time $150 cleaning fee, plus $10 per night.

Port Jefferson
Ransome Inn, Cliff Rd. (631-474-5019; innkeeper@ ransomeinn.net; www.ransome inn.net); $85–175 per night. The Ransome Inn is a homey North Shore accommodation with one guest room and one larger suite. Both have private baths, air-conditioning, and cable television; a full breakfast is served each morning. Those traveling to Long Island by ferry can also enjoy a complimentary pickup at the in-town dock. Well-behaved dogs are welcome for an additional $35 per stay.

Quogue
Inn at Quogue, 47-52 Quogue St. (631-653-6560; innatquogue@ aol.com; www.innatquogue. com); $135–215 per night for pet-friendly rooms. This Hamptons

BOB THE DOG SUPERVISES CHECK-IN AT THE ATLANTIC IN SOUTHAMPTON.

A GUEST SUITE AT THE BENTLEY IN SOUTHAMPTON

country inn offers an outdoor swimming pool, air-conditioning, massage therapy, sports courts, fireplaces, a front porch, and bicycles. The individually decorated guest rooms have comfortable, updated furnishings; some have kitchens, and several can be joined together for groups. Dogs are welcome in designated rooms for an extra $50 per night.

Riverhead
Best Western East End,
1830 Rte. 25 (631-369-2200; bestwesterneastend@aol.com; www.bestwesterneastend.com); $109–189 per night. The 100 guest rooms at the Best Western East End have air-conditioning, cable television, and in-room movies and video games. Other amenities include a swimming pool, a fitness center, a restaurant, a lounge, and conference facilities. Four-legged guests are welcome without extra charges.

Shelter Island Heights
Stearns Point House,
7 Stearns Point Rd., P.O. Box 648 (631-749-4162; www.shelter-islandgetaways.com); $95–165

per night. Your dog will be welcome without extra charges at Stearns Point House, a recently restored farmhouse with four guest rooms, private baths, canopy and king-size beds, a light-and-airy décor, complimentary daily breakfasts, and air-conditioning. The beach is a five-minute walk down the road.

Southampton
The Atlantic, 1655 County Rd. 39, Rte. 27 (631-287-0908; info@hrhresorts.com; www. hrhresorts.com); $120–550 per night. One of three Hampton Resorts properties in Southampton to allow pets, The Atlantic is a motel-style accommodation with 57 rooms, 5 suites, tennis courts, a swimming pool, complimentary coffee and breakfast items, air-conditioning, and in-room hair dryers, irons, and ironing boards. Pets weighing less than 40 pounds are welcome for an additional $40 per night. The motel participates in the annual "Urban Pooch Getaway" events that take place each April and October.

The Bentley, 161 Hills Station Rd. (631-287-0908; info@hrh resorts.com; www.hrhresorts.com); $180–475 per night. Visitors at The Bentley can enjoy large suite accommodations with exterior corridors, art deco–style furnishings, kitchenettes, and living room areas. The 2.8-acre property also has a swimming pool, sunbathing deck, and tennis courts. Guests of the motel can also take advantage of the complimentary breakfasts and coffee at the other two nearby Hampton Resorts properties, The Atlantic and The Capri. All three participate in the annual "Urban Pooch Getaways" program. Dogs weighing less than 40 pounds are welcome for an extra $40 per night.

The Capri, 281 County Rd. 39A (631-283-4220; info@hrhresorts.com; www.hrhresorts.com); $150–500 per night. For an additional $40 per night, your 40-pounds-or-lighter dog is welcome to join you at this Hampton Resorts motel with 27 rooms, 4 suites, a swimming pool, down comforters, a retro 1950s décor, a restaurant and lounge, and 2.3 acres for exploring. In-room hair dryers, irons, and ironing boards are also available. The Capri is a participant in the "Urban Pooch Getaways" program affiliated with numerous New York City pet businesses and services.

Village Latch Inn Hotel, 101 Hill St. (631-283-2160; 1-800-545-2824; mail@villagelatch.com; www.villagelatch.com); $140–495 per night. Choose from traditional guest rooms or larger suites at Village Latch, a resort hotel with antiques, original artworks, private baths, cable television, voice mail, fireplaces, balconies, and decks. Outside, visitors can enjoy the swimming pool, tennis courts, bike rentals, and manicured gardens. Dogs are allowed in designated rooms for an extra $25 per night.

Westbury
Red Roof Inn Westbury, 699 Dibblee Dr. (516-794-2555); $99–119 per night. Pets are welcome at all Red Roof locations; the large Westbury site offers 163 guest rooms, free local calls, cable television with premium movie and sports channels, voice mail, alarm clocks, fax and copying services, movie rentals, free coffee and newspapers, and lots of nearby restaurants. Children under 18 stay for free.

Campgrounds

Brookhaven
Southaven County Park, River Rd. (631-854-1418); $14 per night for residents, $24 per night for visitors. This Suffolk County Park campground offers opportunities for camping, hiking, fishing, horseback riding, and picnicking. Amenities include a playground, rest rooms with showers, rowboat rentals, and even a miniature train ride. Dogs must be leashed, attended to, and cleaned up after at all times. Be sure to carry proof of vaccinations.

East Hampton
Cedar Point County Park, Alewive Brook Rd. (631-852-7620); $14 for residents, $24 per night for visitors.

Overnight camping, fishing, hiking, bicycle trails, a beach, and picnic areas are all available at this small campground managed by Suffolk County. The site also offers a camp store and rest rooms with showers. Dogs are allowed, but cannot be left unattended at any time. Owners must carry proof of vaccinations and clean up any messes.

Fire Island National Seashore

Watch Hill Campground, Fire Island National Seashore, c/o 120 Laurel St., Patchogue (631-289-9336); $14 per night, two-night minimum. Located across the Great South Bay from Patchogue, Watch Hill is a national park campground that is only accessible by boat. Dockage is available, or you can take the ferry (www.davisparkferry.com). The campground features a National Park Service visitor center, a camp store, a marina, nature trails, and a beach. Leashed dogs are welcome.

Greenport

Eastern Long Island Kampgrounds Rte. 48 (Queen St.), P.O. Box 89 (516-477-0022; mydon1@aol.com; www. easternlikampground.com); $30–40 per night. Tenters and RVers will feel welcome at this family campground, where the amenities include a swimming pool, a camp store, laundry facilities, rest rooms with showers, picnic tables, and planned activities. Dogs are allowed without extra charges, provided owners follow the campground's pet policies. Certain breeds are not allowed; call for details.

Hampton Bays

Sears Bellows County Park, Bellows Pond Rd. (631-852-8290); $14 per night for residents, $24 per night for visitors. Sears Bellows has separate camping areas for tents and trailers, along with three rest room buildings with showers. After you get settled, you and Rover can enjoy picnics, hikes, fishing, bicycling, and old-fashioned exploring. Rowboat rentals and equestrian trails are also available. Your dog is welcome if you bring proof of vaccinations, clean up any messes, and use a leash.

Riverhead

Indian Island County Park, Rte. 105 (631-852-3232); $14 per night for residents, $24 per night for visitors. Indian Island is another Suffolk County park that is friendly to canines, as long as they're leashed, have proof of vaccinations, and are not left alone in the campground. Choose a campsite in sections A through H, then enjoy the playground, picnic areas, rest rooms with showers, a sports field, and hiking, biking, and fishing opportunities.

Shirley

Smith Point County Park, Terminus of William Floyd Pkwy. at Fire Island (631-852-1315; 631-852-1316); $14 per night for residents, $24 per night for visitors. This scenic Fire Island campground has six camping areas, four rest room buildings with showers, outer beach access, a playground, and a snack bar. Popular activities include swimming, hiking, bird-watching, saltwater fishing, and even scuba diving. Dogs must be leashed, cleaned-up after, and attended at all times. Bring proof of vaccinations. Pets are not allowed on lifeguard-protected beach areas.

Smithtown
Blydenburgh County Park,
Veteran's Hwy./Rte. 347 (631-854-3712); $14 per night for residents, $24 per night for visitors. Kids will enjoy the playground, rowboat rentals, and picnic areas at this Suffolk County Park campground, while adults will appreciate the overnight camping facilities, fishing and hiking opportunities, equestrian trails, and rest rooms with showers. Your leashed dog is welcome, provided you show proof of vaccinations, clean up after him, and don't leave him unattended.

Southampton
Shinnecock East County Park,
Dune Rd. (631-852-8899); $14 per night for residents, $24 per night for visitors. The main attraction at Shinnecock is the beach, which can make things a little tricky for you and your dog: Pets are not allowed on lifeguard-protected beaches, and several protected dunes and bird-nesting areas make this campground's ecology sensitive and easily harmed by trampling canine (and human) feet. If you're willing to abide by the restrictions, however, dogs are welcome in some camping areas. Owners are required to bring proof of vaccinations, clean up pet waste, and not leave their animals alone at any time.

Homes, Cottages, and Cabins for Rent

Bridgehampton
Bridgehampton homes (631-725-5217; 516-729-6729; reserve@31islandview.com); $3,000–6,500 per week. One homeowner offers two vacation rental homes in the Bridgehampton area that are pet-friendly: The first, a six-bedroom, five-bath house, can accommodate up to 16 people with a swimming pool, a hot tub, cable television, and a fireplace. The second home can accommodate up to 11 people with four bedrooms, three bathrooms, a swimming pool, and 20 private acres of land.

Bridgehampton Rentals (917-757-3534; ztunick@optonline.net; www.bridgehamptonrental.com); $500 per weekend–$8,500 per week. This rental group has six large, manor-style homes available for rent in Bridgehampton, Southampton, Watermill, and East Hampton—and pets are permitted at five of them. Each home is located adjacent to a nature preserve and offers plenty of privacy. Well-behaved dogs are welcome, provided they stay off the furniture. Security deposits vary at each property; call or visit the web site for details.

East Hampton
Contemporary saltbox (212-847-2979; 516-343-5592; georgia@tryatemp.com); $3,000-3,500 per week or $10,000–12,000 per month. "I'm a big pet fan," says homeowner Georgia Ellis, who welcomes companion animals to

her saltbox rental home with an extra security deposit. Located within bicycling distance to a private beach, the house has three bedrooms, two bathrooms, a washer and dryer, a swimming pool, an outdoor shower, a pool house, air-conditioning, cable television, and a half-acre yard.

East Hampton house (914-879-8411; forcinoesq@aol.com; www.easthamptonhouse.net); call for rate information. Located about 2 miles from Bridgehampton, this four-bedroom contemporary home has a heated swimming pool, air-conditioning, a hot tub, a fireplace, a large deck, and 2 acres of wooded property. The living room has satellite television, a VCR and DVD player, and skylights. Well-behaved dogs are welcome.

Upside-Down House (631-907-9001; 212-645-2133; lscanlong @optonline.net); $2,500–3,500 per week. The most frequently used rooms in this contemporary house are located upstairs, beside the large wrap-around deck. The home has three bedrooms, two bathrooms, an underground "electric fence" for dogs, air-conditioning, cable television, a fireplace, a barbecue grill, and Internet access. A nature preserve is next door, and the beach is a short walk away.

Vacation home (212-397-1021; 631-324-7907; srosenc@ix. netcom.com); $3,500–4,000 per week. Your dog will love this property's fenced-in yard, while you'll love the heated swimming pool, outdoor shower, large deck, sculpture garden, cable television, air-conditioning, fireplace, barbecue grill, washer and dryer, and full kitchen. The contemporary-style home can accommodate up to six people with three bedrooms and two bathrooms.

Montauk
Beach house (631-324-7673; 516-659-8270; mbromley@ hamptons.com); $3,500 per month in summer; call for autumn rates. Up to seven people can stay comfortably in this four-bedroom, two-bath house with cable television, a fireplace, a barbecue grill, a CD player, and an outdoor shower. "The ocean beach is directly across the street, and dogs can freely run and play there before 10 AM and after 5 PM during the summer," says homeowner Kyril Bromley. Pets are welcome.

Pond-view home (917-532-8440; montauksummer@mindspring. com); $1,500–2,000 per week; $4,000–8,000 per month; or $15,000 per season. Modern and open, this two-bedroom vacation home has a full kitchen, a stone patio, air-conditioning, a woodstove, a washer and dryer, a barbecue grill, and cable television. The beach and in-town attractions are all within walking distance. Adult dogs (sorry, no cats) weighing less than 30 pounds are allowed with a $150 nonrefundable cleaning fee.

Remensburg
Historic farmhouse (917-923-6398; 631-325-7798; hogart911@ aol.com); $3,000 per week or $14,000–16,000 per month. With

three bedrooms and two bathrooms, this renovated 1888 farmhouse is decorated in a country style with a swimming pool, a covered front porch, a fireplace, cable television, air-conditioning, a full kitchen, and barbecue grill. Dogs are welcome. The home rents only by the month or by the season during the summer.

Sagaponack
Gibson Beach cottage (540-878-7118; 540-364-1474; osprey landing@earthlink.net); $1,050–7,500 per week. Romp on your own private beach at this three-bedroom, waterfront vacation rental. The cottage has two bathrooms, decks, horse pastures, satellite television, an outside shower, a washer and dryer, a stereo, and a CD player. Dogs (sorry, no cats) are welcome with a refundable $500 security deposit. Horse boarding is also available on-site.

Hamptons home (212-777-7696; 631-537-3394; hampton294@aol. com); $25,000 per month. "Since I have a dog and am very pet-friendly, I do allow pets at my home when I rent," says homeowner Richard McCabe. Amenities include a heated swimming pool, fireplaces, air-conditioning, cable television, a full kitchen, four bedrooms, and a short walk to the ocean. The house is available for rent only during the month between August 1 and Labor Day.

Sag Harbor
Harbor mansion (516-860-6529; 516-860-6528; hamptonsgetaways @aol.com; www.hamptons getaways.com); call for rate information. This dog-friendly eight-bedroom, nine-bath home can accommodate up to 40 people. The property's 2.5 acres offer a swimming pool, a hot tub, a tennis court, a sand volleyball court, and a full-size basketball court. Inside, visitors will find cable television in every room, a full kitchen, air-conditioning, a fireplace, a game room, a DVD player, and a washer and dryer. Group rentals for retreats, parties, and family reunions are welcome.

Wainscott Village
Family home (212-737-8917; 631-537-0915; richlistco@aol.com); call for rate information. Planning a *very* long vacation? Relocating? This year-by-year, long-term rental home has a large lawn area, an underground "electric fence" for dogs, a swimming pool, a porch, and decks with patio furniture. Inside, the home has four bedrooms, four bathrooms, air-conditioning, cable television, a full kitchen, and a fireplace. Dogs are welcome.

Village of Westhampton Beach
Westhampton contemporary (631-898-0191; 917-301-2416; wwwmlsli.com); $4,000–7,000 per week; $15,000–25,000 per month; $55,000 per season. This luxurious house offers six bedrooms, four bathrooms, a tennis court, a heated swimming pool, a hot tub, a big-screen TV, and air-conditioning. Small, housetrained, adult dogs are allowed with a refundable security deposit of twenty percent. This home rents only by the month or by the season during the summer.

OUT AND ABOUT

Beaches. Although the rules vary from town to town, in general your dog will not be allowed on most beaches during peak daytime hours during the summer. In many cases, dog access is restricted to early morning and late evening hours even during the winter, spring, and fall. Gibson Beach in Sagaponack is a popular spot for canines and canine lovers from 6 AM to 8 AM and 5 PM to 8 PM in the summer. In Montauk, however, dogs are only allowed to hit the sand before 10 AM and after 6 PM between September 15 and May 15. If the beach is a big part of your travel plans, check the "dog rules" with the town offices at your destination before making lodging reservations and consider visiting during the spring or fall.

Belmont Lake State Park, Deer Park Ave., Babylon (631-667-5055). Leashed dogs are allowed in "undeveloped areas only" at Belmont Lake, a state park with playgrounds, sports courts, playing fields, a boat rental, and trails for hiking, biking, horseback-riding, and cross-country skiing. Dogs are not allowed in the picnic area. The park is open year-round, seven days a week.

BoatRenting.com, Beaver Dam Marina, South Country Rd., Bellport (631-286-7816; www. boatrenting.com). Despite its cyberspace name, BoatRenting. com is actually a brick-and-mortar destination where visitors rent motorboats of all kinds. Pets are welcome to join their humans on board the Family Sport Speed Deck Boat, a 23-footer that can accommodate 8–10 people. Expect to pay between $250 and $300 for a full-day rental, with slightly higher rates on holidays.

Bridgeport–Port Jefferson Steamboat Company, 102 West Broadway (631-473-0286; 203-335-2040; www.bpjferry.com); $37.50 one-way for car and driver. For commuters and travelers, this ferry service can help avoid several hours of driving between Bridgeport, Connecticut, and Port Jefferson, Long Island. The scenic trip across Long Island Sound takes about an hour and fifteen minutes. In Bridgeport, the ferry is located at the Water Street Dock; in Port Jefferson, you'll find the dock at the end of Rte. 112. Dogs are welcome on the exterior decks.

Camp Hero State Park, 50 South Fairview Ave., Montauk (631-668-3781). Camp Hero can seem like many parks in one: Its 415 acres include wooded areas, beaches, and even a preserved historic military site. Visitors here can fish, boat, have a picnic, hike, ride a mountain bike, explore the bridle paths with their horses, cross-country ski, swim, and sunbathe. At the time of this writing, dogs were welcome on the beach year-round, as long as owners use a leash no longer than 6 feet and clean up after their pets.

BELLE, A LOCAL BLACK LAB, TAKES A REST AFTER ROMPING ON THE ROBERT MOSES FIELD FIVE BEACH ON FIRE ISLAND.

Castello di Borghese Vineyard,
Rte. 48 and Alvah's Lane,
Cutchogue (631-734-5111;
info@castellodiborghese.com;
www.castellodiborghese.com).
"We get many canine visitors!"
says vineyard owner Marco
Borghese, who bought the winery
in 1999 with his wife, Ann Marie.
They produce whites such as
pinot blanc and chardonnay, as
well as reds, roses, and even
olive oil. Sample vintages in the
tasting room and browse through
the gift shop. Pets are welcome in
outdoor areas.

Cold Spring Harbor State Park,
Rte. 25A, Cold Spring Harbor
(631-423-1770). The main attraction of this park is its trail system,
which winds through 40 acres of
forests and offers views of the
harbor. Wildlife-watchers should
keep an eye out for great-horned
owls, red-tailed hawks, and
numerous species of songbirds. In
the winter, the trails are also popular with cross-country skiers and
snowshoers. Visitors can spend
the morning hiking and the afternoon window-shopping in the
nearby village of Cold Spring
Harbor. Dogs must be on a leash
no longer than 6 feet.

Cross Sound Ferry, 2 Ferry St.,
New London, Connecticut (860-
443-5281 in Connecticut; 631-323-
2525 on Long Island; info@long-
islandferry.com; www.longisland-
ferry.com); $37 one-way for car
and driver. Hop across Long
Island Sound between Orient
Point (at the tip of the North
Fork) and New London,
Connecticut, on this ferry offering
daily service for passengers, cars,
and bicycles. Leashed or contained pets are allowed in designated areas on the vessels.

Fire Island Ferries, Inc., 99
Maple Ave., Bayshore (631-665-
3600; www.fireislandferries.com);
$12.50 round-trip for adults; $6
round-trip for children. These
high-speed ferries can get you
across the water to spots like Fair
Harbor, Ocean Bay Park, Ocean
Beach, Dunewood, Atlantique,
and Saltaire. Leashed dogs are
allowed on board; pet owners pay
the child's rate for each animal.

**Fire Island National Seashore,
Field Five Beach** (631-289-4810;
www.nps.gov/fiis). For a year-
round doggy-friendly beach, park
at Robert Moses Field Five (at the
far end) and walk all the way
down the boardwalk. The beach,
straddled on both sides by nude
beaches, is located across from
the beautiful lighthouse. Don't be
thrown by the "no pets" signs:
Dogs are indeed allowed on this
stretch of beach throughout the
year, but confusing signs say pets
aren't allowed on the boardwalk—
which just happens to be the only
way to access the beach. (Go fig-
ure.) In any case, this is an envi-
ronmentally sensitive area with
numerous birds and other species,
so be sure to keep Fido close by
and out of nesting areas. In addition, pet owners should note that
ticks run rampant here: Be sure
to check your pup carefully for
these parasites when it's time to
go home.

Heckscher State Park, Terminus
of Heckscher State Pkwy., P.O.
Box 160, East Islip (631-581-

2100). Dogs are allowed at Heckscher State Park—sort of. Although you and your pooch can roam the trails and other "undeveloped areas," you'll have to steer clear of the beach, the picnic areas, the walkways, and the campground. Luckily, the park's 20 miles of trails provide plenty of scenery and opportunities for hiking, meandering, biking, and cross-country skiing. The park also has a boat launch. Dogs must stay on a leash no longer than 6 feet.

Hempstead Lake State Park, Exit 18 at Southern State Pkwy., West Hempstead (516-766-1029). If you're like most visitors to Hempstead Lake, you'll come here to fish: The lake and two nearby ponds are stocked with trout. Or, you might want to explore the park's trails, which are open to dog walkers, hikers, horseback riders, cross-country skiers, and mountain bikers. Dogs are required to be on a leash no longer than 6 feet, and are not allowed on beaches, in picnic areas, or in the campground.

Hither Hills State Park, 50 South Fairview Ave., Montauk (631-668-2554). First, the bad news: Dogs are not allowed in camping or picnic areas, nor are they allowed on the beach in the summer. But leashed pups are welcome to frolic in the sand during the off-season, and they're also allowed to explore most trails with their humans. Popular activities in the park include sport fishing, biking, cross-country skiing, picnicking, and horseback riding.

Jamesport Vineyards, Rte. 25 (Main Rd.), Jamesport (631-722-5256; www.jamesport-vineyards.com). Open to visitors for tastings, tours, and casual browsers, Jamesport Vineyards has acres of walkways and vines as well as a large, outdoor grassy area with lawn chairs. Well-behaved, leashed dogs are welcome on the grounds. In the summertime, the vineyard even offers live music events every Saturday afternoon. Try the merlot, pinot noir, sauvignon blanc, or Riesling.

Lieb Family Cellars, 35 Cox Neck Rd., Mattituck (631-298-1942; info@liebcellars.com; www.liebcellars.com). Stop by for an indoor or outdoor tasting at Lieb Family Cellars, a fairly new winery that opened in 2001 with a tasting room and ultra modern wine-making equipment. The family also offers a picnic area with tables, umbrellas, and shade trees. "I am a dog lover, and try to allow dogs when we're not too crowded," explains General Manager Gary Madden. Canines may also be restricted if other two-legged visitors are afraid of or allergic to dogs.

Lighthouse viewing. Long Island, as you might expect, is home to an impressive number of lighthouses—22 in all. Lighthouse aficionados will delight in traveling up and down the shore in search of these scenic structures. Perhaps the most famous are the Montauk Point Lighthouse (sorry, no pets allowed on the grounds) and the Fire Island Lighthouse, but others include the Stepping Stones

Light, Old Field Point, Execution Rocks, and Cold Springs Harbor Light, all on the central-northern shore; and Horton Point Light, Orient Point, Race Rock Light, and Gardiner's Point Light, all on the North Fork. For more information and directions to each lighthouse, visit www.LIlight housesociety.org or www.licvb. com/lighthouses.

Macari Vineyards, 150 Bergen Ave., P.O. Box 2, Mattituck (631-298-0100; macari@peconic.net; www.macariwines.com). This vineyard is so animal-friendly it was recently featured in *Animal Fair* magazine; on the grounds, you're likely to run into dogs, cats, a parrot, a goat, cows, donkeys, horses, and more furry and feathered residents. Your pet is welcome to join the fun. Macari produces a wide selection of wines, including merlot, chardonnay, red and white table wines, and others.

Montauk Point State Park, 50 South Fairview Ave., Montauk (631-668-3781). Dogs are permitted in certain areas of this heavily wooded park, which offers walking trails, picnic areas, and views of the Montauk Point Lighthouse and the ocean. Leashed pooches are also allowed on the beach during the off-season and during restricted hours in the summer. Horseback riding, biking, cross-country skiing, and hiking are some of the popular activities on the trails.

North Shore Animal League, 25 Davis Ave., Port Washington (516-883-7575; www.nsalamerica.org). NSAL is probably the most famous animal rescue organization on the East Coast, and one of the better known in the country. Pet lovers come from far and wide to meet the homeless animals—typically as many as 350 dogs and cats—waiting patiently in the league's 17,000-square-foot Adoption Center. The organization headquarters also has a pet-supply store (see "Hot Spots for Spot"), a Veterinary Medical Center, rescue vans, and Pet Outreach programs. Special events and adoption events are held throughout the year; call or visit the web site for the latest schedules and information.

Osprey's Dominion Vineyards, 44075 Main Rd., Peconic (631-765-6188; winemkr@ospreysdominion.com; www.ospreysdominion.com). This North Fork vineyard boasts more than 90 acres of grapes, all of which come together to make the winery's award-winning chardonnay, cabernet sauvignon, merlot, and others. Picnics are popular on the grounds, where you'll also find lawn chairs, tables, and a covered patio. Well-behaved, leashed dogs are welcome, as long as they aren't inclined to bother the resident Maine Coon cat, Spice.

Sayville ferry service, 41 River Rd., P.O. Box 626, Sayville (631-589-0810; www.sayville-ferry.com); $11 round-trip for adults; $5 round-trip for children. Venture to Fire Island Pines, Cherry Grove, the Sunken Forest, and Water Island on board this busy ferry service. Leashed, well-behaved dogs are welcome on the ferry for an extra $3 round-trip.

Shadmoor State Park,

Rte. 27 and Seaside Ave., Montauk (631-668-3781). As long as your pup stays on a leash no longer than 6 feet, the two of you are welcome to explore the 100-or-so acres of forests, beaches, and bluffs of Shadmoor State Park. Birdwatchers, anglers, and botanists will find plenty of wildlife here, including rare and endangered plants. The park is also home to two World War II–era bunkers, designed to fortify the Long Island coast. Come for fishing, biking, or hiking year-round, seven days a week.

Silly Lily Fishing Station,

99 Adelaide Ave., East Moriches (631-878-0247; www.sillylily. com). Pets are welcome to join the fun at Silly Lily, a fishing station and marina with motorboat rentals, kayak rentals, and dockage. Anglers come from far and wide to Moriches Bay in search of flounder and fluke, but you'll also find bluefish, blue claw crab, and striped bass in abundance.

Suffolk County Parks,

Suffolk County Dept. of Parks, Recreation & Conservation, Montauk Hwy., P.O. Box 144, West Sayville (631-854-4949; www.co.suffolk.ny.us). Dog lovers visiting Long Island can thank their lucky stars for Suffolk County parks, where dogs are always welcome as long they're friendly, leashed, picked-up after, and have proof of vaccinations. The county manages 20 parks in a large geographic area, divided into "East End" and "West End" categories. Many of these parks also have dog-friendly campgrounds (see "Accommodations"). In the East End, the parks include Theodore Roosevelt County Park in Montauk, Indian Island County Park in Riverhead, the Pine Barrens Trails Information Center in Manorville, and Cedar Point County Park in East Hampton. In the West End, vacationers can visit sites like Cathedral Pines County Park in Middle Island, West Hills County Park in Huntington, Lake Ronkonkoma County Park in Lake Ronkonkoma, and Lakeland County Park in Islandia. For directions, maps, and trail information, call or visit the Department of Parks' web site. Dogs are not allowed in lifeguard-protected beach areas.

Sunken Meadow State Park,

Terminus of the Sunken Meadow/Sagtikus Pkwy., P.O. Box 716, Kings Park (631-269-4333). You can't visit the picnic or bathing areas at Sunken Meadows with your dog, but you can explore "undeveloped areas" of the park (including 6 miles of trails) as long as you use a leash no longer than 6 feet. Trail visitors include hikers, bikers, dog walkers, cross-country skiers, and horseback riders. The park also has three golf courses, a man-made dam, a playground, and a variety of ecosystems, including marshes, forests, and tidal flats.

"Stroll to the Sea" Dog Walk (annual),

Animal Rescue Fund (ARF) of the Hamptons, Daniels' Hole Rd., P.O. Box 901, Wainscott (631-537-0400; info@arfhamptons.org; www.arfhamptons.org). Bring your favorite pooch for a sea-air stroll and help raise funds for this animal welfare organization. In 2003, the event was moved from its usual spring date to October; call or visit the web site for the latest information on this year's event. Founded in 1974, ARF finds families for homeless dogs and cats and provides veterinary care, obedience classes, spaying and neutering services, and outreach programs in the community.

Window-shopping in Southampton. The clothing boutiques, candy shops, antiques dealers, and casual and upscale eateries seem to continue endlessly in this much-visited shopping mecca. Even if you can't enter most of the stores with a canine in tow, it's still worth a visit to roam the quaint streets and get a peek at the latest fashions, home accessories, and sweet treats displayed in the windows.

QUICK BITES

Café Off Main, 66 Newtown Lane, East Hampton (631-907-8800). Open seven days a week, this cozy café serves breakfast and lunch with items such as salad platters, eggs and omelettes, sandwiches, wraps, and pancakes. A kid's menu is also available, and the sidewalk tables make a great perch for people-watching.

Crabby Jerry's, Main Street Dock, Greenport (631-477-8252). This is the casual, greasy-spoon, seafood restaurant you were hoping to find on your seaside vacation: Order chowder, clam strips, popcorn shrimp, crab cakes, mussels, or French fries and pig out at the outdoor tables.

Drossos Snack Bar, Main Rd., Greenport (631-477-1334). If you're looking for a guilty pleasure, surely this will qualify. Drossos serves up kid-friendly meals and snacks like burgers, French fries, ice cream sundaes,

smoothies, slushes, and buckets of fried chicken. Plenty of outdoor seating is on the premises, as is a miniature golf course.

Funcho's Fajita Grill, 1156 W. Main St., Riverhead (631-369-7277; funchos@optonline.net). This primarily take-out place offers outdoor seating and lots of Mexican favorites. Menu items include tacos, fajitas, salads, chili con carne, nachos, jalapeno poppers, quesadillas, and wraps. Individual meals, platters, and catering are also available.

Hellenic Snack Bar and Restaurant, 5145 Main Rd. (Rte. 25), East Marion (631-477-0138). Locals recommend this casual North Fork restaurant for Greek specialties like Gyros, Greek salads, and souvlaki. An indoor dining room, an outdoor seating area, and a take-out service are all available.

Hewitt's Main Street Café and Carry Out, 782 Main St., Montauk (631-668-2727). Outdoor dining, takeout, and delivery are all available at this Main Street stop. Choose from a large variety of meals and treats like pizza, salad, ice cream, seafood, sandwiches, vegetarian specialties, soup, and a full bar with frozen drinks.

Jerry & the Mermaid Seaside Restaurant and Clam Bar, 469 East Main St., Riverhead (631-727-8489). Located just outside the Treasure Cove Resort Marina, this casual eatery serves up fish, pasta, fried seafood platters, salads, soups, sandwiches, and other quick meals. Order your food to go or enjoy it at one of the outdoor tables.

Orient by the Sea Restaurant and Marina, Main Rd., Orient (631-323-2424). Visitors can join the friendly crowds of locals at this popular waterfront restaurant; menu items include shrimp cocktail, chicken wings, chowder, pasta, steaks, and of course seafood of all shapes and sizes. Don't be surprised to see well-behaved dogs in the outdoor patio seating area.

Rising Tide Natural Market, 42 Forest Ave., Glen Cove (516-676-7895). A market and deli, Rising Tide offers a bakery, a juice bar, all-organic produce, and numerous vegan and vegetarian options for wraps, soups, and sandwiches. Order your meal or snack to go or eat at one of the market's outdoor tables.

Rita's, 81 Adelhaide Lane, East Islip (631-224-4893). Hot enough for ya? Stop into Rita's for some cool refreshment, including Italian ices, ice cream, and shakes. Take your treat on the road or relax for a while in the outdoor seating area.

Tiger Lily Café, 156 East Main St., Port Jefferson (631-476-7080). Vegetarians will appreciate the healthful menu at this "alternative eatery." A few outdoor tables are available out front, or you can order your meal to go. Tiger Lily has a cappuccino bar, a juice bar, soy protein shakes, soups, salads, wraps, and more.

World Pie, 2402 Montauk Hwy., Bridgehampton (631-537-7999). Best known for its wide selection of thin-crust pizzas, this friendly and popular Bridgehampton eatery has plenty of outdoor tables with umbrellas. Expect a wait, and try not to stare at the celebrities—their dogs are much cuter, anyway.

HOT SPOTS FOR SPOT

All Animals Pet Food & Supply, 61 East Main St., East Islip (631-581-5353). In addition to stocking doghouses, kennels, cages, pet beds, and food-storage bins, this pet-supply store also carries well-known pet food brands such as Iams, Eukanuba, Natural Choice, Purina Pro Plan®, and Wellness. Delivery is also available, and the store is open seven days a week.

Barrie Inn, 154 Woodmere Blvd., Woodmere (516-569-1555; www.thebarrieinn.com). This is a one-stop location for pet care, including "cageless" overnight boarding, doggie daycare, full grooming services, a "pet limo" transportation service, pet parties, play dates, and even a boutique selling dog- and cat-themed merchandise.

Dee-Jo's, 345 Rte. 25 A, Miller Place (631-928-5898). Located just outside of Rocky Point, this pet-supply store can help travelers stock up on anything they might need for a dog, cat, gerbil, or goldfish. Choose from your favorite pet-food brands and browse a good selection of toys, treats, leashes, rawhides, and more.

Four on the Floor Pet Grooming, 379 Rte. 25A, Rocky Point (631-744-1000). Before you hop on the Port Jeff ferry, you might want to stop in to the nearby Four on the Floor to clean the vacation grime from Fluffy's coat. The full-service shop offers grooming, clipping, and all-around beautification services.

North Shore Animal League, 25 Davis Ave., Port Washington (516-883-7575; www.nsalamerica.org). In addition to its extensive adoption facilities and special events (see "Out and About"), this animal rescue organization also offers a pet-supply store at its Port Washington headquarters. The name-brand pet foods, training cages, toys, chew treats, and other supplies are all offered at discounted prices.

One Stop Pet Shop, 136 Main St., Amagansett (631-267-7535) and 20 Hampton Rd., Southampton (631-287-6001). Stop in to One Stop for toys, canned and dry name-brand foods, bowls, brushes, and other pet accessories. The Amagansett location also offers grooming services, including a quick bath and flea-dip known as the "$15 Special."

Paws 'n Claws, 47 Newtown Lane, East Hampton (631-324-8995). Though a little tricky to find (it's located in an alley off of Newtown Lane), this grooming shop and pet-supply store is an invaluable stop for vacationers. Fido can get a quick shampoo while you stock up on collars, pet beds, water bowls, and other doggy essentials.

Pet Hampton, Montauk Hwy. (Rte. 27), Wainscott (631-537-7387). Located on the main drag next door to the South Fork Animal Hospital, this shop stocks treats, toys, tie-outs, and fun doggie clothing, along with a wide selection of aquarium supplies.

Stocked pet-food brands include Nutro Max, Iams, Eukanuba, and Canidae.

Riverhead Bed & Biscuit, 1182 W. Main St. (Rte. 25), Riverhead (631-727-2009). Located in a veterinarian's office, the Riverhead Bed & Biscuit is an overnight boarding facility where pet owners can choose from The Single, a private kennel with an indoor/outdoor run, The Double, a kennel for two, and Bed & Biscuit Suites, where pets can roam 200 square feet with an indoor/outdoor run. "Room service" and "maid service" are included in the rates; grooming and obedience classes are also available.

Smitty's Kennels, 103 Curran's Rd., Middle Island (631-345-0000; smittyskennel.com; www.smittyskennel.com). Overnight canine guests at Smitty's Kennels each have an indoor/outdoor sleeping and exercise area; the indoor spaces have radiant heat and ceiling fans. In general, the kennel's drop off/pick up hours are 7 AM to 11 AM and 5 PM to 7 PM.

Three Village K-9 Camp, 200 Wilson St., Port Jefferson Station (631-476-9320; www.lidogcamp.com). Three Village's slogan is "home of the happiest dogs on earth," and your pup might not disagree after her stay here. Whether they've arrived for daycare or for overnight "camping," visiting canines interact and play with each other in outdoor, fenced-in spaces and indoor, temperature-controlled exercise rooms. Staff members provide plenty of TLC, attention, and supervision for all dogs throughout their stay. Full grooming services are also available, including "Day of Fun and Beauty" packages and "spa bath" packages. Call ahead for reservations.

Treat Your Pet, 4397 Austin Blvd., Island Park (516-670-0470; www.treatyourpets.com). In addition to offering a big selection of pet foods, snacks, and standard accessories, this shop also carries harder-to-find items like holistic remedies, dietary supplements, and gift items for pet lovers. Special orders and delivery are also available.

IN CASE OF EMERGENCY

Animal Wellness Center (complimentary/holistic care)
20 West Hills Rd., Huntington Station (631-351-0447)

East Hampton Veterinary Group
22 Montauk Hwy. (631-324-0282)

Fort Hill Animal Hospital
146 East Main St., Huntington (631-427-1655)

Manorville Pet Vet
20 Ryerson Ave., Manorville (631-722-8100)

North Fork Animal Hospital
58605 Rte. 25, Southold (631-765-2400)

Olde Towne Animal Hospital
380 County Rd. 39, Southampton (631-283-0611)

Sayville Hospital for Animals
5262 Sunrise Hwy. (631-589-5120)

Three Village Veterinary Hospital
1342 Stony Brook Rd. (631-689-8877)

West Hempstead Animal Hospital
104 Cherry Valley Ave. (516-483-9720)

Woodbury Animal Hospital (complimentary/holistic care)
141 Woodbury Rd. (516-367-7100)

The Hudson River Valley

THE WARD POUND RIDGE RESERVATION ATTRACTS HIKERS, PICNICKERS, ANGLERS, AND PLENTY OF FOUR-LEGGED VISITORS.

The Hudson River Valley

DOG-FRIENDLY RATING:

Vacationing with your pet in the Hudson Valley has its advantages and disadvantages. On the negative side, visitors will find fewer dog-friendly lodging options and tourist attractions here than in most other regions of New York State. Even state parks and state campgrounds, usually havens for traveling pet lovers, are strangely unwelcoming to companion animals in this region. (Many parks ban dogs altogether; others require, of all things, muzzles.) On the other hand, the valley is ideally located for vacationers who want easy access to New York City as well as the wilder areas to the north and west. Hudson Valley accommodations are pricier than those in the Catskills, but more affordable than those in the city. And where else can you sit by a campfire at night and shop Fifth Avenue by day?

From Wall Street commuters in Westchester to farmers in Dutchess, this is a region more focused on residents than visitors. Of course, you can

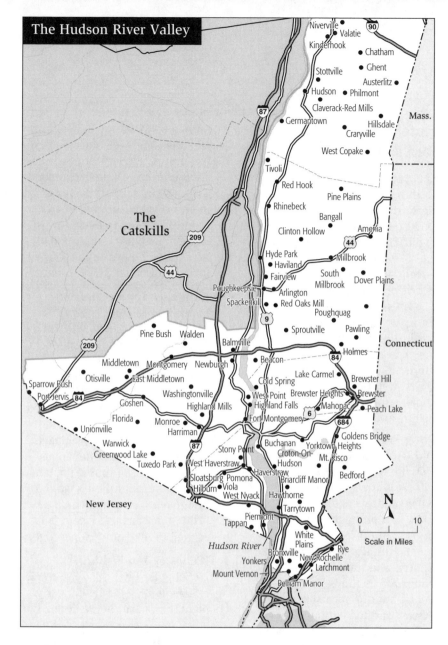

The Hudson River Valley

Niverville
Valatie
Kinderhook
Chatham
Stottville
Ghent
Austerlitz
Hudson
Philmont
Claverack-Red Mills
Mass.
Germantown
Hillsdale
Craryville
West Copake
Tivoli
Red Hook
Pine Plains
Rhinebeck
Bangall
The Catskills
Clinton Hollow
Amenia
Hyde Park
Millbrook
Haviland
Fairview
South Millbrook
Dover Plains
Poughkeepsie
Arlington
Spackenkill
Red Oaks Mill
Poughquag
Sproutville
Pawling
Pine Bush
Walden
Balmville
Holmes
Connecticut
Middletown
Montgomery
Newburgh
Beacon
Lake Carmel
Brewster Hill
Otisville
East Middletown
Cold Spring
Brewster Heights
Brewster
Sparrow Bush
Washingtonville
West Point
Brewster Heights
Mahopac
Peach Lake
Port Jervis
Goshen
Highland Mills
Highland Falls
Florida
Monroe
Fort Montgomery
Unionville
Harriman
Buchanan
Goldens Bridge
Warwick
Stony Point
Yorktown Heights
Greenwood Lake
West Haverstraw
Croton-On-Hudson
Mt. Kisco
Tuxedo Park
Haverstraw
Bedford
Sloatsburg
Pomona
Briarcliff Manor
Hilburn
Viola
West Nyack
Hawthorne
New Jersey
Piermont
Tarrytown
Tappan
White Plains
Hudson River
Bronxville
Rye
Yonkers
New Rochelle
Larchmont
Mount Vernon
Pelham Manor

N

0   10
Scale in Miles

use that to your advantage: While other vacationers are crowding Catskills campgrounds and lakes, you can find yourself visiting well-known historic sites, canoeing down the Hudson River, enjoying some elbowroom in a spacious park, gawking at presidential mansions, and snapping photos of lighthouses. And if you happen to live in the Big Apple, the Hudson Valley has the unsurpassed advantage of being close, close, close. Hop on the highway for an hour (or two), check into a B&B, and let the chorus of crickets sing you and your favorite mutt to sleep.

ACCOMMODATIONS

Hotels, Motels, Inns, and Bed & Breakfasts

Chappaqua
Crabtree's Kittle House Restaurant and Inn, 11 Kittle Rd. (914-666-8044); $127–147 per night. This 1790s inn offers 12 guest rooms with private baths, queen- and king-size beds, cable television, and Internet access. The on-site restaurant is known for its wine cellar and American cuisine, and complimentary continental breakfasts are served each morning in the dining room. Quiet, well-behaved dogs are welcome, although owners will be held responsible for any damages.

Dover Plains
Old Drover's Inn, Old Rte. 22, P.O. Box 100 (845-832-9311; info@olddroversinn.com; www.olddroversinn.com); $150–475 per night. This quaint historic inn offers four guest rooms: the Rose, the Sleigh, the Cherry, and the Meeting. The ambiance includes hardwood floors, antique furnishings, fireplaces, and terry robes. Dogs weighing less than 40 pounds are permitted for an extra $25 per night; advance notice is essential because only one pet is allowed on the premises at a time. Weekend rates are higher than weekday rates and include a full breakfast and full dinner for two.

Fishkill
Homestead Studio Suites, 25 Merritt Blvd (845-897-2800); $79–159 per night. Formerly known as MainStay Suites, this all-suite hotel welcomes guests for long- and short-term stays. Each unit has a full-size kitchen, a desk with data ports, voice mail, irons and ironing boards, a fitness center, free local calls, laundry facilities, and free daily breakfasts. Your dog can join you for an additional $25 per night.

Residence Inn by Marriott Fishkill, 14 Schuyler Blvd. (845-896-5210; 1-800-331-3131); $169–239 per night. Ideal for those looking for a long-term stay facility, the Residence Inn of Fishkill offers studio suites and 2-level penthouse suites. Each suite has a full-size kitchen, a living and dining area, a coffeemaker, and access to free continental breakfasts, a swimming pool, and laundry facilities. If you want to bring your dog along, you'll pay a $200 nonrefundable cleaning fee, as well as an extra $20 per night.

Wellesley Inn Fishkill, 20 Schuyler Blvd. (845-896-4995; 1-800-444-8888); $81–109 per night. Guests at the Wellesley Inn enjoy interior corridors, free newspapers, air-conditioning, free continental breakfasts, business services, a wake-up service, and safe-deposit boxes. All rooms feature coffeemakers, in-room movies, hair dryers, irons, and ironing boards. Dogs are allowed in first-floor smoking rooms without extra charges, provided that owners do not leave them unattended in the rooms.

High Falls

High Falls Motel, 1061 Rte. 213 (845-687-2095); $80–85 per night. This plain-and-simple, clean motel provides nine rooms (some nonsmoking), air-conditioning, an outdoor swimming pool, and televisions. Major credit cards are accepted. Dogs are welcome, although their owners are asked to follow some commonsense rules and regulations; inquire about details at check-in.

Hillsdale

Celerohn Motel, 9350 Rte. 22 (518-325-3000; www.celerohn-motel.com); $65–125 per night. This 1950s retro-style motel has nine rooms, private bathrooms, free local calls, a swimming pool, televisions and VCRs, and 4.5 acres for meandering. Dogs are welcome in designated rooms, though pet owners can expect a pre-visit "interview" to screen out unfriendly or aggressive animals. To help with planning, the web site will even tell you which upcoming dates are sold out.

Holiday House Motel, 2871 Rte. 23 (518-325-3030; www.holiday-housemotel.com); call for rate information. Located beside a trout-fishing stream, the Holiday House Motel offers individually decorated rooms with double or king-size beds, air-conditioning, cable television, and coffeemakers. Dog lovers will also appreciate the motel's lawns and picnic area. Well-behaved, leashed pets are welcome for an additional $10 per night.

Hudson

St. Charles Hotel, 16-18 Park Place (518-822-9900); $89–119 per night. This historic hotel, built in 1868, provides guests with updated facilities along with unique touches like tin ceilings and an antique mahogany bar. The 34 rooms have air-conditioning and cable television; other amenities include a restaurant, a bar with live entertainment, a banquet room, and meeting facilities. Your pooch is welcome without extra charges.

Middletown

Days Inn Middletown, Rtes. 17 West and 6 (845-374-2411; 1-800-544-8313); $71–89 per night. The Middletown Days Inn provides guests with free daily continental breakfasts, a 24-hour front desk, a swimming pool, free local calls, alarm clocks, and cable television. The recently renovated Executive Rooms also have oversized desks, microwaves, and 25-inch televisions. Your dog is welcome in designated smoking rooms without extra charges.

Middletown Motel, 501 Rte. 211 East (845-342-2535); $59–89 per night. Guests at the Middletown Motel enjoy free daily breakfasts, an outdoor swimming pool and hot tub, air-conditioning, cable television, in-room movies, smoking and nonsmoking rooms, and a game room. Golf courses, tennis courts, fishing, and horseback-riding opportunities are all nearby. Well-behaved dogs are welcome for an extra $15 per night.

Super 8 Motel Middletown, 563 Rte. 211 East (845-692-5828; 1-800-800-8000); $59–89 per night. There are no extra charges for your dog at this pet-friendly motel, where amenities include a

THE PET-FRIENDLY COTTONWOOD MOTEL IN MILLBROOK OFFERS ROOMS, SUITES, AND COTTAGES ON A 3.5-ACRE PROPERTY.

24-hour front desk, a wake-up service, complimentary continental breakfasts, laundry facilities, modem lines, cable television, and smoking and nonsmoking rooms. Several restaurants and Stewart Airport are nearby.

Mount Kisco

Holiday Inn Mount Kisco, 1 Holiday Inn Dr. (914-241-2600); $119–159 per night. Located about 30–45 minutes from Manhattan, this full-service hotel has a fitness center, an outdoor swimming pool, laundry facilities, a restaurant and bar, air-conditioning, safe-deposit boxes, a 24-hour front desk, room service, a wake-up service, and a concierge desk. In the rooms, guests will find alarm clocks, coffeemakers, modem lines, irons, and ironing boards. Those traveling with a dog pay a one-time fee of $25.

Millbrook

Cottonwood Motel, Rte. 44 (845-677-3283; www.cottonwoodmotel.com); $89–250 per night. Choose from standard rooms, deluxe rooms, suites, or cottages at this friendly motel conveniently located near the Taconic State Parkway. Children stay free, and well-behaved pets are welcome with prior approval in all rooms and cottages.

Nanuet

Candlewood Suites Nanuet, 20 Overlook Blvd., (845-371-4445; 1-888-226-3539); $119–199 per night. Designed for long-term stays, this all-suite hotel provides full-size kitchens and living areas, laundry services, alarm clocks, voice mail, speakerphones, modem lines, free local calls, VCRs and CD players, a fitness center, and a 24-hour convenience store. Numerous restaurants are located nearby. Pet owners pay $35 for a stay of up to two weeks or $75 for longer stays.

Days Inn Nanuet, 367 Rte. 59 (845-623-4567; 1-800-544-8313); $79–99 per night. For an extra $8 per night, your pooch is welcome to join you at this full-service Days Inn. Amenities include a restaurant and bar, a fitness center, express checkout services, microwaves and refrigerators, a swimming pool, cable television, free newspapers and local calls, coffeemakers, and daily continental breakfasts.

Newburgh

Super 8 Motel Newburgh, 1287 Rte. 300 (845-564-5700; 1-800-800-8000); $69–89 per night. Like the Super 8 location in Middletown (see listing above), this site offers a 24-hour front desk, free parking, smoking and nonsmoking rooms, cable television, and laundry facilities. The Newburgh location is also convenient to West Point, Stewart Airport, and several historic sites. Dogs are welcome guests for an additional $10 per night.

New Rochelle

Residence Inn by Marriott New Rochelle, 35 Le Count Place (914-636-7888; 1-800-331-3131); $157–204 per night. Like other Residence Inns, the New Rochelle location offers small and large suites for long- and short-term stays. Guests will find kitchens, dining areas, laundry facilities, meeting rooms, a 24-hour front desk, a fitness center, a swimming pool, and safe-deposit boxes. Dog owners pay a $75 initial charge, plus $15 per night.

Peekskill

Peekskill Inn, 634 Main St. (914-739-1500; 1-800-526-9466; www.peekskillinn.com); $117–199 per night. Choose from suites or guest rooms with full-, queen-, and king-size beds at the Peekskill Inn, a scenic accommodation with balconies, air-conditioning, premium movie channels, a swimming pool, a restaurant and bar, daily continental breakfasts, and a 24-hour "Lobby Beverage Bar and Bedtime Cookie Depot." Your dog or cat is welcome to join the fun for an extra $15 per night.

Poughkeepsie

Econo Lodge Poughkeepsie, 2625 South Rd. (Rte. 9) (845-452-6600); $79–129 per night. This 2-story Econo Lodge has 112 rooms and efficiency units, along with banquet facilities, a restaurant, laundry facilities, and free daily continental breakfasts. Shops, colleges, and tourist attractions are all nearby. Guests paying in cash pay an additional $50 refundable security deposit for pets; dog owners using a credit card pay no additional security deposit or fees.

Red Hook

Grand Dutchess Bed & Breakfast, 7571 Old Post Rd. (845-758-5818; www.grand dutchess.com); $95–155 per night. Room rates include a homemade daily breakfast at the Grand Dutchess, a Victorian B&B with formal parlors, two porches, and guest rooms and suites. Canine guests are welcome for an extra $15 per night, as long as owners bring a dog bed and don't leave pets alone in the rooms. Only one dog is allowed in the house per weekend, so try to make your reservation as far in advance as possible.

Tarrytown

Hilton Tarrytown, 455 South Broadway (914-631-5700; 1-800-HILTONS; www.tarrytownhilton.

com); $99–269 per night. Hilton Tarrytown guests can choose from standard rooms, junior suites, one-bedroom suites, or two-bedroom suites. Other amenities include room service, a swimming pool, sports courts, a fitness center, business services, laundry facilities, an ATM, and cribs and high chairs for children. Guests traveling with a dog don't pay any extra charges, but they do sign a "pet contract" agreement upon check-in.

Wallkill
Audrey's Farmhouse Bed & Breakfast, 2188 Brunswyck Rd. (845-895-3440; 1-800-501-3872; audreysfarmhouse@aol.com; www.audreysfarmhouse.com); $95–160 per night. Dogs are not only allowed at Audrey's, they're enthusiastically welcomed and treated as special guests by the staff. The restored 1740s saltbox has mountain and meadow views, beautifully landscaped grounds, antiques, percale sheets, down comforters, cathedral ceilings, a swimming pool and deck, a hot tub, a library, and full country breakfasts each morning. During your visit, don't forget to check in with the four-legged "staff members" Kiva, a Shi Tzu, and Shawnee, a golden retriever.

Warwick
Meadowlark Farm Bed & Breakfast, 180 Union Corners Rd. (845-651-4286; meadow@ warwick.net; www.meadow-larkfarm.com); $75–100 per night. Friendly dogs are welcome at Meadowlark for an extra $15 per night—horse stabling is also available for $25 per night. The

B&B offers three guest rooms with private baths, cable television, a front porch, a library, landscaped grounds, and full breakfasts served each morning in the dining room or on the terrace. Dogs cannot be left unattended in the rooms.

White Plains
The Esplanade, 95 South Broadway (914-761-8100; esplanadeinfo@aol.com; www.esplanadecorporate.com); $119 and higher per night or $1,700–2,500 per month. Designed with business travelers in mind, this hotel and corporate housing facility is ideal for long-term stays. Each studio and one-bedroom apartment has a kitchenette and cable television with premium movie channels; other amenities include laundry facilities, free parking, a business center, a fitness center, and complimentary daily breakfasts. Dogs and cats are welcome with a one-time nonrefundable fee of $250 and an extra $250 refundable security deposit. Owners must also sign a pet-policy agreement form.

Renaissance Westchester Hotel, 80 W. Red Oak Lane (914-694-5400; 1-800-468-3571); $99–269 per night. This large, posh hotel boasts 350 guest rooms, an indoor swimming pool, conference facilities, a restaurant, a fitness center, a sauna, in-room movies and video games, air-conditioning, cable television, modems, business services, tennis courts, and 30 acres of landscaped and forested property for exploring. Dogs are allowed for an additional $60 per stay. New

DOGS ARE WELCOME WITHOUT EXTRA CHARGES AT THE BLUE SPRUCE INN & SUITES IN VALATIE.

York City is just 30 minutes away.

Summerfield Suites by Windham, 101 Corporate Park Dr. (914-251-9700); $149–259 per night. Your pet is welcome to join you for a short- or long-term stay at Summerfield Suites, a hotel offering one- and two-bedroom suites with laundry facilities, a swimming pool, a fitness center, sports courts, daily continental breakfasts, and a barbecue area. Pet fees are $50 for 1 to 4 nights, $150 for 5 to 13 nights, $200 for 14 to 29 nights, and $250 for 30 nights or more.

Valatie
Blue Spruce Inn & Suites, Rte. 9 (518-758-9711; service@ bluespruceinnsuites.com; www. bluespruceinnsuites.com); $60–95 per night. Located in the northernmost reaches of the Hudson Valley region, this motel-style accommodation offers exterior corridors, a swimming pool, a coffee shop serving breakfast each morning, and 10 acres with woods and wildflowers. Dogs are welcome without extra charges in designated rooms; be sure to let the manager know ahead of time if you plan to bring an animal. Pets should be crated if left alone in a room.

Campgrounds

Cross River
Ward Pound Ridge Reservation Campgrounds, Intersection of Rtes. 35 and 121 South (914-864-7317; 914-864-7318); $15–35 per night. Westchester County's largest park offers several different camping areas; huddle up under a lean-to or bring your own tent. During the day, you and your favorite mutt can hike the trails, scope birds through binoculars, relax by a fishing stream, or enjoy a snack in one of the many picnic areas. For more information on the reservation, see "Out and About."

Elizaville
Brook-N-Wood Family Campground, Country Rd. 8 (518-537-6896; 1-888-588-8622; www.brooknwood.com); $25–30

per night. Tent and RV campers will each find something to love about Brook-N-Wood; the secluded tent sites are near the water, and the 150 RV sites are large and level. Sports courts, playgrounds, a camp store, and a swimming pool keep all members of the family busy. Dogs are always welcome, provided they are leashed, cleaned-up after, and not left alone at campsites.

Hopewell Junction

Sylvan Lake Beach Park, 18 McDonnells Lane (845-221-9889; sylvanL100@aol.com; www.gocampingamerica.com/sylvanlake); $30 per night. Each campsite at Sylvan Lake is at least 40 feet wide; some are wooded, some are open and sunny. Visitors will also find group camping sites, full hook-ups, a snack bar, a game room, playing fields, a beach, and plenty of opportunities for fishing, swimming, and boating. Keep an eye out for the resident pooch, who patrols the grounds daily in "her" golf cart.

Middletown

Korn's Campground, 60 Meyer's Rd., P.O. Box 579 (845-386-3433); $25–30 per night. Campers at Korn's will find a fishing stream stocked with trout, wooded and open sites, a game room, a playground, laundry facilities, a camp store, and a recreation building. Pet owners pay an additional $10 per night, though many breeds—including terriers—are restricted. Call ahead of time to make sure your dog will be welcomed. Day visitors are not allowed to bring pets into the campground.

Plattekill

Newburgh/New York City North KOA, Rte. 32, P.O. Box 134D (845-564-2836; 1-800-562-7220; nnycnkoa@aol.com; www.newburghkoa.com); $30–39 per night. Campers at this KOA will find extensive facilities, including two swimming pools, a game room, a miniature golf course, a playground, a game room, a camp store, special events, sports courts, a fishing pond, a nature trail, bicycle rentals, and regularly scheduled tours into New York City. Dogs are welcome without extra fees, as long as owners clean up any messes and don't leave animals alone at campsites.

Rhinebeck

Interlake RV Park, 428 Lake Dr. (845-266-5387; interlake@inter-lakervpark.com; www.interlake-rvpark.com); $25–32 per night. Two golden retrievers will greet you at check-in at Interlake, a family-friendly and dog-friendly campground located on a 20-acre lake. Other features include a swimming pool, a game room, a recreation hall, sports courts, a snack bar, a camp store, rest rooms with showers, a fishing pond, laundry facilities, and a dump station. Well-behaved pets are welcome, as long as they are never left unattended on the grounds.

Homes, Cottages, and Cabins for Rent

Ghent

Guest cottage (212-466-6329; 646-279-7206; optimvsmaximvs@

yahoo.com); $100–120 per night; $650–700 per week; or $2,300–2,500 per month. This cozy one-bedroom cottage is located on a lavish estate near a stone castle. Guests can roam the property's two-and-a-half acres, swim in the pool, sunbathe on the decks, and enjoy the landscaping and flower gardens. The cottage has a washer and dryer, a coffeemaker, a microwave, a television, and provided linens. Dogs (sorry, no cats) are welcome.

Highland Falls
Highland Falls cottage (mrand@email.arizona.edu); $100 per night. West Point visitors will appreciate the convenient location of this nearby two-bedroom cottage. Located beside a scenic brook, the cottage can accommodate up to six people with one queen bed, two twin beds, and a pull-out couch. Other amenities

include a fireplace, cable television, a VCR, a CD player, a washer and dryer, a dishwasher, and provided linens. West Point cadet parents receive a discount: Call for details. Dogs are welcome, and will no doubt enjoy romping in the fenced-in backyard.

Millerton
Fieldstone home (212-254-9660; treiter2@rcn.com); $800 per week. "This is a very dog-friendly house," says homeowner Tina Reiter, who rents the two-bedroom, one-bath house to vacationers. Located on 4 acres of private land, the home can accommodate up to six people with a full kitchen, hardwood floors, satellite television, a deck, a stone porch, gardens, an art studio, a fireplace, provided linens, and a barbecue grill. One well-behaved dog is welcome per stay.

OUT AND ABOUT

Tallman Mountain State Park, Rte. 9W, Bear Mountain (845-359-0544). Out beyond the swimming pool, tennis courts, and picnic areas (where pets are not allowed), Tallman State Park offers pristine hiking trails with views of the Hudson and Piermont Marsh. The wetlands are part of the Hudson River National Estuarine Research Reserve, and provide ample opportunities for peering at wading birds and other species through your binoculars. Unfortunately, dogs are required

to be muzzled and on a leash no longer than 6 feet.

Bear Mountain State Park, Intersection of Palisades Pkwy. and Rte. 9W, Bear Mountain (845-786-2701). Although companion animals are allowed at this great park, the welcome comes with a caveat or two. Firstly, dogs at Bear Mountain are officially required to wear a muzzle. (In reality, few do, but that's nonetheless the dictum handed down from the state parks department.) Secondly, they are not allowed in the picnic areas, on the beaches, in the water, or on the walkways. If you can deal with all that, however, Bear Mountain does offer some of the most spectacular views and hiking trails in the Hudson Valley, along with a boat launch, a dock, and a road leading to an overlook. It's definitely worth a visit. Canines are required to stay on a leash no longer than 6 feet.

Cascade Mountain Winery, Flint Hill Rd., Amenia (914-373-9021; cascademt@mohawk.net). Founded in 1972, the Cascade Mountain Winery is now home to an upscale restaurant and award-winning wines, including Baco Noir, Seyval Blanc, and Private Reserve White. Your pooch is welcome to roam the vineyard and lawns as you both take in the scenic views. Tastings and tours are available.

Cole Palen's Old Rhinebeck Aerodrome, Norton Rd., Rhinebeck (845-752-3200; info@oldrhinebeck.org; www.oldrhinebeck.org). Aviation buffs won't want to miss the weekend airshows at the Old Rhinebeck Areodrome: Saturday "History of Flight" shows feature barnstorming and other performances by pilots in aircraft manufactured from 1909 to 1939, while the Sunday "World War I" show spotlights the Fokker Triplane, the Sopwith Camel, and other craft flown during the conflict. Drama, comedy, and crazy characters make the entertaining performances even more fun. Your leashed, well-behaved dog is welcome, as long as he isn't easily frightened by loud noises and overhead excitement.

Columbia-Greene Humane Society Events, Columbia-Greene Humane Society, 125 Humane Society Rd., Hudson (518-828-6044; www.cghs.org). This Catskills animal welfare organization holds numerous fundraising events throughout the year for pet lovers: Call or visit the web site to learn about this year's event dates and times. Past gatherings have included walkathons, tag sales, spring raffles, and Open House Barbecues. Locals and visitors alike can join the fun and benefit the shelter's efforts.

Clarence Fahnestock State Park, Rte. 301, Carmel (845-225-7207). Most people come to this state park for Canopus Beach, a huge day-use area with a sandy beach, a snack bar, showers, and rest rooms. Unfortunately, your dog is not allowed in that section of the park, but it's just as well: Avoid the crowds and head to the quieter trails, where dogs are welcome on a leash. The site also has a boat launch, boat rentals, ice skating, and cross-country skiing trails. Dogs are not allowed in the campground.

Franklin D. Roosevelt State Park, 2957 Crompond Rd., Yorktown Heights (914-245-4434). Alas, four-legged visitors are not allowed in the campground, picnic area, or swimming area at this popular park. But you and Rover can boat and fish in Mohansic Lake and Crom Pond, rent a rowboat, or hike, bike, and cross-country ski on any of the trails. Leashes are required.

George's Island Park, Dutch St., Montrose (914-737-7530). Look out over the beautiful Hudson River at this waterfront park. At 208 acres, it's fairly small, but it packs a punch with wetlands, walking trails, a pond, picnic areas, playing fields, a playground, and great views. All that water access also makes George's Island a great spot to launch a boat. The trails range in difficulty from flat and easy to steep and rough. Dogs are welcome, but must be leashed.

Harriman State Park, Exit 17, Palisades Interstate Pkwy., Bear Mountain (845-942-2560). Also known as the Anthony Wayne Recreation Area, this park has lots of appeal—and lots of restrictions—for animal lovers. Canines are banned from the campgrounds, beaches, water, walkways, and picnic areas in Harriman. In addition, you may be surprised to learn that your dog is required to wear a muzzle within park grounds. That said, the 50,000-acre park does have seemingly endless trails, scenic views, lakes, and opportunities for fun. Make a day of it. Dogs are required to be on a leash no longer than 6 feet.

Home of Franklin D. Roosevelt National Historic Site, Rte. 9, Hyde Park (845-229-9115). The Roosevelts were dog people, so perhaps it's no surprise that leashed, well-behaved pets are welcome to visit the grounds at the home of FDR, America's only four-term president. In addition to the home, known as "Springwood," and the Presidential Library, the 300-acre property also has gardens, trails, and dramatic views. Canines are not allowed inside the buildings and cannot be left alone anywhere on the property.

Hudson Highlands State Park, Rte. 9D, Beacon (845-225-7207). At last, a Hudson Valley park where dogs are welcomed throughout! Mostly rustic and undeveloped, Hudson Highlands boasts more than 25 miles of trails for hiking and biking, as well as plenty of boating and fishing opportunities. Many of the trails round corners with sweeping vistas of the valley and the river. Dogs must be on a leash no longer than 10 feet.

Hudson Valley Humane Society Events, Hudson Valley Humane Society, 150 McNamara Rd., Spring Valley (845-354-3124; www.hvhumane.org). You and Spot can have some fun and help homeless animals by participating in one of this humane society's special fundraising events, including the annual Outdoor Garage Sale and the annual Dog Walk in the Park. Dates, times, and locations vary from year to year; for the latest information, call the society or visit its web site. Founded in 1891, this historic group shelters animals, educates the public about spaying and neutering, and finds new, permanent homes for the animals in their care.

Hyde Park Station, 34 River Rd., Hyde Park (845-229-2338). Once slated for demolition, this historic station was taken over and refurbished by the Hudson Valley Railroad Society starting in 1975. The site has exhibits, rest rooms, dedicated staffers and volunteers, and even nice views of the Hudson River. Next door, the town's Riverside Park provides more diversions with picnic tables, open grassy areas, and a gazebo.

James Baird State Park, 122D Freedom Rd., Pleasant Valley (845-452-1489). This is another New York state park that adheres to the perplexing rule of "no dogs in the picnic area." You'll just have to enjoy your sandwich somewhere on the trails, which are plentiful and relatively easy to navigate. The park also offers recreational programs, a playground, playing fields, and cross-country skiing trails. Dogs are not permitted on the golf course or in any buildings.

Lighthouse viewing. The Hudson River's seven remaining lighthouses provide great sightseeing opportunities for visitors and locals alike. Traveling from north to south, lighthouse peepers can view the Hudson-Athens Light in Hudson, a brick lighthouse with a working fog horn; the Saugerties Light, which now operates as a B&B; the Rondout Light in Kingston, a restored 1915 lighthouse with a museum; the Esopus Light, the last remaining wooden lighthouse on the river; the Stony Point Light, built in 1826 and the Hudson River's oldest lighthouse; the Tarrytown Light, which can be viewed from

Kingsland Point Park; and the Little Red Lighthouse in Jeffrey's Hook, the subject of a popular children's book and the site of an annual lighthouse festival.

Lyndhurst, 635 South Broadway, Tarrytown (914-631-4481; Lyndhurst@nhtp.org; www. lyndhurst.org). This National Trust Historic Site is called an estate, but it looks more like a fairy-tale castle. Overlooking the Hudson River, the Gothic structure has housed several of America's wealthiest families and was taken over by the National Trust for Historic Preservation in 1961. Lyndhurst members are allowed to walk their leashed dogs on the grounds; dogs are not allowed inside the building, and visitors are prohibited from leaving a pooch in a parked car.

Margaret Lewis Norrie State Park, Old Post Rd., P.O. Box 893, Staatsburg (845-889-4646). Like too many state parks in the Hudson Valley region, this one bans companion animals in the campground and picnic areas. You and Spot can still roam the trails, which join up with the neighboring Ogden Mills and Ruth Livingston Mills State Park (Old Post Rd., Staatsburg; 845-889-4646) to form more than 1,000 acres of undeveloped forestland. Accepted uses on the trails of the two parks include dog-walking, jogging, mountain biking, horseback riding, snowmobiling, and cross-country skiing. Without too much effort, you'll also stumble across sweeping views of the valley and the Hudson River. Dogs must be on a leash no longer than 10 feet.

New Croton Dam, Rte. 129, Croton-on-Hudson. After the original Croton Dam washed away in 1841, this "new" structure was built to contain the Croton River. Today you can enjoy dramatic views from the top of the dam, then relax in the picnic area of the park below. It's a picturesque stop for travelers and a great place to stretch your legs.

Old Croton Aqueduct Trail. Otherwise known as OCA, this unpaved path stretches through the lower Hudson Valley and into the Bronx. In addition to providing a beautiful, winding route for walking, jogging, and biking, the trail also has the distinct advantage of passing directly by many of the Hudson Valley's most famous historic sites. Plan to catch a glimpse of the Rockefeller State Park Preserve, the Old Dutch Church in Sleepy Hollow, Sunnyside, the Van Cortlandt Park and Mansion, the New Croton Dam, and others. Like many of the region's long-distance trails, however, this one is carry-in/carry-out with few or no services along the way. If you plan to go more than a mile or two, be sure to pack plenty of extra supplies. Leashed dogs are welcome. For maps and trail information, contact the Old Croton Trailway State Park office at 914-693-5259.

Rockefeller State Park Preserve, Rte. 117, P.O. Box 338, Tarrytown (914-631-1470). Perhaps the most famous feature of this state park is its carriage paths, which wind through the property along with miles of unpaved trails. Open year-round, the Rockefeller Preserve is home to a variety of wild species living in numerous ecosystems, including open fields, a lake, forestlands, wetlands, and meadows. Popular activities here include birdwatching, fishing, hiking, biking, dog-walking, cross-country skiing, horseback riding, and jogging. Dogs must be on a leash no longer than 10 feet.

Sleepy Hollow sites (Sleepy Hollow/Tarrytown). Long before writer Washington Irving made this area famous with his spooky tale "The Legend of Sleepy Hollow," the region was home to settlements dating from the mid-1600s. While you're in the area, check out some of the area's best-known historical attractions, including the Old Dutch Church on Rte. 9, the oldest church in New York State, which was featured prominently in Irving's tale. The burial ground on the property is also of great interest to history buffs; free walking tours are held on Sunday afternoons during the warmer months. Another well-known house of worship is the Union Church of Pocantico Hills, located at 555 Bedford Rd. The church boasts lovingly maintained stained-glass windows created by none other than Henri Matisse and Marc Chagall. You can't access the grounds of Sunnyside, the former home of Washington Irving, and other noteworthy estates with a dog in tow, but you can catch a glimpse of the impressive architecture of many of these historic sites from the **Old Croton Aqueduct Trail** (see listing above). For more information, contact the Historic Hudson Valley offices at 914-631-8200 or visit the group's web site at www.hudsonvalley.org.

Sterling Forest® State Park, 115 Old Forge Rd., Tuxedo (845-351-5907). This wild and woolly park encompasses more than 17,000 acres of undeveloped forestland. Birdwatchers and wildlife enthusiasts will find plenty of species to peer at, including hawks, songbirds, and even black bear. Fishing, ice fishing, hiking, and snowshoeing are popular activities. The park also has a boat launch. Dogs must be on a leash no longer than 6 feet.

Taconic State Park, Copake Falls Area (Valley View Rd., Copake Falls, 518-329-3993) and Rudd

Pond Area (Rte. 62, P.O. Box 99, Millerton). The two areas of Taconic State Park offer plenty of fun and activities for visitors—unfortunately, however, your dog will not be allowed in the campgrounds, beach areas, or picnic areas. The Copake Falls Area has Pit Pond, popular with anglers, and challenging trails for hikers and bikers. The Rudd Pond Area offers a boat launch and boat rentals on its namesake pond, as well as more nature trails. Dogs must be on a leash no longer than 10 feet.

Vanderbilt Mansion National Historic Site, Rte. 9, Hyde Park (845-229-9115). Leashed dogs are welcome on the grounds, but not in the buildings, at the Vanderbilt Mansion Historic Site. It's worth a visit just to gawk at the exterior of this impressive mansion, built by industry titan Frederick

A SCOTTIE ENJOYS A SATURDAY MORNING FARMERS' MARKET ON HUDSON STREET IN KINDERHOOK.

Vanderbilt, but you can also stroll on pedestrian-only walkways and trails, wander through formal gardens, and take in views of the Hudson River and Catskill Mountains.

Ward Pound Ridge Reservation, Intersection of Rte. 35 and Rte. 121 South, Cross River (914-864-7317). If you're passing through the area, even for a short time, make sure this park is on your list of things to do. Whether you want to have a quick picnic, stay overnight, spend the afternoon fishing, or get lost down a beautiful nature trail, the reservation can provide a backdrop for your four-legged adventures. With 4,700 acres, Ward Pound Ridge is Westchester County's largest park: Expect to see sparkling streams and rivers, sweeping vistas, numerous wildlife species, picnic tables, lean-to facilities, a nature museum, bikers, hikers, couples, and families. Leashed dogs are welcome, provided that owners pick up any messes. For more information on the campgrounds, see "Accommodations."

Westchester and Rockland Farmers' Markets, Community Markets (914-923-4837). For fresh produce, flowers, baked goods, and just good old browsing, try one of these Hudson Valley Farmers' Markets: Bronxville Farmers' Market, held on Saturday mornings at Stone Place off of Paxton Rd.; Hastings on Hudson Farmers' Market, held in the Public Library parking lot on Saturday mornings; the Mt. Vernon Farmers' Market, held Wednesday mornings in the parking lot of the Neighborhood Family Health Center on W. 4th St.; the Ossining Farmers' Market, held at the intersection of Main and Spring Sts. on Saturday mornings; the Pleasantville Farmers' Market, held on Saturday mornings at the Memorial Plaza off of Manville Rd.; the Spring Valley Farmers' Market, held Wednesday mornings at the corner of Rte. 45 and North Church St.; and the Tarrytown Farmers' Market, held Saturday mornings at Patriot's Park on Rte. 9.

Wilderstein, 330 Morton Rd., Rhinebeck (845-876-4818; www.wilderstein.org). Leashed, friendly dogs are welcome to explore the grounds at Wilderstein, a historic Queene Anne estate formerly owned by Margaret Lynch Suckley, a cousin of Franklin Delano Roosevelt. The property includes wooded walking trails, gardens, and of course wonderful exterior views of the enormous mansion. Every other year, the preservation society holds a special event just for dogs called the "Fala Gala," named after the famous Scottish terrier that Suckley gave to Roosevelt as a gift.

QUICK BITES

Allyn's Restaurant and Café, Rte. 44A, Millbrook (845-677-5888). Allyn's is an upscale eatery serving hungry travelers and locals alike with lunch, dinner, and brunch menus. Weddings and other special occasions are also held on the premises. Dogs are allowed in the outdoor patio seating area, provided they are not "walked" on the grounds.

Bagel Café, 41 Main St., Chatham (518-392-7388). Stop by and order a sandwich made on an H&H bagel from New York City; the Main Street café also serves salads, soups, baked goods, coffee, and cold drinks.

Brandow's and Company, 340 Warren St., Hudson (518-822-8938). This restaurant, café, and bakery serves up coffee, gourmet jams, cookies, muffins, sandwiches, specialty foods, and other wholesome treats that will satisfy a hungry traveler's stomach. Order your lunch or snack to go and enjoy a stroll through Hudson.

Ireland Corners General Store, 551 Rte. 208, Gardiner (845-255-8883). Stock up on snacks and groceries at this small store, or order a sandwich, a salad, or even breakfast items at the deli and breakfast grill. A few tables are available on the outdoor covered porch.

Julia & Isabella Restaurant & Bar, Rte. 9 North, Red Hook (845-758-4545). The owners of this restaurant have a dog-friendly attitude, outdoor seating, take-out service, and menu items like empanadas, quesadillas, calamari, salads, grilled chicken, seafood, steak, lamb, pasta, and vegetarian dishes.

Pandemain Bakery, 18 Garden St., Rhinebeck (845-876-2400). Not only is your dog welcome at Pandemain's outdoor seating area, the staff has also been known to provide visiting canines with fresh-baked doggie cookies. Have a quiche, panini sandwich, or bowl of soup and wash it all down with sweet treats and baked goods from the bakery counter.

Pippy's at the Square, 2 Delafield St., Poughkeepsie (845-483-7239). Weather permitting, you and your well-behaved canine can relax at Pippy's outdoor seating area. Choose Italian items like chicken casa, *fusilli ciambotta,* and seafood ravioli from a reasonably priced menu and wine list.

South Side Grille, 3 Mahopac Plaza, Mahopac (845-621-8710; www.thesouthsidegrille.com). At the time of this writing, the owners of the South Side Grille were planning on opening a new location on the waterfront with outdoor tables and beachfront seating. The new site was scheduled to open by late summer 2004. Menu items at the original South Side include seafood, salads, sandwiches, and steaks. For the latest information, call or visit the web site.

Stoneleigh Creek Restaurant, 166 Stoneleigh Ave., P.O. Box 864, Croton Falls (845-276-0000). Stoneleigh Creek offers indoor seating, outdoor seating, and takeout; menu items change frequently, but typically include dishes such as crab bisque, foie gras, seafood risotto, soft-shell crabs, rack of lamb, and stuffed chicken breast. A brunch menu is also served on Sundays.

Sweetwaters, 577 North Broadway, White Plains (914-328-8918). Sweetwaters serves continental cuisine in an indoor dining room as well as a large outdoor seating area with tables and umbrellas. Stop by for brunch, lunch, or dinner and choose from dishes such as smoked Norwegian salmon, Etruscan salad, a portabella sandwich, chicken Capriciossa, penne à la vodka, and shrimp scampi. Your dog is welcome to sit nearby, just outside the seating area.

The Would Restaurant, 120 North Rd., Highland (845-691-9883). This dog-friendly eatery welcomes you and your pooch at the patio seating area, where you can choose from grilled tenderloin of beef, grilled smoked tofu, sautéed scallops, mixed grilled vegetables, lobster spring rolls, and other dishes made with organic ingredients. Sinful desserts and an extensive wine list are also available.

HOT SPOTS FOR SPOT

Aardvark Pet Supplies, 58 Washington Ave., Pleasantville (914-747-4848). Whether you're looking for food for your dog or a gift for yourself, Aardvark most likely has it in stock. The stocked pet-food brands at this pet and gift store include Iams, Wellness, Canidae, Innova, Natural Choice, and Science Diet; browsers will also find toys, supplies, and home-baked canine treats. For two-legged shoppers, the store offers animal-themed clothing, mugs, calendars, statuettes, and other items.

Educated Dog, Rhinebeck/Hyde Park area (845-876-3671). This "dog vacation camp" is a step away from the ordinary for canines: "The dogs play and socialize all day in a fully fenced half-acre and live in my home with me," explains owner Barbara Whan, who has worked in the animal-care business for more than 23 years. "There are no cages here." A doggie romper room in the house keeps the pets busy on rainy or hot days, and individualized diets can be followed. Only dogs with good temperaments are accepted. Many of Whan's clients are from New York City and take advantage of her transportation services, as well. Daycare and long-term boarding are both available.

Grace Lane Kennels, 46 Grace Lane, Ossining (914-762-6188; 1-888-PET-CAMP; www.grace-lane.com). This large and friendly boarding facility has more than 150 private indoor/outdoor runs for dogs, as well as a separate overnight facility for cats. All indoor areas are heated and air-conditioned. Pooch pickup and delivery is available, as are baths. Visitors are welcome anytime during business hours. The facility, built in 1911, also holds the honor of being the oldest continually operating kennel in America.

L&M Pets Plus, 300 Fairview Ave. (Rte. 9), Hudson (518-828-8764). Pet beds, chew toys, aquarium supplies, treats, and other accessories are in stock at this convenient stop for pet owners. You'll also find food for dogs, cats, reptiles, fish, birds, and hamsters.

Nancy's Professional Dog Grooming, 250 Ridgebury Rd., Slate Hill (845-355-6234). When all that traveling has made your pooch grimy, Nancy's can provide a bath, cut, nail trim, and other clean-up services. Located just south of Middletown, this full-service shop is staffed by animal-loving professionals with more than 30 years' experience.

Paradice Kennels, 8 Silver Fox Lane, Hyde Park (845-229-7488; www.paradicekennels.com). Doggie visitors at Paradice have access to private indoor/outdoor runs, a heated interior area, grooming services, and supplies.

Cats are boarded in a separate "Cat Condo" area. Pickup and delivery is also available, as is 24-hour emergency veterinary service and a "flea-free guarantee."

The Pet Set, 737 Main St., Poughkeepsie (845-485-5790). This small, family-owned shop carries pet food in bulk, aquarium supplies, and a variety of companion animal accessories, toys, and treats. Boarding is also available for all kinds of pets, including reptiles and birds.

Tropical World and Pet Center, 5208 Rte. 9W, Newburgh (845-863-0900) and 2424 Rte. 32, New Windsor (845-534-9672). Open seven days a week, the two locations of this pet-supply store can provide traveling pet owners with all the basics on the road. In addition to stocking fish and aquarium necessities, the stores also sell supplies, food, chew toys, and other treats for dogs and cats.

We Sit 4 All Paws, Rockland County (845-371-4223; www.wesit4allpaws.com). Heading out for a nice meal? Hoping to catch a movie? While you're visiting Rockland County, this pet-sitting service can help out with your short-term sitting needs. For those who live in the area, the service provides in-home pet care, baths, taxi service to vet appointments, walks, and more for pet owners who are working long days or taking a vacation.

IN CASE OF EMERGENCY

Animal Care Clinic
1959 Rte. 9H, Hudson (518-828-9911)

Copake Veterinary Hospital
Rte. 22, Copake Falls (518-329-6161)

County Animal Clinic
1574 Central Park Ave., Yonkers (914-779-5000)

Croton Animal Hospital
7 South Riverside Ave., Croton-on-Hudson (914-271-6222)

Middletown Veterinary Hospital
189 Wawayanda Ave., Middletown (845-343-7012)

Pawling Animal Clinic
550 Rte. 22 (845-855-3316)

Pet Care Animal Hospital (complimentary/holistic care),
70 Pleasant St., Monticello (845-794-0780)

Pine Plains Veterinary Associates (complimentary/holistic care)
2826 Church St. (518-398-9494)

Rhinebeck Animal Hospital
6450 Montgomery St. (845-876-6008)

Rockland Holistic Veterinary Care (complimentary/holistic care)
626 Rte. 303, Blauvelt (845-348-7729)

The Catskill Mountains

THE BAVARIAN MANOR COUNTRY INN IN CAIRO WELCOMES WELL-MANNERED PETS.

The Catskill Mountains

DOG-FRIENDLY RATING:

Dog lovers, gather your gear: This unique, hospitable region offers just the pet-friendly getaway you've been searching for. That ringing endorsement applies to outdoorsy-types, luxury seekers, canoeists, honeymooners, skiers, families, anglers, and just about anyone else who could use a bit of fun and adventure. From feather beds to tent sites, flea markets to train rides, and cabins to chalets, the Catskills run the gamut from rustic to refined. Best of all, most of the animal-friendly lodgings listed here are affordable, accessible, and ultra accommodating to you and your four-legged traveling buddy.

It's hard to believe such a wild and woolly place exists just a few short hours north of New York City. Catskill Park encompasses nearly 300,000 acres of land in four counties, including rivers, lakes, forests, wetlands, and 98 mountain peaks. A little more than half the land is privately owned, and the rest is public, state-owned preserves. Wildlife-watchers

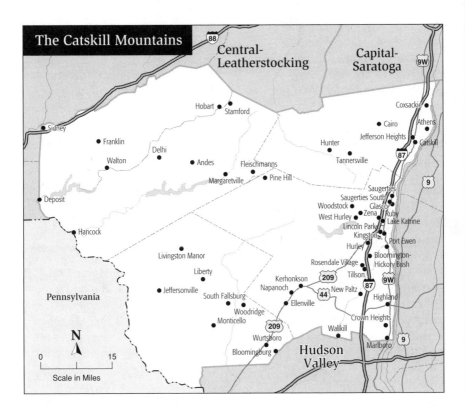

will find few better places in the state to get a glimpse of unique species and habitats. Take a train ride, float down the Delaware River, cross a covered bridge, fish for trout, have a picnic, visit the site of the 1969 Woodstock Music and Arts Festival, or catch sight of majestic eagles through your binoculars. No matter what you decide to do in the Catskills, you can rest assured that you probably won't have to leave your best friend behind.

ACCOMMODATIONS

Hotels, Motels, Inns and Bed & Breakfasts

Barryville
All Breeze Guest House, 227 Haring Rd. (845-557-6485); $40 per night. The four guest rooms at

All Breeze are simple, clean, and affordable; each has a private bathroom and a private entrance, and is located within a cottage next to the main house. Breakfast is served each morning in the farmhouse dining room. Pets are welcome, provided they stay off the furniture and are not left alone in the rooms. The innkeepers can also arrange Canoe-and-Stay packages for $90–100 per couple.

Big Indian

Cold Spring Lodge, 530 Oliverea Rd. (845-254-5711; bobcsl@ catskill.net; www.coldspring lodge.com); $130–195 per night or $800 per week. Located under towering pines and nestled between two Catskill mountains, Cold Spring Lodge offers eight two- and three-bedroom cottages surrounded by miles of trails. Other amenities include a swimming pool, a restaurant, a pond, and a screened-in deck. Dogs are welcome for an additional $10 per night, with a maximum charge of $40 per stay.

Starlite Motel, Rte. 28 (845-254-4449; 1-888-218-6467; info@starlite-motel.com; www. starlite-motel.com); $70–95 per night. Leashed dogs are welcome at Starlite for an extra $10 per night, although they must be crated when left alone in the rooms. The motel offers eight units, including six efficiencies with kitchenettes. Guests enjoy a complimentary breakfast basket and great views of the surrounding mountains. Ski-and-Stay packages for the nearby Belleayre Mountain ski area are also available.

Callicoon Center

Apple Pond Farming Center & Guest House, P.O. Box 371 (845-482-4764; applepon@catskill.net; www.catskill.net/applepon); $200–300 per weekend or $500–600 per week. "Dogs are most welcome as part of the rental of our guest house," says Apple Pond's Sonja Hedlund. "Our dogs love having visitors, too." The guest house has two apartments: one with one bedroom, and one with three bedrooms. The farm is organic, horse-powered, and visitor-friendly. Dog owners are asked to keep their pets away from the sheep, goats, chickens, and other farm animals.

Cairo

McBride's Sunset Motor Court, 166 Rte. 145 (518-634-7681); $60–125 per night. Accommodations at McBride's include motel rooms and efficiencies, all with air-conditioning, cable television, and complimentary continental breakfasts. Outside, guests will find a swimming pool and sports courts. For an extra $5–10 per night, most breeds of dogs are welcome; call to see if yours qualifies. Guest dogs must be friendly with other canines (especially the resident keeshond) and owners must clean up after them.

Catskill

Quality Inn and Conference Center, Rte. 23B (518-943-5800); $79–349 per night. The Catskill Quality Inn has 74 guest rooms, air-conditioning, cable television, in-room movies, a swimming pool, a restaurant and lounge, banquet rooms, and smoking and nonsmoking rooms. Some rooms also come equipped with hot tubs and kitchenettes. Two ski resorts are nearby. Your dog is a welcome guest for an additional $20 per night.

Resort Prostokvashino, 5207 Rte. 32 (518-678-9643; www. resort-prostokvashino.com); $55–100 per night or $270–500 per week. "Our name, Prostokvashino, is the name of a village in a very popular Russian cartoon about a kid, a dog, a cat, and a cow," explains proprietor Vitaliy Bobkov. "Therefore we are family-friendly, pet-friendly, and kid-friendly." Guests choose from standard motel rooms, two-bedroom efficiencies, and one- and two-bedroom cottages. Other amenities include a swimming pool, playgrounds, and a game room. Pet owners pay an extra $10 per day.

Earlton

Nightingale Inn Bed & Breakfast, 2371 Rte. 81 at Peat Beds Rd. (518-634-2507; 518-634-7305; info@nightingaleinn.com; www.nightingaleinn.com); $75 per night. The five rooms at this historic B&B have feather beds and shared baths; guests can also take advantage of full daily breakfasts and a large porch overlooking a lake. The inn also specializes in Murder Mystery Weekends. Small- to medium-size dogs are welcome without extra charges, as long as owners agree to keep pets off the feather beds.

Fleischmanns

River Run Bed & Breakfast Inn, 882 Main St. (845-254-4884; riverrun@catskill.net; www. catskill.net/riverrun); $75–165 per night. Built in 1887, this Queen Anne–style manor offers eight guest rooms with private and shared baths, as well as a suite that can accommodate larger families. Guests can enjoy breakfast in the dining room, read a book in the parlor, sip ice tea on the lawn, or gather in a private picnic area next to a stream. Well-behaved dogs are welcome; call for details.

Forestburgh

Inn at Lake Joseph, 162 Saint Joseph Rd. (845-791-9506; inn2@lakejoseph.com; www. lakejoseph.com); $260–385 per night. For an extra $20 per night, dogs (sorry, no cats) are welcome in the Carriage House and Cottage rooms at the Inn at Lake Joseph, a luxurious getaway with cathedral ceilings, whirlpool baths, stone fireplaces, sun decks, and an Adirondacks "great camp" ambiance. During a visit, guests can take a canoe out on the 250-acre lake, relax by the swimming pool, or hike, bike, and ski on the property's many trails.

Greenville

Birmann's Rainbow Lodge & Restaurant, Rte. 26 (518-966-5213; rainbolodge@aol.com, www.rainbow-lodge.net); $55 per night. The Rainbow Lodge has motel-style guest rooms with two double beds, air-conditioning, cable television, and private baths. An on-site restaurant and cocktail lounge is open every night of the week, serving traditional American fare. (Pet owners will appreciate the takeout service.) Well-behaved dogs are welcome at the lodge without extra charges.

Hensonville

Apple Tree Bed & Breakfast, Rte. 296 (518-734-5555; plsrskr@aol.com; www. windham-area.com/appletree. htm); $60–185 per night. This old-fashioned B&B has a quaint front porch, antique furnishings, and three guest rooms, two of which can be joined to form a large suite for bigger families or groups. Ski Windham is located just down the road, and a full breakfast of French toast, pastries, or other treats is included in the rates. Dogs more than two years old (sorry, no cats or puppies) are welcome for an additional $25 per night.

Highmount

Gateway Lodge Bed & Breakfast Inn P.O. Box 397, Highmount (845-254-4084; www.gateway-lodgebandb.com); $75–155 per night. The Gateway Lodge innkeepers not only welcome your dog, but also provide pet-sitting services, a dog run, and even some pet-centered activities. The B&B is located on three acres with five guest rooms, two larger suites, full country breakfasts, and an activities room. Downhill skiing trails are located just across the road at Belleayre Mountain, while other mountains are a half-hour's drive away. This place is a real find for animal-toting travelers.

Kingston

Rondout Bed & Breakfast, 88 West Chester St. (845-331-8144; www.rondoutbandb.com); $75–115 per night. Two resident pooches, Bruno and Brunhilde, will welcome you and your pet to this B&B on 4 acres with four guest rooms—two have private baths and two share a bathroom. Other amenities include daily full breakfasts, air-conditioning, hardwood floors, and a location that's

within walking distance to shops, restaurants, and activities. Dogs and children are always welcome without extra charges.

Lexington

Echo Valley Motel, 11985 Rte. 23A (518-989-6511; 1-800-822-6211); $65–90 per night. Located just down the road from the Hunter Mountain ski slopes, the Echo Valley Motel has eight rooms, all of which have cable television and two of which have kitchenettes. All major credit cards are accepted. The motel is located directly on the Schoharie Trout Creek. Pets are welcome without extra charges.

Liberty

Days Inn Liberty, 52 Sullivan Ave. (845-292-7600; 1-800-544-8313); $57–69 per night. Friendly, well-behaved pets are welcome in smoking rooms without extra charges at this Days Inn. Visitors will find an outdoor swimming pool, a lounge, a 24-hour front desk, laundry facilities, cable television with premium movie channels, a game room, and recently renovated guest rooms. Restaurants and golf courses are nearby.

Econo Lodge, 2067 Rte. 52 East (845-292-7171); $49–159 per night. Guests at the Liberty Econo Lodge enjoy complimentary breakfasts, a swimming pool, interior corridors, and a game room. Each guest room comes equipped with air-conditioning, cable television, private baths, and alarm clocks. Most major credit cards are accepted. Companion animals are welcome for an additional $10 per pet, per night.

Livingston Manor

The Guest House, 408
Debruce Rd. (845-439-4000;
andrea@theguesthouse.com;
www.theguesthouse.com);
$162–245 per night. This very
pet-friendly B&B offers five guest
rooms with private baths, cable
television and air-conditioning,
three romantic cottages, full daily
breakfasts, and 40 acres with
woods, trails, ponds, and a river.
Your dog is welcome for an additional $10 per night, provided
you pick up any messes and
don't leave him alone in the
rooms. The innkeepers can also
arrange pick-up and drop-off
grooming services.

Mt. Tremper

La Duchesse Anne, 1564
Wittenberg Rd., P.O. Box 49
(845-688-5260; info@laduchesse
anne.com; www.laduchesseanne.
com); $80–175 per night. *Condé
Nast Traveler* called this one of
America's top-25 "eating inns,"
based on La Duchesse Anne's
award-winning French restaurant
and antiques-filled guest rooms.
It's not exactly the kind of place
you'd expect pets to be allowed,
but discriminating animal lovers
will be happy to learn that well-
behaved dogs (with well-behaved
owners) are welcome without
extra fees. A daily continental
breakfast is included in the rates.

Lodge at Catskill Corners, 5368
Rte. 28 (845-688-2828; 1-877-688-
2828; www.catskillcorners.com);
$125–400 per night. This spa-
cious, upscale lodge offers Deluxe
and Luxury rooms, Junior and
Luxury suites, and Family suites.
A continental breakfast is

included in the rates. Shopping,
dining, and spa services are all
nearby in the Catskill Corners
marketplace area. Well-behaved,
quiet dogs are welcome in designated rooms; pet owners pay a
cleaning fee of $25 per stay.

Narrowsburg

Gable Farm Bed & Breakfast,
90 Gables Rd. (845-252-7434;
1-888-866-7434); call for rate
information. This 106-acre working farm and B&B offers comfortable guest rooms, open fields, a
large back porch, an in-ground
swimming pool, and resident
sheep and goats. The owners also
breed poodles on-site: If you're
lucky, you might arrive not long
after a litter does. "Smaller" dogs
(sorry, no cats) are welcome in
designated rooms without extra
fees.

Narrowsburg Inn, 176 Bridge St.
(845-252-3998; www.narrows-
burginn.com); $65–135 per night.
According to the owners, this is
the oldest continuously operating
inn in New York, having first
opened in 1840. Luckily the furnishings and décor are more up-
to-date: Choose from recently
renovated rooms with shared
baths or a suite with a private
bath, then hang out in the restaurant and lounge for a bite to eat
or a drink with friends. Well-
behaved, quiet pets are welcome.
(For more information about the
restaurant, see "Quick Bites.")

New Paltz

Dorinda's, 50 Marakill Lane
(845-255-6793); $125 per night.
For an additional $10 per night,
your pet is welcome to join you
at Dorinda's Garden Suite, a pri-

vate suite with a bedroom, a kitchenette, a living area, a full bathroom, and satellite television. Outside, guests can enjoy mountain views, an in-ground swimming pool, gardens, a barbecue grill, and a patio with furniture. Visitors will also find their refrigerator stocked with breakfast treats, including fruit, bread, granola, bacon, and eggs. Skiing, biking, dining, and shopping opportunities are nearby.

North Branch
La Serayna Bed & Breakfast, 526 Jeff-North Branch Rd. (845-482-3446; postmaster@laseraynabandb.com; www.laseraynabandb.com); $95–110 per night. La Sarayna is a stone cottage B&B with two guest rooms: the Cloud Room and the Nature Room. Pets are allowed only if the guest rents both rooms, or if the second renter knows the first and doesn't mind the presence of companion animals. The innkeepers serve a full breakfast each morning; other amenities include tennis courts, walking and hiking trails, ponds, streams, and woodlands.

Oliverea
Shangri-La at Mountain Gate, 212 McKinley Hollow Rd. (845-254-6000; info@mountaingate-lodge.com; www.mountaingatelodge.com); $59–149 per night. For an extra $10 per night, your dog is a welcome guest at this 16-room lodge with mountain views and spa services. Choose from standard double rooms, rooms with queen-size beds, or a family suite. Shangri-La is perhaps best known for its on-site

authentic Indian restaurant, serving breakfast, breads, and rice and vegetable specialties.

Parksville
Best Western Paramount Hotel, 1 Tanzman Rd. (845-292-6700; 1-800-922-3498; www.bestwesternparamount.com); $79–169 per night. This 181-room Best Western offers interior corridors, alarm clocks, business services, and in-room coffeemakers, hair dryers, irons, and ironing boards. Kosher meals and catering are also available. In general, only pets weighing less than 20 pounds are allowed, though general manager Bella Farquhar says occasional exceptions are made (call for details). Pet owners pay a refundable security deposit of $150 per stay.

Pine Hill
Belleayre Village, Main St. (845-254-4200; belleayreh@aol.com); $75–175 per night. Belleayre Village (formerly known as Belleayre Hostel) is a quiet getaway located in the tiny hamlet of Pine Hill. Recently renovated accommodations include one-room cabins with kitchenettes and porches, and three-room log cabins with two bedrooms, kitchenettes, and living rooms. All cottages have air-conditioning. Well-behaved pets are welcome with proof of vaccinations; there's also a fenced-in dog run on the property.

Ithaka House, 28 Pine Hill Rd., P.O. Box 615 (845-254-4417; www.ithakahouse.com); $75–250 per night. For an extra $15 per night, pets are welcome in the Garden Suite, the Cathedral Glen apartment and the Roaring Brook apartment at Ithaka House. Guests can also congregate in the Green Room for continental breakfasts, Karaoke, meditation hours, television and books. Children are welcome. Up to two pets are allowed per apartment, and the Garden Suite can accommodate one small dog only.

Purling

Bavarian Manor Country Inn & Restaurant, Purling/Cairo, County Rte. 24 (518-622-3261; Bavarian@ mhonline.net; www.bavarian-manor.com); $79–189 per night. "If your pet can vouch for you, you're welcome too!" So says the Bavarian Manor's Pet Guide, an agreement signed by guests who arrive with a four-legged friend. Each room in the historic 1865 house has a private bathroom, cable television, and air-conditioning. Guests can also hike or ski the trails on the inn's 100 acres, fish on the 6-acre lake, enjoy a drink in the lounge, or sample German specialties in the restaurant.

Tumblin' Falls Bed & Breakfast, Country Rte. 24 (1-800-473-0519; tfallsbb@francomm.com; www.tumblinfalls.com); $85–165 per night. As its name implies, Tumblin' Falls is indeed located next to a scenic waterfall, in full view of the front porch. It also offers one guest room and a falls-view suite, along with full breakfasts served on the porch in warm weather. For an extra $10 per night, your pet is welcome, although only two visiting canines are allowed at any one time. Two resident dogs also live on the property.

Rock Hill

Lodge at Rock Hill, 283 Rock Hill Dr., P.O. Box 858 (845-796-3100; 1-866-RHLODGE; info@lodgeatrockhill.com; www.lodgeatrockhill.com); $109–179 per night. For a one-time fee of $25, your dog is a welcome guest at the Lodge at Rock Hill, where you'll find recently renovated rooms and suites with coffeemakers, hair dryers, voice mail, and cable television with premium movie channels. Some suites also have hot tubs. Guests also enjoy free continental breakfasts, hiking and skiing trails, an indoor swimming pool, a fitness center, and an on-site restaurant.

Shandaken

Rose Mountain Cottages, 120 County Rte. 47, P.O. Box 541 (845-688-6825; rosemtcottages@ aol.com; www.rosemt.com); $60–120 per night. Surrounded by 62 private acres, the one- and two-bedroom efficiency cottages at Rose Mountain are popular with families and pet owners. Guests can spend their time exploring the nature trails, swimming in the in-ground pool, splashing around Esopus Creek, enjoying a picnic, or just relaxing. Dogs must be leashed on the grounds.

Shinhopple

Pepacton Cabins, River Rd. (607-363-2091; pepacton@catskill.net; www.pepactoncabins.com); $95 per night or $475 per week. Pepacton's three golden retrievers, Logan, Dakota, and Kade, welcome friendly canine visitors for an extra $20 per night or $100 per week. Each cabin has a covered porch, a full-size bathroom, a kitchenette, a fireplace, a picnic table, and a fire pit. Fishermen will enjoy easy access to the east and west branches of the Delaware River and the Beaverkill Stream.

South Fallsburg

My Retreat, Lincoln Rd. (www.myretreat.net); $125–250 per weekend or $375–700 per week. Not an ordinary vacation destination, My Retreat was designed to accommodate writers, artists, and others looking for inspiration and a quiet spot to work. The setting is rustic; guests check themselves in and out and manage their own housekeeping. Singles, couples, and small groups are welcome—many guests also visit the nearby SYDA yoga ashram. Pets are allowed in one of the four on-site cabins.

Spring Glen

Gold Mountain Chalet Resort, Tice Rd., P.O. Box 456 (845-647-4332; 1-800-395-5200; www.goldmtnresort.com); $279–469 per night. Designed with couples in mind, this romantic retreat offers indoor and outdoor swimming pools, a hot tub and sauna, a stocked fishing stream, hiking trails, mountain views, champagne brunches, and fireplaces. Meals are included in the rates. Pets are welcome in the private chalets as well as in the Victorian Lower Suite for an additional $15 per night.

White Lake

Parise's Cottages, Rte. 17B, (845-583-6489; parisescottages@aol.com); $50–70 per night or $350–420 per week. The dog owners and animal lovers at Parise's will welcome you and your leashed, well-behaved pooch for one night, a week, or even a whole season. The fully furnished one- and two-bedroom cottages are located on 18 private acres with a swimming pool, a recreation hall, picnic areas, a play-

THE KENYA ROOM IS ONE OF SEVERAL COZY ACCOMMODATIONS AT AUDREY'S FARMHOUSE B&B IN WALLKILL.

ground, and sports courts. Fishing and boating are available at nearby White Lake.

White Sulphur Springs

Fox Mountain Bed & Breakfast, 628 Fox Mountain Rd. (845-292-0605; foxmountainbandb@ yahoo.com; www.foxmountain bandb.com); $65–250 per night. Get away from it all at this restored farmhouse with antique barn-board walls, quilts, stained-glass windows and an old-fashioned country kitchen. Guest rooms and larger suites are available; some have hot tubs and decks. "Small" pets (call to see if yours qualifies) are welcome for an additional $20 per stay.

Woodridge

Rosemond Campground and Motel, 253 Rosemond Dr. (845-434-7433); $45–55 per night for motel rooms. Your pet is welcome at campsites as well as in motel rooms at Rosemond, which offers 12 rooms and bungalows with private bathrooms and kitchenettes. There are no extra fees for dogs, although owners will be held responsible for any damage to the room or furniture. (For more information on Rosemond's camping facilities, see listing under "Campgrounds.")

Wurtsboro

Valley Brook Motor Inn & Cottages, 201 Kingston Ave. (Rte. 209) (845-888-0330; www.valley brookinn.com); $60–115 per night. Guests at Valley Brook choose from motel rooms and cottages, all with air-conditioning. The cottages also have knotty-pine walls, kitchenettes, and porches. Outside, children can

play at the playground while their parents relax on the deck or explore the brook that runs through the property. Housebroken pets are welcome, provided that their owners clean up any messes.

Yulan

Washington Lake Retreat, Rte. 21 (845-557-8776; 917-376-1831; washingtonlakeretreat@yahoo. com; www.geocities.com/ washingtonlakeretreat); $55–625 per night. The accommodation choices at this getaway retreat are varied: Choose from B&B-style rooms with shared bathrooms, motel-style rooms, cottages, cabins, and a large guest rooms. At mealtime, retreat visitors enjoy vegetarian and vegan meals made with organic ingredients. On-site activities include swimming and sunning at the beach, volleyball, basketball, rafting, sailing, canoeing, sailing, hiking, cross-country skiing, and snowshoeing. Leashed dogs are welcome, although they cannot be left alone in the rooms.

Campgrounds

Barryville

Kittatinny Campgrounds, 3854 Rte. 97 (845-557-8611; 845-557-8004); $8–14 per site, per night and $10.95 per person, per night. Many visitors at this 250-acre campground also take part in Kittatinny Canoes river trips (1-800-FLOAT-KC); those campers enjoy access to the "prime sites." The campground offers a stocked trout stream, a playground, sports courts, hiking trails, a camp store, a deli and grill restaurant, a swimming pool, laundry facilities, and rest rooms with showers. One leashed dog per site is allowed.

Bloomingburg
Rainbow Valley Campground, 61 High St. (845-733-4767); $29–32 per night. Rainbow Valley can accommodate even the largest RV with 85 sites, full hook-ups, a dumping station, a camp store, a playground, a recreation hall, a swimming pool, picnic tables, rest rooms with showers, laundry facilities, and pay phones. Cabin rentals are also available. Your leashed, well-behaved dog is welcome without extra charges.

Cairo
Gordon's Torchlite Campsites, 4529 Rte. 23, P.O. Box 626 (518-622-9332; torchlite@hotmail.com; www.torchlite.org); $20–28 per night. Every member of the family will find something to do at Torchlite, where the facilities include a swimming pool, a game room, a camp store, a playground, laundry facilities, sports courts, and large wooded sites with picnic tables and fire pits. Leashed dogs are welcome, provided they are never left unattended in the campground.

Downsville
Bear Spring Mountain State Campground, East Trout Brook Rd. (607-865-6989); $12 per night. Managed by the New York State Department of Environmental Conservation, the Bear Spring Mountain camping area offers secluded, primitive camping with 41 sites, a picnic area, a beach, a boat launch and boat

rentals, and hiking trails. Among equestrians, the park is best known for its miles of horse trails. Dogs are not allowed on the beach or in the picnic area, and owners must use a leash and provide proof of vaccinations. For more park and day-use information, see "Out and About."

Gardiner
Yogi Bear's Jellystone Park Camp-Resort at Lazy River, 50 Bevier Rd. (845-255-5193; www.lazyriverny.com); $42–47 per night. Pets are allowed at this Jellystone Park campground—sort of. You can bring your dog if you're planning to stay in your own motor home, but not if you're renting a campsite or cabin. Activities include splashing around the swimming pools, fishing, putting on the miniature golf course, munching a treat at the snack bar, and playing in the game room, playgrounds, or sports courts.

Haines Falls
North-South Lake State Campground, County Rte. 18 (518-589-5058); $16 per night. With 219 sites, two lakes, two beaches, rest rooms with showers, two picnic areas, a recycling center, a dump station, a playing field, organized recreational programs, and a rental area for canoes, rowboats, and kayaks, this is the largest and busiest state-run campground in the Catskills. Motorboats are not allowed. Your leashed dog is welcome, as long as you clean up after him and bring vaccination records. For more park and day-

use information, see "Out and About."

Hunter
Devil's Tombstone State Campground, Rte. 214 (845-688-7160); $10 per night. This campground, managed by the state Department of Environmental Conservation, gets its spooky name from early settlers' legends about a huge boulder that rests on the property. The primitive park has 24 tent and trailer sites, a lake, two picnic areas, a playground, and several well-known hiking trails. Your pooch is welcome as long as you have vaccination records, clean up any messes, and use a leash. Dogs are not allowed in the picnic areas. See "Out and About" for more park information.

Livingston Manor
Covered Bridge Campsite, 68 Conklin Hill Rd. (845-439-5093; campsite@catskill.net; www.coveredbridgecampsite.com); $25–41 per night. Peace and quiet is the overriding theme at Covered Bridge—the campground recently transformed its 125 smaller sites into 70 larger ones to give campers more privacy. The facilities include rest rooms with showers, hiking trails, play areas, and a petting zoo. Dogs are welcome, but visitors should note that eight breeds are restricted, including some you might not expect. Call to make sure your four-legged friend will be welcomed.

Little Pond State Campground, Barkaboom Rd. (845-439-5480); $16 per night. If your dog is leashed and has vaccination records, he's welcome to join you at this 67-site campground. Choose from sites near the activity or more secluded camping areas on the opposite side of the pond. Amenities include canoe rentals, a boat launch (no motor boats allowed), a picnic area, rest rooms with showers, a beach, and a dump station. The campground is operated by the New York State Department of Environmental Conservation. Dogs are not allowed on the beach or in the picnic area. Noncampers can also visit the park for day-use activities (see "Out and About").

Mongaup Pond State Campground, Mongaup Rd. (845-439-4233); $16 per night. Managed by the Department of Environmental Conservation, this campground is located beside the largest natural body of water in the Catskills, the 120-acre Mongaup Pond. Campers will find 163 tent and trailer sites, a picnic area with barbecue grills, a recycling center, a dump station, rest rooms with showers, hiking trails, a beach, a boat launch, and organized activities during the warmer months. Dog owners must use a leash, bring vaccination records, and clean up any messes. Canines are not allowed in the picnic area or on the beach. See "Out and About" for day-use information.

Mt. Tremper
Kenneth L. Wilson State Campground, Wittenberg Rd. (845-679-7020); $16 per night. This Department of Environmental Conservation campground

has 76 sites for tents and trailers, rest rooms with showers, a picnic area with barbecue grills, a recycling center, a dump station, a swimming beach with a bathhouse, hiking and biking trails, and boat rentals. Motorboats are not allowed, although canoes and rowboats are plentiful. Canines must be leashed and be accompanied by vaccinations records; dogs are not allowed on the beach or in the picnic area.

Phoenicia

Woodland Valley State Campground, 1319 Woodland Valley Rd. (845-688-7647); $14 per night. Woodland Valley sits at the base of the tallest peak in the Catskills. Camping facilities include 72 sites for tents and trailers, rest rooms with showers, hiking trails, a picnic area, a dump station, a recycling center, and pay telephones. The campground, which is managed by the Department of Environmental Conservation, opens for the season in mid-May and closes in mid-October. Pets must be leashed, and owners must clean up after them and have vaccination records handy. Dogs are not allowed in the picnic area. For more park information, see "Out and About."

Roscoe

Beaverkill State Campground, 792 Berry Brook Rd. (845-439-4281); $14 per night. Located alongside the Beaverkill trout stream, this campground attracts anglers as well as anyone hoping for a quiet outdoor experience. Campers choose from 108 sites for tents and trailer and have

access to rest rooms with showers, a dump station, and a picnic area with barbecue grills. A historic covered bridge is also located on the property. Dog owners must use a leash, show proof of vaccinations, and clean up after their animals. The campground is operated by the state Department of Environmental Conservation.

Roscoe Campsites, Rte. 17A, P.O. Box 160 (607-498-5264); call for rate information. Visitors to this private family campground will find more than 50 sites for tents and RVs, rest rooms with showers, a dump station, pay phones, a playground, camp supplies, sports courts, religious services, and a fishing stream. Many sites have full hook-ups. Pets are welcome without extra fees; dog owners must use a leash and carry vaccination certificates.

Saugerties

New Life Campground, 432 Old Kings Hwy. (914-706-5797; newlifecamp@optonline.com; www.newlifecamp.bravepages. com); $14–25 per night or $160 per week. New Life owners Bill and Gail Carlock pride themselves in providing a tranquil and relaxing experience for visitors; they just built a new playground and remodeled the picnic area. Canoe rentals are also available. Leashed dogs are welcome as long as owners clean up after them and don't leave them unattended in the campground.

Swan Lake

Swan Lake Camplands, Fulton Rd., P.O. Box 336 (845-733-0604; www.swanlakecamplands.com);

$30–32 per night or $210–224 per week. Catering primarily to RV owners, Swan Lake Camplands offers full and partial hook-ups as well as RV rentals by the night or week. Campers can enjoy a 75-foot swimming pool, sports courts, a dance hall, playgrounds, paddleboat rentals, a camp store, laundry facilities, a game room, and sites with a view of the pool, the pond, or the woods. Dog owners are asked to use a leash, clean up any messes, and have vaccinations records handy.

Woodridge

Rosemond Campground and Motel, 253 Rosemond Dr. (845-434-7433); $26–30 per night for campsites. Leashed pets are welcome to join the fun at Rosemond, a campground with 200 sites, a swimming pool, a camp store, a playground, a pond, rest rooms with showers, a boat launch, cabin rentals, laundry facilities, a dumping station, and a recreational building. (For more information on Rosemond's motel facilities, see listing under "Hotels, Motels, Inns, and Bed & Breakfasts.")

Wurtsboro

Catskill Mountain Ranch & Camping Club, 538 Mt. Vernon Rd. (845-888-2161; 845-888-0216; info@catskillmountainranch.com; www.catskillmountainranch.com); $22–36 per night for campsites and $40–50 per night for rental units. The most talked-about feature of this campground is its new skate park, but visitors will also find an adult lounge, a teen lounge, a playground, laundry facilities, a restaurant, a stocked fishing lake, lots of planned activities, and rental cabins and trailers. Leashed pets are allowed, as long as owners have vaccination papers and clean up after them.

Homes, Cottages, and Cabins for Rent

Accord

The Woods (845-331-8144; www.thewoods-catskills.com); $500 per weekend. This large contemporary home is owned by the innkeepers at Rondout B&B in Kingston (see listing under "Hotels, Motels, Inns, and Bed & Breakfasts"). The recently built rental home has 1500 square feet of living space, a fireplace, a whirlpool tub, a dramatic sloped roof, and 40 acres of woods for exploring. For more information, including weekly and monthly rates, contact Rondout B&B at the phone number listed above.

Andes

Inspiration Peaks (845-676-4881; inspirationpeaks@aol.com); $700–900 per weekend or $1,200–1,400 per week. "We absolutely welcome pets," says homeowner Joseph Massa. "And we truly have the best view in the Catskills." Massa's Inspiration Peaks home sits high in the mountains overlooking the Pepacton Reservoir; other amenities include four bedrooms, three bathrooms, a full kitchen, a breakfast area, a playroom, a piano room, and pillow-top beds. A maximum of two pets are welcome with an extra $100 cleaning fee. Companion animals are not allowed on the beds.

Barryville
Mountain cabin, (646-337-4111; nyemilyevans@hotmail.com); $150 per night or $800 per week. "We have little or no restrictions for pet owners and even have dog dishes available for use," explains homeowner Emily Allen, whose two-bedroom cabin has a deck, a stone patio, and a barbecue grill. The home is fully furnished with one bathroom, a sleeping loft, a large yard, and a woodstove. The Delaware River is located about one mile away.

Bethel
Secluded country home (301-808-9187; crivers@erols.com; www.erols.com/crivers); $950–975 per weekend or $1,450–1,500 per week. Surrounded by 7 wooded acres, this rental home has a landscaped yard, a volleyball court, a horseshoe pit, a playground, a basketball court, and a large deck with a barbecue pit. Inside, renters will find five bedrooms, five bathrooms, a pool table, ceiling fans, a den, a recreation room and a full kitchen. Dogs and cats are welcome to join the fun with no particular restrictions.

Bovina Center
Getaway Cabin (617-835-4201; becca0923@yahoo.com); $350–450 per weekend or $600 per week. "I have always been a pet person and feel good when I can allow an owner to bring their pet with them on vacation," says Rebecca Griffin, the owner of this cozy two-bedroom cabin. Besides the animal-friendly welcome, other amenities of the cabin include cathedral ceilings, an open floor plan, a washer and dryer, a barbecue grill, a VCR, a CD player, and 13 private acres to explore.

Callicoon Center
Country Cottage Center (646-256-8121; 514-844-6730; brussen57@msn.com); $400 per weekend or $700 per week. Guests at this three-bedroom chalet can cook meals in the fully equipped kitchen, explore the gardens and stream, watch satellite television under the cathedral ceiling in the living room, build a bonfire in the fire pit, barbecue outside, or just relax in front of the wood-burning stove. House trained pets are welcome.

Catskill
Cauterskill Creek Farm (845-795-5706; cauterskill@msn.com); $600–750 per weekend or $1,050–1,250 per week. This 200-year-old rambling farmhouse can accommodate up to eight people with three bedrooms, two bathrooms, a library, an eat-in kitchen, a greenhouse, satellite television, air-conditioning, a barbecue grill, and a porch overlooking the creek. Pets are welcome, although the homeowners request an extra security deposit for some types of pets; call to see if yours qualifies.

Claryville
Mountain home (317-722-1570; 317-255-7655; felicity.kelcourse@cts.edu); $1,800–3,500 per month. If you're looking for a long-term rental, this home might be for you. The five-bedroom farmhouse can accommodate up to nine people with five bathrooms, a recently renovated

kitchen, a wrap-around porch with a stone floor, a woodstove, a private swimming hole, gardens, apple trees, and frontage on the Neversink River. Dogs and declawed cats are welcome. The owners prefer to rent by the year.

Claryville cabin

(516-946-6469; 516-753-1733; plankfarm@aol.com); $275–400 per weekend or $600–700 per week. Anglers will flip for this two-bedroom, secluded cabin located beside a trout stream. The house has log sides, interior knotty-pine walls, a fireplace and woodstove, a full kitchen, a dining room, a covered front porch, a barbecue grill, satellite television, and provided linens. The cabin can accommodate up to eight people. Dogs and cats are welcome without extra charges or restrictions.

Cochecton Center
Catskills farmhouse

(845-252-7430; 973-271-3720; dscharf@commonhealth.com); $100 per weekday, $400 per weekend or $600 per week. "We allow dogs—and cats—because we love dogs and know how much they mean to other dog lovers," say Dean and Krista Scharf, the owners of this three-bedroom farmhouse located near the Delaware River. The Arts and Crafts–style home has hardwood floors, one bathroom, a generous front porch, and a location that's convenient to golf, fishing, swimming, and antiquing opportunities. Pets are welcome without extra charges.

Eddy
Our Love Nest (212-463-0043; 1-917-952-9662; keith@tesa.com; www.ourlovenest.freeservers.com); $500–600 per weekend or $1,000 per week. Built in 1998, this two-bedroom home has a great room, a fireplace, satellite television, an outdoor hot tub, a full kitchen, exercise equipment, hardwood floors, stone walls, views of the Delaware River, and four private acres. Pets are welcome without extra charges, though the home-owners request that animal owners enter through the lower terrace and clean pets' feet before entering the main house.

Grand Gorge
Catskill cabin (212-532-9322; info@catskillcabin.com; www.catskillcabin.com); $1,050–1,850 per week. Your dog is a welcome guest at this two-bedroom cabin surrounded by 30 private acres. Although secluded, the rental has all the modern amenities you might need, including a six-person hot tub, satellite television, a deck with mountain views, and a swimming pool. The cabin is also the home of the Herbal Bear, where educational herbal healing classes are held on some weekends. Dogs are not allowed in the pool or hot tub, and owners are asked to clean up any messes.

Phoenicia
Contemporary home getaway (917-627-1057; bdcange@aol. com); $485 per weekend or $900 per week. This two-story, two-bedroom home has a master bedroom with skylights, two fireplaces, air-conditioning, satellite

television, a washer and dryer, a barbecue grill, country-style furnishings, mountain views, and two private acres with woods and streams. Skiers will find Bellayre Mountain and Ski Hunter just a few miles away. "Small to medium-sized" canines are welcome (call to see if yours qualifies).

Saugerties

Villa at Saugerties (845-246-0682; upstatevilla@aol.com); $1,700–2,500 per week or $6,800–$7,500 per month. Perhaps the most unusual amenity at this vacation villa is the 40-foot swimming pool lined with stainless steel; renters will also find a sauna, a screened-in barbecue room, a patio, two brooks, a pond, flower gardens, a full kitchen, and satellite television. The four guest rooms can also be rented individually, B&B style (call for details). Clean, well-behaved dogs are welcome for an additional $50 per stay.

Swan Lake

Swan Lake Rentals, (201-869-9876; rowcats@netscape.net); $500–550 per weekend or $1,300–2,000 per week. The homeowner of a vacation cabin and two-bedroom cottage, both located on Swan Lake, often allows pets as rental guests. The cottage has a private dock and rowboat, along with a fireplace, woodstove, barbecue grill, cable television, a doggie door and a fenced-in side yard. The log cabin rental offers a stone fireplace, a large deck overlooking the lake, dormered windows, a

patio, a full kitchen, a hot tub, a private beach, a dock, and a rowboat. Pet owners typically pay an extra fee; call for details.

Tannersville

Colgate Lake farmhouse (850-527-0550; amjamjor@netscape.net); $975–1,175 per weekend or $1,875 per week. This eight-bedroom farmhouse can accommodate up to 16 people, making it a great locale for family reunions or other group events. The large lawn opens up onto a lake; the home also offers a deck, picnic tables, a barbecue grill, a pool table, a fireplace, hiking trails, a creek, and plenty of privacy. The rental is pet-friendly.

Log cabin (212-721-8000, ext.113; lsugar@davisllp.com); $500 per weekend or $4,500 per week. Up to 10 people can comfortably stay at this recently built cabin with four bedrooms, two baths, wood-beamed ceilings, tile floors, a full kitchen, a front porch, a deck, leather couches, a big-screen television, a washer and dryer, a woodstove, and provided linens. Seasonal rentals are also available; call for details. "We're pet friendly, and have no extra charges for animals," explains homeowner Lindsey Sugar.

Windham

Ski chalet (516-328-2876; 718-347-9485; mjaroslaw@aol.com); $200–300 per night. After a day on the slopes or the golf course, stretch out and relax at this three-bedroom chalet with a fireplace, a wraparound deck, two bathrooms, cable television and a DVD player, a washer and dryer, a barbecue grill, and a fully equipped kitchen. Housetrained dogs are welcome; the owners just ask that you treat the house and furnishings as you would your own.

The Windham House (850-527-0550; amjamjor@netscape.net); $775 per weekend or $1,375 per week. The owners of the Colgate Lake Farmhouse in Tannersville (see above) also offer this five-bedroom home for rent in the village of Windham. Dating from the 1800s, the renovated house has three bathrooms, a hot tub, a barbecue grill, a full kitchen, a wood-burning stove, a washer and dryer, linens, and more than 2 acres of land, including a landscaped backyard. Pets are welcome.

Woodstock

Luxury cabin (646-322-8568; 917-691-9788; nyproperties@hotmail.com); $850 per week or $2,500 per month. This isn't exactly roughing it: Visitors to this loft-style cozy cabin will find an old-fashioned claw-foot bathtub, slate floors, a marble bathroom, a full kitchen, a TV/VCR, a barbecue grill, linens, and mountain and forest views. Cats and dogs are welcome guests, although the homeowners sometimes require an additional $200 security deposit, depending on the type of pet.

Mountain chalet (646-322-8568; 917-691-9788; nyproperties@hotmail.com); $1,100–1,300 per weekend or $1,500–2,000 per week. The owners of the Woodstock luxury cabin (see above) also welcome pets to this four-bedroom, three-bathroom chalet on a quiet and secluded street. The home has a hot tub, a patio, a fireplace and woodstove, a washer and dryer, two kitchens, stainless-steel appliances, cable television, a barbecue grill, and two acres with brooks.

Woodstock Getaway (212-807-9109; woodstockrental@aol.com); $300 per weekend; call for discounts on weekly or monthly rates. The owners of this three-bedroom vacation rental are animal lovers and always welcome dogs. (Due to allergies, cats are not permitted.) Located near the town center, the house has two bathrooms, a living room and dining room, a full kitchen, a fireplace, cable television, a VCR, a CD player, and provided linens.

Rental Agencies

A House Around the Bend, Catskills (607-832-4589; info@ahousearoundthebend.com; www.ahousearoundthebend.com. This vacation rental agency manages about 12 Catskills properties, give or take a few from year to year. Pets are allowed at most rental homes, which range from farmhouses to chalets, townhouses, and mountaintop hideaways. Many short-term and long-term rentals are available. Call or visit the web site for detailed, updated information on the latest listings. The agency is a real find for vacationing pet owners.

YOUR DOG IS WELCOME ON BOARD THE SCENIC DELAWARE & ULSTER RAILROAD TRAIN RIDE IN ARKVILLE.

OUT AND ABOUT

Bald eagle–watching. Take bird-watching to the next level in Sullivan County, where up to 100 bald eagles migrate each winter in search of fish. In addition to these transitory visitors, local experts estimate that eight to ten breeding pairs are living and raising chicks in Sullivan County. For your best chances of spotting the magnificent birds, bring your binoculars to these sites during the winter months: Rio Reservoir and Mongaup Falls Reservoir Observation Hut, both in Forestburgh; Rondout Reservoir in Grahamsville; Basha Kill Wildlife Management Area in Wurtsboro; and the Delaware River from Hawk's Nest to Narrowburg, along Rte. 97. If you happen to arrive in the spring, the same sites might be frequented by ospreys.

Bear Spring Mountain, East Trout Brook Rd., Downsville (607-865-6989). This Department of Environmental Conservation park offers a campground (see "Accommodations") as well as day-use facilities. Although dogs are not allowed in the picnic area or on the beach, you and your pooch can enjoy 24 miles of trails, rowboat and canoe rentals, fishing, and beautiful views of Launt Pond. The park, which also offers 24 horse stalls, is especially popular with equestrian enthusiasts. Canines must be leashed and cleaned-up after, and owners must carry proof of vaccinations.

Covered bridges. Perrine's Bridge on Rte. 213 in Rifton is the last remaining covered bridge in Ulster County, and also the last Burr Arch Truss bridge in the state. The pedestrian-only bridge crosses the Wallkill River, providing a nice photo opportunity during any journey through the area. Visitors will also find a picnic area on-site. The Beaverkill Covered Bridge (sometimes called the Conklin Bridge) is located on Beaverkill

Camp Road within Beaverkill State Park. It was built in 1865 and boasts a 98-foot span.

D&H Canal Heritage Corridor, Ulster County. This ongoing rails-to-trails project includes about 35 miles between Ellenville and Kingston. The trail is popular with joggers, dog-walkers, mountain bikers, horseback riders, and cross-country skiers; organized races and other events are also held here regularly. For detailed maps and other information, contact the D&H Heritage Corridor Alliance at P.O. Box 176, Rosendale, NY, 12472 (845-331-2102).

Delaware and Ulster Railride, Rte. 28, Arkville (1-800-225-4132; www.durr.org); $10 per adult; $6 per child. All aboard! Friendly dogs are always welcome on the D&URR train rides—they even get their own tickets, known as "pooch passes." The ride traverses the 45-mile Scenic Trail through two counties and seven towns, providing relaxing and scenic views. The railroad is managed by the nonprofit Catskill Revitalization Corporation, which aims to promote the history of the railroad industry in the region.

Devil's Tombstone Park, Rte. 214, Hunter (845-688-7160). Early settlers' thought the devil roamed this wild area and perhaps even carried the seven-by-five-foot boulder—the Devil's Tombstone— that still rests in the grounds today. (The boulder was more likely to have been moved by glaciers or a landslide.) Some visitors come here to camp (see

"Accommodations"), while others want to hit the hiking trails, including the infamous "Devil's Path," that start in the parking area. Motorboats are not permitted. Pets are not allowed in the picnic areas; owners must carry vaccination records and use a leash at all times.

Huguenot Street, New Paltz. One of the oldest streets in the United States, Huguenot Street is still home to several original stone homes dating from the late 1600s. Although dogs are not allowed in the historic buildings, it's worth a visit just to gape at the exteriors of these homes, which were built by refugees from France. You'll also find picnic facilities, public bathrooms, and a 300-year-old burial ground on the street. For more information, contact the Huguenot Historical Society at 18 Broadhead Ave., New Paltz (845-255-1660). You will also pass by Huguenot Street if you're hiking on the **Wallkill Valley Rail Trail,** which traverses several scenic and historic areas in town. For more detailed information about the Rail Trail, write to P.O. Box 1048, New Paltz, NY, 12561, or visit www.gorailtrail.org.

Kenneth L. Wilson Park, Wittenberg Rd., Mt. Tremper (845-679-7020). Perhaps best known for its campground (see "Accommodations"), the Kenneth L. Wilson Park also offers day visitors plenty of diversions. Some of the most popular include fishing for yellow perch, largemouth bass, sunfish, and other species, grilling up a meal in the picnic area, playing in the baseball field or volleyball court, renting a canoe or rowboat, hiking, and enjoying the views. Motorboats are not permitted, and dogs are not allowed in the picnic area or on the beach. Pet owners must carry proof of vaccinations.

Kingston self-guided tours, Kingston. Show yourself around this historic city via the Heritage Trail, a route that highlights sites like the Rondout Waterfront, the Uptown Stockade District, and Midtown. Self-guided maps and brochures are available from the City of Kingston (www.ci. kingston.ny.us; 1-800-331-1518). You can also take a self-guided "talking" tour of the uptown area by tuning your car radio to the designated frequency and cruising around town. Call or visit the web site for updated information.

Kirkside Park, Main St., Roxbury. You'll find this reno-vated, 11-acre park behind Roxbury's famous Gould Church on Main St. The park has been the center of the town's activities and gatherings for more than 100 years, and residents still like to commemorate its history by dressing in period clothing and reenacting historic baseball games and other events. With or without a parasol, visitors can cross graceful bridges and stroll paths beside the Delaware River. Dogs must be leashed.

Lake Superior State Park, Rte. 55, Monticello (845-794-3000). Managed by Sullivan County, this park allows dogs—though, oddly, your pet is officially required to be muzzled while on park property. It's doubtful that most dog owners adhere to this strange rule (how many of us actually own a muzzle?), but it's a rule nonetheless. The main appeal of Lake Superior State Park is the boat launch and boat rentals. Dogs must be leashed and are not allowed in picnic, camping, or bathing areas. All in all, this scenic park probably isn't the best choice for dog lovers, but it will do in a pinch.

Little Pond, Barkaboom Rd., Livingston Manor (845-439-5480). Although most visitors come to Little Pond for its campground (see "Accommodations"), you can also visit the park during the day to take advantage of the beautiful views, fishing opportunities on the 13-acre pond, canoe rentals, beach, picnic area, and numerous hiking trails, including one that leads to the ruins of a now-defunct farm. The park has a few downsides for dog lovers, though: Your pet is not allowed in the picnic area or on the beach. Motor boats are also not allowed. Be sure to use a leash and keep your dog's vaccination records handy.

Mohonk Preserve, 3197 Rte. 44/55, Gardiner (845-255-0919; www.mohonkpreserve.org). This unusual site offers more than 60 miles of carriage roads, hiking trails, forest groves, streams, ponds, cliffs, and towering rock formations. The preserve is partic-ularly popular among rock climbers, equestrians, cross-country skiers, hikers, birdwatch-ers, and nature lovers. Leashed pets are welcome as long as owners clean up after them; dogs are not allowed to swim at Duck Pond or Split Rock, and are not allowed on the trails during cross-country skiing season. Parking is somewhat limited, and fills quickly during the warm months. Consider carpooling if possible.

Mongaup Pond, Mongaup Rd., Livingston Manor (845-439-4233). Your leashed dog is welcome to join you on a visit to Mongaup Pond, as long as you bring vaccination records and clean up after her. You'll both find plenty to keep you busy, including hiking trails, a campground (see "Accommodations"), and rowboat and canoe rentals. Anglers can fish the 120-acre pond in search of brook trout, golden shiner, smallmouth bass, yellow perch, yellow sucker, and other species. Motorboats are not allowed. Dogs must stay clear of the picnic area and the beach.

Monticello Raceway Flea Market, Rte. 17B, Monticello (845-796-1000; 516-897-5396; www.monticellofleamarket.net). Open every Saturday and Sunday from the end of June to the beginning of September, this famous flea mart offers plenty of browsing opportunities for locals and vacationers in the area. You'll see plenty of visiting pets, too: Dogs are welcome on a "short" leash, provided that owners clean up after them.

Mower's Saturday Market, Maple Lane, Woodstock (845-679-6744). "Some days it seems like there are more dogs at the market than people!" says Janine Mower,

owner of this long-running and popular attraction. Search for hidden treasures at the numerous vendors' tables and exhibits, selling everything from furniture to clothing, housewares, antiques, and memorabilia. Dogs must be leashed and cleaned-up after.

North-South Lake, County Rte. 18, Haines Falls (518-589-5058). Managed by the state Department of Environmental Conservation, this popular park has a campground (see "Accommodations"), picnic areas, pavilion rentals, two beaches, and two lakes. Don't miss Alligator Rock (which seems to more closely resemble a piranha than an alligator), Sunset Rock, Newman's Ledge, and sweeping scenic views in every direction. Motor boats are not allowed, but you should have no trouble renting a canoe, rowboat, or kayak on-site. The hiking trails lead to the best views, including those of Kaaterskill Falls—the highest waterfalls in the state at 250 and 260 feet. (The waterfall trail starts on Rte. 23A.) Dogs are not allowed in the picnic areas or on the beach; pet owners are required to use a leash, clean up any messes, and bring vaccination records.

Paradise Lake Fishing Preserve, Old Rte. 17 West, Livingston Manor (845-439-4618; 845-439-4990; docaddiction@catskill.net). Anglers and their families can enjoy a fun afternoon at Paradise Lake fishing for bluegills, catfish, trout, and largemouth bass. No fishing license is necessary. After you reel a few in, you can cook up your catch in the picnic area. Companion canines are welcome on a leash, although owners can let the dog run free if no other people are around.

Sam's Point Dwarf Pine Ridge Preserve, off of Rte. 52, Hamlet of Cragsmoor, Town of Wawarsing (845-647-7989). Managed by The Nature Conservancy, this 4,600-acre preserve is home to some of the world's last remaining dwarf pine barrens. Visitors can get a glimpse of the unique habitat on Sam's Point Trail, the Verkeerderkill Falls Long Path, and numerous other trails, all of which are detailed on the maps and brochures available at the entrance kiosk and Visitor Center (open from April through October). Leashed dogs are welcomed, though they are not allowed in the ice caves. Because hiking conditions can be challenging, field officers at the preserve recommend that pet owners bring plenty of extra water and keep an eye on their dog's physical condition.

Sullivan County Farmers' Markets, various locations (845-292-6180; www.scafm.org). Browse fresh produce, baked goods, herbs, cheeses, apple cider, maple syrup, flowers, pottery, jams and jellies, and even jewelry at the outdoor county farm market. The locations vary by day: On Thursday, you'll find the market at Second in Wurtsboro from 2 to 6 PM; on Fridays, you can shop at the Municipal Parking Lot on Darbee Lane in Liberty from 3 to 7 PM;

on Sunday, there are two locations, one at the intersection of Audley Dorrer Dr. and Main from 11 AM to 2 PM and the other at Highland Ave. in Roscoe from 11 AM to 2 PM. Most markets open in May and close in October. Locations and times might vary from year to year; call or visit the web site for the latest information.

Winter Carnival, Rotary Park, Livingston Manor (845-794-3000). This annual event celebrates brisk air and fallen snow with figure-skating demonstrations, ice and snow sculptures, hot food and drinks, ice-skating races, and even dogsledding. The festival is typically held on the third Sunday in January. Call for this year's updated schedule.

Woodland Valley, 1319 Woodland Valley Rd., Phoenicia (845-688-7647). A Department of Environmental Conservation park, Woodland Valley offers a picnic area with barbecue grills, a campground (see "Accommodations"), and a vibrant fishing stream filled with brook trout, brown trout, rainbow trout, white sucker, cutlips minnow, and other species. Two well-known hiking trails, the Slide-Wittenberg and the Valley-Denning, take visitors up into the surrounding mountains. Dogs are not allowed in the picnic area and must be leashed at all times. Owners are required to have vaccination records on hand.

Woodstock Festival site, Hurd Rd., Bethel. Despite its name, the famous Woodstock Music and

A MEMORIAL MARKS THE SPOT OF THE 1969 WOODSTOCK MUSIC AND ARTS FESTIVAL IN BETHEL.

Arts Festival of 1969 took place not in Woodstock, but in another Catskills town: Bethel. You can still visit the open fields of the site that came to represent the flower child love-fest movement of the '60s; the current owners have even erected a memorial. Check it out in its original form while you still can: Plans are in the works to build a new performing-arts and cultural center on the site.

QUICK BITES

Ann Marie's, Main and Partition Sts., Saugerties (845-246-5542). Gourmet sandwiches, baked goods, cold and hot drinks, salads, soups, and other belly-filling favorites are available at this take-out café. Ann Marie's adjoining bistro offers pasta, seafood, steaks, and a wine list. The sidewalk tables are a good spot for people-watching.

Armadillo Bar & Grill, 97 Abeel St., Kingston (845-339-1550). Armadillo's owner is the former vice president of the local S.P.C.A. (Society for the Prevention of Cruelty to Animals); with pet owners in mind, she designed a large outdoor seating area at the restaurant. The eatery also offers a kid's menu, weekly specials, special events, and tasty items like fajitas, black-bean soup, nachos, enchiladas, burritos, tacos, and vegetarian dishes.

Bun 'N Cone, 86 Bridge St., Margaretville (845-586-4440).

Order your burger, ice cream, beer, and even breakfast at the take-out window, then relax with your treats at the outdoor seating area. The restaurant is located near the intersection of Rte. 30.

Buster's, Rte. 17B, White Lake (845-583-4222). Named after the owner's rottwieller (whose mug is featured on the menu), Buster's is a barbecue "joint" with pulled pork, ribs, burgers, Cajun-style seafood, baked beans, smoked potatoes, collard greens, and even veggie burgers and portabella mushroom burgers. Indoor and deck seating is available, and all of the menu items are available for takeout.

Candy Cone, Intersection of Routes 17B and 55, White Lake (845-583-6232). Nothing fancy but oh so convenient, this take-out place offers ice cream cones and sundaes along with hot and cold sandwiches, burgers, hot dogs, fried seafood dinners, mozzarella sticks, onion rings, and other quick snacks. Order your meal at the window and enjoy it (with Rover) at one of the picnic tables.

The Flour Patch, 75 Bridge St., Margaretville (845-586-1919). Eat in or take out at this café serving gourmet coffees, specialty sandwiches, homemade soups, chef salads, and a variety of bagels. Breakfast and lunch are available Tuesday through Sunday.

Last Chance Antiques & Cheese Café, Main St., Tannersville (518-589-6424). This unique stop offers browsing and food all rolled up into one: The gourmet shop offers a selection of more

than 100 cheeses and 300 beers, while the restaurant serves soup, appetizers, sandwiches, burgers, and quiche. Your pooch is welcome to hang out with you on the front porch.

Ming Moon Restaurant, 121 East Broadway, Monticello (845-791-7712). Hoping to enjoy some chow mein, fried rice, or chicken wings in front of the campfire? Locals recommend this take-out Chinese restaurant located in the Shop Rite Plaza.

Narrowsburg Inn, 176 Bridge St., Narrowsburg (845-252-3998; www.narrowsburginn.com). Friendly pets are sometimes allowed on the outdoor deck of this recently renovated restaurant serving meat, fish, and pasta dishes and a wide assortment of beers. For more information about the inn's accommodations, see "Hotels, Motels, Inns, and Bed & Breakfasts."

New Paltz Public House, 215 Huguenot St. (845-255-1960). Though you'll enjoy the food at this homey Public House, you might like the location even better: The restaurant is perched on historic and scenic Huguenot St. (see "Out and About" for more information). Well-behaved, friendly dogs are welcome in the outdoor seating area.

Pizza the Rock, Rock Hill Dr., Rock Hill (845-796-0700). This oddly named local favorite keeps 'em coming for—you guessed it—pizza in every variety. Order a pie with pepperoni, mushrooms, peppers, or just plain cheese to bring back to your hotel room or campsite. Sandwiches, ice cream, and other treats are also available.

Railroad Pizza & Deli, 8776 Rte. 28, Big Indian (845-254-4500). This casual restaurant provides packed lunches for skiers and sightseers; hungry visitors can also order a whole pizza, a slice or two, soups, salads, or an ice-cream cone. Bellaeyre Mountain is located just down the road. The restaurant is open year-round.

Spotted Dog Firehouse Restaurant, 5340 Rte. 28, Mt. Tremper (845-688-7700). What canine lover wouldn't love a restaurant with a name like this? Menu items at the family-friendly spot include steak, chicken and pasta dishes, vegetarian meals, sandwiches, fajitas, burgers, and

"spotted dogs" with chili. Takeout is available.

Sullivan County Feast, 334 Broadway, Monticello (845-791-4555). This New York–style deli serves up thick sandwiches, wraps, salads, soups, and imported cheeses. Relax at the outdoor tables or pack a picnic lunch to go.

Woodstock Candy & Fudge Store, 60 Tinker St., Woodstock (1-877-383-4311; info@woodstock candy.com). When that sweet tooth acts up, head straight to this fun shop for fudge in every flavor, hard candies, sugar-free candy, and gift boxes. The store also specializes in "retro" hard-to-find candies from decades past.

HOT SPOTS FOR SPOT

Bed & Biscuit, Saugerties (845-246-6340; dogs@bednbiscuit. com; www.bednbiscuit.com). This ultracasual doggie daycare service, located in a private home, can provide daycare, "cageless" overnight boarding, playtimes, nutritional counseling, and walks and outings. Visiting dogs can enjoy an organic treat, a whole-food diet, or whatever food you normally provide.

Bed & Chow Pet Lodge & Salon, 11289 Rte. 9 West, Coxsackie (518-731-6859). The Bed & Chow provides overnight boarding with covered indoor and outdoor runs,

along with complete grooming services for all breeds. An on-site pet boutique sells food, toys, treats, and other accessories. The owners have more than 20 years' experience in pet care and grooming.

Catskill Morning Farm, 87 DeBruce Rd., Livingston Manor (845-439-4900). This place qualifies as a Hot Spot for Spot *and* for Spot's people: Dog lovers will find organic treats, chew toys, pet shampoos, doggie breath fresheners, hand-painted water bowls, and other animal goodies at Catskills Morning

Farm. But they'll also find candles, antiques, birdfeeders, and a farm stand and café serving up fresh organic foods for two-legged travelers.

Gardeners & Their Companions, 14 North Chestnut St., New Paltz (845-255-0156). As the paw-print "o" on the sign out front indicates, the "Companions" mentioned in this shop's title are the four-legged variety. The upscale gift shop carries unique and whimsical gift items for gardeners and homeowners, but pet lovers will especially appreciate the shop's stock of premium pet foods and gifts for animal admirers of all stripes. Soap dishes, jewelry, books, hats, clothing, clocks, chew toys, organic biscuits: You name it, this store probably has it. Your well-behaved dog is welcome inside, but watch for wagging tails around the breakables!

GebirgsHaus Kennel, 218 East River Rd., Walton (607-865-4398; www.adogshome.com). Whether Fido needs a quick bath or a place to stay, the staffers at GebirgsHaus aim to please. They offer complete grooming services and individual kennels with covered, outdoor runs. The kennels are air-conditioned. One of the company's more unique services is Camp Pak-A-Nap-Sak, where dogs have individual "bunk areas" and access to a fenced-in play area for running and retrieving. A pick-up and drop-off service is also available.

The Golden Paw Pet Sitting, Stone Ridge (845-687-8751;

info@thegoldenpaw.biz; www.thegoldenpaw.biz). The Golden Paw provides playtime, walks, feedings, and lots of individual attention for your pet when you can't be there; the business is bonded and insured. "Our clients leave their pets at home, the hotel, or the B&B and we visit them there," says Golden Paw owner Danielle Liotta. "That way, they can stay in their own familiar environment, so they are much happier!"

Liberty Pet Center, 6 Ontario St., Liberty (845-292-1255). This Agway store specializes in pet, home, and garden supplies. If you're on the road and running out of food, you'll find brands like Iams, Science Diet, Eukanuba, Blue Seal, and Big Red stocked here. Chew toys, treats, and aquarium supplies are also available.

Pawprints & Whiskers Pet Boutique, 292 Wall St., Kingston (1-888-495-2150; www. pawprints-n-whiskers.com). You and your pooch will enjoy browsing through the gift baskets, treats, toys, and novelty items for animals (and animal lovers) at this fun shop. The company also offers an extensive on-line catalog of pet products, including gift baskets like the "Football Team Basket for Dogs," the "Birthday Greetings Box," and "The Cat's Meow Gourmet Sampler."

Siam Kennels and Grooming, 59 Siam Rd., Windham. Located just down the road from Ski Windham, this small boarding and grooming facility provides a solution for vacationers hoping to hit the slopes. Dogs can romp in separate indoor areas as well as outdoor runs and a doggie playground. Shampoos, flea dips, and cuts—along with basic obedience lessons—are also available for all breeds. The kennel is open seven days a week, year-round. Clients can also feel free to stop by anytime to visit their pet or take him out for a hike.

IN CASE OF EMERGENCY

Catskill Animal Hospital
601 Kings Rd. (518-943-4340)

Delhi Animal Hospital
15891 State Hwy. 28 (607-746-2230)

Four Paws Veterinary Center
100 Mill Hill Rd., Woodstock (845-679-9445)

Jeffersonville Animal Hospital
89 Schoolhouse Rd. (845-482-5500)

Kingston Animal Hospital
456 Albany Ave. (845-331-0240)

Monticello Animal Hospital
267 East Broadway (845-791-4400)

New Paltz Animal Hospital
230 Main St. (845-255-5055)

Wurtsboro Veterinary Clinic
251 Sullivan St. (845-888-4884)

The Capital-Saratoga Region

CAPITAL PLAZA IN ALBANY

The Capital-Saratoga Region

DOG-FRIENDLY RATING:

And they're off: Capital-Saratoga is a region full of animal lovers, though the animal of choice is usually a racehorse instead of a puppy dog. Still, you should have a relatively easy time finding enough pet-friendly accommodations and activities to fill a fun vacation, especially considering that noteworthy historic sites, protected forestlands, Lake George, and Great Sacandaga Lake are all nearby or a short drive away. Popular Saratoga Springs is a tony place—even the motels here have spas. Most of the action is centered on the summertime races, starting in July. But if equestrian pursuits aren't your thing, you can cut your lodging rates in half by visiting at any other time of the year. The best known Saratoga Springs hotels, dramatic and historic structures, are largely unwelcoming to dogs; luckily, there are plenty of friendly, if less deluxe, accommodations to fill the void for pet-loving travelers.

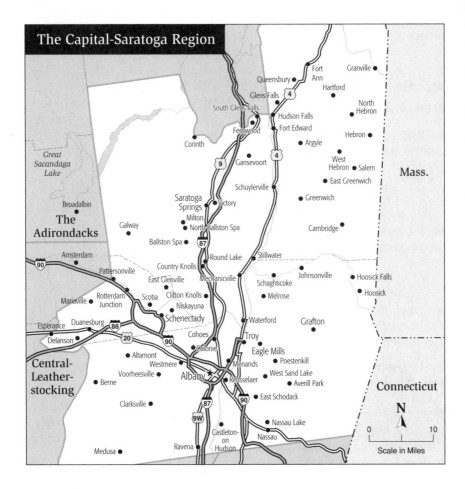

The Capital-Saratoga Region

Albany, the state capital, is noticeably overrun with bureaucrats, business-men and women, and other nine-to-fivers. But it's also rich in history, cul-ture, recreational facilities, parks, gourmet and casual restaurants, great architecture, and other attractions that travelers cherish. (And who couldn't love a city where the local baseball team is called the Diamond Dogs?) Though geographically small, this region is surprisingly packed with things for canines and people to do and see—visit the statehouse, stroll through a preserved early-American neighborhood, pitch a tent, run for your own roses in a spring garden, or watch for eagles at a state park. Out-of-town-ers may especially appreciate a visit to one of Albany's memorials to the state's fallen firefighters and police officers: It's a poignant stop for New Yorkers visiting their state capital.

ACCOMMODATIONS

Hotels, Motels, Inns, and Bed & Breakfasts

Albany

Ambassador Motor Inn, 1600 Central Ave. (518-456-8982; 1-800-950-STAY); $59–89 per night. Guests at the Ambassador receive free daily continental breakfasts and newspapers; each of the 56 units also has cable television, in-room movies and video games, Internet access, and air-conditioning. Smoking and nonsmoking rooms are available. Pet owners pay a refundable $5 security deposit.

Best Western Albany Airport Inn, 200 Wolf Rd. (518-458-1000; 1-800-780-7234); $89–129 per night. With an emphasis on convenience, this hotel is located 2 miles from the airport and offers park-and-fly packages and seven meeting rooms. Overnight guests will find cable television, alarm clocks, in-room movies and coffeemakers, a restaurant and lounge, a swimming pool, and a 24-hour front desk. Dogs weighing less than 15 pounds are welcome.

Best Western Sovereign Hotel, 1228 Western Ave. (518-489-2981; 1-800-780-7234); $78–105 per night. Most of the 195 guest rooms at this Best Western are nonsmoking and offer cable television, alarm clocks, and in-room coffeemakers and hair dryers. Guests can also take advantage of a restaurant, room service, free daily newspapers and breakfasts, a swimming pool, a fitness center, laundry facilities, and business services. Dogs are allowed in designated rooms for an extra $10 per stay.

Cresthill Suites Albany, 1415 Washington Ave. (518-454-0007); $96–239 per night. This high-end hotel has a swimming pool, valet services, free daily newspapers, continental breakfasts, a 24-hour front desk, alarm clocks, in-room hair dryers and coffeemakers, free airport shuttles, vaulted ceilings, and cable television. Only dogs weighing less than 20 pounds are allowed; pet owners pay an extra $150 nonrefundable fee per stay.

Motel 6 Albany, 100 Watervliet Ave. (518-438-7447); $50–59 per night. Pets are always welcome at Motel 6; the Albany location offers cable television with premium movie channels, free morning coffee, laundry facilities, free local calls, smoking and nonsmoking rooms, a "Kids Stay Free" program, and a location that's convenient to the airport. There are no extra charges for companion animals.

Ramada Inn Downtown Albany, 300 Broadway (518-434-4111; 1-800-2-RAMADA); $74–86 per night. Typical amenities at the Ramada chain include cable television, restaurants and lounges, alarm clocks, 24-hour front desks, smoking and nonsmoking rooms, in-room coffeemakers, safe-deposit boxes, free local calls, and air-conditioning. Dogs weighing less than 50 pounds are welcome at this location.

Ramada Limited Albany, 1630 Central Ave. (518-456-0222; 1-888-298-2054); $62–79 per night. This more economical member of the Ramada hotel chain provides free daily newspapers and local phone calls, cable television, a fitness center, a 24-hour front desk, alarm clocks, modem hook-ups, laundry facilities, and banquet facilities. Your dog is welcome to join you for an additional $10 per stay.

Red Roof Inn Albany, 188 Wolf Rd. (518-459-1971); $49–99 per night. Like the Motel 6 chain, all Red Roof Inns welcome well-behaved pets without extra charges. The Albany location has a 24-hour front desk, cable television, modem hook-ups, free morning newspapers and local phone calls, express-checkout services, banquet facilities, plenty of parking, and in-room hair dryers upon request.

State Street Mansion Bed & Breakfast, 281 State St. (518-462-6780); $75–125 per night. This upscale accommodation has 12 guest rooms, fireplaces, cable television with in-room movies, an on-site restaurant, a game room, free parking, complimentary daily breakfasts, modem hook-ups, air-conditioning, discounts for children and seniors, and a location that's convenient to the State Capital and Empire Plaza. Dogs weighing less than 20 pounds are welcome guests.

Super 8 Motel Albany, 1579 Central Ave. (518-869-8471; 1-888-316-7870); $59–89 per night. The 59 rooms at this Super 8 come equipped with cable television and air-conditioning. Elsewhere in the motel, guests will find a 24-hour front desk, a restaurant, free parking, laundry facilities, and fax and copy services—shops, other services, and golf are nearby. Dogs are welcome without extra charges.

TownePlace Suites by Marriott Albany, 1379 Washington Ave. (518-435-1900; 1-800-257-3000); $109–169 per night. Convenient to the SUNY Albany campus, this all-suite hotel offers smoking and nonsmoking rooms, studios and one- and two-bedroom suites, full kitchens, furnished living and dining areas, desks, laundry facilities, valet services, a 24-hour front desk, a swimming pool, and a fitness center. Dog owners pay an extra $75 nonrefundable fee per stay.

Berlin

Sedgwick Inn, 17971 State Rte. 22, P.O. Box 250 (518-658-3998; sedgwickin@aol.com; www.sedgwickinn.com); $75–195 per night. This charming B&B and restaurant is located in a 200-year-old country home on 12 wooded acres. Pets are allowed in the neighboring motel-style annex building, which offers six guest rooms with quilts, cable television, and front-porch areas with tables and chairs. Dog owners pay an additional $10 per night.

Cohoes

Hampton Inn Albany-Latham, 981 New Loudon Rd. (518-785-0000); $79–149 per night. Located within walking distance and short driving distance to more than eight restaurants, the Hampton Inn offers a swimming pool, cable television, laundry facilities, valet services, a fitness center, meeting and banquet rooms, connecting rooms, and in-room hair dryers, irons, and ironing boards. There are no extra fees for pets; dogs must be crated if left alone in the rooms.

Guilderland

Governor's Motor Inn, 2505 Western Ave. (518-456-3131); $39–49 per night. Conveniently located near Albany and the airport, this 2-story motor inn has 43 rooms, cable television, air-conditioning, smoking and non-smoking rooms, in-room telephones and daily maid service. Your dog is welcome to join you at Governor's for an additional $5 per night.

Latham

Century House Hotel, 997 New Loudon Rd. (518-785-0931); $85–105 per night. Located just outside of Albany, the Century House welcomes pets for an additional $15 per night. The hotel has 68 guest rooms and deluxe suites on two floors, cable television, air-conditioning, a fitness center, tennis courts, walking trails, an on-site restaurant, and complimentary daily breakfasts. Dogs should be leashed on the property.

Econo Lodge Latham, 622 Rte. 155 East (518-785-1414); $55–99 per night. Formerly known as the Latham Travelodge, this hotel offers balconies, free morning coffee in the lobby and in-room coffeemakers, laundry facilities, express checkout services, an outdoor swimming pool, a fitness center, fax and copy services, and a convenient location that's close to the airport and shopping malls. Dogs are welcome for an additional $5 per night.

Holiday Inn Express Albany-Latham, 946 New Loudon Rd. (518-783-6161); $89–134 per night. This dressed-down, more affordable version of a Holiday Inn has guest amenities like an outdoor swimming pool, free airport shuttles, cable television, a fitness center, alarm clocks, copy and fax services, courtesy cars, modem hook-ups, safe deposit boxes, and in-room hair dryers and coffeemakers. Companion animals are allowed for an extra $20 per night, per pet.

Residence Inn by Marriott Albany Airport, One Residence Inn Dr. (518-783-0600; 1-800-331-3131); $99–154 per night. All Residence Inn guests can take advantage of free daily hot breakfast buffets, a swimming pool, and a 24-hour front desk, as well as studios and one- and two-bedroom suites with full kitchens, cable television, and valet services. Penthouse suites are also available. Pet owners pay an extra $100 cleaning fee, plus $5 per day.

Malta

Post Road Lodge, 2865 Rte. 9 (518-584-4169; postroadlodge @msn.com; www.postroad lodge.com); $79–200 per night.

The Post Road Lodge offers motel-style guest rooms and well-landscaped grounds with flower beds, fountains, picnic areas, and wooded walking trails. Efficiencies with tables, refrigerators, coffeemakers, and sinks are also available. "Most" dogs (call to see if yours qualifies) are welcome, although they cannot be left alone in the rooms at any time.

Northville

Flip Inn, 214 Hwy. 152 (518-725-7277; flip@flipenterprises.com; www.flipenterprises.com); $53–70 per night. "As an animal lover and president of the local animal shelter, of course I allow pets!" says Debby Hupkes, the enthusiastic innkeeper at the Flip Inn. (The name is an acronym for "Feels Like I'm in Paradise.") The inn offers motel-style accommodations on the shores of the Great Sacandaga Lake, and is located within walking distance of a restaurant, a golf course, and boat dockage.

Saratoga Springs

Adirondack Inn, 230 West Ave. (518-584-3510; adironinn@ aol.com; www.adirondackinn. com); call for rate information. At the time of this writing, this self-described "pet-friendly place" was expanding to provide 26 units. Amenities include a swimming pool, a gazebo, and large decks with tables and chairs. There is no extra charge for pets, although the motel has a limit of one pet per room. Guests must use a credit card to reserve a room; the card is charged if the pet causes any damage.

Community Court Motel, 248 South Broadway (518-584-6666; 1-800-322-7856; www.saratoga communitycourt.com); $49–159 per night. This 42-room motel is located within walking distance to shops, restaurants, parks, a museum, and the Saratoga Race Course. Guests can also enjoy free continental breakfasts in the lobby each day. Dogs are welcome without extra fees, although owners will be held responsible for any damages.

Country Club Motel, 306 Church St. (518-584-4780; www.country-clubmotel.com); $60–150 per night. Choose from traditional guest rooms and larger efficiencies at Country Club, a 12-unit motel offering cable television, quilted bedspreads, air-conditioning, kitchenettes, refrigerators, coffeemakers, microwaves, picnic areas, and outdoor barbecue grills. Pet lovers will appreciate the wooded walking trails and grassy yard; dogs are welcome for an extra $5 per day.

Grand Union Motel and Crystal Spa, 120 South Broadway (518-584-9000; www.grandunion-motel.com); $53–240 per night. Standard rooms at Grand Union have cable television, air-conditioning, and Internet access; deluxe rooms also have tiled bathtubs and a sitting area. Guests can also enjoy the on-site spa services, including mineral baths, body wraps, facials, and massages. Leashed dogs are allowed for an extra $25 per stay, although they cannot be left alone in the rooms.

Robin Hood Motel, 2205 Rte. 50 South (518-885-8899; robinhood-motel@spa.net;www.saratoga.org/robinhood); $50–55 per person. There's no need to rob the rich to pay for this affordable and clean accommodation, where guests will find an outdoor swimming pool, cable television, air-conditioning, and in-room refrigerators. Pets weighing less than 20 pounds are allowed for an extra $5 per night, as long as they stay off the furniture and are not left alone in the rooms.

Springs Motel, 165 Broadway (518-584-6336; gailm@springs-motel.com); call for rate information. The Springs Motel has a convenient location, a swimming pool, and in-room coffeemakers and refrigerators. Recent bad experiences with irresponsible dog owners have led the managers to reconsider their former pet-friendly policies, although they sometimes allow "small" pet guests on weekdays.

Union Gables Bed & Breakfast, 55 Union Ave. (518-584-1558; 1-800-398-1558; information@uniongables.com; www.union-gables.com); $120–295 per night. This is one of the more upscale pet-friendly accommodations in the area; Union Gables is a B&B in a 1890s Queen Anne–style Victorian home. Guests can relax in the outdoor hot tub, enjoy a meal in the elegant dining room, read a book on the expansive front porch, or unwind in one of 12 large guest rooms in the main house or carriage house. The three resident pets, Max the dog and Butch and Sally the cats, will welcome you and your pooch.

Schenectady
Days Inn Schenectady, 167 Nott Terr. (518-370-DAYS); $59–139 per night. For an extra $10 per night, your dog can join you at this Days Inn, where amenities include cable television with premium movie channels, free daily newspapers and continental breakfasts, kitchenettes, smoking

THE UNION GABLES B&B IN SARATOGA SPRINGS WELCOMES CANINE GUESTS.

and nonsmoking rooms, air-conditioning, discounted rates for children and seniors, and a 24-hour front desk. Some guest rooms also have hot tubs.

Ramada Inn Schenectady, 450 Nott St. (518-370-7151; 1-800-2-RAMADA); $89–149 per night. (See listing under "Albany.") Dogs are welcome without weight restrictions or extra fees.

Troy

Best Western Rensselaer Inn, 1800 6th Ave. (518-274-3210; 1-800-528-1234); $59–89 per night. The large guest rooms at this Best Western have cable television, in-room movies, and air-conditioning; other amenities include a swimming pool, a restaurant and lounge, a coffee shop, discounts for seniors and children, a fitness center, and a game room. Dogs are welcome for an extra $10 per stay.

Campgrounds

Austerlitz

Woodland Hills Campground, 386 Fog Hill Rd. (518-392-3557); $20–26 per night. Woodland Hills offers 200 shady and sunny campsites for RVers as well as tenters. Other amenities include a beach, paddleboat rentals, two playgrounds, playing fields, sports courts, a game room, rest rooms with showers, a camp store, and laundry facilities. Your dog is welcome to join you as long as you use a leash, keep her with you at all times, and clean up any messes.

Cherry Plain

Cherry Plain State Park Campground, 26 State Park Rd., P.O. Box 11 (518-733-5400); $10–13 per night. This fairly cozy campground has just 20 sites; 10 for trailers and 10 for tents. Visitors will also find a playground, picnic tables, scheduled recreational programs, pavilions, hiking trails, and boat rentals. Campsites are available from mid-May to mid-October. For more park information, see "Out and About."

Gansevoort

Moreau Lake State Park Campground, 605 Old Saratoga Rd. (518-793-0511); $13 per night. The lake provides the views and boating opportunities, while the campground provides the accommodations at this beautiful state park. Tents and trailers are nestled in the woods with access to rest rooms with showers, a playground, walking trails, recreational programs for kids and adults, pavilions, and a dumping station. Dog owners must have proof of vaccinations and keep animals leashed at all times. For more information on the park, see "Out and About."

Saratoga RV Park, 4894 Rte. 50, P.O. Box 14 (518-798-1913; reservations@saratogarv.com; www.saratogarv.com); $25 per night or $150 per week. "We are a pet-friendly park," explains proprietor Marge Legac. "We just ask that dogs be leashed, picked up after and never left unattended." The campground offers extra-large sites for extra-large RVs, group camping sites, wooded and sunny areas, laundry facilities, a camp store, and discounts to nearby attractions. RV sales are also available.

Petersburg
Aqua Vista Campground, 82 Armsby Rd. (518-658-3659; aquavistacampground@hotmail.com); $23–27 per night. Leashed, quiet dogs are welcome without extra fees at Aqua Vista, a campground with an in-ground swimming pool, a miniature golf course, a playground, laundry facilities, a camp store, sports courts and fields, a game room, a dump station, and organized activities like hayrides. The tent and RV sites all have picnic tables and fire pits.

Broken Wheel Campground, 61 Broken Wheel Rd. (518-658-2925; brokenwheel1971@aol.com; www.brokenwheelcampground.com); $15–18 per night. Campers at Broken Wheel have access to rest rooms with showers, a camp store, a pavilion, a recreation room, playgrounds, a swimming pool, sports courts, and an on-site stream. Pet owners must bring proof of vaccinations and walk their dogs away from the campsites. There are no extra charges for companion animals.

Homes, Cottages, and Cabins for Rent

Middle Grove
Suburban home
(terryhut@nycap.rr.com; www.members.tripod.com/contemporaneous/index); $9,350 per racing season. Located about 15–20 minutes from the Saratoga Racetrack, this three-bedroom home sits on a 2-acre lot with three bathrooms, a swimming pool, flower gardens, air-conditioning, a screened-in porch, and a large master bedroom with cathedral ceilings. "Small" dogs (call to see if yours qualifies) are welcome with an additional $200 refundable security deposit.

Saratoga Springs
Luther Forest home
(518-899-7311; 518-461-0618; jparker@peomgtsys.com; www.peomgtsys.com/saratoga-rental); $1,800–3,000 per week. Available from June to October, this large contemporary home has cathedral ceilings, an outdoor hot tub, a master bedroom suite with an indoor hot tub, a two-car garage, a washer and dryer, and a private location. Pre- and post-season discounts are available. Pets are welcome; there's even a fenced-in dog run in the back yard.

Poller Family Rentals,
(201-320-4884; 212-696-0770); $1,000–2,000 per week; $2,250–2,750 per month; or $10,000–14,000 per racing season. The horse-loving Pollers offer three homes for rent in the downtown Saratoga Springs area where your companion animals are welcome. "You could not have found a more pet-friendly family!" says Brad Poller. Each house has five bedrooms, three bathrooms, fireplaces, eat-in kitchens, dens, living rooms, and dining rooms. Two of the homes also have swimming pools and fenced-in yards.

Russell Street apartment, Russell St. (msong@rent101.com); $3,800 per season. Available during the summer racing season only, this three-bedroom apartment has one full bathroom, central air-conditioning, a dishwasher, a washer and dryer, a private balcony, off-street parking, and a convenient in-town location. Well-behaved dogs are welcome.

Saratoga home, East Broadway (518-580-2387); $1,000–3,000 per week. This two-bedroom home will be available for rent starting in the summer of 2004; pets are welcome with a refundable security deposit, and the house is even equipped with a doggie door. Other features include a sauna, a fireplace, a patio with furniture, a washer and dryer, off-street parking, a dishwasher, a microwave, and a quiet neighborhood.

Summer cottage, Saratoga Lake (914-723-6185); $900–1,150 per week, $550 per weekend, or $6,500 per race season. You can walk to a sandy beach and dock from this two-bedroom, one-bath cottage. The rental has a new sunroom, a recently remodeled kitchen, a deck, hardwood floors, a barbecue grill, and air-conditioning. Downtown Saratoga Springs is about 10 minutes away. "Small" pets (call to see if yours qualifies) are welcome.

Victorian townhouse, Woodlawn Ave. (msong@rent101.com); $6,000 per season. Located in a 2-story Victorian home, this townhouse rental offers three bedrooms, two bathrooms, a gas fireplace, central air-conditioning, a washer and dryer, a front porch with wicker furniture, and off-street parking. The downtown area is three blocks away, and Skidmore College is five blocks away. Dogs are welcome.

OUT AND ABOUT

Albany memorials. While you're visiting the capital district, be sure to check out at least a few of the numerous sites and sculptures commemorating the past and present heroes of New York State, including the Fallen Firefighters Memorial (State St.), the State of New York Police Officers Memorial (plaza level between Agency Building 4 and Swan St.), the Vietnam Veterans Memorial (Lafayette Park), the Korean War Memorial (west of the Cultural Education Center at Empire State Plaza), the New York State Women Veterans Memorial (Empire State Plaza along Madison Ave.), and the Spanish-American War Monument (Empire State Plaza at Washington and Central Aves).

Albany walking tours, Albany Heritage Visitors Center, 25 Quackenbush Square, Boradway and Clinton Ave. (518-434-0405; 1-800-258-3582). You can pick up maps for self-guided walking tours of the city's notable and historic sites at this visitor center, which also offers a gift shop, trolley tours, and a planetarium.

AnimaLovers' Annual Fall Festival, Animal Welfare League of the Greater Capital District, P.O. Box 6426, Albany (518-448-5468; www.animalovers.org). This welfare league, also known as AnimaLovers, typically holds its yearly festival in September. Local and visiting pets are welcome to join in the fun: Events often include games, contests, kid's activities, raffles, craft and bake sales, animal psychic readings, cook-offs, and even a Blessing of the Animals. Call or visit the web site for this year's date, time, and location.

Art on Lark Street, Lark St., Albany (518-434-3861; www. larkstreet.org). This free, open-air festival celebrates local talent with artists' demonstrations and works for sale in various media. Visitors will also find live music and entertainment, kid's activities, and hands-on art projects for families. The festival is typically held in June, but the neighborhood, which has shops, restaurants, and historic brownstones, is also worth a visit throughout the year.

Bog Meadow Brook Nature Trail, Rte. 29, Saratoga Springs (www.openspaceproject.org). This picturesque 2-mile trail was created by volunteers and includes significant stretches of boardwalks through wetland areas. You can meander slowly or traverse the paths with snowshoes or cross-country skis. Parking is available at either the Rte. 29 entrance or the Weibel Ave. entrance.

Champlain Canal Tour Boats, Canal House, end of the towpath, Schuylerville (518-695-5609; info@champlaincanaltours.com; www.champlaincanaltours.com). Although dogs are not allowed on regularly scheduled public cruises, this company does welcome leashed companion animals on private charters. These tours are often arranged by small or large groups hoping to explore the historic canal on board the 18-passenger *M/V Sadie* or the 60-passenger *M/V Caldwell Belle.* A $25 cleaning surcharge applies when animals are on board.

Cherry Plain State Park, 26 State Park Rd., P.O. Box 11, Cherry Plain (518-733-5400). In addition to camping facilities (see "Accommodations"), Cherry Plain State Park offers 175 acres with a beach, a boat launch that's popular with anglers, picnic areas, and trails for walking, cross-country skiing, mountain biking, and snowmobiling. Dog owners must keep animals leashed and provide proof of vaccinations. Pets are not allowed on the beach.

Cohoes Falls, Cohoes. The most popular way to see these graceful falls is from the overlook at School St., off of North Mohawk St. You can also get a bit closer by accessing a small, unmarked park at the end of Mohawk St. To get there, look for the driveway located at the intersection of

Mohawk and Remsen Sts. The falls become more impressive when the river stage reaches 15 to 20 feet.

Covered bridges. They're not just in New England: Visitors to Cambridge will find the Buskirk Covered Bridge, a 160-foot single span on Old First Northern Tpke., and the Eagleville Covered Bridge, a 100-foot double cord with a town patent lattice truss on Eagleville Rd. Edinburg is home to the Copeland Covered Bridge on Rte. 30, a smaller 1870s structure built by a farmer to get his cows over the water. Salem offers the Rexleigh Covered Bridge, a 107-foot span on Rexleigh Rd. And the town of Shushan offers the Shushan Covered Bridge Museum on Rte. 61 (518-677-8251), located—where else?—within a covered bridge.

Dakota Ridge Farm, 189 East High St., Ballston Spa (518-885-0756; llamawhisp@aol.com). Interested travelers are welcome to stop by Dakota Ridge, a training and boarding facility for horses and llamas. Visitors can enjoy picnics and day hikes, with or without llamas, on the 42-acre farm. Dogs are allowed on the property, as long as they're leashed and keep their distance from the llamas, who are sometimes frightened of unfamiliar canines.

Eagle Mills Cider Company, Eagle Mills Rd., Rte. 138, Broadalbin (518-883-8700; craig@eaglemillsfun.com; www.eaglemillsfun.com). Much more than a cider-manufacturing company, Eagle Mills welcomes visitors with nature trails, gem mining, a pond, a bakery, a covered bridge, and attractions like Dino Dig, the Nature Discovery Train Ride, and Kidsville. In the fall, the waterwheel-powered cider mill is in full operation on weekends. "We allow any type of pet here, and only ask that dog owners use a leash," says Eagle Mills owner Craig Boyko.

Empire State Plaza, bordered by Swan, State, and Madison Sts., Albany. Popular with tourists and city residents, this large Mall area (reminiscent of the Mall in Washington, D.C.) has rectangular reflecting pools, sculptures, and walkways, and is surrounded by high-rise government buildings, a cultural education center dubbed "the Egg" because of its odd shape, and the 1867 State Capital Building—still gorgeous after all these years. The plaza's 1970s-era architecture and design are alternately criticized and praised: Too impersonal? Too dated? A crowning achievement in urban renewal? Visit and decide for yourself.

Glens Falls Feeder Canal Trail, Glens Falls. You can access this 9-mile biking, walking, and cross-country skiing trail at Warren and Oakwood Sts.; most of the stone-gravel trail is set away from the road. The route was once part of a canal system built in the 1820s.

Grafton Lakes State Park, Long Pond Rd., P.O. Box 163, Grafton (518-279-1155). There's lots to do at this 2,300-acre park, including sailing, fishing for perch and bass, sunbathing, building sand castles on the beach, enjoying a picnic, horseback riding, canoeing, cross-country skiing, ice skating, and hiking. The park has miles of trails and five ponds; boat rentals are also available. Dogs are welcome as long as they're on a leash no longer than 6 feet and have proof of vaccinations, although they are not allowed on the beach.

Hudson River Islands State Park, Hudson River Islands (518-872-1237). Accessible only by boat, this park is primarily located on Gay's Point and Stockport Middle Ground islands. The picnic areas are equipped with tables and barbecue grills, and the trails wind past endangered and threatened flora and fauna. (Dog owners are asked to stay on trails and use caution in sensitive nesting areas.) Leashes and vaccination records are required.

John Boyd Thatcher State Park, Rte. 157, Voorheesville (518-872-1237). The highlight of this park is the Helderberg Escarpment, which is chock-full of fossils. Limestone cliffs are joined by forestlands, open fields, expansive valley views, and miles of trails. Guided tours are also available. Although the park is open year-round, its best known trail, the Indian Ladder, is only open from May to November. Dogs are welcome as long as owners have proof of vaccinations and use a leash no longer than 6 feet.

Moreau Lake State Park, 605 Old Saratoga Rd., Gansevoort

(518-793-0511). Whether you're camping at Moreau Lake (see "Accommodations"), or just visiting for the day, the park will provide plenty of opportunities for sightseeing and relaxation. The facilities include a beach, a boat launch, boat rentals, pavilions, and trails for hiking, biking, and cross-country skiing. If you're bringing a canine along, you must have proof of vaccinations handy and use a leash. Dogs are not allowed on the beach.

Paws for the Cause, SPCA of Upstate New York, P.O. Box 171, Hudson Falls or 454 Queensbury Ave., Queensbury (518-798-3500; info@spcauny.org). This fun event includes a walkathon and doggie talent contest; the society's other annual activities include pet calendar contests and a telethon. The group also organizes an annual Mutt Strut fundraising walk in May and participates in the popular yearly Kiwanis Kid's Day Million Dollar Duck Race in Glens Falls. Contact the SPCA for updated events and information.

Petrified Sea Gardens, Petrified Sea Gardens Rd., P.O. Box 5076, Saratoga Springs (518-691-0150). Definitely one of New York State's most unusual attractions, the Petrified Sea Garden is exactly that: a 500-million-year-old ocean reef known as a *Stomatolite.* Visitors can walk the trail that winds past the ancient fossils as well as massive rock formations, rock gardens, a sundial garden, a labyrinth, and a 300-year-old pine tree. There's also a gift shop on site. Leashed dogs are welcome; the staff even provides fresh drinking water for four-legged visitors.

Saratoga ARC Festival & Dressage, Saratoga Racetrack, Saratoga Springs (518-587-0723; www.saratogaarcfestival.org). Usually held at the end of May, this annual event is one of New York State's largest and most popular outdoor festivals. Animal lovers will enjoy the horse shows, pony rides, and llama and alpaca parades, although "dog people" will especially appreciate the canine agility competitions and "People and their Animals" pet shows. The event also includes regional crafters and artists showcasing their works, along with music, food, entertainment, and saddlery demonstrations.

Saratoga National Historic Park, 648 Rte. 32, Stillwater (518-664-9821; sara_info@nps.gov). Leashed pets are welcome to join their owners on an exploration of this 4-square-mile battlefield park, which commemorates the first American military triumph of the Revolutionary War. Popular activities here include hiking, bird-watching, biking, cross-country skiing, and attending staged demonstrations of the famous battle. The park also includes two other sections: the historic home of General Philip Schuyler in Schuylerville; and the Saratoga Monument in Victory.

Saratoga Spa State Park, 19 Roosevelt Dr., Saratoga Springs (518-584-2535). Unlike most other state parks, many of the attractions at Saratoga Spa are indoor, including a performing arts center, a museum of dance, a hotel, a theater, and mineral baths. The park also includes a vast swimming pool complex with fountains, slides, and a children's wading pool. The extensive property even has two golf courses. Dogs, as you may imagine, are not allowed in the buildings or pool areas, although Rover can join you in admiring the historic architecture and exploring the scenic terrain, which includes walking trails, picnic areas, and a playground. Listed as a National Historic Landmark, the park is worth a visit—even if just from the outside. Dogs must be leashed.

Schodack Island State Park, 1 Schodack Way, Rte. 9J, Schodack Landing (518-732-0187). Bird-watchers, naturalists, boaters, and anglers make good use of this 1,000-acre park that lies along the Hudson River. Interpretive signs describe resident species that visitors are likely to see in protected areas, including blue herons, cottonwood trees, and bald eagles. The facilities also include picnic tables, boat launches, and walking trails. Leashed pets are welcome, provided their owners have proof of vaccinations. The park is located just south of Albany on Rte. 9J.

Stockade Historic District, Front St., Schenectady. This well-preserved historic neighborhood provides a glimpse into a 17th-century settlement of Dutch immigrants. About 200 buildings give passersby a look at facades from Revolutionary War times all

the way up to the 1930s, as well as the largest grouping of pre-Revolutionary buildings anywhere in America. The area's Riverside Park also provides a greenway for walking or biking. ("Scoop the Poop" signs remind dog lovers not to leave a mess behind.) For more information and maps, visit the Stockade Association's web site at www.historicstockade.com.

Peebles Island State Park,

P.O. Box 219, Waterford (518-237-8643). In addition to being an impressive park in its own right, Peebles Island also serves as the headquarters for the state's Bureau of Historic Sites. As such, it provides visitors with information (including flyers, videos, and exhibits) on all the state's historic sites. The park also offers miles of walking and jogging trails along the Hudson and Mohawk Rivers, picnic areas, and fishing opportunities. Dogs must be leashed at all times, and owners must have proof of vaccinations handy. Though its home address is in Waterford, access to the park is located in Cohoes: Take Ontario St. to Delaware Ave.

Thompson's Lake State Park,

68 Thompson's Lake Rd., East Berne (518-872-1674). Visitors at Thompson's Lake can sunbathe, launch or rent a boat, frolic in the playground, fish, swim, play on the sports courts and fields, enjoy a picnic, or walk and cross-country ski on the trails. Canines

must be leashed and have proof of vaccinations to enter the park. Dogs are not allowed on the beach or in the on-site Emma Treadwell Thacher Nature Center.

Wilton Wildlife Preserve & Park, Rte. 50, Gansevoort (518-587-1939). Leashed dogs are welcome to join their owners at this wildlife preserve and park located about halfway between Saratoga Springs and Lake George. Visitors will find walking trails through the woods, a lake, and lectures and presentations on local flora and fauna. The park is a bit tricky to find, but you can get there by taking Exit 16 off of I-87 North, taking a right off the exit and then another quick right onto Edie. When you reach Rte. 50, take a left. You'll soon see the park entrance on your left. The property is owned and managed by The Nature Conservancy.

QUICK BITES

Broadway, Saratoga Springs. This street is where all the action's at in Saratoga Springs, including a dozen or so restaurants. Choose from Mexican, Italian, American-style grills, coffee shops, and more. Many of the eateries offer outdoor seating, though some ask that your pooch stay on the sidewalk-side of the railings or other barriers surrounding the seating area. Takeout is also plentiful.

Café Mangia, 1652 New Scotland Rd., Slingerlands (518-439-5555); Western Ave., Stuyvesant Plaza, Albany (518-482-8000); and 15 Park Ave., Shoppers World Plaza, Clifton Park (518-383-6666). All three Café Mangia locations have outdoor patio seating in the spring, summer, and fall. The Tuscan-inspired menu includes items like wood-fired oven pizza, pasta, calzones, focaccia, salad, and meat dishes.

C. H. Evans Brewing Company at the Albany Pump, 19 Quackenbush Square, Albany (518-447-9000). The outdoor seating area here is small but lovely; if you can't find a seat, everything on the menu is available for takeout. In addition to its home-brewed beers, C. H. Evans also offers favorites like crab cakes, Caesar salad, steak sandwiches, traditional and vegetarian burgers, meatloaf, fish-and-chips, and pasta dishes.

Giffy's Bar-B-Q, 1739 Rte. 9, Clifton Park (518-373-9800; www.giffysbarbq.com). The outdoor seating area at Giffy's has no table service, but you're welcome to order any item as takeout and eat it out at the open-air tables. Baked potatoes, chicken wings, sweet-potato fries, onion straws, pork ribs, and salads are just some of the available menu items; the restaurant's trademark barbecue sauce is also available to go.

Good Times Lakeview Restaurant, 175 Lake Rd., Ballston Lake (518-399-9976). Order your sandwich, soup, salad, burger, or root-beer float to go and enjoy it under the gazebo down by the water. You and your pooch are also welcome to sniff around the restaurant's 4,000 square-foot property and enjoy the views.

I-Go-Inn Restaurant & Bar, 241 South Shore Rd., Edinburg (518-883-8900). This casual, fun restaurant recently constructed a new deck area that provides plenty of outdoor seating for diners; a garden patio has even more. Menu items include burgers and sandwiches, appetizers, and meat and pasta dinners.

Mr. Ed's Ice Cream Station and Pizza Shop, 588 Lake Ave., Saratoga Springs (518-581-8633). Pop inside for a frozen yogurt, ice cream cone, milkshake, sundae, or cold drink—or perhaps a slice of cheese or pepperoni—and then relax on Mr. Ed's picnic tables with your treat.

Saso's Japanese Noodle House, 218 Central Ave., Albany (518-436-7789). There's no outdoor

seating area at Saso's, but all of the homemade Japanese dishes are available for takeout, and boxed lunches are available during the day. Choose from items such as sushi, sashimi, steamed vegetables, tempura, rice bowls, Ramen and Udon noodle dishes, and seafood and chicken teriyaki.

Village Pizzeria and Ristorante, 2727 Rte. 29, East Galway (518-882-9431; www.villagepizzeria.com). Located just down the street from Saratoga Springs, this casual spot serves garlic bread, fried calamari, salads, pasta and seafood entrees, calzones, sandwiches, and a wide variety of pizzas. Order your meal to go or enjoy it at the outside patio.

Wheatfields Restaurant, 440 Broadway, Saratoga Springs (518-587-0534; www.wheatfields.com). The patio sidewalk seating area at Wheatfields is open from May through Labor Day. Lunch and dinner items like zuppa del giorno, tortellini salad, lasagna classico, eggplant sandwich, and chicken parmesan are also available for takeout year-round.

HOT SPOTS FOR SPOT

Altamont Country Kennels, 220 Brandle Rd., Altamont (518-861-8391; www.altamontkennels.com). Boarding and grooming are the specialties at Altamont Country Kennels, which

offers heated and air conditioned kennels, indoor and outdoor spaces, large exercise areas for pets, and complete grooming services. There are no breed restrictions, and the owners live on the premises. The kennel is open seven days a week.

Benson's Pet Centers, 3073 Rte. 50, Saratoga Springs (518-584-7777); 1701 Rte. 9, Clifton Park (518-373-1007); and 197 Wolf Rd., Colonie (518-435-1738). This Capital/Saratoga-area chain carries premium brands like Innova, California Natural, Canidae, Nutro, and Solid Gold. Animal lovers will also have fun browsing the three shops' wide selection of pet supplies and treats.

Four Seasons Professional Pet Sitting, Rensselaer and Eastern Albany (518-479-3155; buckhoff@nycap.rr.com; www.fourseasonspetsitting.com). Business partners Karen Buckhoff and Cathy Laraway recently joined forces to create this pet-sitting service for residents and visitors to the capital area. Whether you're gone for an hour or the whole day, Karen and Cathy can keep your pet exercised, well fed, and happy. Call in advance for reservations.

Homebuddies Professional Pet Sitting, 1197 Glenwood Blvd., Schenectady (518-382-7740; rrowney@nycap.rr.com; www. homebuddies.net). Serving the greater Schenectady area, petsitter Rita Marie Rowney can provide your dog with exercise and companionship while you're off enjoying a "people-only" activity. "We keep our clients' pets as close to their regular routine as possible, providing feeding, exercise, TLC, and medication administration when necessary," Rita says.

Park Avenue Pets, 113 Park Ave., Mechanicville (518-665-0557). Located about halfway between Albany and Saratoga Springs, this pet-washing and grooming service caters to all breeds with shampoos, nail cuts, and specialized grooming. The shop also offers a discount for senior citizens. Reservations are recommended.

Petcetera's Bed & Biscuit, 2417 Rte. 9, Ballston Spa (518-899-4194; petbandb@aol.com; www.petceterasbandb.com). For more than 20 years, this business has been serving local and visiting dog lovers with doggie daycare and overnight boarding services. (The owners also raise and show champion Siberian huskies and miniature poodles at their Skrimshaw Kennels.) The boarding facility has 22 indoor/outdoor heated runs for dogs and "kitty condos" for the cats. Dogs in daycare are able to socialize and play with each other in fenced-in yards.

Pet Supplies Plus, University Plaza, 1235 Western Ave., Albany (518-438-1040). While you're visiting the big city, stop by this store to grab a quick treat for Fluffy or stock up for the road: The selection includes foods like Iams, Alpo, Science Diet, Purina, Nutro, and Pedigree, along with numerous chewy treats, toys, pet clothing, cleaning and grooming supplies, bowls, and pet-related books and magazines.

Putting on the Dog, 959 Albany-Shaker Rd., Latham (518-783-0557; www.puttingonthedog.net).

Certified as a National Master Groomer, Putting on the Dog owner Karen Greenman provides obedience training as well as scissoring, styling, and washing. Call ahead for an appointment; the shop is open Tuesday through Saturday.

Reigning Cats and Dogs, 759 Rte. 9W, Glenmont (518-767-9718; 1-888-220-3788; www.reigning-catsanddogs.com). Serving the Capital area residents and visitors, this unique business has expanded from a retail store into an extensive facility offering doggie daycare, overnight boarding, dog training, and pet transportation. The store continues to offer companion animal food, supplies, and accessories, as well. Senior pets or others with special needs stay in the Pampered Pets Unit, which is secluded from the other areas with music, a TV, and a separate exercise yard.

IN CASE OF EMERGENCY

Amsterdam Animal Hospital
191 Wallins Corners Rd. (518-842-0540)

Cambridge Valley Veterinary Hospital
42 McMillan Rd. (518-677-8815)

Glens Falls Animal Hospital
66 Glenwood Ave. (518-792-6575)

Guilderland Animal Hospital
4963 Western Turnpike. (518-355-0260)

Parkside Veterinary Hospital
172 Morton Ave., Albany (518-463-0418)

Upstate Veterinary Hospital
415 Maple Ave., Saratoga Springs (518-583-0609)

The
Adirondack
Mountains

A VISITING PUP EXPLORES TUPPER LAKE'S DOWNTOWN WATERFRONT PARK.

The Adirondack Mountains

DOG-FRIENDLY RATING:

Dog lovers, welcome to paradise. This region is home to the 6-million-acre Adirondack Park (yes, that says 'million') as well as numerous pet-friendly lodges, motels, hotels, and campgrounds. Prefer to rent a private home or cottage? Take your pick: The Adirondacks are generously dotted with rustic cabins, waterfront cottages, and contemporary lakefront homes where dogs are welcome guests. Most accommodations here blend in with their peaceful surroundings, providing water and forest views, old-fashioned "Great Camp" ambiance, and, of course, plenty of Adirondack chairs for lazy lounging.

In the south, families flock to the Lake George area for camping, boating, hiking, water parks, and relaxation. To the west and north, majestic lakes like Piseco, Raquette, Tupper, Saranac, and Champlain provide limitless recreational opportunities and impressive views. Lake Placid, best known as the site of the 1932 and 1980 Winter Olympics, still attracts visitors with downtown shopping, restaurants, water and mountain vis-

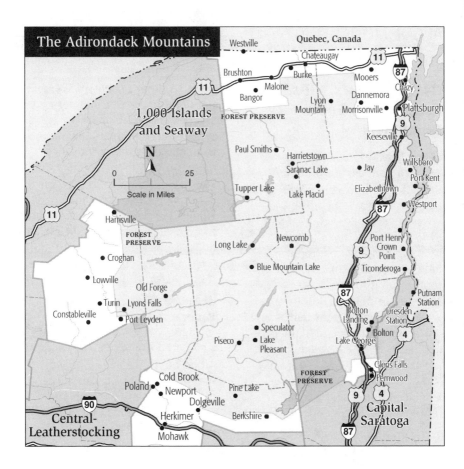

The Adirondack Mountains

tas, and the excitement of Olympic Village—where two-legged visitors can take a stab at winter sports like bobsledding. The main attraction of the region, however, is the Adirondack Park itself: a huge expanse of peaks, valleys, rivers, and deep woods that surrounds each village and resort. The locals here take pride in their unique surroundings, and most will enthusiastically welcome you and your pup to explore all their home has to offer. You can't see it all in a week, but you can taste a vacation-size sample of Adirondack charm—and then hopefully come back for more.

ACCOMMODATIONS

Hotels, Motels, Inns, Lodges, and Bed & Breakfasts

Chestertown
Atateka Lodges, 393 Atateka Dr., Friends Lake (518-494-2768; boggia@netheaven.com; www.atatekalodges.com); $85 to $135 per night. Close to Lake George, these two-bedroom lodges have full kitchens, living room/dining room areas, screened-in porches, knotty-pine walls, fireplaces, cable television with premium movie channels, and VCRs. Pets are welcome during the fall, winter, and spring seasons. Animal owners pay a $50 cleaning fee and a $250 refundable damage deposit.

Twin Pine Lodge, Rtes. 8 and 9 (518-494-4355; mail@twinpinelodge.com; www.twinpinelodge.com); $100–140 per night or $525–775 per week. Twin Pine guests stay in full-size cabins and cottages spread throughout 25 acres with a swimming pool. Each accommodation has four to six rooms, a full kitchen, cable television and heat; some have screened-in porches, balconies and woodstoves. Dogs are welcome with prior notice, provided they are leashed at all times.

Hague
Trout House Village Resort, 9117 Lakeshore Dr. (518-543-6088; 1-800-368-6088; inquiry@trouthouse.com; www.trouthouse.com); $59–450 per night or $630–2,900 per week. This resort offers a vast array of accommodations options, from standard motel rooms to deluxe cottages, log cabins, and country inn rooms. Located on the Lake Geroge shoreline, Trout House has a private beach, a putting green, and sailboats. Leashed dogs are welcome in certain units from mid-September to mid-June for an extra $20 per night.

Hampton
Panorama Motel, Rte. 22A (518-282-9648; 1-800-423-9648); $45–54 per night. The Panorama Motel has 12 roomy units with mountain views, air-conditioning, cable television, smoking and nonsmoking rooms, and private bathrooms. Nearby, guests can enjoy golf, fishing, boating, cross-country skiing, and downhill skiing. For an extra $6 per night, your dog is a welcome guest.

Indian Lake
Mountain Chalet Café and Cabins, 111 W. Main St. (518-648-0242; amarini@capital.net; www.adirondacks.com/mtchalet); $55–60 per night. The log-style, one-room cabins at Mountain Chalet can each accommodate up to four people with private bathrooms and televisions. An on-site café serves breakfast and lunch. Leashed dogs are allowed with prior approval; owners pay an additional $7 per night and must have proof of vaccinations.

Smith's Cottage, Rte. 30 (518-648-5222); $65–315 per night or $315–1,575 per week. Smith's Cottage is actually a lodge with seven neighboring cottages available for rent. The main lodge can accommodate a party of up to 14 people; the cottages each can accommodate two to eight guests. Dogs are allowed with prior approval for an additional $10 per night. Owners must use a leash, show proof of vaccinations, and not leave their pets unattended in the cottages. Dogs are not allowed in the beach area.

Jay

Fourpeaks Adirondack Camps and Guest Barn, Stonehouse Rd. (1-800-373-8445; martin@4peaks.com; www.4peaks.com); $300–500 per three days or $600–1,000 per week. "We don't just accept pets—we invite them for a fun outdoor vacation they'll never forget!" says Fourpeaks owner Martin Schwalbaum. The resort's six housekeeping cottages can accommodate two to eight people with lots of privacy; some have extras like a sauna, a screen house, cathedral ceilings, and sleeping lofts (the 400-page web site gives more than a few details). Pet owners pay an extra $25 per stay.

Keene Valley

Trail's End Inn, Rte. 73, HC1 Box 103 (518-576-9235; 800-281-9860; tei@kvvi.net;www.trailsendinn.com); $135–195 per night. For an additional $20 per dog, per night fee, dogs are welcome in two of Trail's End's suites as well as three nearby cottages. Two of

the cottages are located on the Ausable River; all have two bedrooms. The suites have separate entrances, private baths, peaceful views, and updated furnishings. Inn guests enjoy daily full breakfasts, hardwood floors, and fireplaces.

Lake George

Best Western Lake George, Rte. 9N (518-668-5701; 1-800-234-0265; reservations@fortwilliamhenry.com; www.bestwesternlakegeorge.com); $74–399 per night. Dogs weighing less than 20 pounds are allowed at this Best Western, a motel offering standard rooms, premium rooms, poolside suites, deluxe suites with hot tubs, and one "ultra" suite—a two-bedroom loft. Other amenities include indoor and outdoor swimming pools, a hot tub, a wading pool, and a "Kids Stay Free" program.

Blair House of Lake George, 2734 Canada St., Rte. 9 (518-668-2871; blairhse@adelphia.net; www.lakegeorgeblairhouse.com); $47–150 per night. For an extra $10 per night, dogs (sorry, no cats) are welcome in some of Blair House's motel rooms, suites, and cottages. The homey motel has been owned by four generations of the same family for more than 60 years; the rooms have cable television, air-conditioning, and refrigerators. Dogs should not be left unattended and should be leashed at all times.

Fort William Henry Motor Inn, 48 Canada St. (518-668-3081);

ROSIE'S COUNTRY CABINS IN LAKE GEORGE

$89–429 per night. Your pet is welcome at Fort William Henry, a motor inn with a swimming pool and sun deck. Guests can watch the fireworks over Lake George in one of the recently renovated suites with separate living and sleeping areas. A sandy beach is within walking distance of the hotel; other amenities include a 24-hour front desk, air-conditioning, cable television, and in-room hair dryer, irons, and ironing boards.

Rosie's Country Cabins & Lakeview Cottages, 1779 Rte. 9L, P.O. Box 223 (518-668-2743 in summer; 518-793-3869 in winter; rosie@albany.net); $65–180 per night. Rosie's lakeview cottages are motel-style accommodations that can house two to seven peo-

ple and are located near the lake and the Million Dollar Beach. The country cabins are located nearby on Rte. 9N; these can accommodate two to eight people and share access to a swimming pool and a picnic area. Dogs are welcome with prior approval.

Lake Luzerne
Elms Waterfront Cottages, Rte. 9N, P.O. Box 95 (518-696-3072; elmscottages@juno.com; www. elmscottages.com); $90–135 per night in spring and fall or $705–955 per week in summer. This family resort on the Hudson offers one- and two-bedroom cottages for rent along with boating, fishing, swimming, hiking, and kayaking opportunities. Dogs are welcome for an additional $50 per week; cats are welcome for

an extra $25 per week. An on-site kennel is also available free of charge.

Hide-A-Way Waterfront Cottages,

138 Hidden Valley Rd. (518-696-2248; www.hideaway waterfrontcottages.com); $100–125 per night or $550–750 per week. The housekeeping cottages at Hide-A-Way have one- to two-bedrooms and share access to a private beach, picnic tables, outdoor fireplaces and play areas. Pets are welcome in some of the two-bedroom cottages; cat owners pay an additional $25 per week or $5 per night, while dog owners pay an extra $50 per week or $10 per night.

Lake Placid

Best Western Golden Arrow Hotel,

150 Main St. (518-523-3353; info@golden-arrow.com; www.golden-arrow.com); $89–369 per night. This deluxe hotel has a restaurant and lounge, a dance club, an indoor swimming pool, lake access, a health club, a con-

ference center, and in-room refrigerators and coffeemakers. Choose from standard rooms, deluxe rooms, suites, and extended-stay suites. Dogs are welcome in rooms with private entrances for an extra $25 per stay.

Cobble Mountain Lodge,

Northwood Rd., Rte. 86 (518-523-2040; innkeeper@ cobblemountain.net; www.cobblemountain.net); $45–135 per night. Cobble Mountain Lodge rooms and cabins have private bathrooms, cable television and coffeemakers. Guests also have access to playground equipment, fire pits, and of course plenty of Adirondack chairs. Pets are welcome—nearby trails are great for dog-walking.

Howard Johnson Resort Inn,

90 Saranac Ave. (518-523-9555; 800-858-4656; www.howard-johnson.com); $82–165 per night. This Howard Johnson Inn offers a 24-hour front desk, free newspapers, an on-site restaurant,

A GUEST SUITE WITH KITCHENETTE AT THE NORTHWOODS INN ON LAKE PLACID

cable television, a picnic area, hiking and cross-country skiing trails, alarm clocks, and free use of the hotel's rowboats, paddleboats, and canoes. There are no extra charges or deposits for dogs, although owners are asked not to leave them alone in the rooms.

Lake Placid Lodge, Whiteface Inn Rd., P.O. Box 550 (518-523-2700; 1-877-523-2700; info@ lakeplacidlodge.com; www.lake-placidlodge.com); $350–800 per night. Pets and their people get the royal treatment at this luxury lodge built in the traditional Adirondack "great camp" style with elaborate woodwork, large stone fireplaces, antiques and Oriental rugs. Animals are welcome in all 19 cabins, where they are treated to pet beds, treats and toys. Dog owners pay an extra $50 per pet, per night fee.

Lake Placid Resort Hotel & Golf Club, 1 Olympic Dr. (518-523-2556; 1-800-874-1980; info@ lpresort.com; www.lakeplacid resort.com); $69–219 per night. For a one-time fee of $25, dogs, cats, and other pets are all welcome at this hotel located within the Olympic Village. Amenities include a restaurant and bar, an indoor swimming pool and hot tub, tennis courts, and a fitness center. Pets are not allowed in chalets or Lakehouse units and should not be left alone in the rooms.

Northwoods Inn, 122 Main St. (518-523-1818; info@northwoods-inn.com; www.northwoodsinn.

com); $46–159 per night. Close to everything, this modernized historic hotel welcomes all kinds of pets for an extra $25 per stay. Guests can dine in the hotel restaurant and lounge, play in the game room, walk to shops and the Olympic Village, or just relax in condo suites, extended-stay suites or deluxe suites—all have great mountain and lake views. Dogs should not be left unattended. The inn is located within walking distance to all Main St. gift stores, coffee shops, and restaurants.

Prague Motor Inn, 25 Sentinel Rd. (518-523-3410); $50–125 per night. Guests at the lakefront Prague Motor Inn can choose from standard rooms, cottages, and suites with kitchenettes, fireplaces, and hot tubs. All accommodations have air-conditioning. There are no extra charges for dogs, although the managers reserve the right to limit the number of animals staying in each room.

Swiss Acres Inn, 189 Saranac Ave. (518-523-3040; 1-800-464-4690; info@swissacres.com; www.swissacres.com); $49–199 per night. Choose from standard rooms (16 of which are newly built), two-room suites, and the deluxe Whiteface Suite at Swiss Acres. The inn has an outdoor swimming pool, a hot tub and sauna, an ice skating rink, gardens, a basketball court, and a game room with a big-screen television. Pet owners pay a $50 refundable security deposit and a one-time fee of $20.

Long Lake
Morning Star Inn, North Point Rd. (518-624-5522); $40–60 per night. The room rates at this Long Lake inn include breakfast for two. Close to the lake and renowned Buttermilk Falls, Morning Star has westerly views, fireplaces, beautiful grounds and flower gardens, and a laid-back atmosphere. Blue Mountain Lake is 6 miles to the south. Most breeds are welcome: "We've had everything from Chinese water spaniels to retired greyhounds," says innkeeper Bill Moore.

Old Forge
Old Forge Motel, Rte. 28, P.O. Box 522 (315-369-3313); $58–80 per night. There are no extra charges for Fido at this pet-friendly motel offering an outdoor swimming pool, cable television, and a convenient location close to shops and restaurants. Some rooms also have air-conditioning and patios. In 2003, the owners started construction on an indoor swimming pool that was scheduled to be completed by 2004.

Palmer Point Cottages and Boat Rentals, Rte. 28 (315-357-5594; palmerpt@yahoo.com; www.adirondacktravel.com/ppt/cottages); $310–370 per week. For an extra $3 per day, dogs are permitted at Palmer Point's Surprise Cottage, a housekeeping cabin in the pines that overlooks a pond and can accommodate up to five people. Guests can also take advantage of the on-site boat-rental facility, complete with powerboats, fishing boats, pon-toon boats, sailboats, canoes and rowboats.

Plattsburgh
Best Western Inn at Smithfield, 446 Rte. 3 (518-561-7750; 1-800-243-4656); $70–99 per night. Your dog is welcome without extra fees at the 120-room Inn at Smithfield, where guests enjoy an on-site restaurant and lounge, an indoor swimming pool, a game room, free daily newspapers, a playground, a gift shop, cable television, free local calls, and in-room coffeemakers, hair dryers, and alarm clocks. A nearby ferry service shuttles guests to and from Vermont across Lake Champlain.

Marine Village Cottages, 82 Dickson Point Rd. (518-563-5698; info@marinevillagecottages.com; www.marinevillagecottages.com); $75–125 per night or $475–700 per week. The 25 housekeeping cottages at Marine Village each have three bedrooms, a fireplace, a kitchen, a .25-acre lot, and views of the mountains and Lake Champlain. Dogs are welcome, but must be leashed and cleaned-up after and are not allowed on the beach between 9 AM and 5 PM.

Raquette Lake
Risley's Rush Point Cottages, Rte. 28, P.O. Box 112 (315-354-5211; rushpt@aol.com; www.rushpt.net); $660–760 per week. The eight rental cottages at Risley's vary in size and style, although each has a fireplace or furnace, a full kitchen, and a porch or sundeck. Popular activities include fishing, boating and hiking on nearby trails. "We specialize in families and are dog lovers ourselves," explains owner

Barbara Risley Allen. Owners are asked to clean up after their animals and to keep them leashed.

Saranac Lake

Adirondack Motel, 23 Lake Flower Ave. (518-891-2116; 1-800-416-0117; info@adirondackmotel. com; www.adirondackmotel.com); $50–220 per night. Guests here choose from motel rooms, efficiency units in the boathouse, and fireplace suites. Amenities include free daily continental breakfasts, a picnic area with barbecue grills, and cable television with premium channels. Dogs (sorry, no cats) are welcome, provided they are leashed, quiet, and crated when left alone in a room.

Cochran's Cabins, 303 Kiwassa Rd. (518-891-5721; Douglas@ northnet.org; www.adirondack cabin.com); $600–1,100 per week. At Cochran's, guests choose from 11 cabins, varied in size and style, spread across 20 acres on Lake Kiwassa. Each rustic cabin has a dock and a clean outhouse (no indoor plumbing). Pets are welcome with prior permission and should be leashed, quiet, cleaned-up after, and not left alone in the cabins. Nightly rates are also available for some cabins.

Doctor's Inn, Trudeau Rd., P.O. Box 375 (518-891-3464; 1-888-518-3464; docsinn@adelphia.net; www.docsinn.net); $75–200 per night. "We are dog-friendly, and just ask that the dogs are people-friendly," explain Alan Brown and Susan Moody, who run this historic B&B. The Doctor's Inn has individual guest rooms and

suites, a wraparound porch, a cheerful décor, and a tucked-away location.

Hotel Saranac, 101 Main St. (1-800-937-0211; hotelin@ paulsmiths.edu; www.hotel-saranac.com); $55–195 per night. Owned and run by Paul Smith's College, this 75-year-old grand hotel offers a 24-hour front desk, room service, voice mail, cable television, and a restaurant, café, bakery and coffee bar. The hotel is also renowned for its gift shop—the largest in the Adirondacks. Dogs are welcome for an additional $15 per night, although they cannot be left alone in the rooms.

Speculator

Cedarhurst Motor Lodge, Rtes. 8 and 30 (518-548-6064 or 518-548-8427; lodge@klink.net; www.speculatorny.com/ cedarhurst); $49–65 per night. This 10-room motel offers a dog-walking area for guests, many of whom come to the area for skiing, hiking, boating, fishing, and leaf-peeping. Pets cannot be left unattended in rooms; shorthaired, nonbarking dogs are preferred.

Tupper Lake

The Wawbeek on Upper Saranac Lake, Panther Mountain Rd., Rte. 30 (518-359-2656; 1-800-953-2656; info@wawbeek.com; www.wawbeek.com); $125–445 per night or $625–2,660 per week. The Wawbeek, a traditional "great camp" resort, boasts 1,400 feet of shoreline with a sandy beach, lodge rooms, cabins and cottages, boats and canoes, tennis courts, and trails for walking, biking, or cross-country skiing. Dogs are welcome in most rooms and cottages for an extra $25 per night.

Warrensburg

Route 9 Motel, 4046 Main St., Rte. 9 (518-623-2955; desk@ route9motel.com; www.route9-motel.com); $47–75 per night. Accommodations at this convenient motel include standard rooms with two double beds and efficiencies with microwaves and refrigerators. All rooms have cable television, heat, and air-conditioning. The motel is popular with families and close to all Lake George attractions. Dogs and cats are welcome for short stays; pet owners pay an additional $10 per stay.

Wevertown

Adirondacks Cabins at Mill Creek, Johnsburg Rd., Rte. (718-726-4622; info@adirondacks-cabins.com; www.adirondacks-cabins.com); $300–375 per weekend or $600–750 per week. Guests here choose from six cabins: The main house cabin, which can accommodate up to 10 people; Sparrows Nest, a two-bedroom with a full kitchen; cabins 1, 2, and 3, which each sleep up to six people; and the Honeymoon Cabin, a cozy and secluded one-bedroom. Pet owners pay a $50 cleaning fee.

Whiteface Mountain

Ledge Rock at Whiteface, Rte. 86, P.O. Box 34 (1-800-336-4754; ledge_rock@yahoo.com; www. ledgerockatwhiteface.com); $89–179 per night. Quiet, well-behaved dogs are welcome at Ledge Rock for an extra $10 per night. The motor inn offers mountain views, standard rooms and larger two-bedroom units with kitchenettes, exterior corridors, a swimming pool, and a gathering room with a fireplace, big-screen TV, books, a pool table, and board games.

Wilmington

North Pole Campground and Motor Inn, Rte. 86 (518-946-7733; 800-245-0228; info@northpoleresorts.com; www.northpoleresorts.com); $49–129 per night in motor inn rooms. For an additional $3 per night, one dog per room is allowed at North Pole's motor inn. Choose from economy rooms with either one queen bed or two double beds, deluxe rooms with refrigerators and microwaves, and family suites with wet bars, dining tables and VCRs. (For more information about on-site camping, see "Campgrounds.")

Willkommen Hof Bed & Breakfast, Rte. 86 (518-946-SNOW; 1-800-541-9119; willkommenhof@whiteface.net; www.lakeplacid.net/ willkommenhof); $63–165 per night. Guests at this farmhouse B&B choose from two rooms with a shared bath, three deluxe rooms with private baths and lofts, and a suite with two bedrooms, a sitting room, and a whirlpool bath. Whiteface Mountain is just down the road. Friendly, leashed pets are welcome with a refundable security deposit of $25 and a $10 per night, per pet fee.

Campgrounds

Ausable Chasm

Ausable Chasm Campground, Rte. 373, P.O. Box 390 (518-834-7454; 1-800-537-1211; www.ausablechasm.com); $18–39 per night. Although pets are not allowed on Ausable Chasm tours (which generally involve a raft ride), they are welcome to join their families at the chasm campground. In addition to miles of trails, the property also offers sites for tents and RVs, a swimming pool, movies, cabins, and a game room. The campground is open in spring, summer, and fall.

Ausable Forks

Douglas on Silver Lake, 18 Douglas Lane (518-647-8061; 1-800-201-8061; douglascampsites@aol.com; www.douglasresort.com); $20–25 per day at the campground; $75–250 per night or $350–900 per week in the cottages. Leashed pets are welcome at the Douglas resort's camping areas and 19 housekeeping cottages, all of which are near hiking trails, rivers, and lakes. The cottages can accommodate 2 to 11 people; some have screened-in porches, fireplaces, or a beach-front location.

Colton

Higley Flow State Park Campground, 442 Cold Brook Dr. (315-262-2880). $19–25 per night. The campsites at Higley Flow are laid out along the Raquette River and surrounded by pine forests, providing plenty of opportunities for fishing, boating, swimming, hiking, and canoeing. Picnic tables and rest rooms with showers are also available to campers. Dogs are allowed with a leash and proof of vaccinations, although they are not allowed in picnic and bathing areas. For more information on the state park, see "Out and About."

Hinckley

Trail's End Campground, South Side Rd., P.O. Box 60 (315-826-7220; info@trailend.com; www.trailend.com); $20–30 per night. Campers here choose from the rustic tent area, the RV area, the Back Park, or the Lakeside RV area. Amenities include lake and pond access, a picnic grove, rest rooms with showers, and a camp store. Pets are not allowed on the beach, but they are welcome to swim in an area near the boat launch. Dog owners pay an extra $2 per pet, per stay; some breeds are not allowed.

Lake George

Lake George Escape, 175 East Schroon River Rd. (518-623-3207; 1-800-327-3188; info@lakegeorgeescape.com; www.lakegeorgeescape.com); $19–46 per night. Up to two pets per site are welcome at this large campground resort with two ponds, two swimming pools, river access, a beach, laundry facilities, a café with outdoor seating, rest rooms with showers, gem mining, and wagon rides. Dogs must be leashed at all times.

Lake George RV Park, 74 Rte. 149 (518-792-3775; www.lakegeorgervpark.com); $35–42 per night. In many ways, this large property resembles a small village more than a campground:

With more than 390 sites for every size RV, three swimming pools and two kiddie pools, four playgrounds, seven tennis courts, two ponds, hiking trails, and two arcades, families should have trouble staying busy. Dog owners must keep their pets leashed and clean up after them.

Long Lake

Hoss's Country Campground, Lake St. (1-800-952-HOSS; hoss@capital.net; www. hossscountrycorner.com; call for rate information. This RV park (no tent sites available) has 14 waterfront sites on Jennings Park Pond, a miniature golf course, and a game room. Hoss's Country Corner, an old-fashioned general store with ice cream, sandwiches, and souvenirs, is next door. Dogs are welcome without extra fees as long as their owners keep an eye on them.

Lowville

Happy Hollow Campground, Rte. 1, P.O. Box 233 (315-376-4345; diller@northnet.org; www.happyhollowcg.com); $16–20 per night. Happy Hollow is popular with families and provides campers with tennis courts, a pond, a recreation hall, a pavilion, rest rooms with showers, a camp store, and 175 shaded and sunny sites on 90 acres. Quiet, leashed dogs are welcome, although they are not allowed on the beach or at the playground.

Malone

Deer River Campsite, 123 Deer River Dr. (518-483-0060; deerriver@westelcom.com; www.deerrivercampsite.com); $23–54 per night. Campers at

Deer River will find tent and RV sites, camping cabins, walking trails, a playground, a volleyball court, recreation rooms, laundry facilities, a café and library, boat and canoe rentals, and rest rooms with showers. Leashed, quiet dogs are welcome, as long as owners are considerate of others on the property who may not be dog lovers.

North Hudson

Yogi Bear's Jellystone Park at Paradise Pines, Blue Ridge Rd., P.O. Box 180 (518-532-7493; 1-800-232-5349; office@paradise pines.com; www.paradisepines. com); $34–44 per night. No need to "rough it": This Jellystone Park has rest rooms with showers, a swimming pool, a miniature golf course, movies and hayrides, and even Internet access. Dogs are welcome with prior approval at campsites (but not in rental units), as long as they are leashed and picked-up after.

Peru

Iroquois RV Park and Campground, 270 Bear Swamp Rd., Rte. 442 (578-643-9057; iroquois@westelcom.com); $23 per night. Iroquois, located just down the road from Lake Champlain, offers 170 sites for tents and RVs, a fishpond, a par-3 golf course, paddleboats, planned activities, and a swimming pool. There are no extra fees for pets, although dog owners must show proof of vaccinations and clean up any messes.

Schuyler Falls

Macomb Reservation State Park Campground, 201 Campsite Rd. (518-643-9952); $13–19 per night.

Visitors relaxing at the wooded and open campsites at Macomb Reservation have access to rest rooms with showers, picnic tables, a boat launch, pavilions, sports fields, dumping stations, and planned recreational activities. Dogs are welcome on a 6-foot leash everywhere except the beach and picnic area. Bring proof of vaccinations. For more information on the park, see "Out and About."

Various locations
New York State Department of Environmental Conservation Campgrounds (518-402-9428; www.dec.state.ny.us/website). The DEC operates 45 campgrounds within the Adirondack region, and pets are allowed in all except the Lake George Islands camping area. The campgrounds vary in size and amenities provided. Some examples include: Ausable Point in Peru, which has 123 sites, a beach and Lake Champlain access; Nicks Lake in Old Forge, where campers will find 112 sites for tents and trailers, a picnic area, lake access, and a quiet atmosphere without powerboats; Hearthstone Point in Warrensburg, which offers a junior naturalist program, 250 campsites, boating, and rest rooms with showers; Eighth Lake in Inlet, a shoreline campground with picnic areas, a beach, and hiking trails; and Meacham Lake in Paul Smiths, a secluded campground on a 1,200-acre lake with a boat launch, a playground, and 224 sites. For more information or to make reservations, call the DEC or visit the web site, where you'll also find a complete listing of the campgrounds with rates, descriptions, and contact information. Pets will not be permitted in any camping area without rabies vaccination certificates. Dogs are not allowed in any beach or picnic areas and should be on a leash (no longer than 6 feet) at all times. Pet owners also cannot leave their animals unattended and must clean up after them.

Warrensburg
Daggett Lake Campsites, 660 Glan Athol Rd. (518-623-2198; daggetlake@aol.com; www.daggettlake.com); $20–29 per night. This 400-acre campground is unusually pet-friendly: Canines will love Dog Beach, a stretch of sand devoted just to them, and their owners will also enjoy the annual Daggett Dog Days event in June. Close to Lake George, the property also has an 80-acre lake, wooded sites, rest rooms with showers, boats and canoes, a camp store, laundry facilities, hiking and biking trails, and housekeeping cottages. Bring your pet's vaccination records.

Warrensburg Travel Park, Schroon River Rd., P.O. Box 277 (518-623-9833); $20–26 per night. Companion animals are welcome at this family campground located beside the Schroon River. Amenities include wooded sites for tents and RVs, a camp store, a swimming pool, boat rentals, laundry facilities, rest rooms with showers, a boat launch, a beach, sports courts, a game room, and daily trash pickup. Miniature golf courses, go-cart tracks, shops, and other attractions are located nearby.

Westport
Barber Homestead Park,
68 Barber Lane (518-962-8989; www.barberhomesteadpark.com); $22–25 per night. Tenters and RVers can unwind at this campground offering shady and sunny sites, rest rooms with showers, a recreation hall, volleyball and basketball courts, and a camp store. "We consider ourselves very pet-friendly," says park owner Billie Marsh. Campers and spectators are welcome to attend the campground's annual dog-agility event and picnic every July.

Wilmington
Lake Placid/Whiteface Mountain KOA Kampground,
Fox Farm Rd., P.O. Box 38 (1-800-562-0368; www.koa-campground.com); $26–65 per night. RVers and tenters each have their own separate areas at this KOA, which also offers river access, boat rentals, a miniature golf course, a swimming pool, hayrides, and a game room. A maximum of two pets are allowed at each campsite and one pet weighing less than 40 pounds is allowed in each Kamping Kabin.

North Pole Campground and Motor Inn,
Rte. 86 (518-946-7733; 800-245-0228; info@north-poleresorts.com; www.north-poleresorts.com); $28–32 per night for campsites; $38–50 per night for camping cabins; $89–119 per night for housekeeping cottages. This family resort offers sites for tents and RVs, camping cabins and cottages, swimming pools, a picnic area, game rooms, a playground, a miniature golf course, rest rooms, and boat rentals. There are no extra fees for pets in the campground. (For more information about the on-site motor inn, see "Hotels, Motels, Inns, and B&Bs.")

Homes, Cottages, and Cabins for Rent

Ausable Forks
Silver Lake Waterfront Camp,
Richards Rd. (518-647-8226); adkmts@frontiernet.net); $75–150 per night or $500–800 per week. With great lake and mountain views, this two-bedroom home has a sleeping loft, a family room, a large front deck, and an enclosed porch. Despite some previous negative experiences with visiting pets, the homeowners still allow well-behaved dogs as long as they are cleaned-up after.

Big Moose/Old Forge
Northern Lights, Higby Rd.
(910-470-9897; 910-271-5209; shvaisey@charter.net; www.webpages.charter.net/shvaisey); $1,589 per week. Northern Lights is a large waterfront house with a private beach and great views of Big Moose Lake. The vacation rental also has a master bedroom with a private deck, a sleeping loft with two beds, a formal dining room, a full kitchen, and a barbecue grill.

Chestertown
Loon Lake Waterfront Cottage,
State Rte. 9 (212-628-7862; loonlakecottage@cs.com; www.ourworld.cs.com/loonlakecottage); $400–525 per week. With 180 feet of private

frontage on Loon Lake, this cottage can accommodate up to five people with a full kitchen, a barbecue grill, a woodstove, a television and VCR, a beach, a dock, a swim float, and mountain views. Dogs and cats are welcome without extra fees.

Indian Lake

Anchors A'Hoyes, Lake Abanakee Rd. (315-652-1485; dhoyes@twcny.rr.com); $125 per night or $850 per week. Located just steps from the lake, this three-bedroom cottage has an enclosed front porch, satellite television, a furnished sundeck, a dock with canoes, a barbecue grill, hardwood floors and a full kitchen. Dog owners pay an additional $50 per week.

Thornbush Acres,
Big Brook Rd. (518-648-5843; gputerko@telenet.net); $140 per night. Located on the property of the Thornbush Acres RV Park and Farm, this five-bedroom home comes complete with antiques, country furnishings, two porches, a full kitchen, and even a resident horse. Dog owners are asked to just use common sense while looking after and cleaning up after their animal at the rental.

Inlet

Inlet Lodge and Chalet Rentals, Seventh Lake (315-738-0608; seventhlakelodge@cs.com); $1,200–1,800 per week. These two vacation homes provide cozy waterfront getaways for Inlet-area vacationers: The chalet has three bedrooms, a large front deck, cathedral ceilings, and a fireplace, while the lodge offers a knotty-pine interior, a covered

deck, and three bedrooms. Both properties sit directly on Seventh Lake. Responsible pet owners are always welcome.

Island Camp, Sixth Lake (585-396-1826; 585-394-8023; dfinchhd@aol.com); $1,800 per week. The rental fee for this secluded vacation home includes the use of a 20-foot pontoon boat. Located on a private island on Sixth Lake, the home has two bedrooms, a knotty-pine finish, and a large living room with a fireplace. Guests have free reign of the entire island. Dogs are welcome for an extra $100 per stay.

Jay

Ausable Valley Farmhouse (518-674-1416; nerenbus@aol.com); $250 per weekend or $675 per week. Located within walking distance to the Ausable River, this three-bedroom house is centrally located to popular Adirondack attractions and provides guests with a screened-in porch, a full kitchen, a woodstove, and a washer and dryer. Well-behaved, well-groomed, house-trained dogs are welcome with prior notice.

Sugar Mountain Cabin, Ausable Cascade Rd. (518-647-5869; cripplecrkcabins@aol.com); $600–850 per week. This new log cabin rental is set on 2 private acres with access to the Ausable River. The cabin offers a whirlpool tub, a wood-burning stove, a full kitchen, a washer and dryer, and sleeping accommodations for up to six people. Dogs are welcome with no extra fees or restrictions.

Keene

Pine Cottage, Rte. 9N (518-576-4497; pinecottage@addr.com); $180 per weekend or $650 per week. Located directly on the Ausable River, Pine Cottage can accommodate up to four people with two bedrooms, a porch, a washer and dryer, a full kitchen, a television, and a VCR. House-broken dogs are welcome as long as they stay off the furniture and are not left alone in the cabin.

Lake Clear

Ted's Cabin, Upper St. Regis Lake (518-327-3470; info@adkguideboat.com); $1,200–1,500 per week. Accessible only by water, this one-bedroom cabin has a private dock, a covered porch, and a TV/VCR. Boat transportation on your days of arrival and departure is free. "We are happy to have dogs as cabin guests," says homeowner Lynn Cameron. Pet owners pay an additional $50 cleaning fee per week.

Waterfront Vacation Rental, McMaster Rd., McCauley Pond (508-228-4225; bambi@nantucket.net); $150 per night or $925–1,150 per week. "We have a dog, so we know how nice it is to find a place that welcomes pets," explains Bambi Mleczko, the owner of this two-bedroom cottage located on a pond. The property's amenities include a kitchen and living room, a fireplace, an outdoor fire pit, and 50 acres of trails.

Lake George

Lake George Rental Homes (518-668-5545; thevitos@global2000.net; www.lakehouse-onlakegeorge.com and www.lakegeorgehouse.com); $550–1,000 per weekend or $1,000–2,000 per week. The Vito family welcomes visitors and their dogs to these two rental homes: The Ski/Lake House on Lake George can accommodate up to 10 people with large bedrooms and common areas; the Lake George House is set on 50 private acres and offers four bedrooms, four bathrooms, and central air-conditioning. Up to two dogs are welcome at a time in each house for an extra $40 per weekend or $75 per week.

Lake Placid

Paradise Point on Paradox Bay (518-523-4433; jslcpa-wpreston@northnet.org); $400-2,200 per week or $110–550 per night. Paradise Point is a boathouse divided into two rental units: East (1,370 square feet) and West (1,740 square feet). Both can accommodate up to seven people with boat slips, canoes and paddleboats, full kitchens, TV/VCRs, living room/dining room areas, woodstoves, and barbecue grills. The West unit also has a sunroom, and the East unit has a sleeping loft. Dogs (a maximum of two) are welcome for an additional $10 per day, per pet fee.

Loon Lake

The Loony Bin (518-580-0209; 1-518-580-0008; wolfmojo@earthlink.net; www.loony-bin.net); $750–1,050 per week. Located on the lakeshore, this Adirondack-style camp has two bedrooms, a large waterfront deck, satellite television, a VCR, a new stove, a canoe, and a row-boat. The small lake, about 2.5-miles long, is quiet and peaceful. A golf course is located just down the road. Well-behaved dogs are welcome.

North River

Gore Mountain ski area log cabin (212-750-8977; gharper@rcn.com); $450–600 per weekend or $650–800 per week. Recently updated, this home can accommodate up to six people and offers mountain views, a fireplace, a screened-in porch, a full kitchen, a washer and dryer, a canoe, and lake access. The Gore Mountain ski area and miles of cross-country trails are nearby. Well-behaved dogs, cats, and other pets are welcome.

Peru

Miller Homestead, Hallock Hill Rd. (508-946-3433; rpcassoc@aol.com; www.millerhomestead.com); $1,200–1,400 per week. This stone house, originally built by the Quakers and listed on the National Register of Historic places, offers a unique vacation experience with five bedrooms, a kitchen, a washer and dryer, and a fireplace. One well-behaved dog or cat is allowed per stay; short-haired dogs are preferred.

Piseco

Adirondack Lakefront Camp, Old Piseco Rd. (518-548-3508; 847-428-4042; esvet75009@aol.com); $800 per week. With the mountains on one side and Piseco Lake on the other, this cozy two-bedroom cottage can accommodate up to six people with a screened-in porch, a beach, a canoe, a barbecue grill,

a living room with a fireplace, and great views. Up to two dogs are welcome at a time without extra fees.

Four Season Home, Pawling Rd. (518-474-5892 or 518-346-0799; mms01@health.state.ny.us); $650–1,400 per week. This three-bedroom home has sweeping water and mountain views, a private sandy beach, two porches, a barbecue grill, a picnic table, and a paddleboat. One dog (sorry, no cats) is welcome without extra fees; additional dogs are welcome for an additional $25 per dog, per night.

Rainbow Lake

Camp Oxbow, Clark Wardner Rd. (847-356-7636; rentoxbow@hotmail.com); $1,200 per week. Guests here enjoy a sandy beach, a screened-in porch, a full kitchen, a great room with a cobblestone fireplace, wood-beam ceilings, three bedrooms, a floating raft, a dock, and a canoe. Pet owners pay a $500 refundable security deposit and are asked to keep dogs off the furniture.

Saranac Inn

Rock Ledge, Church Pond (607-776-2714; saintly@linkny.com); $170–210 per night or $1,000–1,400 per week. This chalet-style home abuts a golf course and a pond; amenities include three bedrooms, a deck, and a canoe and kayak. "I've been very fortunate to have responsible renters and pet owners in the past," says homeowner Susan St. Louis. Dogs (sorry, no cats) are welcome for an additional $100 per week.

Saranac Lake

Camp Hum-In-A, Branch Farm Rd. (518-891-4052; adklabs@ northnet.org); $100–130 per night or $650–850 per week. This newly built log cabin can accommodate up to four people with a knotty-pine interior, a covered porch, one bathroom, lake access and a dock, a barbecue grill, cable television, and a stereo. Well-behaved, housebroken dogs are welcome without extra fees.

Lake Flower Vacation Home, Fox Run (845-647-6485; ruthdetar@aol.com); $230 per night or $1,500 per week. A large deck and picture windows make it easy to enjoy the lake views at this three-bedroom home with a laundry room, a full kitchen, a crib, and a great room with a fireplace. A maximum of two dogs are allowed in the home at a time; pet owners pay a one-time fee of $25 per dog.

Severance

Paradox Lake Vacation Rentals, Paradox Lake (914-666-4767; paradoxlaker@aol.com; www.adirondacklakefronthomes. com); $1,500–2,300 per week. John Flynn offers four full-size vacation homes for rent on Paradox Lake: The CJ House has contemporary styling, three bedrooms, and a dock; Nanny's House was built in the 1800s and has three bedrooms, a screened-in porch, and a private beach; the Kristen House offers four bedrooms, a dock, and satellite TV; and the Adele House has three bedrooms, a stone patio, and a screened-in porch. Well-behaved dogs are welcome (a maximum of two per house) for an additional $100 per dog, per week.

Star Lake

Seldom Inn (315-848-9917; kanneo@lycos.com; www.seldominn.com); $350 per weekend or $850 per week. Dogs (sorry, no cats) are welcome to join their families at this three bedroom cottage with lake access, a woodstove, a barbecue grill, a piano, screened-in porches, a full kitchen, a washer and dryer, a deck, and a canoe. Dog owners pay a refundable $150 deposit and cannot leave their animals alone in the house.

Upper Jay

Hemlock Lodge (585-624-2043; hemlocklodge@brandforward. com); $120–145 per night or $750–900 per week. Surrounded by hiking trails, wildflower meadows, and a beaver pond, this house is popular with dog owners and others looking to "get away from it all." The two-bedroom rental also has a sleeping loft, full furnishings, a washer and dryer, a rustic Adirondack décor, and access to the Ausable River.

Wilmington

Willard House, Whiteface (518-946-7682; dayv@frontiernet.net); $75 per night for cottage rental and $220 per night for house rental. The Willard House property includes a rustic cottage with accommodations for two guests and a three-bedroom home with a fireplace, a full kitchen, and a TV/VCR. Both have views of the Whiteface mountain and ski resort. Well-behaved dogs are welcome for an extra $20 per stay.

Woodgate
White Lake Vacation Rental,
Rte. 28 (315-668-3221;
Jennifer@rchgrd.com); $600 per
week. Well-behaved, housebroken dogs are welcome at this waterfront cottage with two bedrooms, one bathroom, cable television, a full kitchen, a washer and dryer, a pull-out couch, and a barbecue grill. Overlooking the lake, the house also provides water access and storage for up to two snowmobiles.

Rental Agencies

Adirondack Mountain Properties, 5074 Rte. 28, Old Forge (315-357-5302). Adirondack Mountain Properties works with private homeowners to offer cabins, lodges, chalets, and other homes for rent. Some are cozy and rustic, while others are spacious, waterfront homes with decks, docks, and lake rights. Most of the time, the agents can find you a pet-friendly property or two on the list; call for the latest listings.

Merrill L. Thomas, Inc., 65 Main St., Lake Placid (518-523-2519; 800-244-7023; rentals@lakeplacid vacations.com; www.lakeplacid-vacations.com). Offering services for those looking to buy or rent in the Adirondacks, this agency lists waterfront properties, condominiums, townhouses, cottages and estates. Some of the rental property owners do allow pets, though the number varies from year to year. For updated listings, contact the agency or visit the web site.

OUT AND ABOUT

Adirondack Loj Trailhead,
Adirondack Loj Rd., Lake Placid. Owned by the Adirondack Mountain Club, this large parking area can accommodate more than 100 cars at a time—and often does. From here you can access Marcy Dam, MacIntyre Range, Mt. Jo, Indian Pass, and other popular hiking routes. For more information and the latest parking rates, visit Adirondack Mountain Club's web site at www.adk.org or call the group's headquarters at 1-800-395-8080.

You'll also need to contact the club to reserve one of the Loj's wilderness campsites or lean-tos.

Adirondack Park, Paul Smiths Visitor Interpretive Center, Rte. 30, Paul Smiths (518-327-3000; adkvicpr@yahoo.com) and Newcomb Visitor Interpretive Center, Rte. 28N, Newcomb (518-582-2000; adkvic@telenet.net). Encompassing much of northeastern New York State, this 6-million-acre park includes wetlands, marshes, forests, peat bogs, small towns, lakes, rivers, dirt roads, hiking trails, mountains, valleys, gorges, public preserves, and private land. You'll also find historic sites, like Camp Santanoni, primitive wilderness areas, like the St. Regis Canoe area, "intensive use" areas, such as the Gore and Whiteface ski areas, state campgrounds (see "Out and About"), and wild forest areas, including the Aldrich Ponds Wild Forests. For more information, tips, and trail maps, visit one of the two interpretive centers in person or on-line at the Adirondack Park Agency's web site: www.northnet.org/adirondackvic. The Adirondack Mountain Club (www.adk.org) can also provide many helpful hints and suggestions for planning a visit. Dogs are not allowed on designated ski trails during the winter, but they are welcome in other areas provided they are on a leash at all times. Park rangers ask that owners take pains to keep their pets away from wildlife and sensitive sites

like nesting areas. Outside of the resort areas, much of the Adirondacks are considered "backcountry" areas with few services: Use caution while exploring and always be prepared with a tent and extra food and water for you and your dog.

Beaver Brook Outfitters, Junction of Rtes. 8 and 28, P.O. Box 96, Wevertown (1-888-45-GUIDE, www.beaverbrook.net). Although this company specializes in whitewater rafting trips—not the best outing for most pooches—the staff can also run shuttles, provide you with canoe rentals, and even arrange guided canoe trips up to a week in length. The Beaver Brook store also stocks rental snowshoes, skis, and snowboards, along with books, maps, and fishing equipment.

Crown Point State Historic Site, 739 Bridge Rd., Crown Point (518-597-4666). Walk the grounds of Fort St. Frederick, explore the

THE FORT RUINS AT CROWN POINT STATE HISTORIC PARK IN CROWN POINT

ruins, and learn the history of this much-battled-over structure: First in the hands of the French, it was captured by the British in 1759 and then by local Colonists in 1775. The State of New York bought the land and preserved it as a historic site in 1910.

Cumberland Bay State Park, 152 Cumberland Head Rd., Plattsburg (518-563-5240). Cumberland Bay's large beach and picnic area on Lake Champlain are renowned—unfortunately, pets are not allowed at either. But who needs a beach? Animal lovers can take advantage of 200 campsites for tents and trailers, along with hiking and cross-country skiing trails, playing fields and great views. Dog owners must show proof of rabies vaccinations.

Dog Equipment Rentals, 2590 Stillwater Rd., Lowville (315-376-2110). With a name like this, it has to be good, right? No, you won't find rental leashes and kennels here, but you will find boats, canoes, kayaks, snowshoes, and more available for short-term use. The office is located within a general store and gift shop called the Stillwater Shop.

Higley Flow State Park, 442 Cold Brook Dr., Colton (315-262-2880). Best known for its campground (see "Accommodations"), this state park also has access to the Raquette River (popular with canoeists), a beach, a boat launch, and the Beaver Pond Nature Trail used for hiking and cross-country skiing. Pet owners should have rabies vaccination certificates and keep their animal on a leash no longer than 6 feet. Dogs are not allowed on the beach or in the picnic area.

Lake Champlain ferries, Headquarters: King St. Dock, Burlington, Vermont (802-864-9804; lct@ferries.com; www. ferries.com). Leashed or crated pets are allowed on board Lake Champlain Transportation Company's ferries running between upstate New York and Vermont. The three main routes are Burlington, Vermont to Port Kent, New York; Grand Isle, Vermont to Plattsburgh, New York; and Charlotte, Vermont to Essex, New York. Visit the web site for schedules, directions to each port, and rate information.

Long Lake and Raquette Lake outdoor adventures, Long Lake Department of Parks, Recreation and Tourism, P.O. Box 496, Long Lake (518-624-3077, longlake @telenet.net, www.longlake-ny. com). The Long Lake parks department publishes an excellent set of free brochures detailing the many hiking, fishing, cross-country skiing, snowmobiling, boating, birdwatching, and biking opportunities on Long and Raquette Lakes. Call or e-mail for the information before you leave home; the helpful brochures provide complete directions, lengthy descriptions of each trail and waterway, local rules and regulations, and descriptions of the flora and fauna you're likely to encounter.

Lowville Demonstration Area and Forestry Nature Trail,

Rte. 812, Lowville (315-376-3521). Managed by the New York State Department of Environmental Conservation, this 98-acre site is the former home of the Lowville Tree Nursery, which closed in 1971. Today you can follow a wonderful self-guided trail that winds past a fire tower, a picnic area, bluebird nest boxes, orchards, wetlands, and open fields. Dogs must be leashed. Insect repellant and long pants are recommended.

Macomb Reservation State Park,

201 Campsite Rd., Schuyler Falls (518-643-9952). Open from Memorial Day to Labor Day, this state park offers wooded campsites (see "Accommodations"), a pond, hiking, snowshoeing and cross-country skiing trails, play areas, and access to the Salmon River. Pet owners must show proof of vaccinations; dogs are not allowed at beach or picnic areas.

Oswegatchie Education Center,

Long Pond Rd., Croghan (315-346-1222; info@oswegatchie.org; www.oswegatchie.org). Owned by the Future Farmers of America, this 1,200-acre recreational and education center offers a summer camp for kids, conference facilities for family reunions and other gatherings, numerous environmental education programs, an annual Duck Derby and pancake breakfast, and tenting and hiking areas. Leashed dogs are welcome as long as their owners clean up after them.

Paws for the Cause Pet Walk and Talent Contest,

SPCA of Upstate New York, 454 Queensbury Ave., Queensbury (518-798-3500; info@spcauny.org; www.members.fortunecity.com/hospitaldog/spcauny). This fun event is just one of the regular fund-raising and awareness-raising gatherings hosted by the SPCA of Upstate New York, an organization which houses homeless animals and runs a low-cost spay-neuter program. Call or visit the web site for upcoming events in the Lake George area.

Point Au Roche State Park,

19 Camp Red Cloud Rd., Plattsburg (518-563-0369). Just up the road from Cumberland Bay State Park, this state refuge offers a boat launch, open fields and forests, a volleyball court and softball field, a nature center, and numerous trails for hiking, biking, and cross-country skiing. Dogs are not allowed at the beach or picnic areas and must be leashed; owners must provide proof of updated vaccinations.

Sacandaga River Pathway,

Speculator. Great for kids, this short but informative nature trail winds through the village of Speculator: Along the way, you'll encounter a picnic area and nearly 40 placards providing information about local history, flora, and fauna. The trail, which was created entirely by volunteers, starts at the baseball diamond in Speculator Municipal Park, which is located just east of scenic Rte. 30.

Saranac Lake Winter Carnival, Saranac Lake Area Chamber of Commerce (518-891-1990; 1-800-347-1992; www.saranaclake.com). Buy a button and enjoy outdoor festival events all around town at this annual winter party. Activities change from year to year, but you can expect lots of ski and inner tube races, concerts, snow and ice sculptures, food, and fireworks. Call the Chamber or visit the web site for this year's schedule.

Scenic drives. In the Lake George area, try Rte. 28 from Warrenburg to Indian Lake, Rte. 9 from Lake George to Chestertown (Prospect Mountain Veteran's Memorial Hwy.), or Rte. 9N from Lake Luzerne to Stony Creek. Rte. 86 in Wilmington (the Whiteface Mountain Veteran's Memorial Hwy.) is a 5-mile toll road with great mountain views. Rte. 30, known as the Adirondack Trail, spans a wilderness area that runs from Montreal, Canada all the way down to Amsterdam, New York, passing through many small towns and backcountry areas.

St. Regis Canoe Outfitters, Floodwood Rd. at Long Pond Portage, Lake Clear and 9 Dorsey St., Saranac Lake (518-891-8040 or 518-891-1838; info@ canoeoutfitters.com; www. canoeoutfitters.com). St. Regis's two locations are both very pet-friendly: Well-behaved dogs are welcome in the retail store in Saranac Lake and in all rental canoes. Dogs transported to put-in sites in the vans are charged the same rate as a person, and

are welcome to join the group on any custom-guided trips.

Tupper Lake Municipal Park, Demars Blvd. (Rte. 3), Tupper Lake. You'll run into many other dog walkers at this waterfront area offering a municipal park with playgrounds, ball fields, a scenic trail along the water, and picnic areas—the park also serves as home base for Tupper Lake's famous Woodsmen's Days, the Masonic Craft and Flea Market and the Championship Tinman Triathalon. Pooper-scooper bags are provided for pet owners. For more information, visit www. tupperlakeinfo.com.

Warren County Bikeway, Warrensburg. Easy to navigate, this meandering 12-mile path is paved and passes through forested areas from Lake George to the Glens Falls Feeder Canal trail. Don't miss the bike bridge recently built over Quaker Rd. Access free maps on-line at www.warrencountydpw.com/ parks-rec, or call the Warren County Department of Public Works at 518-623-2877.

Westport Marina on Lake Champlain, 20 Washington St., P.O. Box 410, Westport (518-962-4356; 1-800-626-0342; thecrew@ westportmarina.com; www. westportmarina.com). This pet-friendly, full-service marina provides powerboats for rent, available for individuals, families or large groups. The staff also leads narrated boat tours of the area. An on-site restaurant offers nourishment after a long day of boating: See "Quick Bites."

Whetstone Gulf State Park, Off Rte. 26, RD 2, Lowville (315-376-6630). The high point of Whetstone Gulf is the park's impressive 3-mile-long gorge with a waterfall and 350-foot-high stone walls. Visitors will also find shady campsites, a reservoir stocked with fish, and trails for hiking and cross-country skiing. Leashed pets are welcome as long as owners bring proof of vaccinations; dogs are not allowed in beach or picnic areas.

QUICK BITES

Adirondack Family Buffet, Rte. 28, Old Forge (315-369-6846). In addition to its dining room and eat-in buffet, this restaurant also has an extensive deli and bakery offering take-out orders of sandwiches, pizza, hot subs, salads, bagels, cold beverages and sweet treats. You'll find it right across the street from the Strand Theatre.

Brown Dog Deli, 3 Main St., Lake Placid (518-523-3036). Now, how could we leave this one out? Choose from specialty sandwiches like the Timone (avocado, tomato, onion, sprouts, cucumber and tomato chutney on a multi-grain roll) while admiring the canine-themed art on the walls, including woodcut prints by well-known Vermont artist Stephen Huneck.

Cate's Italian Garden, 7054 Main St., Bolton Landing (518-644-2041). This Mediterranean-influenced eatery offers pizza, pasta, and other Italian dishes for hungry travelers and locals. In warm weather, ample shady outdoor seating is available.

Eagle's Nest, 5496 Rte. 28, Eagle Bay (315-357-3898; nester@eaglesnestny; www.eaglesnestny.com). The owners of this restaurant and bar welcome leashed dogs to romp and play in their large lawn area; all of the menu items, including Philly cheese steaks, calzones, pizza, and finger foods, are available for takeout.

Fire and Ice Bar & Grill, 175 Canada St., Lake George (518-668-9673). Watch the world walk by on this busy street while relaxing in the outdoor seating area of this popular bar and restaurant. Diners can choose from BLTs, chicken salad and club sandwiches along with salads, hot dogs, burgers, onion rings and fried chicken baskets.

Firehouse Pizza and Restaurant, Main St., Westport (518-962-4878). Charming and friendly, this small restaurant serves up specialty pies, calzones, strombolis, salads, pasta dinners, hot and cold sandwiches, and appetizers like chicken wings, fried shrimp, and fried mushrooms. Your well-behaved pup is welcome at the shady outdoor seating area. Takeout is also available.

Island View Café, Rte. 9N, Hague (518-543-6367). Enjoy take-out sandwiches, burgers, ice cream, or breakfast, or relax with your meal at the café's outdoor patio area. The restaurant is easy to find in the center of town.

The Galley Restaurant and Bar, 20 Washington St., Westport (518-962-4899). Located at the Westport Marina (see "Out and About"), this lively eatery has seating available on an outdoor deck and famous barbecue dinners. The casual restaurant also has live music on weekends, an annual Lobsterfest each Labor Day, and lunch and dinner throughout the year.

Naked Turtle Holding Co., 1 Dock St., Plattsburgh (518-566-6200). Park your boat or your car at the Naked Turtle for fun casual dining. The large outdoor patio has umbrellas, great lake views and waiters serving up steak, chicken, seafood, sandwiches, chowder and salads. (Dock St. is located at the Boat Basin.)

Route 9N, Lake George Village. Always hopping, this downtown streetscape is filled with places to fill your belly. Numerous restaurants here offer outdoor seating in the summer and take-out service. If you're just hoping for a snack, you won't be disappointed: Taffy, popcorn, pizza, fudge, ice cream, candy, and other goodies are plentiful. You'll need the energy to tackle the other activities that the street has to offer, including arcades, wax museums, and other kid-friendly fare.

Tail-o-the-Pup BBQ, Sara Placid Rd., Ray Brook (518-891-5092). Located about 5 miles west of Lake Placid, this casual spot is so popular the staff can sometimes be seen directing traffic in and out. Outdoor tables are everywhere. Be prepared to get down-and-dirty with gooey barbecue favorites like ribs, hot dogs, burgers, and even lobster-and-clambakes.

HOT SPOTS FOR SPOT

Adilaska Kennels, P.O. Box 81, Long Lake (518-624-2050). Doggie guests at Adilaska have heated indoor/outdoor runs, an exercise area for fun socializing, and plenty of personal attention. Vet records are required at check-in; call for details and reservations.

Adirondack Park Pet Hospital, 150 River St., Saranac Lake (518-891-3260). In addition to providing emergency medical care (including house calls), this vet-erinary hospital also provides boarding services. Call for reservations and more information if you're planning to be in the area.

Bow Wow Boutique, 15 Fire Fly Lane, Westport (518-962-4353). Opened in 2001, this grooming business provides cuts, washes, and clips in a waterfront location on Lake Champlain.

Church Street Enterprises, Church St. Ext., Saranac Lake (518-891-5364). This store's main enterprise is pet supplies: Browse Eukanuba, Iams, Sun Seed and Blue Seal cat and dog foods, along with birdseed, reptile supplies, leashes, collars, and chew toys and treats.

Clendon Brook Pet Care Plus, 20 Cone Mountain Dr., Queensbury (518-792-0303 or 1-888-323-9111). Clendon Brook provides traditional overnight boarding as well as in-home pet-sitting and grooming services. The kennel facility has indoor/outdoor runs, a fenced-in play area, and a separate area for cats.

The Fish Bowl, 331 Cornelia, Plattsburgh (518-566-9700). Despite its fishy name, this shop stocks food and supplies for furred and feathered pets as well as for the scaled variety. Rawhide bones, cat treats, cages, popular brands of food, and squeaky toys are all available.

For Paws Trading Co., 3 Wilmington Rd., Lake Placid (518-523-0323). Passing through Lake Placid? This shop can help you stock up on food, accessories and supplies for dogs, cats, birds, rodents and reptiles. They'll even deliver supplies upon request.

Kibbles and Sits Pet Sitting Service, Lake Luzerne (518-260-4596; kibblesandsits@hotmail.com; www.kibblesandsits.com). Serving Lake Luzerne, Queensbury, Hadley, Corinth, Glens Falls and other nearby towns, Gail McLaughlin's pet care business provides visitation, walks, cuddles, feedings, a pet-taxi service, and other short-term services for local and visiting animals. Gail is also certified in American Red Cross Pet First Aid.

Schroon River Animal Hospital, 150 Schroon River Rd., Warrensburg (518-623-3181). A member of the American Animal Hospital Association, Schroon River provides overnight boarding, grooming services, and full healthcare services. For boarding, call ahead for a reservation.

Stone Edge Acres Kennels, Lake Luzerne (518-696-5016; info@stoneedgeacres.com; www.stoneedgeacres.com). Billed as "the Adirondacks' finest bed and biscuit," this kennel has indoor/outdoor runs for dogs, kitty condos, 10 acres of trails, a fenced-in exercise area, and optional grooming and training services. Visitors receive complete address information after making a reservation or requesting a tour.

Stony Acres Kennels, 3927 Main St., Rte. 9, Warrensburg (518-623-3046; 518-623-2100). Also the home of Bella Dog Grooming, this boarding and grooming facility offers dog-sitting and bathing services in addition to a gift shop with pet-related novelties and ceramics.

IN CASE OF EMERGENCY

Adirondack Park Pet Hospital
150 River St., Saranac Lake (518-891-3260)

Animal Clinic of Malone
185 W. Main St. (518-483-9080)

Champlain Valley Veterinary
408 Rte. 3, Plattsburgh (518-563-5551)

Chester Veterinary Hospital
Rte. 9, Chestertown (518-494-5116)

Countryside Veterinary Clinic
Utica Blvd., Lowville (315-376-6563)

Glens Falls Animal Hospital
66 Glenwood Ave. (518-792-6575)

Westport Veterinary Hospital
Pleasant St. (518-962-8228)

1,000
Islands
and Seaway

GUESTS AT CAPTAIN'S COVE MOTEL IN HENDERSON HARBOR ENJOY A DECK AND BOAT DOCKAGE.

1,000 Islands and Seaway

DOG-FRIENDLY RATING:

This is the road less traveled for New York vacationers. A daunting distance from New York City and somewhat overshadowed by its next-door neighbor, the Adirondacks, the 1,000 Islands and St. Lawrence Seaway region remains a fairly isolated, off-the-beaten path destination. Of course, that's exactly what makes it appealing for travelers hoping to avoid touristy attractions and crowds.

The 1,000 Islands' name is more than just a pretty-sounding moniker: There really are that many islands (and more) punctuating the St. Lawrence River. Not surprisingly, water is the focus of most activities here, from power-boating to kayaking, swimming, and freighter-watching. Canadian attractions lie just across the river, though you won't have to leave the U.S. to enjoy a wide variety of parks and natural areas. Accommodation choices are somewhat limited in this small region, and the problem is exacerbated for those traveling with an animal. The good news is, most of the area's pet-friendly hotels, motels,

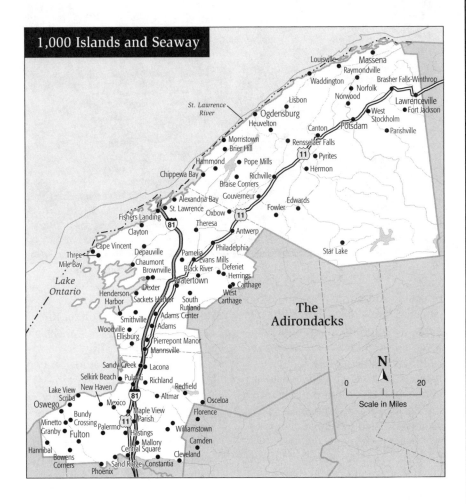

1,000 Islands and Seaway

and cottages are on the water (or close to it) and many provide docking facilities or access to a marina and boat rentals. For budget-conscious travelers, families, boaters, fishermen, and those just looking for a peaceful walk in the woods, the 1,000 Islands and Seaway corridor is worth a second look.

ACCOMMODATIONS

Hotels, Motels, Inns, Cottages, and B&Bs

Alexandria Bay
Ledges Resort Motel and Marina,
71 Anthony St., P.O. Box 245

(315-482-9334; 1-877-233-9334; ledges@thousandislands.com; www.thousandislands.com/ledges) $58–168 per night. Situated just across the river from the historic Boldt Castle, this 6-acre resort

THE FAMILY-SIZE "FLOATING CHALETS" AT LEDGES RESORT AND MARINA ARE ON THE DOCKS IN ALEXANDRIA BAY.

offers air-conditioned rooms, efficiencies, cable television, refrigerators, a swimming pool, a picnic area, and free morning coffee. Another unique feature is the resort's "floating chalets," 2-story-house rentals located directly on the dock. Boat dockage and rentals are also available. Dogs are welcome, though owners must pick up after them and can't leave them alone in the rooms.

Pine Tree Point Resort,

Anthony St. (1-888-746-3229; info@pinetreepointresort.com; www.1000islands.com/pinetree); $59–159 per night. The Pine Tree Point Resort is located on a 15-acre peninsula on the St. Lawrence River and offers water access, wooded trails, and 96 guest rooms in buildings like The Chalet, The Cove, The Evergreen, and The Spruce Lodge. Many have private balconies and either water or woods views. Well-behaved pets are welcome in designated rooms.

Boonville

Headwaters Motor Lodge, Rte. 12, P.O. Box 337 (315-942-4493); $45–75 per night. The Headwaters has 38 rooms on two floors; amenities include air-conditioning, free coffee in the lobby, laundry facilities, a game room, cable television, refrigerators in some rooms, and fax and copy services. There are no extra charges for pets, although they must be quiet enough to not disturb other guests.

Cape Vincent

Buccaneer Motel and B&B, 230 North Point St., P.O. Box 332 (315-654-2975); $60–185. Pets are welcome in the motel rooms at this animal-friendly motel and B&B located within walking distance of shops and restaurants. Overlooking the St. Lawrence River, the Buccaneer also offers a private marina and free docking for guests. The front lawn is a relaxing spot for watching sunsets or enjoying a picnic: Many of the local restaurants offer take-out service.

Dodgebay Farmhouse Bed & Breakfast, Rte. 12 East (315-654-2084); call for rate information. "This is a great place to walk and run," say Charlie and Sally, the innkeepers at this 1829 farmhouse. "We have paths through the fields, a pond, and a riverfront beach. It's very quiet and open for pets." Two cats live on premises, so visiting dogs must be feline-friendly and well behaved. Guests enjoy full daily breakfasts in the dining room.

Chaumont

Little T's Resort, 9474 Rte. 125 (315-649-2433); $47–55 per night or $235–325 per week. Fishermen and families are the most frequent guests at Little T's, a facility offering an 8-room motel, cable television, a playground, five cabins, RV campsites, a boat launch, and a bait shop. Open year-round, it's also a popular spot for ice fishing. Leashed dogs are welcome as long as owners provide proof of vaccinations and clean up any messes. Dockage is available for $5 per day or $30 per week.

Chippewa Bay

Sojourn Cottages and Boatel, 97 New Rd., P.O. Box 175 (315-324-5229; 1-800-480-9742; www.sojourncottages.com); $345–545 per week. These fully furnished, riverside cottages vary in size and can accommodate five to nine people. Each has a full kitchen, a screened-in patio, double beds and bunk beds, and a barbecue grill. Fishermen, boaters, and divers can enjoy on-site boat rentals and dockage for Sojourn guests. Dogs are welcome without extra charges.

Clayton

Calumet Motel, 617 Union St. (315-686-5201); $50–60 per night. Guests at this homey motel will find quilts, cable television, heat and air-conditioning, standard rooms and larger efficiencies, and a location that's close to French Creek, a public boat launch, and the downtown area. All eight units were recently remodeled. Dog owners pay an additional $5 per night.

Gananoque, Ontario, Canada

Houseboat Holidays, R.R. 3 (613-382-2842; www.gananoque.com/hhl); $750–1,850 per week (in Canadian dollars). This Canadian rental company provides visitors with a unique and fun way of exploring the 1,000 Islands area: in pontoon-style houseboats. The vessels vary in size and can accommodate 6 to 10 people with bathrooms, deck chairs, kitchens, water tanks, and other amenities. Dogs are welcome; management reserves the right to charge a $50 cleaning fee if necessary. The boats are docked at Clark's Marina, located about 11 miles from U.S./Canada border.

Hammond

Black Lake Marine Cottages, 3732 Country Rte. 6 (315-375-4953; droll@tsf.com; www.blacklakeny.com/blmc); $365–650 per week. Boaters, anglers, and families enjoy these lakefront cottages featuring two or three bedrooms with picnic tables, cable television, air-conditioning and heat, barbecue grills, coffeemakers and refrigerators, docking space, and boat rentals.

Well-behaved dogs are welcome with no extra fees.

Fisherman's Landing, 3490 Country Rte. 6 (315-375-4953; droll@tsf.com; www.black-lakeny.com/fishermanslanding); $365–600 per week. Managed by the Roll family, who also own the Black Lake Marine Cottages down the street, these six cottages provide screened-in porches, cable television, electric heat, microwaves and coffeemakers, and share access to a fish-cleaning house. Pets are welcome as long as they are cleaned-up after.

North Country Cottages and Campground, 2628 Country Rd. 6, Black Lake Rd. (315-375-4671; www.blacklakeny.com/northcountry); $395–425 per week for cottages. Each of these two-bedroom housekeeping cottages has an outdoor deck, a barbecue grill, a picnic table, cable television, and a full kitchen. Well-behaved dogs (sorry, no cats) are welcome with prior approval. (For more information on North Country's campground facilities, see "Campgrounds.")

Toti's Cottages, 2692 Country Rte. 6, Black Lake Rd. (315-375-4443; www.toticottages.com); $85–125 per night or $35–415 per week. These two- and three-bedroom cottages on Black Lake have full kitchens, full bathrooms, screened-in porches, barbecue grills, and picnic tables. Leashed, quiet pets are welcome as long as their owners clean up after them. Boat rentals and docking facilities are also available on-site.

Henderson Harbor

Captain's Cove Motel, 13179 Harbor Rd. (1-800-824-FISH; jonboy738@cs.com; www.jon-boy.com/motel); $57–70 per night. Captain John welcomes dogs to his "pet-friendly, biker-friendly, bicycle-friendly, and computer-friendly" motel located directly on Henderson Harbor. Guests here can enjoy air-conditioning, cable television with premium movie channels, free morning coffee, a sun deck, and free docking facilities.

Henchen Marina and Fishing Camp, P.O. Box 36 (315-938-5543; 1-888-848-3821; henchmen@imcnet.net); $55–77 per night. Accommodations at this casual fishing camp include housekeeping cabins with air-conditioning, one housekeeping trailer, an apartment, and several B&B/motel-style rooms. Well-behaved, housetrained dogs are welcome. "We've had a lot of people stay with animals, and we haven't had a problem yet," explains owner Diane Gamble.

West View Lodge and Marina, 13499 Country Rte. 123, P.O. Box 440 (315-938-5285; www.wvlodge.com); $60–70 per night. Open from May 1 through October 15, West View offers guest rooms with two double beds or one queen bed, air-conditioning, and cable television—some also have harbor views. Lodge guests can also take advantage of free boat dockage, a full marina, and an on-site restaurant offering daily breakfast buffets.

Massena

Bob's Motel, 228 Trippany Rd., Rte. 37 (315-769-9497); $40–55 per night. Guests at this 30-room motel can enjoy a 24-hour front desk, cable television, in-room movies, free daily continental breakfasts, air-conditioning, alarm clocks, refrigerators, and free local calls. Restaurants, a shopping mall, and a casino are all nearby. Well-mannered dogs are welcome for an additional $5 per night.

Econo Lodge, 15054 State Hwy. 37 (315-764-0246; 1-800-424-4777); $72–92. This 44-room budget hotel offers air-conditioning, in-room coffeemakers, a restaurant and lounge, cable television, a fitness center, copy and fax services, and a wake-up service. Well-behaved dogs are welcome in certain rooms for an additional $5 per pet, per night fee, though they cannot be left alone in the rooms at any time.

St. Lawrence Hotel, Main and W. Orvis Sts. (315-769-2441; 1-800-654-6212; www.st-lawrencehotel.com); $49–200 per night. This 4-story hotel has 123 recently renovated rooms and suites, cable television with premium movie channels, air-conditioning, business services, a concierge service, and an on-site restaurant and lounge. Dogs are allowed in designated rooms for an additional $10 per night.

Ogdensburg

Days Inn Ogdensburg, 1200 Paterson St. (315-393-3200); $59–69 per night. For an extra $7 per night, your dog is a welcome guest at this Days Inn offering cable television, a 24-hour front desk, wake-up calls, a restaurant and lounge, safe-deposit boxes, copy and fax services, on-site jogging and walking paths, exterior corridors, in-room coffeemakers, and ice and vending machines.

Ramada Inn River Resort, 119 W. River St. (1-888-298-2054); $59–149 per night. This waterfront hotel has a 24-hour front desk, an indoor swimming pool, a hot tub, fax and copy services, air-conditioning, cable television, safe deposit boxes, wake-up calls, ice and vending machines, and river views. Guests can also arrange sightseeing tours and other activities at the front desk. Dogs are welcome for an additional $10 per night.

Potsdam

Nomad Motel, 7575 Hwy. 11 (315-265-6700); $40–65 per night. The Nomad provides a 24-hour front desk, air-conditioning, free continental breakfasts, alarm clocks, cable television, in-room movies, refrigerators, and free local calls. Several restaurants are nearby, as are Clarkson and Saint Lawrence Universities and attractions like miniature golf, batting cages, and bumper cars. Dogs are allowed in designated rooms for an extra $10 per night.

Sackets Harbor

Ontario Place Hotel, 103 General Smith Dr., P.O. Box 540 (315-646-8000; 1-800-564-1812; hotel@imcnet.net; www.ontario-placehotel.com); $59–79 per night. Guests at Ontario Place choose from minisuites with refrigerators, microwaves, and whirlpool baths, or Sportsman and Family Suites that can each accommodate up to five people. Rooms are air conditioned with cable television and harbor or village views. Dogs are welcome in designated rooms for an extra $10 per night.

Waddington

Riverview of Waddington, 12508 Rte. 37 (315-388-5912); $55–65 per night. Well-behaved dogs are welcome in the 15 rooms and 5 cottages at Riverview, which offers satellite television, refrigerators, complimentary coffee and cold drinks, barbecue grills, and picnic tables. Fishermen enjoy the easy access to the St. Lawrence River. Animals cannot be left alone in the rooms at any time.

Watertown

Best Western Carriage House Inn, 300 Washington St. (315-782-8000); $59–130 per night. This Best Western hotel offers 150 recently renovated guest rooms, 10 suites, two restaurants, a lounge, an indoor swimming pool, a sauna, an exercise room, and banquet facilities. Well-behaved dogs are allowed in designated rooms for an additional $10 per night.

Ramada Watertown, 6300 Arsenal Rd. (315-788-0700); $60–95 per night. This 4-story hotel has 145 guest rooms, cable television with premium movie channels, pay-per-view movies, a restaurant and lounge, and an outdoor swimming pool. Downtown stores and restaurants are within walking distance, and Fort Drum is 8 miles away. Dog owners pay a $200 refundable deposit at check-in.

Campgrounds

Alexandria Bay
Keewaydin State Park Campground, Rte. 12 (315-482-3331; 1-800-456-CAMP); $13–17 per night. The 41 sites at Keewaydin are all designed to accommodate tents. Open from May through September, the waterfront campground has a swimming pool, a boat launch and dock, a playground, rest rooms with showers, handicap access, and picnic tables. Dogs are allowed with a leash and proof of vaccinations.

Boonville
Pixley Falls State Park Campground, Rte. 46 (315-942-4713); $10 per night. Admire the thundering waterfall and then relax at your streamside campsite at Pixley Falls, a relatively small and rustic campground. The park has just 22 sites for tents and trailers, along with picnic tables, walking trails, and plenty of opportunities for splashing around in streams and the Black River Canal. There are no rest rooms or showers on-site. Dogs are welcome, as long as you have proof of vaccinations and keep them on a leash.

Clayton
Burnham Point State Park Campground, 34075 Rte. 12 East (315-654-2324); $13–20 per night. Campers here can choose a wooded site or one overlooking the St. Lawrence River; 30 sites are designated for tenters and 18 have hook-ups for RVers. The campground also offers rest rooms with showers, a picnic

area, a boat dock and launch, a playground, and a dumping station. Dogs must be leashed and have proof of vaccinations. Animals are not allowed in beach or picnic areas.

Cedar Point State Park Campground, 36661 Cedar Point State Park Dr. (315-654-2522); $13–20 per night. This fairly large campground has 84 sites for tents and more than 80 sites for RVs. Leashed dogs are permitted with proof of vaccinations; amenities here include rest rooms with showers, a sandy beach, a marina with dockage, a boat launch, and a playground. Dogs are not allowed in beach or picnic areas. For more information on the park, see "Out and About."

Dexter
Black River Bay Campground, Foster Park Rd., P.O. Box 541 (315-639-3735); call for rate information. Leashed pets are welcome at Black River, a family campground featuring large sites for tents and RVs, water access with boat rentals, a playground, laundry facilities, planned activities, a camp store and tackle shop, rest rooms with showers, basketball, volleyball and horseshoe courts, and picnic tables.

Fishers Landing
Grass Point State Park Campground (315-686-4472; 1-800-845-CAMP); $16–22 per night. This state park campground has 77 sites for tents and RVs, a beach, a dumping station, a boat launch and boat rentals, rest

THE WATERFRONT CAMPGROUND AT CEDAR POINT STATE PARK IN CLAYTON

rooms with showers, a playground, and laundry facilities. Dogs must be on a leash no longer than 6 feet, are not permitted in beach or picnic areas, and must have proof of vaccinations.

Hammond
North Country Cottages and Campground, 2628 Country Rd. 6, Black Lake Rd. (315-375-4671; www.blacklakeny.com/ northcountry); $25 per night for campsites. Popular with fishermen, this family campground has sites for tents and RVs, laundry facilities, boat dockage and rentals, and rest rooms with showers. "Controlled" dogs are welcome, as long as owners clean up any messes. (For more information on North Country's housekeeping cottages, see Hotels, Motels, Inns and Bed & Breakfasts.)

Henderson Harbor
Association Island RV Resort and Marina, Snowshoe Rd., Association Island (315-938-5655; 866-223-2244; airvresort@msn. com; www.associationisland resort.com); $30–55 per night. Spread out on an island in Lake Ontario, this RV resort has 300 water-view sites, full hook-ups, laundry facilities, a swimming pool, and tennis courts. Two well-behaved dogs are welcome per site, as long as owners keep them leashed and provide proof of vaccinations. Certain breeds are not allowed; call for details.

Willows Campground, Rte. 3, P.O. Box 63 (315-938-5977; capp135@aol.com); call for rate information. For an extra $5 per night, outdoorsy dogs are welcome at Willows, a seasonal family campground on Lake Ontario. Visitors will find 30 sites for tenters and RVers (20 with full hook-ups), a dump station, five rental cottages, and a boat launch. Owners must provide proof of vaccinations and clean up after their animals.

Mary Island
Mary Island State Park Campground (315-482-2722; 1-800-456-CAMP); $10 per night. This remote campground, located just east of Wellesley Island, is accessible only by boat and has 12 tent sites, a dumping station, a dock, water views, basic rest rooms, picnic tables, barbecue grills, and a genuine escape from the busy outside world. Your dog is welcome to join you on a leash as long as you can provide proof of vaccinations.

Massena
Massena International Kampground, 84 CR 42 Extension (315-769-9483); $20–28 per night. Campers can choose from sunny or wooded tent and RV sites at this getaway offering laundry facilities, rest rooms with showers, a camp store, a playground, swimming and fishing opportunities, planned activities for kids and adults, and full hook-ups. Leashed dogs are welcome without extra fees, as long as owners agree to clean up after them.

Robert Moses State Park Campground, Barnhart Island Rd., P.O. Box 548 (315-769-8663); $13–20 per night. This large state park (see "Out and About" for more information) is open to RV and tent campers from May through Columbus Day; the campground has 168 sites, rest rooms with showers, a playground, a tennis court, a bathhouse, a marina with boat rentals, and a dump station. Dog owners must bring proof of vaccinations and keep animals leashed and out of picnic and beach areas.

Pulaski

Rainbow Shores Campsites and Motel, 348 Rainbow Shores Rd. (315-298-4407; www.pulaskiny.com/rainbowshores); $24 per night. Leashed pets are welcome at the campsites, though not the motel, at Rainbow Shores, a family-owned campground with 147 sites. Amenities include a private beach, a swimming pool, a playground, laundry facilities, a miniature golf course, planned activities, a pond, a basketball court, and a baseball field.

Selkirk Shores State Park Campground, Rte. 3 (315-298-5737); $13–20 per night for campsites and $66–100 per night for rental cabins. You can't beat the views at this campground, where sites sit on a ledge overlooking Lake Ontario. Amenities include sites for tents and trailers, a playground, rest rooms with showers, dumping stations, rental cabins, picnic tables, a boat launch, and trails for hiking and biking. (For more information on the park, see "Out and About.") Your pooch is welcome with proof of vaccinations and a leash no longer than 6 feet.

Redwood

Kring Point State Park Campground, 25950 Kring Point Rd. (315-482-2444; 1-800-456-CAMP); $13–22 per night. Some of the 107 sites at Kring Point have hook-ups for RVs; campers will also find eight camping cabins, picnic tables, barbecue grills, a playground, a beach, a dock, a boat launch, and rest rooms with showers. Your dog is welcome to join you on a leash if you can provide proof of vaccinations.

Waddington

Coles Creek State Park Campground, Rte. 37, P.O. Box 442 (315-388-5636); $13–22 per night. Campers at Coles Creek can choose from 228 sites, including some RV sites with hook-ups. Amenities include rest rooms with showers, a playground, hiking trails, picnic areas, and a nearby marina and boat launch. Dogs must be leashed, have proof of vaccinations, and are not allowed in picnic or beach areas. For more information on the park, see "Out and About."

Wellesley Island

DeWolf Point State Park Campground, Cross Island Rd. (315-482-2012; 1-800-456-CAMP); $13–40 per night. Cozy with just 28 tenting sites (no hook-ups), DeWolf Point also offers camping cabins, a waterfront area with a dock and boat launch, rest rooms with showers, picnic tables, and fire pits. Pets must be on a leash no longer than 6 feet and have proof of vaccinations. They are not allowed in beach or picnic areas. For more park information, see "Out and About."

Wellesley Island State Park Campground, Cross Island Rd. (315-482-2722; 1-800-456-CAMP); $13–20 per night. You can visit this large state campground from April through October to take advantage of more than 420 sites for tents and RVs (many with hook-ups), ten camping cabins, a beach, picnic tables and fire pits, a camp store, a playground, rest rooms with showers, a dock, a boat launch, and boat rentals. Dogs are not allowed in beach and picnic areas and must be leashed and have proof of vaccinations.

Homes, Cottages, and Cabins for Rent

Grindstone Island
Grindstone Island home
(781-449-6462; sandywilder@ rcn.com); $2,000 per week. "Dogs love swimming here and running on our 800 acres," says homeowner Sandy Wilder, who welcomes pets with a $500 security deposit. The five-bedroom house can accommodate up to 11 people with expansive views, two bathrooms, a living/dining area with a fireplace, a porch with an awning, a barbecue grill, a TV/VCR, a full kitchen, and a sailboat. The home is accessible by boat only; ask Sandy about nearby rentals if you don't have your own.

OUT AND ABOUT

Bay Drive-In Theatre, Bailey Settlement Rd., Alexandria Bay (315-482-3874); $5 per person. The staffers at this retro-cool drive-in theater not only welcome dogs, they also greet them with a doggie biscuit at the ticket window. It's a great way for you and your pooch to enjoy a night out with the latest movie releases and an extensive snack bar. Owners are asked to keep their canines quiet and leashed.

Boldt Castle, Wellesley Island (1-800-847-5263; info@boldt castle.com; www.boldtcastle. com). Many local boat-tour companies (including those listed here) provide trips to this historic castle and yacht house, which is only accessible by water. Leashed, friendly dogs are allowed on the grounds, stone walkways, and gardens, though not in the buildings. The castle is managed by the Thousand Islands Bridge Authority.

Burnham Point State Park, 34075 Rte. 12 East, Clayton (315-654-2324). At 12 acres, this relatively small park is comprised primarily of its campground (see "Accommodations"), a playground, several walking trails, docks, and a boat launch. It's a good launching spot for fishermen and boaters. No dog will be allowed in the park without a leash and proof of vaccinations.

Cedar Point State Park,
36661 Cedar Point State Park Dr., Clayton (315-654-2522). The campground is the primary attraction here (see "Accommodations"), but visitors also come to the 46-acre Cedar Point to launch their boats, watch the freighters float by, swim, have a picnic, or relax in the playground. Dogs are allowed, but must be on a leash no longer than 6 feet and are not allowed in picnic or beach areas. Owners must show proof of vaccinations.

Coles Creek State Park, Rte. 37, P.O. Box 442, Waddington (315-388-5636). Open from mid-May through October, this 1,800-acre park located on the south shore of Lake St. Lawrence has a campground (see "Accommodations"), a playground, walking trails, a marina with a store, and a boat launch. The river is used to generate electricity for the New York Power Authority. Fish and other wildlife, including deer, coyote, and songbirds, are plentiful. Pets must be on a leash no longer than 6 feet and are not allowed in picnic or beach areas.

DeWolf Point State Park, Cross Island Rd., Wellesley Island (315-482-2012). This park, located on an island off the coast of Alexandria Bay, is open from April to September with a boat launch, picnic areas, a campground (see "Accommodations"), boat dockage, and wonderful views. Dogs with proof of vacci-

nations are permitted, but they must be leashed and are not allowed in beach or picnic areas.

Empire Boat Lines, 4 Church St., Alexandria Bay (1-888-449-ALEX; empireboats@northweb.com; www.empireboat.com); $6–17 per person. "People-friendly" dogs are welcome on board Empire Boat Lines cruises and tours along the St. Lawrence River. Choose from the Two Nations Tour, which winds around the 1,000 Islands region with a stop at Boldt Castle, a one-hour Cherry Island Tour, or the simple Boldt Castle ferry service. Children six years old and younger ride for free.

Grass Point State Park, Fishers Landing (315-686-4472). Like so many parks in this scenic region, Grass Park is on the water, making it especially popular with fishermen and boaters. Well-behaved dogs are welcome on a leash, although they are not allowed in picnic or beach areas and must have proof of vaccinations. The park offers a campground (see "Accommodations"), a marina and boat launch, walking trails, and a playground.

Keewaydin State Park, Rte. 12, Alexandria Bay (315-482-3331). Stay overnight at the campground (see "Accommodations") or spend the day at Keewaydin boating, fishing, picnicking, cross-country skiing, hiking, exploring, swimming, or just watching the freighters go by on the St. Lawrence River. Your dog is not allowed in the picnic area, must have proof of vaccinations, and must be on a leash no longer than 6 feet.

Kring Point State Park, 25950 Kring Point Rd., Redwood (315-482-2444). Situated along the St. Lawrence River near Goose Bay, this park provides great views of the water and numerous islands. Park amenities include a boat launch, a dock site, a playground, and trails for walking, hiking, and cross-country skiing. Dogs are not allowed in beach or picnic areas, though they are welcome elsewhere in the park as long as they are leashed and have proof of vaccinations. For more information about the Kring Point campground facilities, see "Accommodations."

Lighthouse viewing. The 1,000 Islands region is dotted with historic and photogenic lighthouses, including these favorites: the Stony Point Lighthouse in Henderson Harbor, a 130-year-old structure with a 73-foot square tower; the Tibbetts Point Lighthouse in Cape Vincent, built in 1827 and still operated by the United States Coast Guard; the Horse Island Lighthouse in Sackets Harbor, another square-towered light and the site of two battles in the war of 1812; the Cape Vincent Light, a tiny, square lighthouse that was moved from a break wall to Market St.; and the Sunken Rock Lighthouse, located off the coast of Alexandria Bay.

Mary Island State Park, Mary Island (315-482-2722; 315-654-2522). Accessible only by water, the 12-acre Mary Island State

Park provides a secluded getaway for those hoping to relax, birdwatch, explore, enjoy a picnic, camp (see "Accommodations"), boat, or fish. The park is open to visitors from May to September. As at other state parks, your dog must be leashed and stay clear of picnic and beach areas. Mary Island is located just east of Wellesley Island.

Pixley Falls State Park, Rte. 46, Boonville (315-942-4713). If your pet is leashed with proof of vaccinations, he's welcome to join you at this day use and camping area located in the inland area north of Rome and south of Lowville. Most visitors come in search of the 50-foot waterfall, though you can also enjoy the picnic area, nature trails, fishing opportunities in trout streams, and campground (see "Accommodations"). One trail is also designated for cross-country skiing.

Robert Moses State Park, Barnhart Island Rd., P.O. Box 548, Massena (315-769-8663). One of the region's largest parks, Robert Moses comprises 2,322 acres in Massena as well as on nearby Barnhart Island. Visitors can reach the park by driving through a tunnel beneath the Eisenhower Lock. Once you arrive, you'll find a campground (see "Accommodations"), a natural history museum, trails for hiking and cross-country skiing, a marina with boat rentals, and wildlife such as beaver, fox, ducks, and several species of fish. Dogs must be kept on a leash no longer than 6 feet and are not allowed in picnic or

THE TIBBETS POINT LIGHTHOUSE IN CAPE VINCENT

beach areas. (Note: This park is sometimes called "Robert Moses State Park—Thousand Islands" to avoid confusion with another New York state park on Fire Island, also called "Robert Moses State Park." For more information on that park, see "Long Island.")

T. I. Adventures, 38714 Rte. 12E, Clayton (315-686-2000; jan@tiadventures.com; www.tiadventures.com). This instruction, tour, and rental company welcomes dogs in its rental kayaks. "We just had a couple who came in and rented a double sit-on-top kayak for three days and went camping with their dog out in the islands," says owner Jan Brabant. Rental time lengths range from a half-day ($25–45) up to five days ($112–177).

Uncle Sam Boat Tours, 45 James St., P.O. Box 398, Alexandria Bay (315-482-2611; 1-800-ALEX-BAY; unclesam@gisco.net; www.usboattours.com); $6.75-16 per person. Though not allowed on dinner and lunch cruises (for obvious reasons), your dog is welcome to join you on board Uncle Sam boats for other trips, including the Seaway Island Tour, the Twilight Hour Tour, and the Two-Nation Tour. You can also charter a boat for a private cruise.

Selkirk Shores State Park, Rte. 3, Pulaski (315-298-5737). Look out over Lake Ontario at this scenic park with a hiking and biking trails, fishing opportunities, a playground, scheduled recreational programs, picnic areas, and a campground (see "Accommodations"). Boaters will

appreciate the boat launch and marina pump-out station. Your dog is welcome to explore the grounds on a leash, as long as you have proof of vaccinations handy.

Surething Fishing Charters, 23683 Pines Park Dr., Alexandria Bay (1-800-432-4665; www.abay.com/surething). Well-behaved dogs with previous boating experience are welcome on board Captain John Slate's fishing charters in search of northern pike, walleye, muskellunge, and small and largemouth bass. The charter's traditional "shore lunch" includes the catch of the day, corn on the cob, potatoes, coffee and French toast.

Wellesley Island State Park, Cross Island Rd., Fineview/Wellesley Island (315-482-2722). Visit this 2,600-acre park to take advantage of great fishing opportunities, a marina with boat rentals, 8 miles of trails for biking and walking, more than 400 campsites (see "Accommodations"), a natural history museum, and a wide variety of wildlife species. This is the largest, and some would say most popular, park in the 1,000 Islands region. Your dog can join you if he has a leash and proof of vaccinations, although not in picnic or beach areas. The park is accessible by car.

Winona Forest Recreation Area, Tug Hill Plateau, Jefferson County. This 9,000-acre public forest is located about halfway between Watertown and Syracuse, just east of Mannsville.

Popular activities here include snowmobiling, hiking, cross-country skiing, horseback riding, dog sledding, and mountain biking. For more information on these or other activities, contact the South Jefferson Chamber of Commerce (315-232-4215) or the Oswego County Department of Promotion and Tourism (1-800-596-3200). Parking areas are available on County Rtes. 13, 50, 90, and 11.

QUICK BITES

Admiral's Inn, James St., Alexandria Bay (315-482-2781). The patio seating area here offers shade and sustenance. Your pooch can sit just outside on the sidewalk; or, if you're lucky enough to get a table next to the rowboat (yes, a real rowboat), your dog can sit inside the boat itself. Choose from sandwiches, salads, seafood, dinners, appetizers, and burgers.

Barracks Inn, Madison Barracks, Sackets Harbor (315-646-2376). Overlooking the bay and harbor, this scenic and historic building has served as an Army post, a hospital, a recruiting station, and now a restaurant offering lunch, dinner, and an outside seating area with great views of the water. (Even if you're not hungry, the 1816 building and grounds are worth a visit.)

Captain Jack's, Ferry Dock, Market St., Cape Vincent (315-654-3333). Locals recommend this casual family restaurant with an outdoor seating area, located at the Wolfe Island ferry dock. Choose from menu items such as sandwiches, seafood, pasta, and burgers.

Castle Dairy Bar & Grill, 750 James St., Clayton (315-686-2753). A casual and family-friendly spot, the Castle offers take-out treats like hard and soft ice cream, hot dogs, hamburgers, chicken fingers, and fried seafood.

Common Grounds, 53 Willow St., Massena (315-769-2183). This gourmet coffee shop has a drive-thru and take-out service with sandwiches, baked goods, soups, and cold drinks, along with a wide variety of fresh-ground coffees, espressos, and cappuccinos.

Harvest Moon Café, 109 Main St., Canton (315-386-5757). Place an order to go from this cute café and walk across the street for a picnic at the Village Park. Menu items include hot and cold sandwiches, breakfast specials, wraps, pizza, calzones, and pasta. The Harvest Moon also delivers.

Rudy's of Lake Ontario, Washington Blvd., Oswego (315-343-2671). For more than 55 years, this seasonal roadside stand/restaurant has been serving up generous portions of Coney dogs, steak sandwiches, French fries, fried seafood, burgers, coleslaw, ice cream, and Rudy's famous hot sauce. Place your order at the counter and then hop outside to enjoy your meal with a great view of the lake.

Scooter's Original Pizza Pie, 62 Church St., Alexandria Bay

(315-482-4821). Packing a picnic lunch? Stop by Scooter's for hot and cold deli sandwiches, soda and beer, chicken wings, calzones, pizza, and a variety of grocery items. Eat in, take out, or call for delivery to your hotel room.

HOT SPOTS FOR SPOT

A Pawsitive Experience, Schultz Rd., Lake View (716-627-9234; k9taxi@earthlink.net; www. 222.pawsitive.biz). Susan Ferry runs this business offering doggie daycare in a fenced-in acre, a "canine bed & breakfast" overnight boarding service, canine massage, doggie birthday parties, and a pet-taxi service to take your dog to the veterinarian's office, the groomer, or anywhere else he might need to go.

Best Friends Doggie Day Spa, 531 Eastern Blvd., Watertown (315-782-3403). At this homey facility, your pooch can be pampered with grooming services, massage, doggie daycare, and boarding in the owner's home. Four-legged visitors can have the run of a 900-square-foot outdoor play area. There's also a self-service dog wash for those who would prefer to do the dirty work themselves.

Blue Seal Feeds, 200 Willow St., Watertown (315-788-0030). Blue Seal has been producing premium animal foods for more than 130 years; this retail center car-

ries the brand for puppies, senior dogs, active dogs, and cats, as well as foods for other pets such as birds, rabbits, horses, and hamsters.

Dog & Biscuit, 31 Nightingale Ave., Massena (315-769-6759). Barbara L.Wing runs this pet-sitting service from her home; while you're at dinner, enjoying a movie, or tending to an emergency, she can keep Fido entertained, exercised, and well fed. Be sure to call ahead for reservations.

Four Paws Pet Motel, 372 East Kirby, Dexter (315-639-6421). This large, friendly facility has been offering overnight boarding, doggie daycare, grooming, and obedience training for more than 34 years. Dogs stay in dry indoor kennels and get access to outdoor runs several times a day. Call in advance for reservations.

Grace Farms Dog Camp, 78 Gunther Rd., Central Square (315-668-3318; www.angelfire. com/ny5/gracefarms0/dogcamp). Located east of Oswego and north of Syracuse, this doggie getaway offers a great kennel alternative. While you're away, your pooch can enjoy interaction with other dogs, agility and obedience training, walks, swims, grooming, and plenty of "cuddle care." The camp is designed for long-term stays only (21 days or more), although you can also stop by for private or group obedience and agility training with award-winning trainer Mary Fowler.

Houghton Farm Supply, 15194 Rte. 193, Pierrepont Manor (315-465-5311). In addition to farm products for people and livestock, this store also sells foods, supplies, and other necessities for dogs and cats.

Maple Ridge Kennels, Pierrepont Rd., Rte. 68, Canton (315-386-3796). A member of the American Boarding Kennel Association, Maple Ridge provides indoor/outdoor runs for dogs and a separate boarding area for cats; reservations are suggested.

Pampered Pets Grooming, 3370 Elm St., Port Leyden (315-348-6669). Located on the border of the Adirondacks and 1,000 Islands regions, this convenient grooming shop can help your pet freshen up with a nail clip or shampoo.

Tina's Pet Palace and Supplies, 35555 Rte. 46, Theresa (315-628-0000). Tina's offers all the pet basics, like food, toys, rawhides, and cages, as well as overnight boarding services for dogs, cats, birds, and other animals. The store's staff also provides animal-themed kids' parties with small animals like guinea pigs and hamsters.

IN CASE OF EMERGENCY

Countryside Veterinary Clinic
7364 Utica Blvd., Lowville (315-376-6563)

North Country Veterinary Services
4592 Rte. 11, Pulaski (315-298-5141)

Seaway Veterinary Services
36005 Rte. 12E, Cape Vincent (315-654-2400)

St. Lawrence Valley Veterinary Clinic
46 Willow St., Massena (315-769-5151)

Thousand Island Animal Hospital
42539 Rte. 12, Alexandria Bay (315-686-5080)

Watertown Animal Hospital
1445 Washington St. (315-788-1711)

The Central-Leather-stocking Region

THE SIGN ON THE HISTORIC BLENHEIM COVERED BRIDGE READS: "$5.00 FINE TO RIDE OR DRIVE THIS BRIDGE FASTER THAN A WALK."

The Central-Leatherstocking Region

DOG-FRIENDLY RATING: 🦴 🦴 🦴

The Central-Leatherstocking region is picturesque, enchanting, and filled with wonderful attractions. It is not, however, particularly welcoming for four-legged travelers. Gorgeous inns and B&Bs are everywhere, housed in restored mansions, graceful Victorians, cute cottages, and Italianate farmhouses, but alas—hardly any allow dogs as guests. (Children are often a hard sell, too.) "I'd say about 95 percent of the B&Bs here don't allow pets," explains one local innkeeper. You might expect better luck at motels and efficiencies, but even most of these seem to adhere to strict "no pets" policies; the same can be said of the local guest houses and apartments. In addition, many of the region's most popular attractions, including the Baseball Hall of Fame, the Boxing Hall of Fame, and numerous museums, opera houses, and theaters, are obviously off-limits to animals.

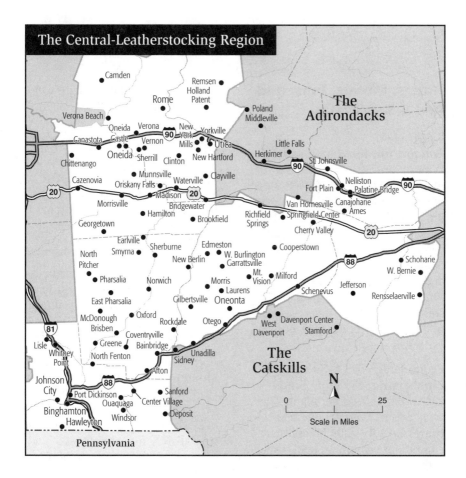

The Central-Leatherstocking Region

But there is good news, too: Even if you and Rover can't stroll among the artifacts of baseball's greats in Cooperstown, you can still spend a fruitful afternoon walking along the village's charming, tree-lined streets, admiring the architecture and catching a peek of Doubleday Field. In the town of Morris, a canine-centered spot known as Glen Highland Farm welcomes you and your pet for an afternoon visit or a week at its Camp Border Collie and Friends. Dogs aren't allowed inside the region's impressive Howe Caverns, but the site does have a short-term kennel where your pooch can relax while you explore the underground tunnels. In Montgomery County, you can browse Amish crafts and learn about the area's Native American heritage. The region's state parks are filled with dog-friendly lakes, picnic areas, and campgrounds. And the Central-Leatherstocking region's innkeepers that allow pets do so with open arms, providing you and your dog with a warm home-away-from-home in this rural, quaint, and unique section of New York.

ACCOMMODATIONS

Hotels, Motels, Inns, and Bed & Breakfasts

Binghamton

Comfort Inn Binghamton, 1156 Upper Front St (607-722-5353; macomfy@aol.com); $59–199 per night. Amenities at this Comfort Inn include 67 smoking and non-smoking rooms, air-conditioning, complimentary daily breakfasts, banquet and conference facilities, and a 24-hour front desk. Kitchenettes are also available in some rooms. Dogs are welcome in designated rooms with no extra fees.

Econo Lodge Inn & Suites Binghamton, 650 Front St (607-724-1341); $49–79 per night. The Binghamton Econo Lodge offers complimentary daily breakfasts, an outdoor swimming pool, cable television, air-conditioning, senior discounts, conference facilities, laundry facilities, a 24-hour front desk, and hot tubs in some rooms. Canine guests are welcome for an additional $5 per night.

Holiday Inn Arena, 28 Hawley St. (607-722-1212); $79–149 per night. Pets are welcome at the Central-Leatherstocking Holiday Inn locations in Binghamton, New Hartford, and Oneonta; the chain's typical amenities include standard rooms and larger suites, restaurants and lounges, fitness centers, business services, laundry facilities, wake-up calls, air-conditioning, and cable television. At the Binghamton

site, companion animals are welcome for an extra $25 per night.

Mansion on Asbury Court, 9 Asbury Court (607-772-2959; info@mansiononasbury.com; www.mansiononasbury.com); $75–105 per night. Guests at this restored Queen Anne Victorian can step back in time and enjoy authentic detailing, antique furnishings and oil paintings, 21 rooms, 11 fireplaces, and meticulously maintained flower gardens. The rates include a full breakfast. Dogs weighing less than 50 pounds are welcome for an additional $15 per night.

Motel 6 Binghamton, 1012 Upper Front St. (607-771-0400); $39–59 per night. Pets are welcome guests in all Motel 6 locations. Amenities vary slightly from site to site, but guests can typically expect to find air-conditioning, cable television with premium movie channels, smoking and nonsmoking rooms, complimentary coffee, a "Kids Stay Free" program, and a convenient location.

Super 8 Motel Front Street, 650 Old Front St. (607-773-8111); $49–105 per night). Super 8 Motel facilities include air-conditioning, smoking and nonsmoking rooms, cable television, and in-room movies and video games. Outdoor swimming pools, kitchenettes, and VCRs are also available at some locations. Dogs are welcome at the Front St. location; pet owners pay a $35 security deposit if paying with cash, but pay no extra fees when using a credit card.

Super 8 Motel Upper Court Street, Upper Court St., Rte. 11 (607-775-3443); $59–79 per night. Guests with dogs at the Upper Court St. site must use a credit card at check-in. If paying in cash, an extra security deposit will be required. (See Super 8 Binghamton listing above.)

Bridgewater
Lake Chalet Motel and Campground, Rte. 8, P.O. Box 22 (315-822-6074; lakechalet@go campingamerica.com; www.lake chalet.com); $49–89 per night in motel rooms. Well-behaved pets are welcome in the Lake Chalet motel, where guests will find a 24-hour front desk, cable television, express checkout services, free daily newspapers, and in-room coffeemakers, refrigerators, and irons and ironing boards. Dog owners must use a leash and clean up after their animals. For more information on the Lake Chalet's camping facilities, see the listing under "Campgrounds."

Canastota
Days Inn Canastota, Rte. 13, Canastota-North Peterboro (315-697-3309); $49–199 per night. This economy hotel provides guests with free continental breakfasts, interior corridors, safe-deposit boxes, a 24-hour front desk, alarm clocks, cable television, air-conditioning, and in-room hair dryers. The Days Inn caters to both business and leisure travelers. There is no extra charge for dogs, although animal owners are required to use a credit card (not cash) at check-in.

Cooperstown
Amanda's Cottage Bed & Breakfast, 37 Walnut St. (607-547-8151 in winter; 607-547-5533 in summer; jonesp2@telenet.net; www.thecottagebandb.bizland. com); $125–200 per night. Guests at Amanda's Cottage choose from one large room with two double beds, a smaller room with one queen bed, or a combination of the two to form a suite. The antique cottage, which is located in a residential neighborhood, also offers flower gardens, antiques, and quilts; the rates include a full breakfast. Children and dogs are welcome with prior approval.

Countryside Lodging, Beaver Meadow Rd. (607-547-2569; cntryent@aol.com; www.coun-trysidelodging.com); $39–84 per night or $700–1,100 per week. Rooms here have names that play on the area's baseball themes: Guests can choose from the Double Play, the Rookie's Corner, and the Dugout Suite, among others. (During peak season, from mid-June to the end of August, the inn offers weekly rentals only.) Some rooms are motel-style with two double beds, while others are suites with living areas. All have private entrances, cable television with premium movie channels, and access to a picnic area with barbecue grills. Pets are welcome.

Frog Hollow Inn, 75 Pioneer St. (607-547-6257; froghollowinn@aol.com; www.froghollowinn.com); $95–135 per night. Joey, the resident pooch at Frog Hollow, will be happy to show you and your

FROG HOLLOW INN'S RESIDENT DOG, JOEY, EAGERLY WAITS TO WELCOME THE NEXT GUEST.

canine friend around this lovingly restored 1812 Federal-style home with off-street parking, large guest rooms, private baths, a parlor, antiques, air-conditioning, and cable television. (For larger groups, the Cal Ripken Room can be combined with the Wye Oak Room to form a suite.) A daily breakfast is served each morning in the dining room. The Baseball Hall of Fame, shops, eateries, and other attractions are located within walking distance. Well-behaved dogs are welcome for an extra $10 per night, as long as they are not left alone in the rooms.

Clinton
The Hedges, 180 Sanford Ave. (315-853-3031; 1-800-883-5883; info@hedgesbb.com; www. hedgesbb.com); $120 per night and higher. This upscale bed & breakfast offers the Federal Suite, with a four-poster bed and marble bathroom, the Hamilton Suite, with two bedrooms and a sitting area, and the Country Cottage Suite, which has a full

kitchen and living room. Outside, guests can enjoy a swimming pool, a patio, and formal gardens. Dogs are welcome with a refundable $100 security deposit.

East Herkimer
Glen Ridge Motel, 5571 State Rte. 5 (315-866-4149; glenridge-motel@yahoo.com; www.glen-ridgemotel.com); call for rate information. This plain-and-simple motel offers cable television, telephones, parking in front of your door, and a location that's convenient to marinas, golf courses, historic sites, and Cooperstown attractions (30 minutes away). Glen Ridge is open year-round. Most dogs are welcome with a security deposit; call for details.

East Springfield
Meadowlark Inn, Hwy. 20 (607-264-3308; meadowlark@ capital.net; www.cooperstown-chamber.org/meadowlark); call for rate information. "Our experience with cat and doggie guests has been great," says Meadowlark innkeeper Joy White. "We think

they're cute, loving, and fun."
Each room has two queen beds, a
private bath, a refrigerator, a
microwave, and cable television.
Owners are asked to walk animals
in the meadow area and not leave
them unattended in the rooms.

Gilboa
Golden Acres Farm & Ranch,
South Gilboa Rd. (607-588-7329;
1-800-252-7787; farmresort@
aol.com; www.goldenacres.com);
$125–210 per night or $490–715
per week for adults; children pay
reduced rates. "We cater strictly
to families with young children,"
explains Golden Acres proprietor
Jerry Gauthier. "It's my personal
opinion that pets are part of the
family." Most guests are Jewish,
with a varying level of obser-
vance from Reform to Orthodox.
Dogs are welcome in rooms and
suites for an extra $10 per night
or $60 per week. The massive
400-acre resort has trails, miniature golf, three swimming pools,
a stocked fishing lake, baby-
sitting services, farm animals,
daily scheduled activities, all-you-
can-eat menus, boats, horseback
riding, and numerous other activities and amenities designed to
keep kids and adults busy.

Greene
Inn at Serenity Farms,
386 Pollard Rd. (607-656-4659;
nyserenity@aol.com; www.
geocities.com/serenityofny/
serenity); $69–89 per night.
Situated on 100 forested and
open acres, this country B&B provides its guests with a swimming
pool, a hot tub, a stocked fishing
pond, a recreation room, fireplaces, and trails for hiking,

snowmobiling, and cross-country
skiing. Some rooms have private
baths, and the rates include a full
breakfast. Your pet is welcome—
the property also has kennels and
a dog run.

Herkimer
Herkimer Motel, Marginal Rd.
(877-656-6835; herkmotl@
mybizz.net; www.herkimermo-
tel.com); $68–125 per night.
Located at Exit 30 on the N.Y.
Thruway, the Herkimer Motel has
been run by the same family for
more than 40 years. Guests can
enjoy an outdoor swimming pool,
cable television with premium
movie channels, a fitness room,
laundry facilities, and free daily
continental breakfasts. Well-
behaved dogs are welcome, but
they cannot be left alone in the
rooms.

Johnson City
Best Western of Johnson City,
569 Harry L Dr. (607-729-9194;
1-800-528-1234; bestwesternjc@
juno.com); $49–79 per night. The
Best Western offers all the amenities of a full-service hotel, including an indoor swimming pool, a
hot tub, a fitness center, banquet
and conference facilities, cable
television, and free daily breakfasts. A shopping mall and
restaurants are within walking
distance. Dogs are allowed in
smoking rooms for an additional
$8 per night.

**Red Roof Inn
Binghamton–Johnson City,**
590 Fairview St. (607-729-8940);
$39–56 per night. The Red Roof
Inn chain offers clean, affordable
lodgings with exterior corridors,

cable television with premium movie channels, pay-per-view movies, vending machines, a "Kids Stay Free" program, and free locals calls. "Small" pets are welcome at all locations, as long as they are not left alone in the rooms.

Johnstown
Holiday Inn Johnstown, 308 North Comrie Ave. (518-762-4686); $69–99 per night. This full-service hotel offers a restaurant and lounge, an outdoor swimming pool, laundry facilities, smoking and nonsmoking rooms, cable television with in-room movies, a 24-hour front desk, banquet rooms, air-conditioning, and in-room irons, ironing boards, coffeemakers, and hair dryers. Your dog will be welcomed without extra fees.

Little Falls
Best Western Little Falls Motor Inn, 20 Albany St. (315-823-4954); $49–99 per night. Renovated in 1997, the Little Falls Motor Inn offers air-conditioning, cable television, 56 smoking and nonsmoking rooms, a dining room, and a banquet hall. "Small and medium-sized dogs" are welcome (call to see if yours qualifies) for an extra $10 per night.

Milford
Country Meadow Inn, 116 North Main St., Rte. 28, P.O. Box 355 (607-286-9496; leeharry@ capital.net; www.cooperstown chamber.org/countrymeadow inn); $85–170 per night or $500–850 per week. Start your day at Country Meadow with a full country breakfast, then head into Cooperstown or nearby state parks and colleges for adventures. The rooms at this 200-year-old farmhouse have air-conditioning and comfortable furnishings. Pets are welcome with prior approval; dogs can stay with owners in the room or in the kennels out back.

Morris
Camp Border Collie and Friends, Glen Highland Farm, 217 Pegg Rd. (607-263-5415; sweetbcrescue@citlink.net; www.glenhighlandfarm.com); $950 per week. All breeds of dogs and people are welcome at this one-week getaway camp designed with canines in mind. Guests can camp at tent and RV sites ($10–30 per night) or stay at nearby hotels, then enjoy daily activities like agility and obedience training, campfires, trail walks, swimming, fishing, Frisbee contests, guest-speaker lectures, and carefree explorations of 175 undeveloped acres. All meals are included in the camp rate. The camp is held at Glen Highland Farm, a Border collie rescue center and sanctuary (see "Out and About").

New Hartford
Holiday Inn Utica–New Hartford, 1777 Burrstone Rd. (315-797-2131); $89–159. Dogs weighing less than 100 pounds are welcome at this Holiday Inn location with a refundable security deposit of $35. (See listing under Binghamton.)

Valley Brook Motel, 100 Seneca Tpk. (315-732-2127); $45–59 per night. Visitors to the 40-room Valley Brook Motel will find a 24-hour front desk, cable television, air-conditioning, smoking and smoking rooms, and in-room refrigerators and microwaves. A restaurant and lounge are also on-site. "Small" dogs (call to see if yours qualifies) are welcome without additional charges.

North Norwich
A Wee Bit of Bonnie Scotland Bed & Breakfast, 7052 State Hwy. Rte. 12 (607-336-8329; www.aweebitofscotland.net); $95 per night. Innkeeper Linda Hartwick, who was born and raised in Edinburgh, brings a genuine Scottish hospitality to this fully renovated B&B with air-conditioning, cable television, and full country breakfasts. Children and pets are always welcome. A percentage of lodging rates are donated to the Glen Highland Farm Border collie rescue facility (see "Out and About").

Norwich
Howard Johnson Hotel Norwich, 75 North Broad St. (607-334-2200); $69–169 per night. All rooms at this Howard Johnson Hotel have cable television with premium movie channels, coffeemakers, hair dryers, irons, and ironing boards. Guests can also take advantage of an indoor swimming pool, business services, and free daily coffee. "Small" dogs (call to see if yours qualifies) are welcome for an additional $10 per night.

Oneonta
Budget Inn Motel, 5059 State Hwy. 23 (607-432-5301); $59–149 per night. Guests choose from smoking and nonsmoking rooms at this Budget Inn, which offers air-conditioning, cable television,

a 24-hour front desk, free daily coffee, and discounts for children. Pets are allowed in two designated rooms for an extra $10 per night.

Celtic Motel, 112 Oneida St. (607-432-0860); $89–125 per night. The 29 rooms at the Celtic Motel have air-conditioning, cable television, and Internet access; hot tubs, kitchenettes, and VCRs are also available in some rooms. Outside, a grassy area is ideal for dog walks and romping. Children's rates are discounted, and most credit cards are accepted. Canine guests are welcome.

Holiday Inn Oneonta-Cooperstown, Rte. 23 Southside (607-433-2250); $69–199 per night. (See listing under Binghamton.)

Super 8 Motel Oneonta, 4973 State Hwy. 23, Oneonta (607-432-9505); $59–139 per night. Well-behaved pets are welcome at this Super 8 as long as they are not left unattended in the rooms. (See listing under Binghamton.)

Richfield Springs
Lake House Restaurant Bed & Breakfast, East Lake Rd. (315-858-2058; 1-877-815-0699; lakehouse1843@netscape.net; www.lakehouse-cooperstown.com); $75–300 per night. Accommodations at the Lake House vary in size and style, ranging from standard-size rooms to 2-story suites large enough to accommodate a family. "We are a sled-dog family with a group of Siberian/Alaskan huskies living here with us," explains innkeeper Chris Corrigan. Guest canines are welcome with prior approval as

long as they get along with the resident dogs, stay relatively quiet, and stay off the furniture.

Rome

American Heritage Motor Inn, 799 Lower Lawrence St. (315-339-3610); $49–69 per night. This 27-room motel has air-conditioning, smoking and nonsmoking rooms, cable television, and a convenient location. Senior discounts are available, and most credit cards are accepted. Canine guests are welcome without extra charges.

Paul Revere Lodge, 7900 Turin Rd. (315-336-1775; 1-800-765-7251; www.thebeeches.com); $66–165 per night. The Paul Revere is located on 52 quiet acres with a French-country décor; some rooms also have whirlpool suites. Adjoining the motor lodge is The Beeches Restaurant, an English manor-style building with dining rooms, breakfast menus, and private meeting rooms. Dogs are welcome for an additional $5 per night.

Quality Inn Rome, 200 South James St. at Erie Blvd. (315-336-4300); $69–119 per night. The Rome Quality Inn location has exterior corridors, a swimming pool, smoking and nonsmoking rooms, and in-room coffeemakers, hair dryers, irons and ironing boards. Visitors can also take advantage of free local calls and free daily newspapers. Your dog is a welcome guest for an extra $25 per night.

Schoharie

Old Wesley Inn, 537 Barton Rd. (518-295-7640; www.oldwesley .com); $65–105 per night. This charming and historic farmhouse B&B has a covered front porch, expansive views of the surrounding 75 acres, two parlors, and a dining room and sunroom where breakfast is served. Howe Caverns and museums are nearby, and Cooperstown is about 45 minutes away. Dogs are sometimes allowed, depending on the season and the occupancy level of the inn; call for details.

Utica

Best Western Gateway Adirondack Inn, 175 North Genesee St. (315-732-4121); $89–129 per night. Your dog is welcome without extra charges at the Gateway Adirondack Inn, a full-service hotel with a fitness center, a gift shop, a game room, laundry facilities and a 24-hour front desk. All rooms have cable television, alarm clocks, coffeemakers, hair dryers, and irons and ironing boards. Suites are also available.

Motel 6, Utica, 150 North Genesee St. (315-797-8743); $48–60 per night. (See listing under Binghamton.)

Radisson Hotel Utica Center, 200 Genesee St. (315-797-8010; www.radisson.com/uticany); $89–129 per night. The 158 guest rooms at the Radisson come equipped with coffeemakers, voice mail, hair dryers, irons, and ironing boards. Other amenities include a restaurant and lounge, a fitness center, an indoor swimming pool and hot tub, a sauna, and banquet facilities. Dogs are welcome with a $10 per-night fee and a $30 refundable security deposit.

Red Roof Inn Utica, 20 Weaver St. (315-724-7128); $44–97 per night. (See listing under Johnson City.)

Super 8 Motel Utica, 309 North Genesee St. (315-797-0964); $59–149 per night. Dogs are welcome at the Utica Super 8 for an extra $10 per night. (See listing under Binghamton.)

Vestal
Residence Inn by Marriott–Binghamton University, 4610 Vestal Pkwy. East (607-770-8500; 1-800-331-3131; binghamtonsales@ innkeepershospitality.com); $69–119 per night. Designed primarily for long-term stays, the suites at Residence Inn have full kitchens, separate living and sleeping areas, cable television, in-room movies, and private entrances. Guests can also enjoy an outdoor swimming pool, a hot tub, and complimentary daily breakfasts. Dogs are welcome for an extra $100 per stay.

Westmoreland
Carriage Motor Inn, Rte. 233 North (315-853-3561); $33–65 per night. Guests at the Carriage Motor Inn enjoy free daily continental breakfasts, free local calls, and free coffee in the lobby. Other amenities include safe-deposit boxes, cable television, smoking and nonsmoking rooms, and refrigerators in some rooms. Weekly rates are also available. Dogs are welcome for an additional $5 per night.

Campgrounds

Bainbridge
Oquaga Creek State Park Campground, Beech Hill Rd. (607-467-4160); $13 per night. Choose from 100 sites for tents and trailers at Oquaga Creek, a state park campground with picnic tables, a playground, nature trails, rest rooms with showers, dumping stations, pavilions, and scheduled recreational programs. Many areas are wheelchair accessible, as well. (For more information about the park, see "Out and About"). Leashed dogs are welcome with proof of vaccinations.

Bridgewater
Lake Chalet Motel and Campground, Rte. 8, P.O. Box 22 (315-822-6074; lakechalet@ gocampingamerica.com; www.lakechalet.com); call for rate information. The Lake Chalet Campground is located on a private 6-acre lake with 50 sites for tents and RVs, rest rooms with showers, laundry facilities, a camp store, sports courts, cabin rentals, a beach, and paddleboats. Dogs must be quiet, leashed and cleaned-up after. For more information on the Lake Chalet Motel facilities, see the listing under "Hotels, Motels, Inns, and Bed & Breakfasts."

Cazenovia
Chittenango Falls State Park Campground, 2300 Rathbun Rd., Rte. 13 (315-655-9620); $13 per night. Campers can enjoy viewing this park's impressive waterfall at their leisure after spending the night in one of 24 sites for tents and trailers. The facilities

here are not extensive, but include rest rooms with showers, public telephones, and picnic tables. Your dog can join the fun, as long as you bring along proof of vaccinations and a leash. See "Out and About" for more information about the park.

Chenango Forks
Chenango Valley State Park Campground, 153 State Park Rd. (607-648-5251); $13–16 per night for campsites and $58–66 per night for cabins. Campers at Chenango Valley will find more than 200 sites for tents and trailers, 24 cabin rentals, dumping stations, rest rooms with showers, picnic tables, a playground, and walking trails. Lake Chenango and Lake Lily, both located within the park's boundaries, provide plenty of opportunities to get out on the water. Leashed dogs are welcome with proof of vaccinations. For more information on the park, see "Out and About."

Cherry Valley
Belvedere Lake Campground and Resort, 270 Gage Rd. (607-264-8182; belvdere@telenet.net; www.belvederelake.com); $22–29 per night. This self-described "dog-friendly" campground has 500 acres with sites for RVs and tents, rental cottages, a 25-acre lake, boat rentals, a camp store, a miniature golf course and a nine-hole standard course, rest rooms with showers, a recreation hall, sports courts, a playground, a petting zoo, a game room, hiking trails, and scheduled activities.

Cold Brook
Adirondack Gateway Campground and Lodge, 244 Burt Rd. (315-826-5335; www.adirondackgatewaycampground.com); $15–23 per night. "We welcome dogs and have never had any problems with our furry guests," says campground owner Stacey Knapp. Adirondack Gateway encompasses 166 acres with scenic vistas, sites for tents and RVs, a playground, a swimming pool, rest rooms with showers, fishing ponds, a driving range, and trails for hiking, biking and dog-walking. Bring vaccination records and be sure to leash and clean up after your animals.

Cooperstown
Cooperstown Beaver Valley Cabins & Campsites, Towers Rd., P.O. Box 704 (607-293-7324; info@beavervalleycampground. com; www.beavervalleycampground.com); $28–31 per night. For an extra $1 per night, dogs are welcome at campsites (but not in cabins) at Beaver Valley, a campground with two baseball fields, stocked fishing ponds, a swimming pool, a wading pool for children, a playground, a game room, a camp store, laundry facilities, and rest rooms with showers. Owners must pick up after their pets and keep them out of the buildings.

Cooperstown Famous Family Campground, 230 Petkewec Rd. (607-293-7766; 1-800-959-CAMP; info@cooperstownfamilycampground.com; www.cooperstownfamilycampground.com); $18–24 per night. Campground amenities include sites for tents and RVs, a swimming pool, stocked fishing ponds, walking trails, a pavilion with a fireplace, laundry facilities, pony rides, playgrounds, a recreation hall, hayrides, a baseball field, and scheduled activities. Vineyards, orchards, and Cooperstown attractions are all nearby. Leashed dogs are welcome.

Glimmerglass State Park, 1527 County Hwy. 31, Cooperstown (607-547-8662); $13 per night. Relatively small and much in demand, this campground fills up quickly. Camping facilities include 37 tent and trailer sites, picnic tables, rest rooms with showers, pavilions, trails, dumping stations, a beach, and a playground. Binoculars would be handy here, as you're likely to see a variety of wildlife species. (For more park information, see "Out and About.") Make sure to bring your dog's proof of vaccinations and use a leash.

Davenport
Beaver Spring Lake Campground, Rte. 23, P.O. Box 64, Davenport (607-278-5293; 1-866-377-5293; bslcg@stny. rr.com; www.beaverspring lake.com); $24–28 per night. Beaver Spring Lake Campground is located on 55 acres with 120 sites, a separate tenting area, rest rooms with showers, a lake, a swimming pool, sports courts, boat rentals, and a camp store. Dogs must be quiet, well behaved, leashed, and cleaned-up after; owners are asked to walk canines on the (ahem) "tinkle trail."

Fultonham
Max V. Shaul State Park Campground, Rte. 30, P.O. Box 23 (518-827-4711); $13 per night.

Although day-use visitors are welcome at Max. V. Shaul, the small park is used primarily by overnight campers. The campground's solitude appeals to those looking for a somewhat secluded experience; the grounds have sites for tents and trailers as well as hiking trails, picnic areas, a playground, rest rooms with showers, and a fishing creek. Dog owners must use a leash and provide proof of vaccinations.

Garrattsville
Jellystone Park at Crystal Lake, 111 East Turtle Lake Rd. (607-965-8265; 1-800-231-1907; coopyogi@ascent.net; www.cooperstownjellystone.com; $33–44 per night. Quiet and secluded yet close to Coopers town, this lakefront family campground has 180 sites for tents and RVs (some on the water), laundry facilities, a camp store, a snack bar, hayrides, a playground, boats, cabin rentals, rest rooms with showers, a swimming pool, and a miniature golf course. Two dogs per campsite are allowed.

Jefferson
Little Lake Campground, 460 North Rd. (607-652-6520; 607-652-3188 buck04@telenet.net); $16–21 per night for campsites and $40 per night for cabin rental. Little Lake has primitive sites available for tents as well as full hook-up sites for RVs. All have picnic tables and fire pits. Visitors will also find a camp store, rest rooms with showers, a playground, walking trails, laundry facilities, and sports courts. Dogs must be leashed and well

behaved; owners must have proof of vaccinations and clean up any messes.

Laurens

Gilbert Lake State Park Campground, County Rte. 12 (607-432-2114); $13–16 per night for campsites and $66–81 per night for cabin rentals. Leashed dogs with proof of vaccinations are welcome at the Gilbert Lake State Park Campground, where visitors will find more than 200 tent and trailer sites, cabin rentals, rest rooms with showers, scheduled recreational programs, picnic tables, pavilions, dumping stations, and more than 12 miles of trails. See "Out and About" for more information about the park itself.

Oxford

Bowman Lake State Park Campground, 745 Bliven Sherman Rd. (607-334-2718); $13 per night. Well known for its camping facilities, Bowman Lake State Park offers nearly 200 sites for tents and trailers, a playground, picnic tables, public telephones, rest rooms with showers, scheduled recreational programs, dumping stations, and of course access to the lake. (For more information on the park, see "Out and About.") Dogs must stay on a leash no longer than 6 feet and have documentation of current vaccinations.

Hunt's Pond State Park Campground, Hunt's Pond Rd. (607-859-2249); $10 per night. Somewhat overshadowed by its larger neighbor, Bowman Lake State Park Campground, this facility would be a good choice for those looking for a more rustic and intimate camping experience. Hunt's Pond has just 18 sites and few facilities (no rest rooms or showers), though you will find picnic tables, a boat launch, and trails for walking, cross-country skiing, and snowmobiling. Pet owners must have proof of vaccinations and use a leash.

Rome

Delta Lake State Park Campground, 8797 Rte. 46 (315-337-4670); $13–19 per night. Although this state park is open year-round, the campground is open seasonally from May through October. The facilities at Delta Lake include more than 100 sites (some waterfront) for tents, trailers, and RVs, picnic tables, rest rooms with showers, a playground, dumping stations, a boat launch, a beach, pavilions, and scheduled recreational programs for kids and adults. Dogs are allowed if owners provide proof of vaccinations and keep them leashed at all times. For more park information, see "Out and About."

St. Johnsville

Crystal Grove Diamond Mine & Campground, 161 Hwy. 114, St. (518-568-2914; 1-800-KRY-DIAM; fun@crystalgrove.com; www. crystalgrove.com); $18–25 per night. Camp facilities at Crystal Grove include tent and RV sites, picnic tables and fire pits, rest rooms with showers, a gift shop, a playground, and sports courts. Leashed, quiet, well-behaved pets are welcome. For an extra fee ($4–6 per day), campers and visitors can dig for diamonds in the on-site mine. Cabin rentals are also available for $50 per night.

Verona Beach

Verona Beach State Park Campground, Rte. 13 (315-762-4463); $13–17 per night. With a great location, Verona Beach State Park Campground is a popular spot that tends to fill to capacity quickly. The campground offers rest rooms with showers, 45 sites for tents and trailers, a beach, a playground, pavilions, scheduled recreational programs, and trails for walking, biking, and horseback riding. Be sure to carry proof of vaccinations for your dogs and use a leash no longer than 6 feet. For more information on the park, see "Out and About."

Homes, Cottages, and Cabins for Rent

Cooperstown

Cary Mede Guest House, Lake Otsego (607-547-9375; carymede@aol.com; www.cary-mede.com); $400–525 per night. This lavish country estate offers a 3,000-square-foot guest house for rent with a private dock on Lake Otsego, flower gardens, a formal dining room, a living room, and a sitting room with a fireplace. The on-site boathouse is also occasionally available for rent. Dogs are welcome for an additional $15 per day.

Deerslayer Appaloosas Rustic Lodge, Kinney Rd. (607-547-5790; 607-547-6125; elizmule@hotmail.com; www.deerslayer-lodge.com); $125 per night or

$1,200 per week. Surrounded by 19 private acres, this rental home has two bedrooms, a full kitchen, a living room with TV/VCR, an enclosed porch and stone patio, a barbecue grill, a hot tub, ponds and woods, a pet play area, and a horse/mule stable. The lodge is rented by the week only during the summer season. Dogs are welcome.

The Suites at 96 Main, Main St. (1-800-528-5775; mickesplce@stny.rr.com; www.webspawner.com/users/96mainstreet); call for rate information. Dogs are welcome to join their owners at these privately owned suites with double beds, cable television with premium movie channels, free local calls, coffeemakers, microwaves, and refrigerators. Guests stop in at Mickey's Place, a baseball memorabilia store located at 74 Main St., to check in and pick up keys.

Dolgeville

Keyser Lake cottage, Keyser Lake Rd. (845-758-8728; gary.kreig@us.nestle.com); $800 per week. A large lawn opens up to the lake at this well-located two-bedroom cottage, which also has a sleeping loft, a pullout couch, a large deck, a barbecue grill, a full kitchen, a television and stereo, a private beach, and two rowboats. Considerate cat and dog owners are welcome without extra fees.

Milford

Cooperstown Connection, 140 East Main St. (607-286-7777; cooperstownconnection@hotmail.com; www.cooperstownconnection.com); $89–129 per night.

These one-, two-, three-, and four-bedroom apartments are within a 100-year-old Victorian home located just down the road from Cooperstown. The apartments have air-conditioning, cable television, ceiling fans, private entrances, hardwood floors, and full kitchens. "Large and long-haired dogs" are not allowed, but "small dogs" are welcome; call to see if yours qualifies.

Paris

Paris cottage, Old Rte. 12 (315-737-9952); call for rate information. This cozy one-bedroom cottage has a living room/dining room area with a fireplace and a full kitchen that comes pre-stocked with breakfast foods and snacks. Small- to medium-size dogs are welcome, as long as their owners clean up after them and keep them off the furniture. (The cottage also happens to be located next door to a veterinarian's office.) There are no extra charges for pets.

Springfield Center

Phoenix Cottage, P.O. Box 182 (607-547-2148; arhclarke@catskill.net; www.cooperstown-chamber.org/phoenixcottage); $150 per night. There's a three-night minimum stay at Phoenix Cottage, a restored and converted carriage house with four bedrooms, three bathrooms, a full kitchen, a living room with fireplace, and a washer and dryer. Cooperstown attractions are about 9 miles away, and a golf course is located within walking distance. Well-behaved cats and dogs are welcome.

Windsor

Farmhouse rental (1-800-484-2551, ext. 7980; dmcgill@farmhouseny.com; www.farmhouseny.com); $450 per weekend or $1,000 per week. "We are more than dog-friendly. We are a dog paradise." So say the owners of this roomy farmhouse with accommodations for up to eight people, 60 acres of forests and meadows, a full kitchen, a dining room and living room, a washer and dryer, a deck with patio furniture, and a fire pit. Your pooch is welcome for an extra $20 per day, and can take advantage of igloo-style doghouses and a fenced-in kennel area.

OUT AND ABOUT

Bear Pond Wines, 2515 State Hwy. 28, Oneonta (607-643-0294; winemaster@nichols.net; www.bearpondwines.com). Leashed dogs are welcome to explore the outdoors areas of this Cooperstown-area winery with a vineyard, a tasting room, a gift shop, and beautiful hillside views. Bear Pond's unique offerings include Grizzly Red, Polar White, Castle Cabernet, Baseball Red, Soccer Ball White, and Grand Slam Champagne.

Blenheim Covered Bridge, Rte. 30, North Blenheim (518-827-

6344). This notable structure is said to be longest single-span covered bridge not only in the United States, but on the entire planet. Built in 1855, the 26-foot-wide bridge has an impressive 210-foot span across Schoharie Creek. Next door, a one-room schoolhouse serves as a museum. The scenic site is definitely worth a stop.

Boat launches. In addition to the many boat launches located within the state parks listed here, you can also find launches at State Hwy. 28 just south of Richfield Springs, and at Fish Rd. in Cooperstown.

Bowman Lake State Park, 745 Bliven Sherman Rd., Oxford (607-334-2718). Birdwatchers frequent the 8 miles of trails at Bowman Lake, where more than 100 species of birds are seen regularly. The woodsy trails also appeal to cross-country skiers, bikers, and hikers, while other visitors flock to the lake beach, playground, boat launch, picnic areas, and campground (see "Accommodations"). Dogs are welcome, but owners must have proof of vaccinations handy and use a leash.

Caverns Creek Grist Mill, Caverns Rd., Howes Cave (518-296-8448; ralphharvey@caverns-creekgristmill.com). Though pets are not allowed inside the mill building itself, they are welcome to join their owners in exploring the grounds. "Our nature trail is a good place for pets or children to stretch their legs," says the mill owner, Ralph Harvey. "It parallels the canal and the creek that feed my mill pond and is very scenic, with a waterfall." Human visitors can shop for gifts, crafts, pancake mixes, honey, maple syrup, and other goodies in the on-site Country Store.

Charlotte's Vineyard, P.O. Box 873, Cooperstown (607-547-2412; questions@charlottesvineyard.com; www.charlottesvineyard.com). Although its mailing address is in Cooperstown, this family-run vineyard is actually located just off Rte. 166 in nearby Middlefield. "We have two ponds, a gazebo, and wide open fields that can accommodate dogs and fishermen," says owner Ginamarie Pugliese. "The dogs can have a swim or a good, old-fashioned run. We even have an informal dog walk just to the right of our wine building." All of the table wines offered in the tasting room and gift shop are made on the premises.

Chenango Valley State Park, 153 State Park Rd., Chenango Forks (607-648-5251). Located just north of Binghamton, this vast state park offers a large campground (see "Accommodations"), two lakes, shaded hiking trails, an 18-hole golf course, a playground, a beach, and boat rentals. The activity doesn't cease in the winter, when ice skating, cross-country skiing, and sledding are popular with locals and visitors alike. As long as they have proof of vaccinations, dogs are welcome on a leash.

Chittenango Falls State Park, 2300 Rathbun Rd., Rte. 13, Cazenovia (315-655-9620). The name says it all: People come to this park for many reasons, but nothing draws visitors more than the 167-foot waterfall. Walking trails and bridges allow views from the bottom, side, and top of the waterfall. After you've had your fill of gawking, relax on the grounds for a picnic, push the kids on a swing in the playground, or hike the trails. (For information on camping at Chittenango Falls, see "Accommodations.") If you can show proof of vaccinations, your leashed dog is welcome.

Cooperstown & Charlotte Valley Railroad, Leatherstocking Railway Historical Society, Oneonta (607-432-2429; lrhs@lrhs.com; www.lrhs.com). Hop on board for a scenic ride of the Central-Leatherstocking area, including Milford-to-Cooperstown trains that help visitors avoid the parking hassles in downtown Cooperstown. Special-events rides include "Santa Express" trains, "Halloween Express" trains, fall foliage excursions, murder-mystery trains, and "Easter Bunny Express" trains. Interested riders can make reservations over the phone or on-line. Well-behaved pets are welcome on board.

Critz Farms, 3232 Rippleton Rd., Cazenovia (315-662-3040; info@ critzfarms.com; www.critzfarms. com). Leashed, friendly dogs are always welcome to join their owners at Critz Farms, a 175-acre agricultural center where activities include maple-syrup collecting, berry picking, cutting-your-own Christmas trees, and gathering at events like the Fall Harvest

Celebration. The on-site gift shop offers fudge, cheese, maple syrup, jams, and Christmas decorations. Don't be surprised to run across the farm's two resident Australian shepherds during your visit.

Delta Lake State Park, 8797 Rte. 46, Rome (315-337-4670). A boon for local residents, Delta Lake also attracts out-of-towners with its large sandy beach, boat launch, picnic areas, trout-, bass-, and pike-fishing opportunities, playground, campground (see "Accommodations"), and trails for hiking, biking, cross-country skiing, and snowshoeing. The boat launch opens for the season in May. Pets must be accompanied by proof of vaccinations and stay on a leash no longer than 6 feet.

Erie Canal. Once called "Clinton's Ditch," this waterway snakes throughout upstate New York and has numerous locks and scenic lookouts in the Central-Leatherstocking region. Watch pleasure boats and fishermen cruise by as cyclists, dog walkers, joggers, and stroller-pushing parents meander along the paved towpaths beside the canal. Each lock has its own park and picnic area; many have boat launches, as well. Locks 10 through 16 are located in Montgomery County, in the towns of Cranesville, Amsterdam, Fort Johnson, Fonda, Canajoharie, Fort Plain, and St. Johnsville. Locks 17 through 22 pass through the Utica and Rome areas on the way to Oneida Lake. For more information and maps, call 1-800-4CANAL4 or visit www.canals.state.ny.us.

Finger Lakes Trail, Chenango County. This 72-mile trail crosses the entire county, winding past forests, meadows, parkland, a fire tower, waterfalls, historic sites, and a gorge. You can jump in at many points along the way, including Rtes. 12, 23, and 220. Although it's primarily designed for hikers, you'll also see mountain bikers and cross-country skiers along the path. It is entirely maintained by volunteers. For more information, contact the Chenango County Land Trust at 607-335-1245 or 607-865-2552.

Fly Creek Cider Mill and Orchard, 288 Goose St., Fly Creek (607-547-9692; bill@flycreekcidermill.com; www.flycreekcidermill.com). Pets are not allowed in the mill building itself, but they can join their owners on the grounds of this extensive orchard and cider mill. The on-site Snack Barn serves up soups, cheese, pie, and, of course, cider; other attractions include a duck pond, a children's play area, a gift shop, and regular special events. Owners are asked to use a leash and keep dogs away from the ducks and geese that roam freely on the property.

General Clinton Canoe Regatta, Bainbridge. For more than 40 years, this annual festival has been drawing canoeists from the United States, Canada, and Europe. Participants paddle 70 miles of the Susquehanna River in one day; if that sounds like too much work, you can watch them sweat while you enjoy food, live music, rowdy crowds, and souvenir shopping. The event is typically held over Memorial Day weekend. For updated information and schedules, call 607-967-8700.

Gilbert Lake State Park, County Rte. 12, Laurens (607-432-2114). With one lake and two ponds, this park is a great spot for vacationers hoping to fish, swim, paddle a canoe, or just enjoy the beautiful views. In addition to conventional attractions like a campground (see "Accommodations"), hiking and biking trails, playgrounds, and a beach, the park also offers a Frisbee-golf course. Your leashed pets are welcome to explore the sights with you, as long as you have proof of vaccinations ready for inspection by park officials.

Glen Highland Farm, 21 Pegg Rd., Morris (607-263-5415; sweet bcrescue@citlink.net; www.glen highlandfarm.com). At their 175-acre farm and animal sanctuary, Lillie Goodrich and John Andersen specialize in the rescue and readoption of Border collies. But dogs of all breeds will appreciate a visit to Glen Highland, which sponsors on-site countryside vacations for inner-city children every summer and maintains the Garden of Resting Spirits pet cemetery. Lillie and John hope to soon expand their rescue efforts to include a "Canine Country Village" for abandoned older dogs. The farm also offers popular one-week camp sessions for people and dogs called Camp Border Collie and Friends (see "Accommodations").

Glimmerglass State Park, 1527 County Hwy. 31, Cooperstown (607-547-8662). This extremely

LILLIE GOODRICH EXERCISES SOME OF THE RESCUED BORDER COLLIES AT HER GLEN HIGHLAND FARM SANCTUARY AND DOG CAMP.

popular park is located just north of downtown Cooperstown and attracts thousands of visitors each year. Trails provide great views of Otsego Lake—the "Glimmerglass" of the park's name—and wind through a variety of habitats, including wetlands, woods, and wildflower fields. Cross-country skiing, ice skating, walking across the covered bridge, relaxing at the beach, and camping (see "Accommodations") are other favorite activities. This is also the site of the Annual Glimmerglass Triathalon, typically held in August. Dogs are welcome, as long as they're on a leash no longer than 6 feet.

Howe Caverns, 255 Discovery Dr., Howes Cave (518-296-8900; www.howecaverns.com). Although dogs are not allowed in the caverns themselves, this popular tourist attraction does provide sheltered kennels for pets to use while their owners take the fascinating underground tour with walkways, limestone formations, and even a boat ride on an underground lake. (The $5 kennel fee is donated to the nearby Animal Shelter of Schoharie Valley.) In addition, visiting dogs and their owners can explore the 400 acres surrounding the historic Howe Caverns Estate.

Iroquois Indian Museum, Caverns Rd., Howes Cave (518-296-8949; info@iroquois-museum.org; www.iroquois-museum.org). Animals are not allowed in the museum building itself, but they are welcome to roam the 50-acre property as long as they're leashed. Five landscaped acres surround the museum, while an additional 45 acres is a designated nature park with marked trails and signs detailing the Iroquois's views about the natural world. In May, the museum hosts an annual out-

THE IROQUOIS INDIAN MUSEUM IN HOWES CAVE OFFERS INDOOR EXHIBITS AS WELL AS SCENIC OUT-DOOR TRAILS.

door festival with Native American food, art vendors, dancers, singers, and children's activities. (A note to visitors: The posted "no pets" sign can cause confusion, but staffers assured us that our dog was welcome on the trails as long as we cleaned up after her.)

Mine Kill State Park, Rte. 30, P.O. Box 923, North Blenheim (518-827-6111). This park's primary appeal is its location at the New York Power Authority's reservoir, which is stocked with fish. Boating, fishing, and even water-skiing are allowed at the reservoir, but swimmers will have to stick to the on-site swimming pools. Campers staying at the nearby Max V. Shaul State Park Campground (see "Accommodations") often make the journey to this park for day-use recreation. Dogs are not allowed in swimming areas or buildings and must be leashed and have proof of vaccinations.

Oquaga Creek State Park, Beech Hill Rd., Bainbridge (607-467-4160). There's something for every type of outdoor enthusiast at this large park with a 55-acre lake: boat rentals, a boat launch, a sandy beach, picnic areas, biking and hiking trails, pavilions, a playground, and a campground (see "Accommodations"). In the winter, visitors enjoy cross-country skiing, ice fishing, and sledding. Your family pet is welcome, provided you have proof of vaccinations and use a leash.

Petpalooza, Chenango County Society for the Prevention of Cruelty to Animals, 6160 County Rd. 32, Norwich (607-334-9724; info@cspca.org; www.cspca.org). In addition to operating a year-round shelter for homeless animals, the Chenango County SPCA also holds a rollicking Petpalooza event each year with Frisbee-catching competitions, food, music, a walkathon, and other pet-related activities, vendors, and attractions. Visitors are always welcome. The event is typically held in August at the Chenango County Fairgrounds; call or e-mail the society for the latest dates and times.

Shako:wi Cultural Center, 5 Territory Rd., Oneida (315-363-1424; info@oneida-nation.org; www.oneida-nation.net). Owned and run by the Oneida Indian Nation, Shako:wi is an educational center designed to teach visitors about Oneida and Iroquois cultures. Very small, well-behaved dogs are allowed inside the center's log building and gift shop, while leashed medium-size and large dogs are welcome on the exterior grounds only. The gift shop houses an impressive collection of Iroquois arts and crafts.

Spring Farm CARES, 3364 Rte. 12, Clinton (315-737-9339; www.springfarmcares.org). Part farm, part animal sanctuary, and part education center, Spring Farm CARES is a nonprofit organization that finds homes for homeless domestic and farm animals, runs a spay-and-neuter program to prevent pet over-population, and leads workshops in "animal communication" that profess to help people and animals better understand each other. The on-site nature sanctuary attracts hikers and bird-watchers with wetlands, open fields, and trails; dogs are welcome on a leash. Daily tours are available by reservation only.

Verona Beach State Park, Rte. 13, Verona Beach (315-762-4463). Pack a picnic and head out to Verona Beach for an afternoon of warm-weather relaxing, hiking, biking, fishing, sunbathing, and wildlife watching. Winter is a quieter season here, so enjoy the respite from the crowds while you cross-country ski, ice fish, or ride a snowmobile. Leashed pets are welcome with proof of vaccinations. The park also has a campground: See "Accommodations" for more information.

Walking tours of Cooperstown, Cooperstown Chamber of Commerce, 31 Chestnut St. (607-547-9983). For 50 cents, you can buy a map at the Main Street Information Center and take a self-guided tour of the town's sites. Cooperstown has been dubbed the "Village of Museums"; dogs aren't allowed in any (even the outdoor Farmer's Museum), but don't let that keep you from enjoying the local scenery.

QUICK BITES

Common Grounds Coffee House, 35 Albany St., Rte. 20, Cazenovia (315-655-4770). In addition to serving up espresso, sandwiches, soups, salads, and baked goods, this convenient coffee shop is also the headquarters for Project Café, a nonprofit organization dedicated to promoting the arts in the greater Cazenovia area.

Garf's Deli, 23 North Broad St., Norwich (607-336-3354). If you're hoping to pack a picnic, Garf's can accommodate: Order a sub, salad, soup, coffee, or even a bowl of chili at this full-service deli and enjoy your lunch on the go.

Heavenly Ham, 201 Oakdale Rd., Johnson City (607-797-9498). Although this chain is best known for providing whole hams and turkeys, travelers are more likely to appreciate Heavenly Ham's box lunches. Each lunch includes a custom-made sandwich with ham, turkey, tuna salad, veggies, or other ingredients on your choice of breads, along with sides like cole slaw, pasta salad, and potato chips—cookies and a drink are also included.

Hoppie's, 2 Lafayette Park, Oxford (607-THE-CONE). This old-fashioned ice cream parlor has unique flavors and creations like the PB&J Sundae, the Chenango Snapping Turtle Sundae, and the Chocoholic Delight Sundae. Hot dogs, sandwiches, and breakfast items are also available. Order your guilty pleasure to go and enjoy it at one of the sidewalk benches out in front of the store.

Hot Diggity Dog with a Lickity Split Bun, Rte. 49, Rome (315-339-3333). You can probably guess what type of food this hot-diggity-spot specializes in. Kids especially love visiting, but you'll no doubt enjoy your own dog, too: with relish, mustard, and maybe an onion or two.

Italian Kitchen, 66 Church St., Oneonta (607-432-2776). All of the menu items at this casual family restaurant are available as takeout: Choose from pizza, hot and cold subs, vegetarian dishes, antipasti, pasta, seafood, and chicken dishes. Cannoli, tiramisu, and tortes finish off the meal.

Portabello's, 6027 State Hwy. 28, Fly Creek (607-547-5145; www. portabellosinflycreek.com). Portabello's sidewalk café opens in May; watch the world go by as

you enjoy dishes like fresh-egg fettuccine, blackened sea scallops, pork chops, and filet mignon. (For dessert, try the Key lime tart.) Meals are also available in the indoor dining room year-round.

Quick Café Snack Bar, Howe Caverns Restaurant, 255 Discovery Dr., Howes Cave (518-296-8900). The indoor dining area of this family restaurant is only open during the busy season, but its adjoining snack bar is open year-round. After you've explored the underground caves, stop in here for a light meal or treat.

Troop's Scoops, Rte. 20 East, Bouckville (315-893-7070). This casual stand is takeout only; order fast treats like burgers, sandwiches, hot dogs, and one of 30 flavors of ice cream and hang out with your pooch in the large picnic area with tables.

HOT SPOTS FOR SPOT

Binghamton Agway, 44 Montgomery St., Binghamton (607-772-1801). Agways are usually handy for pet owners, especially when you're on the road and running low on dog or cat food. The Binghamton Agway is no exception: The shelves here are lined with a good selection of brands, including Iams, ProPlan, ProPet, Eukanuba, Nutro, Big Red, and Purina. You can also find flea-and-tick control products, brushes and shampoos,

treats, toys, and crates.

Canine Care, 7552 Gorton Lake Rd., Waterville (315-861-5215; dogcare@dreamscape.com). Canine Care owner Pat McNamara is also the founder of Canine Working Companions, Inc., an organization that trains dogs to help people with disabilities. Her grooming and boarding facility in Waterville provides overnight boarding and doggie daycare, outdoor play yards, a pet-supply boutique, agility and obedience classes, and all-breed grooming services.

Chenango County Society for the Prevention of Cruelty to Animals, 6160 County Rd. 32, Norwich (607-334-9724; info@ cspca.org; www.cspca.org). The Chenango County SPCA offers a well-stocked gift shop for animal lovers at its Norwich shelter; choose from accessories, toys, dog and cat beds, biscuits, and other pet supplies. Proceeds from all sales benefit the shelter.

Crever's Creatures, 1181 Erie Blvd. West, Rome (315-336-2256). In addition to a large selection of fish, aquariums, and pond supplies, Crever's Creatures also stocks accessories and food for dogs, cats, birds, rodents, and other pets. It's the largest non-chain pet store in the greater Rome area and offers a wide selection of nearly any pet-related item you might need.

From the Heart Pet Sitting Service, Rte. 365, Holland Patent (315-865-6684; yworry@dream-scape.com; www.fromtheheart-petsit.homestead.com). If you're in a pickle and you're staying within a 10-mile radius of Holland Patent (just east of Rome and north of Utica), Kamille Smith would be happy to keep an eye on your pooch for a few hours. In business since 2000, From the Heart specializes in house and pet-sitting and currently has about 85 clients. Advance reservations are required.

Nancy's Pet City and K-9 Motel, 928 Herkimer Rd., North Utica (315-797-6319). For more than 35 years, Nancy's has been providing pet-friendly services in the greater Utica area. The boarding facility can accommodate all types of companion animals, including birds, and the staff also provides grooming for all breeds of dogs and cats. Doggie pickup and drop-off services are available.

Paws Inn Boarding Kennels, Fearon Rd., Morrisville (315-684-7714; pawsinllc@hotmail.com; www.morrisvilleny.com/pawsinn/ index.htm). There's room for 10 dogs at this small family-run kennel; the runs have indoor and outdoor spaces, heat, padded dog beds, and non-tip bowls. Special-needs pets are welcome. Upon request, your pup can also enjoy ice cream and other treats.

Pet Depot, 4700 Vestal Pkwy., Vestal (607-798-6832). This "pet superstore" carries every dog and cat accessory you might need, as well as supplies for birds, fish, reptiles, hamsters, and other companion animals. Food brands include Nutro, Eukanuba, Iams, Pro Plan®, and Science Diet. You can also shop at the Pet Depot Warehouse store, located nearby in Crystal Plaza (607-766-0749).

Pet Supplies Plus, 4488 Commercial Dr., New Hartford (315-768-4488). This large, bright store is part of the national Pet Supplies Plus chain; with a huge selection of food, accessories, magazines, and anything even remotely pet-related, it's a great place to stock up.

VIP Grooming Salon, 640 Varick St., Utica (315-732-8094; info@ vipgroomingsalon.com; www.vip-groomingsalon.com). Traveling can be a dirty business: While you're visiting or passing through Utica, stop in to VIP for a bit of freshening up. All breeds of dogs—and cats—are welcome for plenty of personal attention and a wash, cut, or clip.

IN CASE OF EMERGENCY

Burrstone Animal Hospital
2448 Chenango Rd., New Hartford (315-732-1300)

Cazenovia Animal Hospital
2750 Rte. 20 East (315-655-3409)

Chenango Valley Animal Hospital
1445 Front St., Binghamton (607-722-3392)

Greene Veterinary Clinic
4276 State Hwy. 41 (607-656-4285)

Hamilton Animal Hospital
2402 State Rte. 12 (315-824-5412)

Herkimer Veterinary Associates
121 Marginal Rd. (315-866-9999)

Howes Cave Animal Hospital
Secret Caverns Rd. (518-296-8896)

Leahy Animal Hospital
2959 County Hwy. 8, Oneonta (607-432-8330)

Rome Veterinary Hospital
6161 Lamphear Rd. (315-337-1470)

The Finger Lakes Region

LAMOREAUX LANDING WINE CELLARS OFFERS WINE TASTINGS AND SCENIC VINEYARD PATHS.

The Finger Lakes Region

DOG-FRIENDLY RATING:

According to Native American legend, the Creator pressed his hand against the Earth in a blessing and left the imprints that formed this region's many long, thin waterways. Whatever their origins, the Finger Lakes are certainly considered a blessing by locals and visitors, who flock to the shores of Canandaigua, Keuka, Seneca, Cayuga, Skaneateles, and other lakes for relaxation and adventure. The region is also distinguished by its wineries that dot the landscape around Seneca and Cayuga Lakes and attract oenophiles from across the nation. Your dog is welcome to join you at many of the vineyards (see "Out and About") for tours of the grounds and tastings of fine, homegrown vintages. You can also get a taste of history in Seneca Falls, long considered to be the birthplace of the Women's Rights Movement in America.

Whether you're traversing wine country, learning about American pioneers, or visiting a student at one of the Finger Lakes region's many universities, including Cornell, Syracuse, and the Rochester Institute of Technology, you shouldn't have any trouble finding a pet-friendly place to stay. The majority of the lodgings here are of the chain-motel variety, especially along the busy New York State Thruway (I-90). But the interior towns and villages also host cozy B&Bs, family-oriented campgrounds, and elegant inns. Boat launches and charters are plentiful, as are expansive state parks, hiking trails, and casual eateries. Many of the area's best attractions are outdoors, which means you and Rover can take in as much—or as little—action as you want. Though it's not the most famous tourist region of the state, the Finger Lakes may be one of the best for dog lovers.

ACCOMMODATIONS

Hotels, Motels, Inns, and Bed & Breakfasts

Auburn

Days Inn Auburn, 37 Williams St. (315-252-7567); $59–79 per night. The Days Inn economy hotel chain provides affordable accommodations in convenient locations; guests will typically find 24-hour front desks, cable television, air-conditioning, laundry services, fitness facilities, express checkout services, free local calls, alarm clocks, and complimentary coffee and tea. All the Days Inns listed here welcome pets; some charge a small nightly fee for doggie guests.

Holiday Inn Auburn, 75 North St. (315-253-4531); $107–169 per night. Though the details vary from site to site, the Finger Lakes Holiday Inn locations offer amenities like interior corridors, air-conditioning, 24-hour front desks, swimming pools, on-site restaurants and lounges, laundry facilities, fitness centers, wake-up services, cable television, business services, and deluxe suites. Pets are welcome in designated rooms. Some sites charge an extra fee for animal guests.

Bath

Days Inn Bath-Hammondsport, 330 W. Morris St. (607-776-7644); $65–85 per night. (See listing under Auburn.) Pets are welcome at this location without extra charges.

Super 8 Motel Bath-Hammondsport, 333 W. Morris, Rte. 17 (607-776-2187); $50–75 per night. Like the other Finger Lakes–area Super 8 Motels listed here, the Bath location welcomes well-behaved pets. At all of its locations, the Super 8 chain offers 24-hour front desks, express checkout services, free local calls, smoking and non-smoking rooms, cable television with premium movie channels, and laundry facilities. Pet fees (if any) vary from site to site.

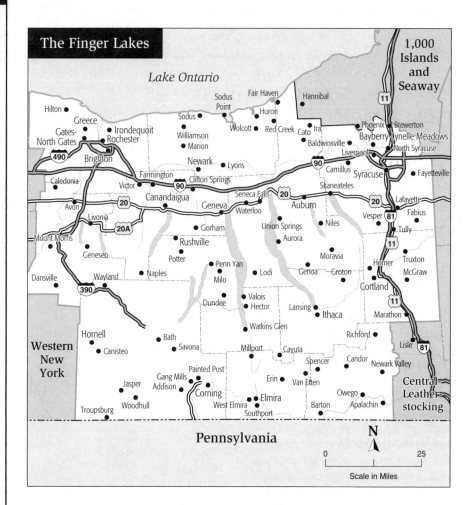

The Finger Lakes

1,000
Islands
and
Seaway

Lake Ontario

Western
New
York

Pennsylvania

N

0   25

Scale in Miles

Central
Leather
stocking

Brewerton

Holiday Inn Express Syracuse–Oneida Lake, 5552 Bartell Rd. (315-676-3222); $69–89 per night. This economy hotel–spin-off of the Holiday Inn chain offers guests features such as complimentary continental breakfasts, standard rooms and larger suites, interior corridors, wake-up services, air-conditioning, safe-deposit boxes, and business services. The Brewerton and Brockport locations welcome pet guests in designated rooms.

Brockport

Econo Lodge Brockport, 6675 4th Section Rd. (585-637-3157); $56–76 per night. Many of the Econo Lodge locations (including all those listed here) welcome guests with pets. Typical amenities include cable television, pay-per-view movies, in-room coffeemakers, irons and ironing boards, swimming pools, picnic areas, on-site restaurants, and fitness centers. Dogs are allowed in designated rooms, and some locations charge a small fee for Fido.

Holiday Inn Express Brockport, 4908 Lake Rd. South (585-395-1000); $89–139 per night. (See listing under Brewerton.) Dog owners pay a one-time fee of $15.

Camillus

Cambridge Inn, 2382 W. Genesee Turnpike (315-672-3022); $39–89 per night. For an extra $5 per night, your dog is welcome at this 10-room motel with free local calls, cable television, smoking and nonsmoking rooms, air-conditioning, and a 24-hour front desk. Syracuse University, the New York State Fairgrounds, golf courses, and walking paths are all nearby.

Canandaigua

Econo Lodge Canandaigua, 170 Eastern Blvd. (585-394-9000); $49–69 per night. (See listing under Brockport.) Pets are allowed at this Econo Lodge, but they cannot be left alone in the rooms at any times. Owners are also required to clean up any messes on the property.

Corning

Radisson Hotel Corning, 125 Denison Pkwy. East (607-962-5000; rd.corn@radisson.com; www.radissoncorning.com); $90–136 per night. Guests at the Radisson will find 177 rooms, an indoor swimming pool, an outdoor hot tub large enough to accommodate 10 people, a restaurant and bar, and a banquet hall. Dogs are welcome in smoking rooms only. There is no extra charge for animals, though owners will be held responsible for any damages and the management prefers that crates are used.

Cortland

Comfort Inn Cortland, 2 Locust Ave. (607-753-7721); $95–119 per night. Comfort Inns typically offer affordable lodging with amenities such as air-conditioning, free continental breakfasts, cable television and pay-per-view movies, interior corridors, fitness centers, and in-room coffeemakers, hair dryers, and irons and ironing boards. Dogs are allowed at each of the Finger Lakes Comfort Inn locations listed here, although the "rules and regs" and pet fees vary from site to site.

Holiday Inn Cortland, 2 River St. (607-756-4431); $62–109 per night. (See listing under Auburn.) Dog owners pay a $20 nonrefundable fee per stay at this Holiday Inn.

DeWitt

Econo Lodge DeWitt, 3400 Erie Blvd. East (315-446-3300); $59–65 per night. (See listing under Brockport.) Your pooch is welcome here for an extra $10 per night.

East Syracuse

Super 8 Motel East Syracuse, 6620 Old Collamer Rd. (315-432-5612); $49–70 per night. (See listing under Bath.) Dog owners at this Super 8 location pay an additional $10 per night, with a maximum charge of $25 per stay.

Endicott

Econo Lodge Homestead Inn, 749 W. Main St. (607-754-1533); $59–129 per night. (See listing under Brockport.) Dogs are welcome guests at this Econo Lodge for an extra $8 per night.

Geneva

Motel 6 Geneva, 485 Hamilton St. (315-789-4050); $49 per night. Dog lovers will be happy to know that all Motel 6 locations welcome pets without extra fees. The economy chain provides cable television with premium movie channels, exterior corridors, free morning coffee and local phone calls, smoking and nonsmoking rooms, vending services, and convenient locations. Let the staff know ahead of time if you're bringing a pet.

Ramada Inn Geneva Lakefront, 41 Lakefront Dr. (315-789-0400); $89–148 per night. The Geneva, Rochester, and Syracuse Ramada locations all welcome pets in designated rooms. Though amenities vary at each site, you'll typically find extras such as swimming pools, restaurants and lounges, room service, standard rooms and larger suites, laundry and valet services, 24-hour front desks, cable television, express checkout services, and fitness centers. Minimal pet fees may apply.

Henrietta

Red Roof Inn Henrietta-Rochester, 4820 W. Henrietta Rd. (585-359-1100); $49–59 per night. All Red Roof Inn locations welcome one "small" pet per room, although owners cannot leave them unattended in the rooms at any time. The Henrietta and Syracuse sites offer amenities typical of the motel chain, including voice mail, cable television with premium movie channels, free local calls, vending services, ice

machines, pay-per-view movies, and a "Kids Stay Free" program.

Super 8 Motel Henrietta-Rochester, 1000 Lehigh Station Rd. (585-359-1630); $49–105 per night. (See listing under Bath.) Pets are allowed in smoking rooms with no extra charges at this Super 8.

Himrod

Rainbow Cove Resort, 3482 Plum Point Rd. (607-243-7535); call for rate information. This waterfront resort motel has a private pier, a swimming pool, a game room, an on-site restaurant serving breakfast, lunch, and dinner, a boardwalk, and great views of Seneca Lake. Supervised dogs are welcome without extra fees, although they cannot be left unattended in the rooms.

Hornell

Econo Lodge Hornell, 7462 Seneca Rd. North (607-324-0800); $49–55 per night. (See listing under Brockport.) Your pup can join you for an extra $7 per night at this Econo Lodge.

Horseheads

Best Western Marshall Manor, 3527 Watkins Rd. (607-739-3891); $59–89 per night. Marshall Manor's amenities include a restaurant and lounge, cable television, smoking and nonsmoking rooms, a 24-hour front desk, free daily newspapers, and a location that is popular with skiers at nearby mountains like Greek Peak and Labrador. Pets are welcome for an additional $4 per night.

Motel 6 Elmira-Horseheads, 4133 Rte. 17 (607-739-2525); $39 per night. (See listing under Geneva.)

Ithaca

Best Western University Inn, 1020 Ellis Hollow Rd. (607-272-6100); $79–199 per night. Guests at the University Inn can enjoy a swimming pool, cable television, a restaurant and lounge, room service, free morning newspapers, baby-sitting services, a 24-hour front desk, daily continental breakfasts, and a complimentary airport shuttle service. The hotel is located on the grounds of Cornell University. "Small" pets (call to see if yours qualifies) are allowed in designated rooms for an extra $10 per night.

Columbia Bed & Breakfast, 228 Columbia St. (607-272-0204; columbiabb@hotmail.com; www.columbiabb.com); $105–205 per night. Visitors at Columbia B&B stay in the Main House, the Carriage House, or the Gazebo. Amenities include custom-designed furniture, vaulted ceilings, a deck, whirlpool baths, satellite television, skylights, and gardens. The Carriage House also offers a private entrance. Dog guests are welcome for an additional $25 per stay.

Holiday Inn Ithaca, 222 South Cayuga St. (607-272-1000); $84–139 per night. (See listing under Auburn.) Dog owners pay an extra $15 per stay at this Holiday Inn location.

La Tourelle Inn, 1150 Danby Rd., Rte. 96B (607-273-2734; info@latourelleinn.com; www.latourelleinn.com); $99–250 per night. Leashed pets are welcome in selected rooms at La Tourelle, a luxury European-style inn with four-poster featherbeds, private bathrooms, and air-conditioning. The designated pet-friendly rooms have king-size beds and patios that open to the inn's 70 acres and the neighboring Buttermilk State Park. Guests must give prior notice if they plan to bring a dog.

Log Country Inn, La Rue Rd., P.O. Box 581 (607-589-4771; 1-800-274-4771; wanda@logtv.com; www.logtv.com/inn); $135–200 per night. The resident dalmations, Twiggy and Nasza, will greet you at this log home-like inn. Visiting dogs are welcome to stay with their companions at the inn's Russian Jacuzzi Suite, which offers two bedrooms, knotty-pine walls, a sitting area, a hot tub, cable television, a kitchen, and garden views. Walking paths on the property offer a setting for peaceful explorations with your pet.

Liverpool

Econo Lodge Liverpool, 401 7th North St. (315-451-6000); $52–77 per night. (See listing under Brockport.) You'll pay a one-time fee of $10 to bring a pet to this Econo Lodge.

Holiday Inn Syracuse-Liverpool, 441 Electronics Pkwy. (315-457-1122); $109–150 per night. (See listing under Auburn.) There are no extra charges for dogs at this Holiday inn, though a $20 refundable security deposit is required.

Super 8 Motel Liverpool, 421 7th North St. (315-451-8888); $49–65 per night. (See listing under Bath.) This Super 8 welcomes canines for an additional $10 per night.

McGraw

Days Inn Cortland, 3775 Rte. 11 (607-753-7594); $66–80 per night. (See listing under Auburn.) For $10 per night, your pet is a welcome guest at this Days Inn location.

Owego

Angels in the Attic Bed & Breakfast, 313 Front St. (607-687-1927; angelsintheatticbb@ angelsintheatticbb.com; www. angelsintheatticbb.com); $75–85 per night. This welcoming home is located in the downtown historic district and offers four-poster beds, quilts, period furnishings, guest rooms with private and shared baths, and a large front porch that's ideal for breakfast or afternoon lounging. The resident boxer, Zoe, can show your pooch the ropes when you arrive.

Painted Post

Best Western Lodge on the Green, 3171 Canada Rd. (607-962-2456; info@lodgeonthegreen. com; www.lodgeonthegreen. com); $59–99 per night. The 135 rooms at the Lodge on the Green come equipped with cable television with premium movie channels, alarm clocks, Internet access, hair dryers, and irons and ironing boards; guests can also enjoy valet laundry services, free daily continental breakfasts, an outdoor swimming pool, and several restaurants. Well-behaved, quiet pets are welcome without extra fees.

Econo Lodge Painted Post, 200 Robert Dann Dr. (607-962-4444); $59–69 per night. (See listing under Brockport.) At this Econo Lodge, dog owners pay a one-time fee of $10.

Erwin Motel, 806 Addison Rd. (607-962-7411; info@erwin-motel.com; www.erwinmotel .com); $29–89 per night. This family-owned motel provides an outdoor swimming pool and 25 clean and simple rooms with either one or two beds. Quiet, well-behaved dogs (sorry, no cats) are welcome with a refundable $10 security deposit and a nonrefundable $10 one-time fee. Pet owners must clean up after their animals and give prior notice that they plan to bring Fido along.

Penn Yan

Viking Resort, 680 East Lake Rd., Rte. 54 (315-536-7061; info@vikingresort.com; www. vikingresort.com); $70–500 per night. Guests at Viking choose from motel rooms, studio apartments, efficiencies, suites, and full-size cottages. The facilities include a sandy beach, boat rentals, docks, a swimming pool and hot tub, and nightly tours of Keuka Lake on board the Viking Spirit. Pets are welcome, and the resort's owners are happy to recommend nearby kennels and veterinarians.

Rochester

Comfort Inn Central, 395 Buell Rd. (585-436-4400); $57–62 per night. (See listing under Cortland.) There are no extra charges for pets at the Comfort Inn Central.

Comfort Inn West, 1501 West Ridge Rd. (585-621-5700); $71–119 per night. (See listing under Cortland.) Dog owners pay a one-time fee of $10 at this Comfort inn location, regardless of length of stay.

Days Inn Thruway, 4853 West Henrietta Rd., Rte. 15 (716-334-9300); $50–65 per night. (See listing under Auburn.) Your pet is welcome for an additional $10 per night at the Days Inn Thruway.

Econo Lodge Rochester, 940 Jefferson Rd. (585-427-2700); $59–125 per night. (See listing under Brockport.) Pet owners at this Econo Lodge pay no extra charges, although they cannot leave their animal alone in the room at any time.

Holiday Inn Rochester-Airport, 911 Brooks Ave. (585-328-6000; 1-800-278-2248); $87–135 per night. (See listing under Auburn.) There are no additional fees for canines at this Holiday Inn location.

Motel 6 Rochester Airport, 155 Buell Rd. (585-436-2170); $39 per night. (See listing under Geneva.)

Ramada Inn Rochester, 800 Jefferson Rd. (585-475-9190); $55–69 per night. (See listing under Geneva.) Upon check-in at this Ramada, guests must sign a pet-policy and liability agreement form. There are no extra charges for your dog.

Skaneateles

Skaneateles Suites, Rte. 20, P.O. Box 912 (315-685-2333; info@skaneatelessuites.com;

SKANEATELES SUITES IN THE VILLAGE OF SKANEATELES WELCOMES PETS IN DESIGNATED BUNGALOWS.

www.skaneatelessuites.com); $125–150 per night. Your dog is a welcome guest at this unique accommodation offering individual bungalows with decks, kitchenettes, and full bathrooms (some with whirlpool tubs). An on-site four-bedroom home is also available for short-term stays for larger groups. The Village of Skaneateles is located about 2 miles down the road. Pet owners pay a one-time fee of $35.

Spencer

A Slice of Home Bed & Breakfast, 178 North Main St. (607-589-6073); $55–200 per night. Dogs (sorry, no cats) are welcome in one of the cottage units located on the 6-acre grounds of this 1840s B&B. The cottage has two bedrooms, a full kitchen, and living room/dining area. A full breakfast is included in the rates. Four state parks and numerous wineries are nearby. Dog owners must show proof that their animal is on an anti-flea treatment and pay a one-time fee of $25.

Syracuse

Comfort Inn Fairgrounds, 7010 Interstate Island Rd. (315-453-0045); $89–109 per night. (See listing under Cortland.) Dogs are permitted at this Comfort Inn for an extra $10 per stay.

Comfort Inn Syracuse, 6491 Thompson Rd. (315-437-0222); $85–139 per night. (See listing under Cortland.) There are no additional charges for companion animals at this Comfort Inn.

Days Inn University, 6609 Thompson Rd. (315-437-5998); $55–76 per night. (See listing under Auburn.) Dog owners at this Days Inn location pay a one-time fee of $10.

Econo Lodge University, 454 James St. (315-425-0015); $52–69 per night. (See listing under Brockport.) For $10 per night, your dog is a welcome guest at the Econo Lodge University.

Holiday Inn Syracuse, 6555 Old Collamer Rd. South (315-437-2761); $81–117 per night. (See listing under Auburn.) The pet charge at the Syracuse Holiday Inn location is $25 per stay.

Holiday Inn Syracuse-Fairgrounds, Farrell Rd. and State Fair Blvd., (315-457-8700); $77–114 per night. (See listing under Auburn.) Guests traveling with an animal pay a $25 refundable security deposit at this Holiday Inn.

Motel 6 Syracuse, 6577 Baptist Way, East Syracuse (315-433-1300); $36 per night. (See listing under Geneva.)

Ramada Limited-University, 6590 Thompson Rd. North (315-463-0202); $50–60 per night. (See listing under Geneva.) Pet owners pay an extra $10 per stay at this Ramada Limited site.

Red Roof Inn Syracuse, 6614 North Thompson Rd. (315-437-3309); $49–59 per night. (See listing under Henrietta.)

Western Ranch Motor Inn, 1255 State Fair Blvd. (315-457-9236); $39–79 per night. Dog guests are welcome without extra fees at Western Ranch, a small motor inn with air-conditioning, cable television, alarm clocks, balconies and terraces, telephones, and smoking and nonsmoking rooms.

Trumansburg

Mom's Place Bed and Breakfast, 5040 Perry City Rd. (607-387-5597; www.momsplacebandb.com); $90–100 per night. Guests at Mom's Place choose from two suites: the Sunflower, with a queen-size bed, a hide-a-bed, and a sitting area; and the Tulip, a loft with a double bed, hardwood floors, a sitting room, and a porch. Both have a private bathroom, air-conditioning, and a TV/VCR. Dogs are welcome without extra charges. An on-site gift shop offers reproductions and original paintings by the innkeeper.

Waterloo

Holiday Inn Waterloo, 2468 Mound Rd., Rte. 414 (315-539-5011); $69–229 per night. (See listing under Auburn.) Pets weighing less than 50 pounds are welcome without extra charges at the Holiday Inn Waterloo.

Watkins Glen

1871 Benjamin Hunt Inn, 305 Sixth St. (607-535-9843; relax@benhunt.com; www.benhunt.com); $89 per night. There are no extra fees for pet guests at this quaint Victorian inn where each of the four guest rooms has a private bathroom, cable television, air-conditioning, a refrigerator, and classic furnishings. Breakfast and afternoon tea are included in the nightly rate. Antiques, a fireplace, Oriental rugs, and stained-glass windows complete the restoration theme.

Farm Sanctuary, 3100 Aikens Rd. (607-583-2225; www.farm-sanctuary.org); $55–75 per night. This nonprofit sanctuary for farm animals gets thousands of visitors each year. Some stop by just for a few hours or a day, but others prefer to stay a while in one of the sanctuary's three on-site "bed & breakfast" cabins. Comfortable and clean, the cabins have views of the farm fields; a full vegetarian breakfast is included in the rates. Well-behaved dogs are welcome without extra charges. For more information on Farm Sanctuary, see "Out and About."

Seneca Lodge, Rte. 329, P.O. Box 272 (607-535-2014; www.senecalodge.com); call for rate information. Quiet, well-behaved pets are welcome in the cabins and A-frame chalets (though not in motel rooms) at Seneca Lodge, a family-owned resort located next to Watkins Glen State Park. An on-site dining room serves breakfast, lunch, and dinner, and the lodge's tavern serves as a popular gathering place. There are no extra fees for four-legged guests.

Campgrounds

Arkport

Sun Valley Campsites, 10740 Poags Hole Rd. (607-545-8388; www.sunvalleycampsites.com); $15–24 per night for campsites; $40 per night for cabins. The extensive facilities at Sun Valley will keep families entertained throughout their stay; amenities

THE B&B CABINS AT FARM SANCTUARY OVERLOOK THE PASTURES AND BARNS.

include a swimming pool, a playground, hiking trails that lead to waterfalls, rest rooms with showers, laundry facilities, a game room, a camp store, sports courts, and organized activities such as clambakes, hayrides, pancake breakfasts, parades, and dances. Owners are asked to keep dogs leashed and clean up after them.

Bath

Hickory Hill Family Camping Resort, 7531 Mitchellsville Rd. (607-776-4345; 1-800-760-0947; camp@hickoryhillcampresort. com; www.hickoryhillcampresort. com); $25–41 per night. Hickory Hill aims to please every member of the family with extras such as hayrides, a game room, a miniature golf course, a camp store, two swimming pools, movie nights, and an activity hall. "We are pet-friendly, and just ask that guests obey the leash law and clean up after their pets," says office manager Cheryl Chely.

Bluff Point

Keuka Lake State Park Campground, 3370 Pepper Rd. (315-536-3666); $13–15 per night. With more than 150 campsites and views of the lake and surrounding vineyards, this seasonal campground is a popular draw. Amenities include rest rooms with showers, a playground, a boat launch, availability for tents and trailers, dockage, and picnic tables and fire pits at each site. Dogs are welcome if owners have proof of vaccinations and keep them leashed, although they are not permitted in the beach area.

Wigwam Keuka Lake Campground, 3324 Esperanza Rd. (315-536-6352; wigwamcamp1 @usadatanet.net; www.wigwam-keukalakecampground.com); $18–22 per night. Campers at Wigwam, a family campground overlooking the lake, can choose from tent sites, RV sites, cabin rentals, and tipi rentals. Amenities include a camp store, a swimming pool, and a fishing pond. Dogs are welcome without extra fees, but they must be leashed, supervised, and cleaned-up after.

Cohocton
Tumble Hill Campground, 10551 Atlanta Back Rd. (585-384-5248; tumblehill@aol.com; www. tumblehill.com); $17–24 per night. Leashed, friendly pets are welcome at Tumble Hill without extra charges. The campground has sites for tents and RVs, a large recreation hall, a playground, 20 acres of trails, scheduled activities like socials, hayrides, and arts-and-crafts gatherings for children. Tent sites have fire pits and picnic tables.

Cortland
Yellow Lantern Campground, 1770 Rte. 13 North (607-756-2959; ylkincort@aol.com); $19–21 per night. Camping dogs love roaming the 40-plus acres at Yellow Lantern, a family campground offering a swimming pool, sports courts, more than 200 campsites with hook-ups, a game room, a playground, and a children's wading pool. Pet owners are asked to use the designated "dog-walk area" and to have vaccination papers ready in case of incident.

Dansville
Stony Brook State Park Campground, 10820 Rte. 36 (585-335-8111); $14 per night. With 125 well-spaced sites for tents and trailers, this campground offers wonderful opportunities for hiking, sightseeing, and cross-country skiing in the park (see "Out and About") along with a playground, rest rooms with showers, tennis courts, picnic tables, a dumping station, and pavilions. Your dog is welcome to join you everywhere except the beach as long as you have proof of vaccinations and use a leash no longer than 6 feet.

Elmira
Newtown Battlefield Reservation, 455 Oneida Rd. (607-732-6067; cvlh@mizar5.com; www.mizar5.com); $12 for country residents, $14 for noncountry residents. You can visit the reservation for the day or for a special event (see "Out and About") or you can take off your coat and stay awhile at the on-site campground. Campers choose from wooded sites for tents and RVs or stay in one of five rustic cabins. Amenities include walking trails, rest rooms with showers, and vending machines. Owners must keep dogs on a leash, clean up after them, and provide proof of vaccinations.

Fair Haven
Shady Shores Campground, 14986 West Bay Rd., P.O. Box 24 (315-947-5488; shadyshs@ redcreek.net; www.shadyshores-campground.com); $17–22 per night. Located on the waterfront at Lake Ontario and Blind Sodus

Bay, Shady Shores offers campers a sandy beach, boat rentals, rest rooms with showers, a camp store, laundry facilities, a recreation hall, and a playground. Dogs are welcome as long as they are leashed and quiet; owners must show proof of vaccinations.

Fayetteville

Green Lakes State Park Campground, 7900 Green Lakes Rd. (315-637-6111); $13–16 per night for campsites and $66 per night for rental cabins. Travel just east of Syracuse and you'll find this expansive campground with 137 sites for tents and trailers, rental cabins, rest rooms with showers, picnic tables, dumping stations, a playground, and scheduled recreation programs. Dogs must be leashed at all times, and owners must provide proof of vaccinations at check-in. For more information about the park, see "Out and About."

Ithaca

Buttermilk Falls State Park Campground, Rte. 13 (607-273-5761); $13 per night. This state park campground offers sites for trailers and tents, rental cabins, picnic tables and fire pits at each site, a playground, walking trails, rest rooms with showers, a beach, a dumping station, and playing fields. Leashed dogs are welcome with proof of vaccinations, although they are not allowed on the beach. See "Out and About" for more information on the park.

Robert H. Treman State Park Campground, Rte. 13 (607-273-3440); $13–15 per night. After you spend the day admiring the park's gorge and waterfalls (see "Out and About"), relax at one of its campsites. There are sites for RVs and tents as well as a beach, recreation programs, a playground, picnic tables and fire pits, and a dumping station. Your dog is not allowed on the beach, though she can accompany you everywhere else as long as she has proof of vaccinations and stays on a leash no longer than 6 feet.

Montezuma

Hejamada Campground and RV Park, McDonald Rd., P.O. Box 429 (315-776-5887; larso692000 @yahoo.com; www.hejamada-campground.com); $19–25 per night. Quiet, well-behaved dogs are welcome without extra charges at Hejamada, where campers can expect to find more than 200 sites for RVs and tents spread out on 85 acres, along with picnic tables, a recreation hall, rest rooms with showers, laundry facilities, a camp store, a snack bar, a swimming pool, sports courts, movie nights, and other scheduled activities.

Moravia

Empire Haven Nudist Resort & Campground, 5947 Sun Lane (315-497-0135; mrobin2459@ aol.com; www.aanr.com/clubs/ ehnude); $13–26 per night. This clothing-optional campground and park caters to families with a swimming pool, a snack bar, nature trails, a hot tub and sauna, a playground, a pond, sun decks, sports courts, and planned activities. Quiet, well-behaved dogs are welcome, as long as owners clean up after them and stay with them at all times. Dogs are not allowed in sunbathing areas.

Filmore Glen State Park Campground, 1686 Rte. 38 (315-497-0130); $13–15 per night.

Open from mid-May to mid-October, this state park campground has 60 sites for tents and trailers, a playground, picnic tables, a dump station, and rest rooms with showers. The nature area provides more than a few diversions for outdoorsmen and women: See "Out and About" for more information about day use at the park. Leashed dogs are welcome if owners can show proof of vaccinations.

Odessa

Cool-Lea Camp, Rte. 228 (607-594-3500; coollea@coolleacamp.com; www.coolleacamp.com); $21–24 per night. RVers and tenters will both find sites at Cool-Lea, a campground beside Cayuta Lake with docks and boat launch areas, rental rowboats and canoes, hayrides, lakefront bonfires, bingo, fireworks, and other scheduled activities for children and adults. The resort is especially popular with fishermen searching for yellow perch, bluegill, largemouth bass, and other species.

Ovid

Ridgewood Campground, 6590 South Cayuga Lake Rd. (607-869-9787; ridgewood@fltg.net; www.ridgewoodcampgrounds.com); $16–25 per night. "We always welcome pets at Ridgewood," says owner Carol Rogers. "We ask owners to have proper vaccination documents,

keep pets on a leash, and clean up after them." The campground offers sites for tents and RVs, a pond, boat dockage, a game room, a miniature golf course, a playground, and rustic cabin rentals.

Seneca Falls

Cayuga Lake State Park Campground, 2678 Lower Lake Rd. (315-568-5163); $13 per night. If one day of exploring the park isn't enough (see "Out and About"), you can also stay overnight at Cayuga Lake's campground. Amenities include picnic tables and fire pits, sites for tents and trailers, rental cabins, rest rooms with showers, hiking trails, and a dumping station. Dogs are welcome as long as owners keep them on a leash no longer than 6 feet and show proof of vaccinations.

Springwater

Holiday Hill Campground, 7818 Marvin Hill Rd. (585-669-2600; 1-800-719-2267; hhcamp@aol.com; www.holidayhillcampground.com); call for rate information. In addition to organized activities like hayrides, ice-cream socials and races, Holiday Hill also offers campers a swimming pool, a playground, a picnic area, a camp store, a recreation hall, hiking trails, and sports courts. A maximum of two pets are allowed per site; dogs must be leashed and supervised at all times.

Trumansburg

Taughannock Falls State Park Campground, 2221 Taughannock Rd., (607-387-6739); $13–16 per night. After you've had a look at the park's impressive falls (see "Out and About"), pitch your tent or set up your trailer for a night of outdoor adventure. The campground offers a playground, rest rooms with showers, picnic tables and fire pits, scheduled recreation programs, a boat launch, and a dumping station.

Watkins Glen

Watkins Glen State Park Campground, Rte. 14, P.O. Box 304 (607-535-4511); $13–17 per night. Join other campers for a night or two in this renowned state park, where you'll find sites for tents and trailers, a playground, rest rooms with showers, a swimming pool, picnic tables, and pavilions. Dog owners must show proof of vaccinations and use a leash no longer than 6 feet; dogs are not allowed in the pool area or on the gorge trail. For more information about the park itself, see "Out and About."

Homes, Cottages, and Cabins for Rent

Auburn

Waterfront cottage (315-252-7970; dreese1@adelphia.net); $800–1,500 per week or $600 per weekend. Up to nine people can stay at this two-bedroom, wooded home located at the edge of Owasco Lake. Amenities include upstairs and downstairs decks, two fireplaces, a full kitchen, lawn furniture, a TV/VCR, a CD player, a dock, a canoe and paddleboat, a gazebo, a barbecue grill, and 150 feet of lake frontage. Dogs are welcome in all rooms except the bedrooms.

Aurora

Cayuga Lake cottage (607-347-6608; tam1@cornell.edu); $500 per week. This seasonal cottage is available for rentals from May to October. Pets are welcome with no extra charges—the owners even have an outside pen available for those occasions when you want to go to dinner or the movies. The one-bedroom cottage is waterfront with a 100-foot beach, a barbecue grill, satellite television, and a kitchen with a coffeemaker and a microwave. Wells College is one mile down the road.

Geneva

Nana's Wine Country Cottage (518-891-6770; gregandlyn@aol.com); $550–700 per week or $450 per weekend. This 2-story house has four bedrooms, ceiling fans, a full kitchen, satellite television, a VCR, patio furniture, a washer and dryer, and 37 acres with a pond. Cayuga State Park, an outlet mall, and many popular wineries are nearby, and the property even has a small vineyard of its own. All renters pay a $75 cleaning fee and a refundable $150 security deposit. Dogs are welcome.

Naples

Canandaigua Lake cottage, Country Rte. 12 (585-374-2176; bjkorts.com); $750–900 per week. Up to nine people can stay at this three-bedroom cottage overlooking the lake, vineyards, and mountains. The bathrooms and kitchen were recently renovated; guests can also enjoy a picnic area, a dining area with a harvest table, and a quiet location that's close to wineries, a boat launch, state parks, Bristol Mountain ski area, and summer stock theater in Naples. Well-behaved dogs are always welcome.

Penn Yan

Keuka House (518-891-6770; gregandlyn@aol.com); $1,000 per week. Greg and Evelyn Miller, who also own Nana's Wine Country Cottage (see listing under Geneva), welcome dogs at this three-bedroom chalet-style home with a fireplace, updated furnishings, and expansive views. "Both of our properties are secluded, private and have lots of acreage away from the main roads," explains Greg. All renters pay a refundable security deposit of $150 and a cleaning fee of $75.

Slice of Heaven Vacation Home (585-352-8254; alfredgibbardo@ hotmail.com; www.gibbardo. com); $950 per week. This Keuka Lake home can accommodate up to eight people with three bedrooms, two bathrooms, a TV/VCR, a stereo and CD player, a barbecue grill, a full kitchen, a woodstove, picnic tables, patio furniture, and 5 acres to roam. The front deck and upstairs balcony both overlook the lake. Pet owners pay a refundable $300 security deposit.

Skaneateles

Lakefront cottage (720-300-0168; mtnlakesides@aol.com); $1,000–1,600 per week. Settle into this waterfront cottage with a boathouse, a dock with patio furniture, decks, and a small motorboat (a larger boat is available for rent). The cottage has three bedrooms, one bathroom, a barbecue grill, a full kitchen, and a TV/VCR. "We encourage our guests to bring their pets," says owner Brad Bailey. "They just have to be respectful of the property and the neighbors."

OUT AND ABOUT

Alcyone **Charters,** 907 Taughannock Blvd., Ithaca (607-272-7963; bcorb80630@aol.com; www.14850.com/web/alcyone); $50–80 per person. Captain Brad Corbitt welcomes well-behaved dogs aboard his 1994 Hunter sloop, the *Alcyone,* for short- or long-term sails. The four-hour "half-day" trip is the most popular; on this tour, passengers set sail from Tremont State Marine Park and enjoy a stop for swim-ming and lunch or dinner. Full-day trips, moonlight trips, and sailing lessons are also available.

Allan H. Treman State Marine Park, Rte. 89, Ithaca (607-272-1460). One of the biggest marinas in the state, this recreational facility (often confused with Robert H. Treman State Park) is primarily geared toward boaters, though you'll also find a picnic area and playing fields on-site. Visitors can use the boat launch or reserve one of the 60 available slips. Dogs are welcome on a leash no longer than 6 feet, and are not allowed in the picnic area.

Bakers Acres, 1104 Auburn Rd., Groton (607-533-8653; info@ bakersacres.net; www.bakers-acres.net). Green thumbs will love this farm and greenhouse complete with display gardens, a tearoom, and a gift shop. In spring and summer, the displays are overflowing with more than 1,000 types of perennials and herbs; in the fall, you can expect to find cider, pumpkins, and lots of apples. "We do welcome dogs, as long as owners keep them on their leash," says Bakers Acres office manager Susan Capista. "We have some beautiful gardens and trails that are available for self-guided tours."

Barktober Fest and Walk for the Animals, Lollypop Farm, Rochester Humane Society, 99 Victor Rd., Fairport (585-223-1330; info@lollypop.org; www.lollypop.org). Held each October, this fun annual event includes a 2-mile walk through Rochester Humane Society's wooded trails at Lollypop Farm, costume contests, doggie day spa activities, pet portraits, children's activities, and agility demonstrations. The event's dates and schedule varies from year to year; call or visit the web site for the latest information. If you can't make it in October, the farm welcomes visitors throughout the year, as well. You can also browse in the on-site gift shop (see "Hot Spots for Spot").

Boat launches. Looking for a spot to hit the water on one of those famous Finger Lakes? Try Dean's Cove Boat Launch (2678 Lower Lake Rd., Seneca Falls; 315-568-5163); Canandaigua Lake State Marine Park (620 South Main St., Canandaigua; 585-394-9420); Seneca Lake State Park (1 Lakefront Dr., Geneva; 315-789-2331); Lodi Point State Park (Lodi Point Rd. off of Rte. 414, Lodi; 315-585-6392); Honeoye Lake Boat Launch State Park (10820 Rte. 36 South, Dansville; 585-335-8111); Long Point State Park—Finger Lakes (1686 Rte. 38, Moravia; 315-497-0130); and Sampson State Park (6096 Rte. 96A, Romulus; 315-585-6392).

Buttermilk Falls State Park, Rte. 13, Ithaca (607-273-5761). Buttermilk Falls park is made up of two general areas: the upper park, which includes hiking trails, a lake, and picnic areas; and the lower park, which has a campground (see "Accommodations"), a swimming pool, and nature trails. Camping is seasonal, but the park itself is open year-round. Pet owners must have proof of vaccinations and keep their dogs on a leash. Pets are not in allowed in beach or picnic areas.

Canandaigua Lady at **Steamboat Landing,** 205 Lakeshore Dr., Canandaigua (585-396-7350; 1-866-9-ANCHOR; www.steamboatlandingonline.com); $12–25 per person. "Small lapdogs" are allowed to join their owners on fall foliage and narrated boat tours on board the *Canandaigua Lady,* a replica of a 19th-century paddlewheel steamboat. (Dogs are not allowed on board for dinner or lunch cruises.) During the journey on Canandaigua Lake, passengers will learn about the local vineyards, local Native American history, and the history of the steamboat itself.

Cayuga Lake State Park, 2678 Lower Lake Rd., Seneca Falls (315-568-5163). A day at Cayuga Lake State Park might include fishing for largemouth bass or carp, launching a boat, frolicking at the playground, tossing the ball in a baseball field, cross-country skiing, or hiking the trails. Leashed dogs are permitted, provided you have proof of vaccinations. Your dog isn't allowed at the beach, but the nearby sunny lawn areas provide equally nice views.

Crossroads Bicycle Rentals, 88 Main St., Penn Yan (315-531-5311). In addition to bike rentals, Crossroads also serves up ice cream and other snacks and provides a picnic area for outdoor eating. Trails are nearby. The shop is located at the junction of Rtes. 14 and 54 and is open seasonally from April to September.

Earle Estates Meadery, 3586 Rte. 14, Himrod (607-243-9011; earle@linkny.com; www.meadery. com). Earle Estates specializes in producing mead, also known as honey wine: Made from boiling honey, it is one of history's first fermented drinks. Visitors can tour the grounds and honey-processing facilities, stop into the gift shop, and taste more than 25 honey and grape wines made on

the premises. Leashed, friendly dogs are welcome to join their owners.

Farm Sanctuary, 3100 Aikens Rd., Watkins Glen (607-583-2225; www.farmsanctuary.org). Animal lovers will enjoy a trip to this sanctuary designed especially for rescued cows, pigs, horses, goats, chickens, and other farm animals. Many of the resident animals had suffered abuse or neglect, and now live out peaceful lives at one of two Farm Sanctuary locations; the other is in California. Visitors to the 175-acre New York site in Watkins Glen can take a tour, stop by the Visitor Center and gift shop, spend time with the animals, or even volunteer for a few hours or a few days. The sanctuary also provides lodging at three bed & breakfast cabins (see "Accommodations").

Filmore Glen State Park, 1686 Rte. 38, Moravia (315-497-0130). This park has some of the best hiking around: The trails wind past five waterfalls, through deep woods and gorge areas, and past lookouts with great views. In the winter, visitors are welcome to use unpaved areas for snowshoeing, snowmobiling, and cross-country skiing. A seasonal campground is also available (see "Accommodations"). Dog owners must have proof of vaccinations and use a leash no longer than 6 feet.

Fox Run Vineyards, 670 Rte. 14, Penn Yan (1-800-636-9786; foxrun@fltg.net; www.foxrun-vineyards.com). Your well-behaved pooch is welcome to join you on the outdoor portion of the tour; those who want to visit the indoor winery or tasting room can take advantage of the frequently used, shady "dog-parking zone" (a tie-out area) near the parking lot. The scenic vineyard is best known for its chardonnay, pinot noir, Riesling, and sparkling wines.

Green Lakes State Park, 7900 Green Lakes Rd., Fayetteville (315-637-6111). Despite the name, there's only one Green Lake at this scenic park; the other is called Round Lake. You're not likely to spend your time worrying about their names, though, while you're enjoying the beach, boat rentals, picnic areas, campground (see "Accommodations"), nature trails, 18-hole golf course, and 10 miles of cross-country skiing trails. Be sure to bring a leash and proof of vaccinations for your dog.

Keuka Lake State Park, 3370 Pepper Rd., Bluff Point (315-536-3666). After visiting the nearby wineries, stop by Keuka Lake for a picnic, a hike, a boat ride, or just a relaxing view. The park offers a boat launch, a playground, pavilions, dockage, and trails for hiking, cross-country skiing, dog walking, or snowshoeing. Dogs are allowed as long as they're leashed and have proof of vaccinations. See "Accommodations" for more information about the on-site camping facilities.

Keuka Spring Winery, 273 East Lake Rd., Rte. 54, Penn Yan (315-536-3147; uncork@keukaspring-winery.com; www.keukaspring-winery.com). "We are a dog-friendly winery," says Keuka Spring owner Judy Wiltberger. Your pooch can join the resident golden retriever on a tour of the grounds, where you'll find lake views, beautiful scenery, and vintages like chardonnay, Riesling, and merlot available for tastings. The vineyard's wines have recently won gold, double gold, and silver medals at the New York Food & Wine Classic, the New York State Fair, and other competitions.

Lamoreaux Landing Wine Cellars, 9224 Rte. 414, Lodi (607-582-6011; llwc@capital.net; www.lamoreauxwine.com). Well-trained and well-behaved dogs are welcome to roam off-leash with their owners throughout the large lawns and vineyards at this expansive Finger Lakes winery. (Don't be surprised by a greeting from the friendly resident yellow lab.) While you're there, try a tasting of some of Lamoreaux Landing's well-known vintages, including reds, whites, sparkling, and dessert wines.

Long Acre Farms, 1342 Eddy Rd., Macedon (315-986-4202; getlost@longacrefarms.com; www.longacrefarms.com). Your leashed dog is welcome to accompany you at this family farm with an ice-cream shop, a produce market, fudge, and farm animals. The farm's highlight is its Amazing Maize Maze, an elaborate 5-acre maze carved out of a cornfield ($5–7 per person). Though dogs are not allowed in the maze itself, Long Acre Farms does have a dog-sitter on-site to keep an eye on Spot while you navigate, which typically takes about 75 minutes. (The dog-sitting service is free, but tipping is appreciated.)

Morgan Marine, 100 East Lake Rd., Penn Yan (315-536-8166; info@morganmarine.net; www.morganmarine.net). "Family dogs are always welcome at our facility and on board our rental boats," explains Morgan Marine owner Kathy Kennedy. Choose from a variety of boats, from simple to souped-up, and hit the water. Pet owners pay an additional $100 cleaning fee.

Newtown Battlefield Reservation and Sullivan's Monument Park, 455 Oneida Rd., Elmira (607-732-6067; cvlh@mizar5.com; www.mizar5. com). Learn Revolutionary War history at this outdoor historic site with scenic overlooks, educational displays, and a campground (see "Accommodations"). The reservation is host to numerous events throughout the year, including a Civil War Weekend, Revolutionary War battle reenactments, music festivals, and Native American Heritage festivals. Leashed pets are allowed at the reservation and at some special events, depending on the decision of that event's committee chairperson. Call or visit the web site for updated schedules.

Pet Walk and Festival, Finger Lakes Society for the Prevention of Cruelty to Animals, 41 York St., Auburn (315-253-5841;

flspca@baldcom.net; www. cayuganet.org/spca). Usually held in the fall, this annual event includes a fundraising pet walk, exhibits, music, food, costume and obedience contests, and Frisbee, agility, and animal first-aid demonstrations. For this year's location, times, and schedule, contact the Finger Lakes SPCA staff and volunteers.

Robert H. Treman State Park, Rte. 13, Ithaca (607-273-3440). Not to be confused with the similarly named Allan H. Treman State Marine Park, Robert's park offers 9 miles of hiking trails that wind past the impressive Enfield Gorge. Highlights include the 12 waterfalls you'll find along the way, including the well-known, 115-foot Lucifer Falls. Stay for the day or overnight at the park campground (see "Accommodations").

South Shore Marina, 2810 Firelane #1, Rte. 38, Moravia (315-497-3006). Dogs are welcome in the marina's rental boats as long as owners clean up any messes; choose from paddleboats, kayaks, canoes, row boats, and inner tubes. South Shore also provides a launch, slips, gas, fishing supplies, and a snack bar.

Stony Brook State Park, 10820 Rte. 36, Dansville (585-335-8111). A great spot for camping (see "Accommodations") or day trips, Stony Brook State Park provides miles of wooded hiking trails, some of which wind past waterfalls and provide gorge views. Snowshoeing and cross-country skiing are popular activities in the winter. There is also a beach on-site, though dogs are not permitted there. Your leashed pooch is welcome in other areas as long as you have proof of vaccinations.

Taughannock Falls State Park, 2221 Taughannock Rd., Trumansburg (607-387-6739). As you might guess from the name, the highlight of this state park is its 215-foot waterfall. You can see the falls and the gorge from the hiking trails on a day trip or spend the night at the campground (see "Accommodations"). The park also has a launch for powerboats, a marina, and a beach. Winter activities include sledding, ice skating, and cross-country skiing. Dogs are not allowed on the beach and must be leashed and have proof of vaccinations.

Tiohero Tours, 435 Old Taughannock Blvd., Ithaca (607-697-0169; 1-866-846-4376; dennis@cayugawoodenboatworks.com). Tiohero Tours is a charter company working to raise awareness of local water quality by providing "floating classroom" boat trips for school groups as well as sightseeing, diving, and fishing trips for individuals and groups. Dogs are welcome on charters with some restrictions; call for details.

Torrey Ridge Winery, 2770 Rte. 14, Penn Yan (315-536-1210; meadery@hotmail.com; www. torreyridgewinery.com). On a visit to Torrey Ridge, guests can explore the grounds and sample the vineyard's special vintages, including Torrey Ridge Red,

Cayuga White, Bandit Blush, Niagara, Blue Sapphire, Summer Delight, and Catawba. "We are animal lovers and have no problem with people bringing pets, as long as they are on a leash and well behaved," says winery owner Esther Earle.

Watkins Glen State Park, Rte. 14, P.O. Box 304, Watkins Glen (607-535-4511). Located at the south end of Seneca Lake, this popular park is the most-visited in the Finger Lakes. A typical walk along the trails will take you past waterfalls (the park has 19 in all), winding streams, a gorge, and scenic wooded areas. Visitors will also find a campground (see "Accommodations"), a gift shop, and trails for hiking, mountain biking, and cross-country skiing. Dogs are not allowed on the precipitous gorge trail, but they can join you everywhere else if they're leashed and have proof of vaccinations. The main park entrance is located within the village of Watkins Glen.

Wegmans Good Dog Park, Onondaga Lake Park (Cold Springs Entrance), Rte. 370, Liverpool (315-453-6712). Sponsored by the local grocery chain Wegmans, this fenced-in park is a real find for local and visiting dog owners. Friendly dogs are welcome to romp off-leash with other canines and enjoy a pet-drinking fountain, agility-course equipment such as tunnels and bridges, and the company of other dog-loving visitors. Pooper-scooper bags are

BIG MEETS SMALL AT THE WEGMANS GOOD DOG PARK IN LIVERPOOL.

also available; dog owners are asked to clean up any messes and to carry proof of vaccinations. Puppies must wait until they are older than four months to visit the park.

Windmill Farm & Craft Market, 3900 Rte. 14A, Penn Yan (315-536-3032; windmill@linkny.com; www.thewindmill.com). Leashed pets are welcome at the Windmill, an open-air market with arts and crafts, fresh fruits and vegetables, baked goods, numerous picnic tables, and great opportunities for people-watching. Dog owners are asked to use the designated dog-walk area when they visit. The market is open every Saturday from the end of April through mid-December.

Women's Rights National Historic Park, 136 Fall St., Seneca Falls (315-568-2991). The town of Seneca Falls was host to the first Women's Rights Convention in 1848, an event that led in no small way to the birth of the women's equality movement in the United States. The 5.3-acre Women's Rights National Park commemorates the efforts of the 300 women and men who attended the convention, as well as notable women like Elizabeth Cady Stanton who helped spearhead the movement. (The park is actually spread out in different areas of the town.) Leashed, friendly dogs are welcome to tour the park with their owners, but they aren't allowed inside any of the park buildings.

QUICK BITES

Bathtub Billy's Restaurant and Bar, 630 Ridge Rd., Rochester (585-865-6510). Serving wings, pasta, lobster, burgers, and sandwiches, "The Tub" is a fun spot with an oversized outdoor seating area. The tables with umbrellas overlook a sand volleyball court; expect music, crowds, and lots of action.

Bob & Ruth's, 204 North Main St., Naples (585-374-5122). Stop into Bob & Ruth's for a full lunch or dinner or just an ice-cream-cone treat; established in 1951, this well-known local restaurant offers indoor dining, outdoor seating, and takeout.

Dinosaur Bar-B-Que, 246 Willow St., Syracuse (315-476-1662). This "genuine honky-tonk rib joint" has been a staple in Syracuse since 1990, attracting college students, bikers, and everyone in between. Eat in, order your meal to go, or chow down at the outdoor picnic tables in warm weather. The owners recently opened another Dinosaur in Rochester (99 Court St.; 716-325-7090).

Doug's Fish Fry, 8 Jordan St., Skaneateles (315-685-3288). This family restaurant has lots of outdoor seating and takeout. As you might guess from the name, specialties here include fried seafood, sandwiches, platters, and ice cream. Beer and wine are also available.

Downtown Deli, 53 Fall St., Seneca Falls (315-568-9943). All that history can make a person hungry: The Downtown Deli

DECLARATION PARK AND THE WESLEYAN CHAPEL AT THE WOMEN'S RIGHTS NATIONAL HISTORIC PARK IN SENECA FALLS

offers bagels, deli sandwiches, ice cream, soups, coffees, and salads, as well as an outdoor deck seating area.

Grapevine Deli & Café, 418 North Franklin St., Watkins Glen (607-535-6141). Stop into this homey café for bagel sandwiches, Caesar and chef salads, soups, vegetarian meals, desserts, coffees, and cold drinks. Grab your meal to go or relax at one of the sidewalk tables in warm weather.

Greenstar Cooperative Market, 701 W. Buffalo St., Ithaca (607-273-9392; www.greenstarcoop. com). This deli and market specializes in all-natural foods, offering sandwiches, coffees, juices, snacks, produce, and other grocery items. Takeout and outdoor seating are available.

Indian Pines Fruit Stand, 2218 West Lake Rd., Penn Yan (315-536-3944). After visiting nearby wineries, stop in to this roadside stand selling pies, cookies, breads, jellies and jams, fruits and vegetables, and other tasty treats.

Linani's Cookie Factory, 6 North Main St., Homer (607-749-9999; www.linaniscookies.com). Linani's ships their gooey confections—from Ultimate Chocolate Chip to Grandma's Old Fashioned Molasses—all over the world, but lucky Finger Lakes visitors can stop in to the company's Homer storefront to grab one fresh out of the oven. Breads, bagels, brownies, coffee and tea are also plentiful.

Little Sodus Inn, 14451 Bell Ave., Fair Haven (315-947-9944). This village bar and grill offers tasty quick meals and treats, great views, a pavilion, and picnic tables overlooking Little Sodus Bay. A boat launch and canoe put-in area are just a few steps away.

Moosewood Restaurant, Cayuga and Seneca Sts., Ithaca (607-273-9610; www.moosewood.com). A mecca for vegetarians, this 30-year-old restaurant is a tourist stop as well as an eatery. Best known for its ever-changing menu and best-selling collection of vegetarian cookbooks, Moosewood also offers T-shirts, mugs, salad dressings, and other merchandise on-line as well as at its brick-and-mortar location. Outdoor seating is available in warm weather.

Tom Wahl's Restaurant and Picnic Pavilion, Rtes. 5 and 20, Avon (585-226-2420). Serving old-fashioned treats like root-beer floats, ice cream cones, burgers, steak sandwiches, and French fries, Tom Wahl's offers an indoor dining room as well as an outdoor seating area that can accommodate up to 280 people.

Village Soft Serve, 7103 North Main St., Ovid (607-869-9912). Located just north of Lodi, this cozy ice cream shop makes for a refreshing stop during a trip to wine country. Enjoy your Hershey's Ice Cream at a picnic table or one of the covered patio tables.

HOT SPOTS FOR SPOT

All Creations Pet Service, 558 Brookwood Dr., Farmington (716-764-3402; info@allcreationspets.com; www.allcreationspets.com). If you need short-term pet care while you're in the area, All Creations owners Frank and Kelly Kibbe can provide overnight and hourly sitting services, dog walks, grooming, and a pet-taxi service. They'll even deliver pet food if you find yourself in a jam.

Al's Pet Shop, 464 Ridge Rd., Rochester (585-865-6040). Pick up pet necessities at this small but well-stocked shop recommended by locals. Browse the selection of leashes, chew toys, collars, and food and supplies for dogs, cats, gerbils, fish, and other pets.

Aristocats & Dogs Pet Boutique, 62 East Genesee St., Skaneateles (315-685-4849). Located on popular Genesee St., this fun shop stocks animal-themed figurines, greeting cards, and clothing, along with pet beds, leashes, bandannas, automatic feeders, tags, and even "Doggles" sunglasses.

Dog Daze Bakery, 2100 Park St., Syracuse (315-457-9595). This unique doggie bakery serves up all-natural canine cookies, premium pet food, chew treats, breath-freshening "Greenies," toys, T-shirts, hats, picture frames, and more. The shop is located across from Carousel Center in the Regional Market.

Fluffy Paws Pet Sitting, Charlotte, Hilton, Irondequoit, Greece, and Spencerport (585-227-2587; 585-455-8055; www.fluffypaw.com). Serving towns just west of Rochester, animal lover Jill Nuciolo will happily keep an eye on your pet while you're out on the town. She can administer medication, take your dog for a walk, keep his belly full, and keep him busy and entertained.

Jungle Critters, 119 W. Market St., Corning (607-936-8422). After you buy animal-themed gifts for *you* at Wags and Whiskers down the street, stop into this shop to buy food, treats, and supplies for your pet.

Lollypop Shop, Lollypop Farm, Rochester Humane Society, 99 Victor Rd., Fairport (585-223-1330; info@lollypop.org; www.lollypop.org). Located at the headquarters of the Rochester Humane Society, this animal-themed gift shop stocks T-shirts, silk ties, hats, books, stuffed animals, umbrellas, tote bags, blankets, mugs, calendars, and myriad other items. Pick up a gift for a pet-loving friend (or yourself!) and help support the society's rescue and adoption efforts.

Orchard Kennels, 1570 Walworth Penfield Rd., Walworth (315-986-1605; kennel@okdirectpets.com; www.orchardkennels.com). This farm-like boarding facility specializes in large canines (weighing more than 35 pounds) and offers heated floors, grooming services, obedience classes, outdoor exercise areas where dogs can interact and play with each other. The kennel also has an on-site pet-supply store selling items like leashes, bowls, collars, and dog food.

Premier Pet Sitting, Rochester (585-546-2266; premierpet@ earthlink.com). Serving local as well as visiting pets in the greater Rochester area, this service provides short-term care on a regular or once-in-a-while basis. Walks, Frisbee games, feedings, cuddles, and scratches behind the ears will keep your dog happy and occupied when you can't be there.

Tweeter Feeders, 8512 Oswego Rd., Rte. 57, Baldwinsville (315-622-4737; www.tweeterfeeders. com). With an emphasis on nutrition, this pet shop supplies pet food brands such as Innova and California Natural, along with toys, chew treats, leashes and runs, and biscuits. Birdseed and handmade birdhouses are another specialty.

Wags and Whiskers Gifts, 24 East Market St., Corning (607-937-9150). This fun shop is packed to the rafters with gifts that dog- and cat-lovers will appreciate, including pet beds, toiletries, carriers, clothing, calendars, magnets, mugs, outdoor gear, and household items.

IN CASE OF EMERGENCY

Brewerton Veterinary Clinic (complimentary/holistic care)
5500-15 Bartell Rd. (315-676-2860)

Briar Patch Veterinary
706 Elmira Rd., Ithaca (607-272-2828)

Broadway Animal Hospital
855 Broadway St., Elmira (607-734-1272)

Center for Specialized Veterinary Care (complimentary/holistic care)
609 Cantiague Rock Rd., Westbury (516-420-000)

Hornell Animal Hospital
22 Wightman Ave. (607-324-1092)

Keseca Veterinary Clinic
1441 Rtes. 5 and 20, Geneva (315-781-1378)

Midstate Veterinary Services
987 Rte. 222, Cortland (607-753-3315)

Stack Veterinary Hospital
5092 Velasko Rd., Syracuse (315-478-3161)

Stoneridge Veterinary Hospital
1908 Ridge Rd., Rochester (585-227-4990)

Western New York

THE MAJESTIC ALLEGANY STATE PARK IS NEW YORK'S LARGEST STATE PARK.

Western New York

DOG-FRIENDLY RATING: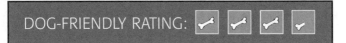

Most people head out this way in search of mighty Niagara Falls, a grouping of waterfalls on the Canadian/American border where more than 100,000 cubic feet of thundering water plunges 180 feet into the gorge every second. It's as impressive as it sounds, and definitely worth the trip. You can see the falls (they're hard to miss) from nearby parks and streets on both the American and Canadian sides of the river, but many of the most popular attractions here, including an observation tower, the *Maid of the Mist* boat ride, the Cave of the Winds, wax museums, and history museums, are off-limits to pets. If you crave an experience with these spots, though, there are several good pet-sitters in the Buffalo–Niagara area (see "Hot Spots for Spot") to watch your dog while you enjoy the show. But visitors traveling with an animal shouldn't neglect the region's other, less well-known sights that can provide the finishing touches on a fun, well-rounded, and pet-inclusive vacation.

For boaters and anglers, the Niagara River, Lake Erie, and Lake Ontario are the launching points for waterlogged adventures. Inland, Allegany State Park (the largest of its kind in New York) and Letchworth State Park attract millions of hikers, campers, rafters, cross-country skiers, snowmobilers, and biking enthusiasts each year. Myriad other parks make up the difference, and you shouldn't have any trouble finding a spot to picnic, bird-watch, bike, stroll, or camp while in western New York. The coastlines of both lakes are dotted with cute small towns and villages, most of which offer shops, restaurants, and great views. The big city of Buffalo is historic, strategically located, and friendly. While you're here, be sure to sample the city's famous chicken wings and try your hand at western New York's most unique sports offering: Frisbee-Disc Golf. The sport is played on a specially designed golf course where "golfers" throw a disc... ah, they putt the disc into a catching device that, um... Well, you're better off visiting and trying it out yourself. Just be prepared for Fido to steal your disc long before it ever reaches its target.

ACCOMMODATIONS

Hotels, Inns, and Bed and Breakfasts

Albion

Dollinger's Motel, 215 South Main St. (585-589-5541); $39–59 per night. Choose from smoking or nonsmoking rooms at this 21-room motel, which also offers air-conditioning, in-room heat controls, laundry facilities, cable television, and irons and ironing boards. Pets are welcome for an additional $5 per night, but must be crated when left alone in the rooms.

Dollinger's Motor Inn, 436 West Ave. (585-589-6308); $39–59 per night. This motor inn is owned by the same family that also runs the nearby Dollinger's Motel; guests can expect to find in-room coffeemakers, smoking and non-smoking rooms, cable television, laundry facilities, air-conditioning, and free local calls. Pet owners pay an extra $5 per night and must keep their pets crated when left unattended in the rooms.

Wishing Well Motel & Restaurant, 15918 Ridge Rd. West (585-638-0911); $49–59 per night. Wishing Well has nine rustic cottages, four with kitchenettes, located next to a restaurant and coffee shop. Cottage amenities include cable television, private bathrooms, and telephones. Children stay free, and golf and boat launches are nearby. Well-behaved dogs are welcome for an additional $5 per night (a dog also lives on-site).

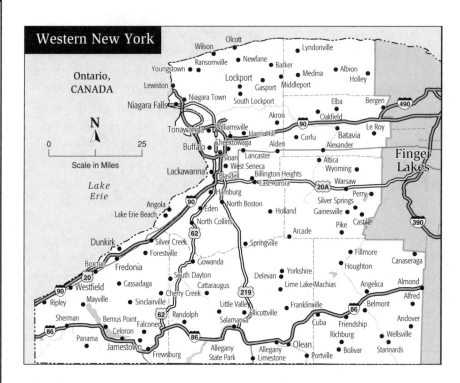

Western New York

Ontario, CANADA

Lake Erie

Finger Lakes

Scale in Miles

Allegany

Gallets House Bed & Breakfast, 1749 Four Mile Rd. (716-373-7493; thegalletshouse@aol.com; www.galletshouse.com); $225 per night. Dogs are welcome in the Gallets House Carriage House apartment suite, which has three bedrooms, a full kitchen, a large bathroom, and a living area. The B&B, a restored Victorian, has a 100-foot front porch, an outdoor hot tub, and monthly murder-mystery events for guests. Animal owners pay an extra $12 per night and are asked to bring pet bedding.

Amherst

Buffalo-Niagara Marriott, 1340 Millersport Hwy. (716-689-6900; 1-800-334-4040); $99–189 per night. This large, upscale hotel has 350 guest rooms on 10 floors, 10 meeting rooms, a restaurant and lounge, room service, a gift shop, business services, laundry services, a Budget rental car desk, cable television, in-room movies, concierge services, and voice mail. Dog owners pay an additional $50 cleaning fee per stay.

Motel 6 Buffalo-Amherst, 440 Maple Rd. (716-834-2231); $58–69 per night. Like all Motel 6 locations, this one welcomes well-behaved pets without extra fees. The motel offers cable television with premium movie channels, Internet access, a 24-hour front desk, free local calls and morning coffee, vending services, smoking and nonsmoking rooms, and exterior corridors.

Red Roof Inn Buffalo-Amherst, 42 Flint Rd. (716-689-7474);

$85–95 per night. The western New York Red Roof Inns in Amherst, Bowmansville, Falconer, and Hamburg welcome pets, as do all of the chain motel's locations. Typical amenities include pay-per-view movies, cable television, exterior corridors, vending services, a "Kids Stay Free" program, and free local calls. There are no extra charges for companion animals.

Batavia

Best Western Batavia Inn, 8204 Park Rd. (585-343-1000); $74–109 per night. Dogs are welcome without extra fees at the Batavia Inn, where guests will find an outdoor swimming pool, a restaurant and lounge, smoking and nonsmoking rooms, cable television, modem hook-ups, a banquet room, and in-room hair dryers. Batavia is located along the New York State Thruway (I-90), about midway between Rochester and Buffalo.

Lee's Motel and Restaurant, 255 W. Main St., Rte. 5 (585-344-4842); $40–50 per night. Lee's Motel has 14 guest units, private bathrooms, air-conditioning, cable television and VCRs, smoking and nonsmoking rooms, some kitchenettes, and an attached family-style restaurant. "Small" dogs (call to see if yours qualifies) are welcome without extra charges.

Bowmansville

Red Roof Inn Buffalo Airport, 146 Maple Dr. (716-633-1100); $64–75 per night. (See listing under Amherst.)

Buffalo

Best Value Inn Buffalo, 475 Dingens St. (716-896-2800; info@bvibuffalo; www. bvibuffalo.com); $45–55 per night. Also known as the Buffalo Motor Inn, this motel has 80 rooms with balconies or patios, an outdoor swimming pool, and a 24-hour front desk. The inn is close to museums, restaurants, theaters, galleries, and shops, and within driving distance to attractions like Niagara Falls and Letchworth State Park. Dogs are welcome without extra charges.

Best Western Inn on the Avenue, 510 Delaware Ave. (716-886-8333; reservations@ innontheavenue.com); $79–149 per night. "We gladly accept man's best friend," explains Inn on the Avenue general manager Dennis Tripi. The 5-story hotel has cable television, free daily continental breakfasts, a glass elevator, free off-street parking, and a location that's within walking distance to shops and restaurants. Dogs weighing less than 50 pounds are allowed in smoking rooms only.

Holiday Motel, 5801 Main St. (716-632-2140); $54–92 per night. The Holiday Motel offers nonsmoking rooms, cable television, refrigerators, safe-deposit boxes, and complimentary coffee each morning. All rooms have either a balcony or a terrace. Dogs are welcome without extra fees, although they cannot be left unattended in the rooms at any time.

Homewood Suites by Hilton, 760 Dick Rd. (716-685-0700; 1-800-225-5466); $119–199 per night. Designed with business travelers and long stays in mind, the Homewood Suites offers apartment-like suites with one or two bedrooms, kitchens, living rooms, high-speed Internet service, cable television with premium movie channels, and pay-per-view movies. Guests also enjoy access to laundry facilities, a 24-hour shuttle service, and complimentary breakfasts each morning. Dogs are allowed for an extra $85 per stay.

Cheektowaga
Four Points by Sheraton–Buffalo Airport, 2040 Walden Ave. (716-681-2400); $76–150 per night. For an extra $50 per stay, your dog can join you at Four Points, where guest rooms are equipped with voice mail, modem hook-ups, coffeemakers, hair dryers, irons, and ironing boards. Other hotel features include an indoor swimming pool, a fitness center, a restaurant and lounge, and free airport shuttles.

Holiday Inn Buffalo–International Airport, 4600 Genesee St. (716-634-6969; 1-800-465-4329); $76–125 per night. Catering to business travelers, this Holiday Inn has high-speed Internet access, fax and copy services, an ATM machine, a bar and grill, 207 guest rooms and 4 suites, laundry facilities, wake-up calls, a 24-hour front desk, and special park-and-fly rates. Pets are welcome for an extra $25 per stay.

Dunkirk
Best Western Dunkirk & Fredonia, 3912 Vineyard Dr. (716-366-7100); $59–129 per night. For an extra $10 per night, your well-behaved dog can join you at this 61-room Best Western. Amenities include an indoor swimming pool, a hot tub and sauna, a fitness center, a 24-hour front desk, cable television, air-conditioning, and in-room movies. Some rooms also have hot tubs. Children 14 and younger stay free.

Dunkirk Motel, 310 W. Lakeshore Dr. (716-366-2200); $40–50 per night. Formerly the Rodeway Inn, this 48-room motel has air-conditioning, cable television, kitchenettes, free continental breakfasts, and smoking and nonsmoking rooms. Golf, tennis, boat launches, and a beach are all nearby. Dogs are allowed for an additional $5 per night.

Ramada Inn Dunkirk, 30 Lakeshore Dr. East (716-366-8350; 1-800-525-8350); $59–179 per night. Located on the water, this Ramada Inn has nice views, indoor and outdoor swimming pools, a hot tub, cable television, air-conditioning, an on-site lounge, modem connections, and free local calls. Some rooms also have hot tubs. For an extra $10 per night, dogs are welcome guests.

Ellicottville
Black Dog Lodge, 7975 Rte. 219 (716-699-6900; blackdoglodge@ novocon.net; www.black doglodge.com); $13–150 per night. The name isn't the only

RESIDENT PUPS MAGGIE AND LOVIE WILL HELP YOU SETTLE IN AT THE BLACK DOG LODGE IN ELLICOTTVILLE.

great thing about this homey B&B offering a gathering room, a stone fireplace, a porch and patio, and 66 acres with a swimming pond and walking trails. Canines are welcome in the Dog House, an efficiency apartment that can accommodate up to four adults that also has a fireplace, a full kitchen, and a private entrance.

Kelly House Lodge, 39 East Washington St. (716-699-4515; info@kellyhouselodge.com; www.kellyhouselodge.com); $60–130 per night. Located within walking distance of restaurants and shops, the Kelly House can accommodate up to 100 people with private and semiprivate baths, a gathering room with cable television, a children's playroom, and a dining area where a full breakfast is served on weekends. Pets are

allowed in the "bunkhouse" area of the lodge with prior notice.

Sugar Pine Lodge, 6158 Jefferson St. (716-699-4855; bandb@ sugarpinelodge.com; www. sugarpinelodge.com); $95–229 per night. Pets are welcome in one of the suites at Sugar Pine: It can accommodate four people with a private entrance, a fireplace, a hot tub, and a minikitchen. "Our inn has a beautiful in-ground swimming pool and a path where pet owners like to walk their dogs," says innkeeper Marilyn Chubb. Dog owners pay a one-time fee of $20 and are asked to bring a sleeping crate.

Telemark Motel, Rte. 219 at Holiday Valley Rd., P.O. Box 1031 (716-699-5161; tektele@msn.com; www.telemarkmotel.com); $49–199 per night. Guests at the Telemark can walk to the lifts at the Holiday Valley ski resort and to a family restaurant that's located next to the motel. One room is set aside for pet owners; there's no additional charge for the animals. All rooms have cable television, double beds, and private baths.

Falconer

Red Roof Inn Falconer, 1980 E. Main St. (716-665-3670); $49–69 per night. (See listing under Amherst.)

Fredonia

Days Inn Dunkirk-Fredonia, 10455 Bennett Rd., Rte. 60 (716-673-1351); $49–79 per night. The Days Inn chain offers amenities such as cable television, air-conditioning, interior corridors, free continental breakfasts, swimming pools, in-room movies and video games, and smoking and nonsmoking rooms. Pets are allowed in smoking rooms only at the Fredonia location.

Grand Island

Chateau Motor Lodge, 1810 Grand Island Blvd. (716-773-2868); $39–119 per night. For an extra $8 per night, your pet is welcome to join you at the Chateau, a motel offering 17 rooms, cable television, alarm clocks, refrigerators, air-conditioning, nonsmoking rooms, a 24-hour front desk, and fax services. Niagara Falls attractions are a short drive away.

Hamburg

Comfort Inn Hamburg, 3615 Commerce Place, Hamburg (716-648-2922); $59–184 per night. Choose from smoking or non-smoking rooms at this Comfort Inn, which also offers cable television, an indoor swimming pool,

complimentary daily breakfast, voice mail, safe-deposit boxes, and in-room coffeemakers, hair dryers, irons, and ironing boards. Friendly pets are welcome for an additional $10 per night.

Red Roof Inn Buffalo-Hamburg, 5370 Camp Rd. (716-648-7222); $69–80 per night. (See listing under Amherst.)

Lewiston

Sunny's Roost Bed & Breakfast, 421 Plain St., P.O. Box 8 (716-754-1161; sunnyroost@adelphia. net; www.sunnysroost.netfirms. com); $70–80 per night. The name of this fun B&B is apt: Each of the guest rooms—the Bantam, the Rhode Island Red, the Ancona, and the Leghorn—are named after rooster breeds. Relax on the front porch or in the dining room, where guests enjoy a breakfast of eggs (of course), pancakes, fruit, homemade breads, and other treats. Well-behaved dogs are welcome, and the resident dachshund, Cinnamon, will make sure you enjoy your stay. Niagara Falls attractions are just down the road.

Mayville

Village Inn Bed & Breakfast, 111 South Main St., Rte. 394 (716-753-3583); $50–70 per night. This European-style, homey inn is furnished with antiques and offers a shady front porch, a breakfast room, and a location that's close to village restaurants and lakes Chautauqua and Erie. Dogs and cats are welcome in the three guest bedrooms, as long as they are not left unattended. (Pampered Pets, a grooming and board-

CINNAMON THE DACHSHUND RELAXES WITH A TREAT IN A GUEST ROOM AT SUNNY'S ROOST B&B IN LEWISTON.

ing facility, is located just down the street: see "Hot Spots for Spot.")

Medina

Dollinger's Courtyard Motel, 11360 Maple Ridge Rd. (585-798-0016); $39–59 per night. Like their motel properties in Albion, the Dollinger's Courtyard Motel welcomes pets for an additional $5 per night. The motel is close to restaurants and offers air-conditioning, cable television, smoking and nonsmoking rooms, irons and ironing boards, refrigerators, and coffeemakers. Dogs must be crated when left alone in rooms.

Newfane

Lake Ontario Motel, 3330 Lockport-Olcott Rd. (716-778-5004); $65–79 per night. The Lake Ontario Motel offers clean, large rooms with two double beds, cable television, air-conditioning, and free local calls.

Guests can enjoy access to the lake and other nearby attractions, including Niagara Falls. Pet owners pay an extra $5 per night, with a maximum charge of $10 per stay.

Niagara Falls

Cascade Motel, 7804 Niagara Falls Blvd. (716-283-3776); $29–59 per night. Close to all the action, this small motel provides 25 rooms, an outdoor swimming pool, a hot tub, air-conditioning, cable television, free parking and local calls, and some kitchenettes. Your dog is welcome for an additional $10 per night.

Coachman Motel, 523 Third St. (716-285-2295; 1-800-335-2295); $39–125 per night. The 18 nonsmoking guest rooms at Coachman have telephones, cable television, and air-conditioning; some also have hot tubs. Niagara Falls attractions and boating, fishing, and golf opportunities are nearby. Children stay free. Pet owners pay a $50 refundable deposit.

Days Inn Riverview at the Falls, 401 Buffalo Ave. (716-285-2541); $49–89 per night. (See listing under Fredonia.) Dogs are welcome for an additional $10 per night.

Rodeway Inn Niagara Falls, 9900 Niagara Falls Blvd. (1-800-843-56440); $49–159 per night. For an extra $10 per night, "small" pets (call to see if yours qualifies) are welcome at this Rodeway Inn, where amenities include 23 smoking and nonsmoking guest rooms, an outdoor swimming pool, cable television, in-room coffeemakers, alarm clocks, hair dryers, irons, and ironing boards. Refrigerators and VCRs are also available upon request.

Sunrise Inn, 6225 Niagara Falls Blvd. (716-283-9952); $35–189 per night. Dogs are allowed for an extra $10 per night at the Sunrise Inn, a 32-room motel with air-conditioning, cable television, nonsmoking rooms, modem connections, and an outdoor swimming pool. Some units have kitchenettes, and VCRs are also available to guests. Walk to attractions, shops, and restaurants.

Travelodge Hotel Fallsview, 201 Rainbow Blvd. (716-285-9321; 1-800-876-3297; www.niagarafalls-travelodge.com); $49–129 per night. Guests at the Niagara Falls Travelodge can choose from 200 rooms and suites and enjoy elegant surroundings, a restaurant and lounge, a gift shop, a game

room, and free parking. Shopping and falls-related attractions are within walking distance of the hotel. Pets are welcome for an additional $10 per night.

Olcott

Bayside Guest House, 1572 Lockport-Olcott Rd. (716-778-7767; 1-800-438-2192); $40 per night. The five nonsmoking guest rooms at Bayside have cable television and shared baths; each looks out over the yard, garden, and marina, and guests enjoy complimentary breakfast each morning. The home is located on a picturesque 18-mile creek. Your well-behaved dog is welcome, as long as she gets along with the resident cats.

Otto

R&R Dude Ranch, 8940 Lange Rd. (716-257-5663; info@ recreationranch.com; www. recreationranch.com); $40–75 per night. Friendly dogs are welcome to join the horses and riders on the trails at this 300-acre working ranch offering swimming, riding, fishing, cross-country skiing, camping ($10 per night), and a B&B. Pets can stay in designated 10-by-12-foot barn rooms; they are also allowed to stay in guest rooms if contained in a crate. Certain breeds are not permitted; call for details. Riding lessons, hayrides, and horse boarding are also available.

Pine City

Rufus Tanner House, 60 Sagetown Rd. (607-732-0213; rthouse@stny.rr.com; www. rufustanner.com); $77–115 per night. "We're a pet-friendly B&B, and we don't have extra charges for people who bring their dogs," says innkeeper Donna Powell. The Rufus Tanner House offers four upscale guest rooms—the Victorian Cottage, the Sleigh Room, the Empire Room, and the Early American—with private baths, period furniture, air-conditioning, cable television, and Internet access. A full country breakfast is served daily.

Sherman

Miller's Angel Inn Bed & Breakfast, 137 W. Main St. (716-761-6795); $35–65 per night. Choose from four guest rooms at Miller's Angel Inn, a B&B offering full country breakfasts, a gift shop, shared baths, cable television, a warm atmosphere, and a downtown village location. Weekly rates are also available. Dogs are welcome for an extra $20 per stay, as long as they are not left unattended in the rooms.

Tonawanda

Microtel Inn, 1 Hospitality Center Way (1-800-227-6346); $39–59 per night. Guests at this Microtel Inn can choose from 100 smoking and nonsmoking guest rooms with air-conditioning, cable television, in-room movies, desks and chairs, irons, and ironing boards. Some rooms also have refrigerators, microwaves, and safe-deposit boxes. Well-behaved dogs are welcome for an additional $10 per night.

West Falls

Pipe Creek Farm Bed & Breakfast, 9303 Falls Rd. (716-652-4868); $50–125 per night. Situated on 200 private acres, Pipe Creek Farm is an animal-friendly place with four guest rooms (one with a private bath), a swimming pool, hiking and cross-country skiing trails, daily continental breakfast and afternoon tea, a fireplace, a gathering room with a television and VCR, and a library. While you're there, don't forget to say hi to the farm's cats, dogs, horses, and the resident potbellied pig, Suzie.

Campgrounds

Akron

Sleepy Hollow Lake Campground, 13800 Siehl Rd. (716-542-4336; 1-866-542-4336); $19–23 per night. Dogs, cats, and even iguanas have stayed at Sleepy Hollow Lake, where the facilities include a camp store, a beach, a petting zoo, laundry facilities, walking trails, a tennis court, playgrounds, picnic areas, cabin and trailer rentals, rest rooms with showers, and a miniature golf course. Pet owners must clean up after their animals, provide proof of vaccinations, and pay a $50 refundable security deposit.

Angelica

Evergreen Trails Campground, 8403 County Rd. 15 (585-466-7993; evergreentrails@msn.com; www.evergreentrails.com); $18–20 per night at campsites and $30–70 per night in cabins. "We consider pets to be part of the family," explains Evergreen Trails' owner Mary Vandewarker. "Dogs are welcome to stay with their owners, even in the cabins, with no hidden charges." The cabins can accommodate two to eight people. Visitors will also find traditional campsites, bath-houses, hiking trails, two ponds, a playground, rest rooms with showers, and laundry facilities.

Barker
Golden Hill State Park Campground, 9691 Lower Lake Rd. (716-795-3885); $13–16 per night. Located on Lake Ontario, the Golden Hill campground has tent and trailer sites, great views, a boat launch, picnic tables, rest rooms with showers, recreation programs, a playground, and pavilions. Leashed dogs are welcome, provided owners can show proof of vaccinations. For more information on the park, see "Out and About."

Batavia
Lei-Ti Campground, 9979 Francis Rd. (585-343-8600; 1-800-445-3484; leiti@leiti.com; www.leiti.com); $22–28 per night. Located about 45 minutes from Niagara Falls, Lei-Ti Campground has rest rooms with showers, a camp store, a snack bar, a beach, laundry facilities, boat rentals, walking trails, a miniature golf course, two play-grounds, a picnic pavilion, and even a petting zoo. Leashed dogs are welcome. (See listing under LeRoy for information about the Lei-Ti, Too! Campground.)

Brockton
Lake Erie State Park Campground, 5905 Lake Rd. (716-792-9214); $13–20 per night. This campground offers nearly 100 campsites for tents and trail-ers, 10 rental cabins, picnic areas, beaches, a playground, rest rooms with showers, dumping

stations, and miles of trails. (See "Out and About" for more park information.) Dogs are not allowed in beach areas or in rental cabins, but they are wel-come at campsites as long as they are leashed and have proof of vaccinations.

Castile
Letchworth State Park Campground, 1 Letchworth State Park Rd. (585-493-3600); $15–16 per night. Extend your visit to this activity-filled state park (see "Out and About") with an overnight stay in the camp-ground; campers can take their pick of more than 270 sites for tents and trailers and enjoy rest rooms with showers, a swimming pool, dumping stations, a play-ground, picnic tables, and fire pits. Dogs are welcome to join their owners at campsites, but not in the on-site rental cabins. Pet owners must show proof of vaccinations.

Darien Center
Darien Lakes State Park Campground, 10289 Harlow Rd. (585-547-9242); $13–16 per night. Darien Lakes campground's 158 sites, 45 of which have hook-ups, are available year-round on weekends and daily from June to October. Campers can enjoy a playground, picnic tables, nature trails, pavilions, and rest rooms with showers. Dog owners must keep pets leashed and show proof of vaccinations; dogs are only allowed in certain camping areas and are not allowed on the beach. For more park informa-tion, see "Out and About."

Franklinville

Triple R Camping Resort, 3491 Bryant Hill Rd. (716-676-3856; triprcamp@aol.com; www. triplercamp.com/campingresort); $21–26 per night. "We love dogs and they are welcome here," says campground manager Laurie Evans. The busy park offers sites for tents and RVs, a camp store, laundry facilities, rest rooms with showers, a pond, two swimming pools, a playground, sports courts, and a miniature golf course. Dogs are not permitted in cabin rentals.

Gainsville

Woodstream Campsite, 5440 School Rd. (585-493-5643; camp@woodstreamcampsite.com; www.woodstreamcampsite.com); $19–24 per night. Located along a creek, this family campground has a miniature golf course, playgrounds, sports courts, a game room, a camp store, laundry facilities, a spring-fed pond, and sites for tents and RVs. Leashed pets are welcome as long as they are attended at all times and are kept out of the swimming area.

Hamlin

Hamlin Beach State Park Campground, 1 Camp Rd. (585-964-2462); $15–16 per night. Visitors can access Hamlin Beach's 264 tent and trailer campsites from May to October; amenities include rest rooms with showers, a playground, scheduled recreational and educational programs, a beach, a boat launch, and 10 miles of hiking, biking, and cross-country trails. For more park information, see "Out and About." Dogs owners must have proof of vaccinations and keep

their animals leashed; pets are only allowed in certain camping areas of the park.

Irving

Evangola State Park Campground, 10191 Old Lake Shore Rd., Rte. 5 (716-549-1802); $13–16 per night. Open seasonally from April through October, Evangola offers more than 80 campsites for tents and trailers. Other amenities include picnic tables, a playground, hiking trails, pavilions, rest rooms with showers, and dumping stations. For more information on the state park, see "Out and About." Dog owners must carry proof of vaccinations and keep their animals leashed. Pets are not allowed on the beach.

Jamestown

Hidden Valley Camping Area, 299 Kiantone Rd. (716-569-5433; hiddenvalley@madbbs.com; www.hiddenvalleycampingarea. com); $22–23 per night. There are sites for tents and RVs alike at Hidden Valley, a family campground with a camp store, shaded and open sites, rest rooms with showers, laundry facilities, group camping areas, and scheduled events and activities—including a pet parade in June. Companion animals are always welcome; past guests have included cats, birds, lizards, ferrets, potbellied pigs, and horses. Dogs must be leashed.

LeRoy

Lei-Ti, Too! Campground, 8101 Conlon Rd. (585-768-4883; leiti@leiti.com; www.leiti.com); $19–23 per night. Not too far from its sister campground in Batavia, this family park offers shaded and sunny sites for tents and RVs, picnic tables and fire pits, a playground, rest rooms with showers, and a full calendar of scheduled events like pancake breakfasts, Halloween costume parties, and Mardi Gras weekends. Leashed dogs are welcome as long as owners clean up after them.

Lockport
Niagara County Camping Resort, 7369 Wheeler Rd. (716-434-3991; camp@niagaracamping.com; www.niagaracamping.com); $19–23 per night. This pet-friendly campground and RV park has 58 acres for roaming, two ponds, a miniature golf course, three playgrounds, a camp store, cabin rentals, rest rooms with showers, sports courts, a petting zoo, and regularly scheduled events and activities. Pet owners must clean up after their animals and show proof of vaccinations.

Lyndonville
Green Harbor Campground & Marina, 12813 Lakeshore Rd. (585-682-9780; www.members.aol.com/ghcampmar2); $20–23 per night. Perched beside Lake Ontario, this campground has tent and RV sites, a game room, paddleboat rentals, scheduled family activities, a camp store, rest rooms with showers, docking, a boat launch, a dump station, and laundry facilities. Cabins are also available for rent ($45 per night). Leashed, well-behaved dogs are welcome.

Salamanca
Allegany State Park Campgrounds, 2373 ASP, Rte. 1

(716-354-9121); $13–20 per night. The three separate camping areas at this enormous state park encompass 300 sites for tents and trailers as well as 300 rental cabins. Relax at your site or enjoy boating, hiking, bird-watching, fishing, snowmobiling, cross-country skiing, picnicking, or just exploring the park's woodlands and lakes. Campground amenities include rest rooms with showers, picnic tables, group camping sites, pavilions, and dumping stations. Leashed dogs are welcome at campsites, but not cabins, with proof of vaccinations. For more information on Allegany State Park, see "Out and About."

Stow
Camp Chautauqua, Rte. 394, P.O. Box 100 (716-789-3435; 1-800-578-4849; info@campchautauqua.com; www.woodalls.com/a/01826_campchautauqua); $27–50 per night. Choose from tent sites, hook-up RV sites, and "executive sites" at this campground, where visitors also enjoy access to Chautauqua Lake, ice fishing, snowmobiling, picnic areas, and scheduled activities, boat rentals, playgrounds, and a beach. One dog is allowed per campsite; each animal must be leashed and attended to at all times. (And don't miss the campground's annual "Mutt Show" event, usually held in August.)

Waterport
Lakeside Beach State Park Campground, Rte. 18 (585-682-4888); $13–16 per night. The large campground at Lakeside Beach has 274 sites for tents and trailers, 4 miles of trails, rest

rooms with showers, a play-ground, athletic fields, dumping stations, picnic tables, and scheduled recreational programs. For more park information, see "Out and About." Dogs are not allowed on the beach and must be leashed at all times; owners must show proof of vaccinations.

Youngstown

Four Mile Creek State Park, Lake Rd. (716-745-3802); $13–15 per night. The 265 campsites at Four Mile Creek are accessible from April to October; campers with tents or trailers can make full use of the facilities, which include rest rooms with showers, picnic tables, dumping stations, a playground, a camp store, and hiking trails. For more information on the park, see "Out and About."

Niagara Falls North KOA, 1250 Pletcher Rd. (716-754-8013; 1-800-562-8715; www.niagarafalls northkoa.com); $23–39 per night. The resident Pomeranian, Pepper, will welcome you and your pooch to this campground with quiet tent sites, pull-through RV sites, rest rooms with showers, a playground, hiking trails, laundry facilities, a camp store, bike rentals, a game room, a dumping station, and a shuttle to nearby Niagara Falls. "We love dogs!" says campground owner Fran Prior. "They are always welcome, as long as they are picked-up after."

Homes, Cottages, and Cabins for Rent

Southshore Vacation Homes, 5040 West Lake Rd., Rte. 5, Dunkirk (716-366-2822; info@southshorevacationhomes. com; www.southshorevacation-homes.com); $55–150 per night. Available for short- or long-term rentals, South Shore rental accommodations include one- and two-bedroom houses, a honeymoon cottage, and three-room suites. All are located on the shore of Lake Erie and share access to a swimming pool, a putting green, barbecue grills and picnic tables, a playground, and a basketball court. Guest pets are welcome with a refundable $50 deposit.

OUT AND ABOUT

Allegany State Park, 2373 ASP, Rte. 1, Salamanca (716-354-9121). The jewel of western New York, Allegany is the largest state park in the system with 65,000 acres of nearly untouched forests. The park's three campgrounds (see "Accommodations") are extremely popular, as are its 90 miles of snowmobile trails. Two semi-developed areas, called Quaker and Red House, support much of the visitor traffic with beaches and well-marked trails for hiking, mountain biking, and cross-country skiing. The park also has three lakes, boat launches, boat rentals, a gift shop, heated cabins for ice fishing, tennis courts, and various scheduled recreational and educational programs. Dogs are welcome with a leash and vaccination records, although they are not allowed on the beaches or on the cross-country skiing trails in the winter.

Arcade & Attica Railroad, 278 Main St., Arcade (585-492-3100; www.anarr.com); $7–10 per person. Take a 90-minute ride into the past on board the A&A, a steam engine that travels between Arcade and Curriers Depot on the same tracks it's been riding since the 1880s. These days, the train carries tourists as well as freight. Passengers are welcome to bring well-behaved dogs on the train, as long as they are leashed or crated. Animal owners will be held responsible for any damages. Dogs are not allowed inside the gift shop, due to food preparation.

Beaver Island State Park, 2136 W. Oakfield Rd., Grand Island (716-773-3271). This day-use park offers myriad recreational opportunities, including an 18-hole public golf course, a large marina, trails for hiking, mountain biking, snowshoeing, snowmobiling, and cross-country skiing, sledding hills, playgrounds, athletic fields, a beach, and picnic areas. Dogs are not allowed on the beach or boardwalk area, but they can sniff around everywhere else as long as they are leashed and have proof of vaccinations.

Boat launches. With all the lakes and rivers winding through and around western New York, you'll no doubt be tempted to get out on the water. Boat launch sites include: Fort Niagara State Park on Lake Ontario (Rte. 18F, Youngstown); the Big Six Mile Creek Marina at Beaver Island State Park (2136 W. Oakfoeld Rd., Grand Island); Conesus Lake Boat Launch at Letchworth State Park (1 Letchworth State Park Rd., Castile); Irondequoit Bay State Park (Culver Rd., Hamlin); Oak Orchard State Marine Park (Archibald Rd., Waterport); and Silver Lake State Park (W. Lake Rd., Silver Springs).

Buckhorn Island State Park, North End of Grand Island (716-773-3271). This largely undeveloped park showcases the region's increasingly rare wetlands and marshes. The state is working on a restoration effort that will increase the number of plant and animal species in the 895-acre park. The visitor facilities are limited but include trails for hiking, bird-watching, and biking. Dogs must be kept on a leash no longer than 6 feet; owners are asked to respect the sensitive nature of the preserve and keep companion animals away from bird-nesting sites and other areas.

Darien Lakes State Park, 10289 Harlow Rd., Darien Center (585-547-9242). Whether you're coming to Darien Lakes for the campground (see "Accommodations") or the day-use facilities, the park has more than enough attractions to keep every family member—including the one with four legs—busy. Boat or fish in the 12-acre lake, ice skate on a pond, relax in the picnic area, play in the playground, hike, bike, ski, or ride a horse on the trails, or take in the view from the lake channel's bridge. The park is open year-round. Dogs are not allowed on the beach and must be leashed and have proof of vaccinations.

Day trip to Niagara Falls, Ontario.

Many would argue that Canada's Horseshoe Falls are the most dramatic; Niagara Falls, Ontario, also has wax museums, several parks, arcades, lots of hotels and theme restaurants, and an overall fun and touristy (if slightly tacky) ambiance. It's definitely worth a trip across the Peace Bridge to see what all the fuss is about, but keep in mind that American/Canadian border crossings are not what they once were before the modern era of terrorism fears. Expect delays. Pets must be free of all communicable diseases, and animal owners are expected to show proof of vaccinations from a veterinarian. Don't forget to bring your own proof of citizenship, such as a birth certificate or passport.

Devil's Hole State Park,

Robert Moses Pkwy. (716-278-1762). Located on the Niagara River just up the street from Whirlpool State Park, Devil's Hole gets its ominous-sounding name from a 300-foot gorge with rapids. Visitors can peer at the spectacle from an elevated walkway or enjoy picnic areas and walkways. Dogs must be leashed.

NIAGARA FALLS, ONTARIO, OFFERS VISITORS GREAT VIEWS, SHOPPING, RESTAURANTS, AND ACTIVITIES.

Downtown Ellicottville. This charming and historic ski village, host to the Holiday Valley downhill ski resort, has much to offer during the other three seasons, as well. Swing your clubs at the 18-hole golf course, swim or play tennis in the park, hit the hiking and biking trails in the nearby hills, or stroll past downtown shops and restaurants. (It also doesn't hurt that Allegany State Park is just down the road.) A self-guided walking tour of Ellicottville's historic sites is available from the Ellicottville Chamber of Commerce; for more information, contact the chamber at 9 Washington St. (716-699-5046; www.ellicottvilleny.com.).

Erie Canal Heritage Trail. Stretching more than 85 miles from Palmyra to Lockport, this scenic pathway winds beside the Erie Canal and forms one of the best recreational opportunities anywhere in the state of New York. Joggers, dog walkers, parents with strollers, and visiting tourists can take it fast or slow, passing by waterfalls, fishing boats, wildlife refuges, locks, farmers' markets, cruise and pleasure boats, restaurants, shops, sunsets, and fall foliage. Some sections are paved; others are made from packed earth or gravel. No matter where you are along the trail, it's worth a visit—even for just a short walk. Dogs are allowed, but must be leashed. For more information and maps, contact the New York State Canal System in Albany at 1-800-4-CANAL-4 or visit www.canals.stste.ny.us.

Evangola State Park, 10191 Old Lake Shore Rd., Rte. 5, Irving (716-549-1802). Although your dog is not allowed at Evangola's sandy beach, you and your pooch will find plenty of other things to do at the park's trails, picnic area, athletic fields, sports courts, and seasonal campground (see "Accommodations"). Dogs must be on a leash no longer than 6 feet and have proof of vaccinations.

Four Mile Creek State Park, Lake Rd., Youngstown (716-745-3802). The main attraction here is the large seasonal campground (see "Accommodations"). But day-use visitors can also take advantage of fishing and wildlife-watching opportunities, scheduled recreational programs, and hiking and biking trails.

Genesee County Park and Forest, Raymond Rd., Bethany (716-344-1122). Leashed dogs are welcome to romp at this park, the oldest county forest in New York. Visitors will find picnic areas, playgrounds, sports courts, and a nature center that offers regular classes in backyard composting, bird identification, and more. The Outer Loop trail is the most popular; park in area B or C on Park Rd. and bike or walk the 2.9-mile loop, which takes about 45 minutes to an hour to complete on foot.

Golden Hill State Park, 9691 Lower Lake Rd., Barker (716-795-3885). Though it houses a campground (see "Accommodations"), this park is also very popular with day-users—especially fishermen. Looking at Golden Hill's attractions, it's easy to see why: The park has a boat launch, athletic fields, picnic areas, a Frisbee-golf course, and trails (some along the shoreline) for snowmobiling, snowshoeing, hiking, biking, and cross-country skiing. Leashed pets are welcome, provided they have proof of vaccinations.

Griffis Sculpture Park, Rte. 219 at Ashford Hollow, East Otto (716-667-2808). Open seasonally from May through October, this unique attraction blends art with nature at open-air sculpture displays set in water, woods, wetlands, and meadows. Visitors are encouraged to get up-close-and-personal with the displays—some are even designed to be climbed on. Leashed dogs are welcome at the East Hill site of the park, but not in the main area.

Hamlin Beach State Park, 1 Camp Rd., Hamlin (585-964-2462). Most visitors at Hamlin Beach come for the campground (see "Accommodations") or the sandy beaches, where pets are unfortunately not allowed. The boat launch is also a draw for fishermen and recreational boaters—once back on dry land, many also take advantage of the park's picnic facilities or visit the on-site environmental education center. Concerns for safety have recently led park officials to close off the bluff known as Devil's Peak. Dogs must be on a leash no longer than 6 feet.

Joseph Davis State Park, 4143 Lower River Rd., Lewiston (716-

754-4596). This day-use park offers forests and ponds, a Niagara River dock used for fishing, a 27-hole Frisbee-golf course, and plenty of trails for dog-walking, cross-country skiing, biking, snowshoeing, and snowmobiling. The park is open throughout the year. Leashed dogs are welcome, although they are not allowed on boardwalks or in buildings.

Kenan Center, 433 Locust St., Lockport (716-433-2617; www.kenancenter.org). This scenic arts and education center has 25 acres with formal gardens, playgrounds, and recreational fields. Dogs are not allowed in the historic buildings, but are welcome to roam the grounds on a leash. There is no charge to visit the center, which is open from May through October.

Lake Erie State Park, 5905 Lake Rd., Brockton (716-792-9214). Unfortunately, pets are not allowed at Lake Erie's long beaches, which are the highlight of the trip for most visitors to this park. Still, the campground (see "Accommodations"), beautiful views, picnic areas, and hiking, biking, and cross-country skiing trails can certainly keep you busy. Dog owners must provide proof of vaccinations and keep their pets leashed.

Lakeside Beach State Park, Rte. 18, Waterport (585-682-4888). Popular summer activities at Lakeside include sunbathing, fishing, biking, hiking, tossing the ball at the park's athletic fields, and camping (see

"Accommodations"). Despite its name, however, no swimming is allowed at Lakeside Beach State Park. In the winter, visitors enjoy cross-country skiing, snowmobiling, and snowshoeing. Dogs must be kept on a leash no longer than 6 feet and are not allowed on the beach.

Letchworth State Park, 1 Letchworth State Park Rd., Castile (585-493-3600). The dramatic scenery of this 17-mile-long park is a must-see for any visit to western New York. The gorge is 600 feet deep; the Genessee River drops at three separate points in the park, forming impressive waterfalls—some as high as 600 feet—and providing plenty of whitewater for rafters. Horseback riding is allowed on some trails; others are reserved for hikers, cross-country skiers, mountain bikers, birdwatchers, leaf peepers, and amblers. An on-site museum details the area's Native American history and tells the tale of early settlers. For information on Letchworth's campground, see "Accommodations." Dogs must be leashed and are not allowed in the museum or cabins. Owners must have proof of vaccinations.

Long Point State Park on Lake Chautauqua, 4459 Rte. 430, Bemus Point (716-386-2722). Fishermen come here in search of huge muskie; hikers come for the chance to walk among forests of maple, spruce, and beech trees. Cross-country skiers and snowmobilers take advantage of winter fun at the park, and recreational boaters crowd the launches and marina in the spring, summer, and fall. And sightseers come just for the picnics and views at Long Point, which juts out into the lake and provides a peaceful, getaway-from-it-all ambiance. Dogs must be leashed and have proof of vaccinations, and are not allowed on cross-country ski trails in the winter.

Mostly Muskies Charters, 268 Harrison Ave., Buffalo (716-833-6739; info@mostlymuskies.com; www.mostlymuskies.com). Captain Larry Jones welcomes dogs on board his fishing charters on the Niagara River: "I think it's a great idea that man's best friends take part in all the adventures in life that we participate in," Jones says. He recommends that dogs have their own life jackets (available in many pet stores) and that owners bring along bowls and extra water and pet food.

Nannen Arboretum, 28 Parkside Dr., Ellicottville (716-699-2377). Dogs are frequent visitors at this expansive 8-acre arboretum, which boasts a lake, a temple garden, nature trails, a composting demonstration, a wildflower meadow, decorative bridges, beautiful views, and numerous species of trees, shrubs, perennials, and herbs. Pet owners are asked to keep dogs leashed and clean up after them. Admission is free, but donations are welcomed; donation cards even include an option for "doggie dues."

Niagara Reservation State Park, Robert Moses Pkwy., Niagara Falls (716-278-1796). This park has two claims to fame: It is the oldest state park in America, and it is also arguably the one with the best views. In one area, you can literally stand on the edge of the gorge and peer down into the mighty falls. An elevator in the observation tower takes visitors 80 feet above the falls—then 180 feet below street level for an up-close-and-personal glimpse of the deafening water. The park also houses a formal garden, picnic tables, a gift shop, nature trails, and a museum. Pets are unfortunately not allowed in the buildings or in the popular Cave of the Winds attraction, but you and your leashed pooch are welcome to take in the sights in all other areas of the park. And this is no mere walk-in-the-park: As you wander along the paved walkways, the water rushes by you in a thundering journey on its way to the falls. This one is definitely a "don't-miss," and probably one of the top-five best attractions in New York State.

Rock City, Rte. 16, Olean (716-372-7790). This geographical oddity makes a great western New York stop: Visitors can gape at huge and strange rock formations, inch down crevice "staircases," and learn about Native American legends on the site's one-hour nature walk. Rock City also has a picnic area, a gift shop, and rest rooms. Leashed dogs are welcome. The site is open daily from May 1 to October 31, although it closes during inclement weather. Call for fee information.

Sparky's Charters, 39 Calvin Court North, Tonawanda (716-837-3146; mmcsparky@aol.com; www.sparkyscharters.com). You and your pooch can head out with Sparky for a day of fishing on Lake Erie, Lake Ontario, and the Niagara River. Popular pursuits include trophy bass in Lake Erie (starting in early May), drift fishing in the Lower Niagara River, salmon in Lake Ontario (starting in May), brown trout, salmon, and lake trout in Niagara Bar. Custom trips on Lake Chautauqua are also available.

Summer Music Concerts, Tonawanda. Hear jazz, rock-n-roll, doo-wop, and other styles under the summer sky at the area's many outdoor concerts held from June through early September. On Wednesday, Friday, and Saturday nights you can catch the show at Gateway Harbor Park, along the canal at Sweeney Street. On Thursday nights the concerts are held at the band shell at Fisherman's Park in North Tonawanda (River Rd.), and on Sundays you'll find the music at the band shell in Niawanda Park in Tonawanda (Niagara Street).

Whirlpool State Park, Robert Moses Pkwy., Niagara Falls (716-278-1762). Start at the upper level of Whirlpool State Park, where you'll have great views of the swirling rapids and access to a picnic area and playground. Then climb down 300 feet into the gorge to see the water from a different perspective and meander along the walking trails. Dogs are welcome, but must be on a leash no longer than 6 feet. Use caution with pets near the powerful water currents.

Wiley's Riverside Marina, 1180 Point Breeze Rd., Kent (585-682-4552). At the time of this writing, marina owners Dick and Peg Wiley had just dockage and a boater's lounge with showers available, but they were planning to add a rental boat service in the near future (call for the latest information). The marina is located on the Oak Orchard River, where the salmon, steelhead, pike, bass, and walleye make it popular with fishermen. Dogs and cats are welcome.

Wilson-Tuscarora State Park, 3371 Lake Rd., Wilson (716-751-6361). This quiet park has a 4-mile nature trail beside Lake Ontario frequently use by hikers, dog walkers, and cross-country skiers. Wilson-Tuscarora's other facilities include a large playground, a boat launch, a marina, picnic areas, and pavilions. Visitors will find forests, marshes, and meadows spread across the park's 400 acres.

QUICK BITES

Allegany Grill, 7993 Rte. 19, Belfast (585-365-8298). Choose from seafood and beef dishes, pizza, subs, chicken wings, salads, and sandwiches at this family restaurant located in the southeastern corner of the region. Delivery and takeout are both available.

Anchor Bar, 1047 Main St., Buffalo (716-886-8920; mail@anchorbar.com; www.anchorbar.com). This is the place where the craze started: In 1964, the bar owner's mother, Teressa Bellissimo, deep-fried some leftover chicken wings, coated them in her own hot sauce, and served them to a group of dubious bar patrons. Buffalo wings were born and continue to be popular to this day. Unfortunately the restaurant does not have outdoor seating, but you can order your wings to go or even have them shipped to your home.

Andriaccio's, Rte. 394, Stow (716-753-5200; www.andriaccios.com). In addition to its indoor dining room, this Italian family restaurant also offers take-out service and delivery. Choose from menu items like traditional and gourmet pizza, calzones, hot and cold subs, chicken wings, and steak, seafood and pasta dishes.

Apple Country Quilt Shop and Café, 51 State St., Rte. 31E, Holley (585-638-5262). This unusual business combines a quilting and fabric shop with a full-service café; all of the café's menu items, including homemade chili, turkey melts, crab cakes, stuffed crepes, quiches, and macaroni and cheese are available for takeout.

Cooling's Ice Cream Café, 10A Washington St., Ellicottville (716-699-8860). While you're strolling down Washington Street, stop into Cooling's for a cone, a hot cappuccino, a sandwich, a bowl of soup, or a fruit smoothie. Eat-and-walk or relax at one of the sidewalk tables.

Cousin Vinny's Doghouse, Isle View Park, 796 South Niagara St., Tonawanda. Okay, so we love the name. But there's more than that to love about Cousin Vinny's, including waterfront open-air dining, a "real wood" barbecue grill, burgers, hot dogs, sandwiches, and ice cream. The restaurant is open seasonally from May through October.

Flavor Haus, 5353 Kilborn Corner Rd., Rte. 242, Little Valley (716-938-9292). Everything on this restaurant's ever-changing menu is available for takeout, including items like seafood dishes, pizza, foot-long submarine sandwiches, French fries, and soft-serve custard.

Mississippi Mudds, 313 Niagara St., Tonawanda (716-694-0787). Located across the street from Niawanda Park, this large and popular take-out stand offers burgers, hot dogs, fried seafood, ice cream, custard, and a great view of Niagara River. Order your treats at the window and then hang out at the park's benches or grassy lawns.

North Tonawanda City Market, Payne Ave. at Robinson St., North Tonawanda (716-693-3746). Browse this open-air market for baked treats, cheeses, and locally grown fruits, vegetables, and flowers. The market is open year-round on Tuesday, Thursday, and Saturday mornings.

Root Five, 4914 Lakeshore Rd., Hamburg (716-627-5551; www.rootfive.com). This waterfront restaurant has some of the best views in town, as well as an extensive wine list, lunch and dinner menus with chicken, pasta, beef, and stir-fry dishes, and a large outdoor patio seating area right beside the water.

The Silo, North Water St., Lewiston (716-754-9680). This distinctive round eatery is hard to miss on the Lewiston waterfront: The pet-friendly place serves up sweet-potato fries, burgers, veggie burgers, salads, barbecue chicken, chili, salads, ice cream, and hot dogs with "Silo Sauce" and cheese. The entire menu is also available for takeout.

Ted's Hot Dogs, various locations, (716-691-3731). A western New York tradition, Ted's has been serving up charbroiled dogs since its founder, Theodore Spiro Liaros, opened his first stand under the Peace Bridge. Today you can get your fill in Amherst (2351 Niagara Falls Blvd.); Cheektowaga (1 Galleria Dr.); Depew (4878 Transit Rd.); Lockport (6230 Shimer Rd.); North Tonawanda (333 Meadow Dr.); Orchard Park (3193 Orchard Park Rd.); Tonawanda (2312 Sheridan Dr.); and Williamsville (7018 Transit Rd.).

T. J.'s Den, Perimeter Rd., Onoville (716-354-2197). Located across the street from the

Onoville Marina and just a few minutes from Allegheny State Park, this casual eatery offers a 60-foot-deck seating area, a bar, model cars, and Italian-inspired meals. The deck overlooks the Kinzua Reservoir.

HOT SPOTS FOR SPOT

Blackwinds Pet Supplies, 2494 Military Rd., Niagara Falls (716-297-1751). Dogs, cats, birds, fish, and small animals will be able to stock up on food, accessories, and supplies at Blackwinds, which also offers a full selection of Feathers-N-Fur products and toys.

Canine Capers, 5310 Southwestern Blvd., Hamburg (716-646-9588; www.canine-capers.us). At this doggie daycare facility and pet boutique, dogs romp and play together in both indoor and outdoor play areas. (Puppies get their own room and obedience training upon request.) Visitors can also browse animal-themed gifts, picture frames, and clothing in the on-site boutique. Call for reservations.

Dog Days of Buffalo, 632 Amherst St., Buffalo (716-886-DOGS; www.dogdaysusa.com). Dog Days started as a doggie day-care facility offering large indoor and outdoor play areas; the com-

VISITING POOCHES LOUNGE, SWIM, AND PLAY AT THE DOG DAYS OF BUFFALO DOGGIE DAY-CARE CENTER.

pany has now expanded its services to include overnight boarding, obedience classes, and grooming services. Five full-time staffers ensure that your dog is well-cared-for and entertained throughout her stay. Call for reservations and be sure to have vaccination records handy—the "kennel cough" vaccination is a must.

Natural Pet Wellness Center, 50 S. Buffalo St., Hamburg (716-646-5673; info@naturalpetwellness.com; www.naturalpetwellness.com). Specializing in all-natural, holistic pet foods and products, the Natural Pet Wellness Center provides a good selection of herbal supplements, dog treats, and pet food brands like Wysong, Sojourner Farms, Azmira, and Dr. Harvey's. In addition to the Hamburg storefront, the company also sells its products on-line.

Pampered Pets, 6314 Portage Rd., Mayville (716-753-3669). Fido can stop by this grooming and boarding facility for a quick bath, a nail clip, or just a good brushing. The staff also provides overnight boarding and doggie daycare.

Petique, S.P.C.A. of Erie County, 205 Ensminger Rd., Tonawanda (716-875-7360). All proceeds of this fun shop benefit the companion and barn animals at the S.P.C.A. shelter and the wildlife undergoing on-site rehabilitation. Browse pet-themed hats, T-shirts, slate welcome signs, magnets, stuffed toys, and other items.

Pet Supplies Plus, 2155 Delaware Ave., Buffalo (716-876-6663). This chain store is a handy stop when you're running low on food; you'll find nearly every brand here, including Purina, Iams, and Pedigree. Biscuits, rawhides, toys, balls, and other supplies are also plentiful.

S.P.C.A. of Cattaraugus County, 2944 Hinsdale Hwy., Olean (716-372-8492). In addition to providing shelter and adoption services for homeless animals, the S.P.C.A. of Cattaraugus County also has a pet-supply outlet: Stock up on food, toys, and other necessities while supporting a good cause.

IN CASE OF EMERGENCY

Amherst Small Animal Clinic
2217 Kensington Ave., Buffalo (716-839-1100)

Batavia Animal Hospital
3699 W. Main St. (585-343-4046)

Countryside Veterinary Clinic (complementary/holistic care)
5860 S. Transit Rd., Lockport (716-434-2838)

Ford Veterinary Association
527 Hyde Park Blvd., Niagara Falls (716-285-5734)

Haskell Valley Veterinary Clinic
2148 Haskell Rd., Olean (716-372-1759)

Holistic Center of Veterinary Medicine (complimentary/holistic care)
9002 Sunset Dr., Colden (716-941-0164)

Nunda Veterinary Clinic
1497 Portage Rd. (585-468-2240)

Springville Veterinary Services
10055 Middle Rd., East Concord (716-592-0070)

Westfield Veterinary Hospital
W. Main Rd. (716-326-3933)

Index